Praise for

WHERE IS THE LONE RANGER
WHEN WE NEED HIM?

"*Where Is the Lone Ranger When We Need Him?* is a major contribution to writing about peacekeeping and, more specifically, security stabilization in postconflict environments—a dimension that has been neglected heretofore. With extensive and unique knowledge of the subject, Perito offers definitive scholarship in this clear, sensible, and insightful volume."

DAVID BAYLEY
Distinguished Professor
School of Criminal Justice, SUNY-Albany

"Most experts and practitioners believe that peace is most durably established and preserved through the rule of law. But how is the rule of law itself established? How is it best preserved? Does it exist in the presence of a police force? A visible judiciary with an active legal docket? Full prisons? When war has destroyed a society's hold on the rule of law, how is it restored? What help can outsiders bring to the process? In *Where Is the Lone Ranger When We Need Him?* Robert M. Perito tackles these thorny questions with a thoroughgoing analysis of the international record over the past dozen years. Carefully researched and methodically argued, this volume fills a gaping void in the literature on postconflict challenges. Perito argues persuasively that military force alone cannot do all that needs doing and that the international community in general, and the United States in particular, must develop a meaningful capacity to deploy the full complement of assets necessary to help establish or restore the rule of law in the aftermath of violent conflict. He rightly maintains that only an integrated approach to restoring law and order—one that links a corpus of legitimately derived laws with corruption-free institutions to uphold them (police forces, independent judiciary, responsive penal system) will lead to genuine stability. His call for a Stability Force deserves serious debate at a time when peacekeeping forces around the globe are stretched thin. This timely volume is important reading for anyone wishing to understand the factors that lead to widespread lawlessness and how the international community—including its most powerful member—can organize to stop madness in its tracks."

JANE HOLL LUTE
Assistant Secretary-General for Missions Support
Department of Peacekeeping Operations, United Nations

"Bob Perito has provided us a unique, badly needed compilation of international policing and constabulary capabilities and description of how they have been used, focused upon Bosnia and Kosovo. Going further, he makes proposals on how they can be used more effectively in the security gap that has so seriously plagued Operation Iraqi Freedom."

ROBERT B. OAKLEY
U.S. Ambassador (Ret.)

WHERE IS THE LONE RANGER WHEN WE NEED HIM?

America's Search for a Postconflict Stability Force

ROBERT M. PERITO

UNITED STATES INSTITUTE OF PEACE PRESS
Washington, D.C.

The views expressed in this book are those of the author alone. They do not necessarily reflect views of the United States Institute of Peace.

UNITED STATES INSTITUTE OF PEACE
1200 17th Street NW, Suite 200
Washington, DC 20036-3011

First published 2004

Printed in the United States of America

The paper used in this publication meets the minimum requirements of American National Standard for Information Sciences—Permanence of Paper for Printed Library Materials, ANSI Z39.48-1984.

Library of Congress Cataloging-in-Publication Data
Perito, Robert, 1942-
    Where is the Lone Ranger when we need him? : America's search
    for a postconflict stabililty force / Robert M. Perito
        p. cm.
    Includes bibliographical references and index.
    ISBN 1-929223-51-X (alk. paper)
    1. Peacekeeping forces. 2. International police. 3. Military police.
4. Peace officers. 5. Constables. 6. Law enforcement—International cooperation. 7. United States—Armed Forces—Foreign countries. I. Title.

JZ6377.U8P47 2004
341.5'84—dc22
                                                    200406129

In memory of
Patricia Campbell Perito

CONTENTS

FOREWORD

IF THERE IS A DISTINCT SET OF IMAGES that brings home the message in *Where Is the Lone Ranger When We Need Him?*, it is the scenes of widespread looting and chaos in the immediate aftermath of post–Saddam Hussein Iraq in the presence of coalition soldiers-cum-peacekeepers. As media accounts have detailed, defense planners at the Pentagon executed a brilliant military campaign, but they seem to have been unprepared to deal with the challenges of stabilizing a society suddenly freed of dictatorial authority. The rapid deterioration of the security environment at the hands of disparate internal forces not only detracted from the joy of the Iraqi people at their liberation from a ruthless and internationally dangerous despot, but it also provided the coalition with some harsh lessons on peacekeeping and stabilizing postconflict environments.

Iraq and Afghanistan are dramatic if not unique examples of the kinds of UN peacekeeping operations that have come to characterize international interventions in the post–Cold War era. Yet all share a common problem: military peacekeepers are able to stop conflict by separating combatants or by ousting hostile, repressive regimes; however, they are not trained or equipped to restore self-sustaining order and stability to a society in a postconflict environment. The author of this book proposes a solution to this peacekeeping paradox.

In the pages that follow, Robert Perito has a straightforward yet compelling argument: military peacekeepers are not trained and organized to provide *sustainable* security to a postconflict environment—whether it is in a peacekeeping mission with a United Nations mandate, or a pre-emptive, unilateral intervention to depose the ruler of a rogue state who appears intent on developing and eventually using weapons of mass destruction. What is required, Perito argues, are the kinds of forces that are structured and trained for the arduous tasks of rebuilding domestic security—specifically, constabularies and international civilian police, as well as legal units, designed to make sure a postconflict society achieves stability and order through the rule of law. Military peacekeepers make up the third element of the postconflict public security triad that Perito outlines, but the military alone, he argues, is not equipped to handle crowds and riots, tackle organized crime, and mediate everyday disputes—the kinds of situations that typically plague postconflict societies. Those are tasks constabularies and police are trained to do.

Perito argues for the creation of a U.S. Stability Force, a combination of military and nonmilitary forces that can effectively put an end to conflict and, more important, facilitate a postconflict society's return to (or arrival at) security and the rule of law. This book examines such a force from an American perspective. The United States is now the largest contributor of peacekeeping forces around the world, so if there is to be a fundamental change in how the international community does peacekeeping, the United States must take the lead. Nevertheless, the kinds of forces Perito calls for make his argument a challenging one for an American readership.

Unlike "core" European countries, the United States, as Perito acknowledges, has a unique and troubled history regarding constabularies—national police forces that combine military and policing duties, such as France's Gendarmerie and Italy's Carabinieri. Indeed, the notion of a constabulary is an ambiguous one in the American experience, although it does not mean that we are without historical examples. As Perito expertly demonstrates in an early chapter of this work, we have had a constabulary in this country in the form of the Texas Rangers, a fictionalized member of which serves as the title character and inspiration for this book. In dangerous situations on the plains or on the frontier, Perito recalls, the Lone Ranger always came to the rescue. Abroad, the U.S. deployed constabularies to restore order in the Caribbean and in postwar Germany and Japan.

In multinational peacekeeping operations in the Balkans, the Europeans understood the benefits of constabularies—specifically, the Special Police Units and Multinational Specialized Units deployed in Bosnia and Kosovo, respectively. Perito recounts and analyzes the various facets of decision making that led up to the deployment and operation of these units, which was for the United States a truly innovative peacekeeping practice. Yet the fact that these units were ultimately frustrated in performing policing duties they were trained for reflects U.S. political and military leaders' misconceptions about the roles of these special formations: Americans and those from other countries lacking constabularies do not seem to understand what constabularies can do in peacekeeping operations. French Gendarmes and Italian Carabinieri who served in these special units had a unique insight into how postconflict tasks in Bosnia and Kosovo should be handled. U.S. military commanders have yet to appreciate the unique capabilities and contributions of such forces.

There is perhaps no one more qualified to author such a study than Robert Perito. He has served in the U.S. foreign policy community for many years as a Foreign Service officer with the State Department and then at the White House as deputy executive secretary of the National Security Council. Before joining the U.S. Institute of Peace, he served as deputy director of the U.S. Department of Justice's International Criminal Investigative Training Assistance Program, which was responsible for training local police forces for stability operations from Panama to Iraq. He completed the research for this work as a senior fellow in the Institute's Jennings Randolph Program for International Peace during 2001–2002.

Where Is the Lone Ranger When We Need Him? is the first book-length study in a growing body of works on managing postconflict environments published by the U.S. Institute of Peace. Beginning in 2001, the Institute has produced several special reports—collaborations of the Professional Training and

Rule of Law Programs—on UN Civilian Police and establishing the rule of law in countries hosting peace operations. The Institute has also published senior fellow Ray Jennings's reports on establishing security and stability in post–Saddam Hussein Iraq. Robert Perito's work is an outstanding contribution to our national effort to rethink the challenges of stabilizing societies disrupted by war.

RICHARD H. SOLOMON, PRESIDENT
UNITED STATES INSTITUTE OF PEACE

ACKNOWLEDGMENTS

This study began as an effort to understand an apparent contradiction in U.S. peacekeeping policy. Why did the U.S. advocate the use of constabulary forces for peacekeeping in the Balkans and oppose their inclusion in America's armed forces? It broadened into an inquiry into how constabulary forces had actually performed in Bosnia and Kosovo; something no one else had thought to do. Finally, it became an effort to look back into our history and ahead into the future for the answer to the question of how to create sustainable security in postconflict societies. The expanding scope of the study brought me into contact with UN officials, diplomats, soldiers, policemen, academics and reporters. The effort to talk directly to people that had been there and listen to their stories was rewarding. It also created a lengthening list of people to whom I owe a debt of gratitude and to whom I wish to express my appreciation for their generosity and support.

First and foremost, I am grateful to the United States Institute of Peace; its president, Ambassador Richard Solomon; and its Board of Directors for my selection as a senior fellow in the Jennings Randolph Fellowship Program. I am greatly indebted to the program's director, Joseph Klaits; my project officer, John Crist; and the program's administrative assistant, Elizabeth Drakulich, for their kindness, good advice, and constant encouragement. Very special appreciation is due to my research assistant, Patricia Taft, who became a full partner in the enterprise and who contributed her talents, enthusiasm, and unfailing energy in making it a success. Special thanks are also due to Christine Herrmann, my first research assistant; and to my colleagues, Ambassador Richard Kauzlarich, Colonel Michael Dziedzic

(U.S.A.F, ret.), Professor Charles Call, and the other senior fellows in the Jennings Randolph Program.

In conducting my field research, I was the beneficiary of the talents and the generosity of many "practitioners" who shared their experiences and their expertise. I am particularly indebted to Michael Jorsback, Joelle Vatcher, and Eric Scheye of the Civilian Police Division of the United Nations Department of Peacekeeping Operations. I also could not have concluded this study without the remarkable support I received from Colonel Gery Plane, adviser on Special Police Units to the commissioner of the United Nations Police in Kosovo, and Warrant Officer Dennis Clement of his staff. I owe special thanks to James Tillman, director of the U.S. International Criminal Investigative Training Assistance Program in Bosnia; to Steven Bennett, director of the Police Service School in Kosovo; and to the Office of the SFOR Historian in Bosnia.

There are also a number of distinguished and courageous individuals who granted interviews. I wish to thank Ambassador Robert Farrand, Commissioner Donald Grady, Colonel James Greer, Sergeant Mike Agate, Major Kimberly Field, Colonel Scott Feil, Colonel Larry Forester, R. Jeffrey Smith, Commissioner Halvor Hartz, Ambassador Robert Gelbard, Colonel Vincenzo Coppola, Chief Mark Kroeker, Lt. Colonel Michael Meese, Colonel Antonio Colacicco, Commissioner Adalbert Gross, Colonel Hameed Iqbal Khaled, Lt. Colonel Oridiu Bratulescu, General William Nash, Ambassador Gary Matthews, Commissioner Thomas Hacker, John Hulsman, Ambassador Jacques Paul Klein, Souren Seraydarian, Martina Vandenberg, Robert Gifford, and General George Joulwan.

For their insights and emotional support, I wish to thank my readers Gregory Schulte, Professor David Bayley, and Colonel George Oliver, and my ever-patient editor Peter Pavilionis.

Finally, I wish to thank my family, Patricia, Robert, Jr., and Samantha for their strength, courage, and support.

LIST OF ACRONYMS

AID: U.S. Agency for International Development
AOR: area of responsibility
CIVPOL: civilian police
CPA: Coalition Provisional Authority (Iraq)
DOD: U.S. Department of Defense
DPKO: UN Department of Peacekeeping Operations
EU: European Union
EUPM: European Union Police Mission (Bosnia)
ICC: International Criminal Court
ICITAP: International Criminal Investigative Training
    Assistance Program
ICTY: International Criminal Tribunal for the Former Yugoslavia
IEBL: Inter-Entity Boundary Line (Bosnia)
IFOR: NATO Implementation Force
IPM: International Police Monitor (Haiti)
IPSF: Interim Public Security Force (Haiti)
IPTF: International Police Task Force (Bosnia)
INC: Iraqi National Congress
INP: Iraqi National Police
ISAF: International Security Assistance Force (Afghanistan)
KFOR: NATO Kosovo Force
KLA: Kosovo Liberation Army
KPC: Kosovo Protection Corps
KPS: Kosovo Police Service
KVM: Kosovo Verification Mission
MIPONUH: UN Civilian Police Mission in Haiti
MNB: Multinational Brigade (Kosovo)
MND: Multinational Division (Bosnia)
MNF: Multinational Force (Haiti)
MP: Military Police

MSU: Multinational Specialized Unit (Bosnia)

NATO: North Atlantic Treaty Organization

NGO: nongovernmental organization

NSC: National Security Council

NSPD: National Security Presidential Directive

OHR: Office of the High Representative (Bosnia)

ORHA: Office of Reconstruction and Humanitarian Assistance (Iraq)

OSCE: Organization for Security and Cooperation in Europe

PDD: Presidential Decision Directive

PIC: Peace Implementation Council (Dayton Accords)

RS: Republika Srpska

SACEUR: NATO Supreme Allied Commander Europe

SFOR: NATO Stabilization Force

SHAPE: NATO Supreme Headquarters Allied Powers Europe

SPU: Specialized Police Unit (Kosovo)

SRSG: Special Representative of the UN Secretary-General

SWAT: special weapons and tactics

UN: United Nations

UNDP: UN Development Program

UNITAF: United Task Force (Somalia)

UNMIBH: UN Mission in Bosnia and Herzegovina

UNMIH: UN Mission in Haiti

UNMIK: UN Interim Administration Mission in Kosovo

UNOSOM I: UN Operation in Somalia I (1992–93)

UNOSOM II: UN Operation in Somalia II (1993–95)

UNPROFOR: UN Protection Force (Bosnia)

UNTAC: UN Transitional Authority in Cambodia

UNTAES: UN Transitional Authority in Eastern Slavonia, Baranja, and Western Sirmium (Croatia)

WMD: weapons of mass destruction

LIST OF ILLUSTRATIONS

FIGURES

MAPS

LIST OF TABLES

Where Is the Lone Ranger When We Need Him?

INTRODUCTION

T
HIS STUDY IS PART OF AN EMERGING LITERATURE on the challenges of establishing sustainable security in postconflict environments. It looks at the subject through the prism of the past role and future potential of international constabulary and police forces in peace operations. Much has been written about the role of the military in peacekeeping, but there are few works in the literature concerning the role of nonmilitary security forces in a postconflict environment. There is also little in the literature about the importance and utility of establishing the rule of law for other aspects of postconflict reconstruction. In postconflict societies, sustainable security and political and economic reconstruction can best be achieved by immediately establishing the rule of law.

This study looks at these issues from an American perspective. The United States has a unique and troubled history with the use of constabulary and police in postconflict environments. It is both the largest contributor of police to international peace operations and the only country where the provision of government assistance to foreign police forces, except under certain circumstances, is literally against the law.[1] It has played the primary role in organizing and leading postconflict stability operations in Somalia, Haiti, Bosnia, Kosovo, and Afghanistan; but Congress, the U.S. military, and the current administration have a deep aversion to peacekeeping. Perhaps for this reason, the United States is woefully ill prepared to accomplish the nonmilitary aspects of postconflict stability operations. It does not have constabulary forces; it uses commercial contractors for UN police missions and has no program to provide the prosecutors, judges, defense attorneys, and corrections officers that are required to establish the rule of law. The study concludes with recommendations for the creation of a U.S. Stability Force composed of constabulary, police, and judicial specialists who would provide the capacity to establish postconflict security in Afghanistan and Iraq.

The need for creating such a force for postconflict operations is compelling. In the wake of the horrific events of September 11, 2001, the United States can no longer afford the luxury of ignoring continuing turmoil in war-torn societies. Weak and dysfunctional states have become the primary source of international instability. The response to the "failed state syndrome"—to intervene militarily, leave behind anarchy, and call it peace—is not the solution. Nor is the solution to be found in military occupation, such as the ever-more-permanent presence of forces from the North Atlantic Treaty Organization (NATO) in Bosnia and Kosovo. Washington has a strategic interest in preventing Afghanistan and other failed states from backsliding to a point where they provide a breeding ground for extremists and safe haven for terrorist organizations. The problem is that countries emerging from crisis lack the mechanisms to end the cycle of impunity for those who commit violence. In states afflicted by ethnic, religious, or political conflict, their own security forces are often among the first victims of the struggle. Either the military and the police are vanquished, or they mutate from protectors of the state and its citizens into predators. In Bosnia, some of the worst cases of ethnic cleansing were perpetrated by the Special Police Units of the Yugoslav Ministry of Interior. In the aftermath of war, international intervention forces must be able to silence the combatants and restore public order. They must also be the leading edge of an effort to institute the mechanism that democracies rely upon to ensure sustainable security—the rule of law.

To accomplish this mission, a triad of international security forces is required, including robust military forces that are capable of compelling the warring factions to cease fighting and abide by terms of the peace agreement. Participation of effective military forces is essential to the success of all stability operations. Military forces are limited, however, by their training, equipment, and experience; they have generally been reluctant to move beyond such tasks as separating and disarming combatants and the cantonment of weapons and former fighters. In particular, military forces are unwilling to tackle situations that involve controlling civil disturbances and law enforcement.

To deal with violent demonstrations, armed gangs, and organized crime, the intervention force needs to include military police and an armed, international civilian constabulary. Such units straddle the line between military and police and have characteristics and capabilities of both types of forces. The benefit of constabulary units in a stability operation is that they can deploy rapidly to respond to situations that require greater force and firepower than can be provided by civil police, but that do not require the firepower of infantry or armored units. Constabulary forces are trained to deal with civilians and are skilled at using the minimum amount of force necessary to control the situation. Constabulary can serve as a bridge between the military and civil police and can handle tasks that do not clearly fall within either camp.

Constabulary forces should support the international civil police who are trained and equipped to take on the patient work of law enforcement. In peace operations, international civil police have proven adept at contributing to public safety, controlling crime, and monitoring and training indigenous police. They have played a critical role in assisting refugees, ensuring free and fair elections, preventing abuse of human rights, and increasing public confidence. The presence of uniformed, international civil police in a community can increase the sense of personal security of local citizens who would be intimidated by or opposed to the presence of armed, foreign troops in their community.

While military and civil police forces have participated in international peace operations since the early 1960s, international constabulary forces in such missions have appeared only relatively recently. This phenomenon is somewhat surprising because the logic of utilizing constabularies in postconflict environments has been so persuasive that America repeatedly turned to such forces throughout its history. From the early colonial period, English and Spanish settlers drew on their respective European traditions to organize local militias that performed both military and police functions. During the Civil War, the Grand Army of the Republic both preserved the Union and dealt with riots and sedition. On the American frontier, settlers banded together to defend their homes against marauders and to provide rough-and-ready justice. The best known example of an American constabulary was the Texas Rangers, who fought Indians, patrolled the Mexican border, and brought law and order to the frontier. The most famous Texas Ranger was the "Lone Ranger," a fictional character created by scriptwriters at a Detroit radio station in the 1930s. In the story line of thousands of radio and television episodes and several motion pictures, the Lone Ranger always came to the rescue.

Drawing on these examples from American history, the United States also used constabularies to restore stability abroad. From the end of the Spanish-American War to the post–World War II occupation of Japan and Germany, the U.S. military created units composed of American and local person-nel that performed both military and police functions. This use of U.S. military forces ended tragically when American troops that performed constabulary duties in Japan were sent into combat against North Korean armored divisions at the begin-ning of the Korean War. Since Korea, the U.S. military has for-sworn creating constabulary units and resisted performing police duties. At the same time, the U.S. government has encour-aged the use of constabulary forces from other countries. Faced with the need to close the "security gap" between military and civil police forces and reduce the U.S. force presence in Bosnia and Kosovo, the Clinton administration called for the creation of European constabulary forces to ensure stability.

The Bush administration also advocated increasing the use of constabulary and police forces as an alternative to the military for peace operations. The events of September 11 added urgency to the administration's call for a drawdown of U.S. troops in Bosnia and their replacement with a European constabulary to fight organized crime.

OVERVIEW

This study looks at the evolution of U.S. policy toward peace and stability operations through the prism of the American experience with constabulary and police forces in postconflict environments. Chapter 1 describes a riot that occurred in the Bosnian town of Brcko on August 28, 1997, that had far reaching implications for U.S. policy on postconflict security. After heavily armed American soldiers were nearly overrun by an unarmed, ethnic Serb "rent-a-mob," the Defense Department determined that European constabulary forces were needed to address civil disturbance in Bosnia. Chapter 2 examines the problem of what a "constabulary" is, as there is no agreed-upon definition; there is also considerable confusion with the term "paramilitary," which is used interchangeably with "constabulary" in the media. The chapter provides a working definition and details the history of U.S. experience with constabulary forces in postconflict environments. Chapter 3 looks at the differences between military and police forces. It also looks at the role of civil police (street cops) in peace operations and examines their shortcomings through case studies of police in peace operations in Cambodia, Somalia, Haiti, and Bosnia. Chapter 4 returns to the story of the U.S. effort to create a European constabulary force for Bosnia. It describes the process through which the United States agreed to maintain military forces in Bosnia, the result of which was a European-led Multinational Specialized Unit (MSU) as part of NATO's Stabilization Force (SFOR) in the war-torn country.

Chapter 5 recounts the checkered history of the MSU in Bosnia. Trained to provide crowd control, the MSU was misunderstood by SFOR commanders and improperly utilized. Chapter 6 details the subsequent use of both military and civilian constabulary forces in Kosovo. As in Bosnia, the history of these forces in Kosovo was one of misunderstanding, misuse, and missed opportunities. Special Police Units (SPUs) in Kosovo have only recently been used for their intended purposes of crowd control, high-risk arrests, and border patrol. Chapter 7 examines the development of U.S. policy toward the use of police and constabulary forces, the end of the UN police mission in Bosnia, and U.S. efforts to include a constabulary force in the new police mission provided by the European Union. Chapter 8 looks at the Bush administration's policy on peacekeeping, the War on Terrorism, Afghanistan, and Iraq. Chapter 9 provides a summary of lessons learned in previous peace operations and concludes with recommendations for the creation of a new U.S. Stability Force that would give the United States the capacity it now lacks to control civil disorder, restore sustainable security, and establish the rule of law in postconflict environments.

1

BRCKO: SFOR vs.

+ + + + + + + + + + + +

THE "RENT-A-MOB"

+ + + + + + + + + + + + +

T HE OLD AIR RAID SIREN SOUNDED at 4:30 A.M. on August 28, 1997. Soon it was joined by a cacophony of church bells. In a well planned and carefully prepared assault, buses loaded with Bosnian Serb women, children, and paramilitaries in civilian clothes rolled into the slumbering market town of Brcko, Bosnia. As sleepy residents emerged from their homes, they were told that NATO forces had occupied the police station. When the mob reached the police station, it was surrounded by heavily armed American troops. The demonstration spiraled rapidly out of control, with the mob venting its fury against the soldiers, the office of the Deputy High Representative, UN vehicles, and the UN police. The radio station in Brcko added vitriol, urging the population to attack the "occupiers."[1] As the day unfolded, American soldiers and UN police faced the most serious incident of mob violence directed against peacekeeping forces in Bosnia.

The members of the arriving ethnic Serb "rent-a-mob" were supporters of Radovan Karadzic, indicted war criminal and hard-line former president of the Republika Srpska (RS), one of two entities that composed the Republic of Bosnia and Herzegovina. The American troops were from "Tiger Base," Camp McGovern, the military facility that housed one thousand U.S. soldiers on the outskirts of Brcko. They were members of Task Force Eagle, the U.S. contingent of NATO's Stabilization Force, which was responsible for the Multinational Division (MND) North sector that included the Brcko region. The UN police officers were members of a special Brcko unit of the International Police Task Force (IPTF), which was created under the Dayton Accords to monitor the local police.

The ostensible target of the mob was the Brcko police station. It had been subject to an attempted takeover by Serb police officers loyal to Biljana Plavsic, the president of the Republika Srpska. Plavsic was a former Serb nationalist who was now receiving international support for her defiance of Karadzic and the president of Yugoslavia, Slobodan Milosevic. With municipal elections scheduled for September 13–14, President Plavsic sought to expand her influence by seizing control of police stations across northern Bosnia. SFOR and the IPTF assisted in this effort by helping to expel policemen who remained loyal to Karadzic. SFOR also seized a television transmitter that was used by the former Serb leader to broadcast propaganda against the international community. The goal of these unusual actions was to break the iron grip that hard-liners in the Serb Democratic Party (SDS) retained more than a year and a half after the arrival of the first NATO peacekeepers in Bosnia.[2]

Already a political and strategic flashpoint, Brcko was at the epicenter of the conflict between Serb political factions. Police stations in towns west of Brcko largely fell to the pro-Plavsic forces. Police in towns to the east remained loyal to Karadzic. In Brcko, the local police chief, who was aligned with Plavsic, intended to take over the local police station, which was held by hard-liners loyal to Karadzic. The police chief had alerted the American SFOR commander at Camp McGovern but asked him to stand by. In the confrontation between opposing groups of Serb police, there was a standoff, but the pro-Plavsic group ultimately lost its nerve and capitulated. During this confrontation, SFOR troops took up positions at the police station allegedly to "prevent violations of the Dayton Accords, which among other things barred police from carrying rifles."[3] SFOR subsequently issued a public statement that it had entered Brcko to deter an outbreak of violence after receiving indications that forces loyal to President Plavsic would try to take control of the police station and local media.[4] Their actions were seen as support for Plavsic by the pro-Karadzic authorities that controlled

Brcko. The arrival of the Serb mob was the hard-liners' response to the SFOR intervention into Serb politics.

The senior international official in Brcko was an American diplomat—Ambassador Robert "Bill" Farrand, Deputy High Representative and International Supervisor of Brcko—who was awakened by the siren. Farrand's bedroom was just down the corridor from his office on the second floor of an unassuming building in the center of town. Having slept with the windows open on a hot August night, Farrand's first thought was that there must be a fire. It then struck him that he had never heard a siren during his four months in Brcko. Moving to the window, Farrand first heard and then made out the darkened forms of numerous people "shuffling" toward the part of town where the police station was located. From earlier reports, he knew the local police commander was a Plavsic loyalist and was intent on removing pro-Karadzic officers from the station. Farrand had expected trouble.[5]

Pulling on his clothes, Farrand went down the hall to his office, where the single guard assigned to watch the building was on duty. The building housing the Office of Brcko Supervisor was a security officer's nightmare. It was right on the street with large glass windows and no protection. Only the window in the Supervisor's office had bulletproof glass, a contribution from the Swedish government. The building had a good-sized meeting room on the first floor and offices for Farrand's twelve-member international staff. The IPTF was previously located in the building but had recently moved its headquarters. Figuring no one would be awake at the Office of the High Representative (OHR) in Sarajevo and doubting he could get through by telephone, Farrand logged on to e-mail. From Brcko the electronic signal went via NATO headquarters in Brussels before returning to Bosnia. In Brussels there was a construction crane on a worksite adjacent to NATO headquarters. When the crane was pointed in the wrong direction, radio and satellite transmissions to NATO headquarters were disrupted and Farrand's e-mail did not work. In the wee hours of August 28, the crane was pointing in the right direction and the message went through.

Sitting in front of his antiquated computer, Farrand sent a report alerting the OHR in Sarajevo that there was trouble in Brcko and describing what he could see from his window. He concluded the first e-mail by promising to send a similar situation report every fifteen to twenty minutes. For the remainder of the day, Farrand stayed in his office, following events by telephone and through reports from staff members who managed to elude the demonstrators and reach the office. The mob vented its wrath on UN and OHR vehicles parked in front of the building but did not attempt to enter. With a bird's-eye view of the growing mayhem below, Farrand had not seen a single police officer.[6]

Donald Grady, the chief of the UN's IPTF unit in Brcko, had also been awakened by the siren and the church bells. Grady was a former chief of police in Santa Fe, New Mexico, with a Ph.D. in applied management, and his six-foot-six-inch athletic frame made him an imposing figure. An African American from Wisconsin, Grady faced the tough challenge in Santa Fe of reforming a police force run by a Hispanic "old-boy network." In Brcko, he had the more daunting task of turning a local police force of Serb thugs into a multiethnic police service.[7] Under the Dayton Accords, IPTF was responsible for reorganizing, retraining, and monitoring the performance of the local police. Unarmed and without "executive authority" to conduct investigations, make arrests, or use force, the IPTF was dependent upon SFOR and the local police for protection.[8] The 257 IPTF officers in Brcko were members of a special unit whose primary tasks were reforming the local police and protecting returning refugees. Chief Grady reported directly to the UN's IPTF commissioner in Sarajevo.

At 5:00 A.M., Grady left his residence and headed for the IPTF station in the center of Brcko. He discovered that SFOR troops supported by armored personnel carriers had taken up positions in front of the local police station, while SFOR helicopters flew overhead. The station was already surrounded by a mob. A week earlier, Grady had been instructed by IPTF headquarters in Sarajevo to make a weapons inspection of the Brcko police station at ten o'clock that morning. Just before 7:00 A.M., Grady received the first of a number of increasingly frantic calls from IPTF Sarajevo ordering him to go ahead with the weapons inspection as quickly as possible. In other towns, SFOR had used the alleged need to protect IPTF weapons inspectors as a pretext for surrounding local police stations and removing pro-Karadzic police officers. Grady tried to plan a snap inspection, but with only the IPTF overnight duty staff available and the streets filling with demonstrators, he quickly realized it would be impossible to comply with the order. At this point, it occurred to Grady that the IPTF headquarters in Sarajevo had advance knowledge of the planned takeover of the Brcko police station, and he had not been informed.[9]

From the IPTF station, Grady made the first of many calls that day to Farrand to brief him on the demonstration. He also sent out vehicle patrols in an effort to determine what was happening in various parts of the town. Demonstrators were moving quickly through the streets, congregating in front of the U.S. military checkpoint on the bridge leading to Croatia, the Deputy High Representative's office, and at various key crossings and access points. They were also blocking roads by building barricades of debris, dumpsters, scrap wood, and destroyed cars, making it impossible to enter or leave town. The barricades channeled SFOR and IPTF vehicles into cul-de-sacs or directly into crowds that climbed on the vehicles and attacked them with stones. Prior to the riot, the Office of the Supervisor and the IPTF had developed a comprehensive plan for the evacuation of all internationals, including the IPTF, in case of an emergency. The plan had been compromised. One of the IPTF local language assistants had passed a copy to hard-liners in the Serb police. Knowing the plan, the demonstration's organizers sent protesters to control the predesignated rallying points and escape routes. There were also well-coordinated mobile teams of rioters with instructions to block roads and prevent SFOR, IPTF, and other internationals from moving.

On the streets, white IPTF police vans with the initials "UN" painted on their sides were magnets for violence. The mob threw rocks, smashed windows, and dented the sides of the vehicles with two-by-fours. With no means of self-defense, those IPTF officers who could flee did so, driving through gauntlets of people throwing rocks and bottles at their vehicles. Except for three officers who suffered bruises and cuts from flying glass, none of the IPTF officers was injured.[10] The media reported that "IPTF officers in blue helmets and flak jackets" were seen fleeing Brcko in "white UN pickups with smashed windows" toward the safety of Camp McGovern.[11]

The IPTF station also came under siege by rock-throwing demonstrators who quickly shattered all the windows. The crowd attacked UN police vehicles in the station's parking lot, removing the radios and then turning over the vehicles and setting them on fire. Altogether, thirty UN vehicles were destroyed and seventy others were vandalized and damaged. Inside the IPTF station, the thirty officers on duty barricaded the doors and windows and hid under their desks, but the crowd made no attempt to enter the building. Telephone calls from IPTF officers and other internationals began to come to the station. Most of the IPTF forces, like other members of the foreign community, were trapped in their homes by hostile crowds that prevented them from leaving.[12] Two IPTF officers, Bill Aycock and Joe Jordan, were protected by their Serb landlord, who put the officers' UN vehicle in his garage and hid the officers in his attic. The landlord told the officers they would be safe, but their vehicle would be destroyed if it was discovered by the mob. When an opportunity to escape presented itself, a group of elderly neighbors formed a protective ring around the UN officers' van as they drove out of the neighborhood.[13]

At about 8:00 A.M., Grady made the first of several attempts to get the RS police to control the disturbance. He found the head of the regional police, Chief Bjelosivic, at the headquarters of the Ministry of Interior Special Police Unit. Grady was unaware Bjelosivic had already tried but failed to take over the main police station and was now completely discredited in the eyes of nearly all of the RS police officers. Bjelosivic told Grady only that there was nothing he could do. Two hours later, the frightened

Bjelosivic fled Brcko for the safety of Camp McGovern. After his departure, Grady's subsequent efforts to rally the RS police also failed because the few pro-Plavsic officers who remained in Brcko were too frightened to intervene.[14]

By midmorning, the mood in Brcko had turned ugly. Shops were shuttered. Angry people roamed the streets. Truckloads of shouting men, some carrying Karadzic posters, roared around town. Roving mobs smashed cars belonging to international agencies. In incendiary broadcasts over the local radio station, Serb authorities accused the United States of assisting in the takeover of the police station and called for the townspeople to oppose the action. Speaking over Radio Pale, Momcilo Krajisnik, the Serb member of the tripartite Bosnian presidency,[15] congratulated the mob, saying, "I hope you will repeat this feat a hundred times." A Serb Orthodox priest broadcast an appeal for those who housed UN personnel to throw them out. The broadcasts also falsely accused SFOR troops of wounding four civilians and killing local people. The broadcasts continued until General David Grange, the commander of MND-North, ordered a helicopter to direct its downdraft at the station's antenna and blow it down.[16]

Grady drove into the town convinced that the demonstrators were highly disciplined and under instructions to frighten representatives of international agencies and destroy their property, but not to directly harm them. To prove the point, Grady, in uniform and accompanied by his female interpreter, left his UN vehicle and walked into a crowd of demonstrators. His UN vehicle was overturned and burned, but Grady and his assistant were virtually ignored. At about the same time, a small group of IPTF officers outside of Brcko had a similar experience. The officers were pursued by a rock-throwing mob, which stopped abruptly and allowed them to escape to the safety of an SFOR vehicle.[17]

THE POLICE STATION

The apparent order not to harm unarmed IPTF officers and other foreign civilians did not apply to SFOR. At 4:30 A.M., SFOR troops from "Team Dog" were already manning observation posts and blocking positions in and around Brcko to prevent the movement of rifles into the city and to support the scheduled IPTF inspection of the local police station. A platoon of U.S. soldiers had fortified their position in front of the main police station with concertina wire as they confronted a hostile mob with women and children in the front ranks and men at the rear. The rioters were armed with brick-size stones and timbers taken from the rubble of war-damaged buildings. The mob threatened the soldiers with clubs and mimed how they would kill them with pistols and knives. They attacked the troops in waves, with women and children throwing stones and men and youths swinging clubs and fists. The struggle lasted until midmorning.[18]

The Americans at the police station, led by Sergeant First Class Phillip Burgess, were members of D Company, Second Battalion, Second Infantry Regiment, First Infantry Division. Burgess and his troops were quickly cut off by the mob from the U.S. soldiers who were guarding the Brcko Bridge. D Company held its position at the police station until about 10:00 A.M., when it was "pretty much overwhelmed."[19] Demonstrators used their bare hands to tear down the barbed wire protecting the troops. Burgess was hit by a club and suffered a cut that closed his left eye. Another soldier, Sergeant Matthew Martin, was more seriously injured when the three-man crew of his Bradley fighting vehicle was besieged by the mob, which put steel pipes in the treads to prevent it from moving. When Martin emerged in an attempt to reason with the crowd, he was struck in the face with a board and suffered a broken nose and damage to his eye. With his position becoming increasingly untenable and Martin needing medical attention, Sergeant Burgess led his platoon away from the police station to a position south of town, where Martin was picked up by vehicles from Camp McGovern for medical evacuation to Germany.[20]

During the confrontation, a seventeen-year-old Bosnian Serb high school student, Mladen Pajic, was shot in the thigh when a U.S. solider fired his sidearm into the pavement and the bullet ricocheted. The boy's brother said: "They didn't shoot right at the people. I guess that is not allowed."[21] The soldiers at the station had authority to use force to disperse the crowds but were not willing to use their weapons against unarmed demonstrators. For their restraint and discipline, eighteen soldiers received medals and other commendations.

EVACUATION OF THE IPTF

From midmorning, the remainder of Grady's day was spent in a running debate with IPTF Sarajevo on whether to evacuate IPTF officers and other internationals from their homes in Brcko. Grady believed people were safer in their homes. Sarajevo disagreed. Trapped by hostile crowds and afraid for their lives, IPTF officers were telephoning Sarajevo and demanding to be rescued. At 1:00 P.M., IPTF Sarajevo ordered an evacuation of all IPTF and other internationals to Camp McGovern. Grady could not reach people in the town, but he devised a plan to evacuate the thirty officers at the IPTF station.[22] One group of SFOR armored personnel carriers (APCs) under the command of Army Second Lieutenant William White of D Company created a diversion by driving away from the station with the crowd in pursuit, as another group of vehicles arrived at the front of the IPTF station from the opposite direction. As the IPTF officers ran to the APCs, the mob ran back to attack the vehicles with rocks. Several officers suffered bruises, but there were no serious injuries. Lt. White was decorated for bravery. Once the IPTF station was unoccupied, it was quickly overrun and completely trashed by the mob. Equipment and furnishings were looted or destroyed and offices were vandalized. The station was a total loss.[23]

After arriving at Camp McGovern, Grady began to work with SFOR to evacuate the eighty-five IPTF officers who remained trapped in Brcko. The rescue operation involved many acts of individual heroism by U.S. forces. Among the most daring was an action conducted by four members of a U.S. Army Force Protection Team from Camp McGovern. The mission began when a German IPTF officer assigned to McGovern received a call for help from two British and four Indian IPTF officers whose residence in Brcko was besieged by a mob. In response, the team, all volunteers, donned civilian clothes and borrowed a van from a local merchant who ran a shop on the military base. The team removed the van's license plates and painted Cyrillic letters on the side to make it look like a local vehicle. With a chief warrant officer at the wheel, a U.S. soldier who spoke the local language along as an interpreter, and the German IPTF officer and his radio, the team, armed and "locked and loaded," left McGovern for Brcko. Their first challenge was to explain their way past an SFOR checkpoint outside the town. Their next encounter was with a group of Serbs armed with pipes and clubs who blocked the road and ordered them out of the van. When the driver refused, one Serb swung a pipe at the windshield but missed as the vehicle lurched forward and sped away, traveling by back roads to reach the IPTF officers' residence.[24]

The team found the house surrounded by an angry crowd. The van drove on for a block and then made a U-turn in front of a large, walled compound before heading back up the street to the residence. At that point, the team became aware of a U.S. Army Apache helicopter gunship hovering above them. Having been told before leaving McGovern that U.S. forces in Brcko were alerted to their mission, the team assumed the gunship was there to protect them. They did not know the helicopter crew was unaware of the mission and was reporting that an unmarked van full of armed Serbs had just turned in front of an arms depot housing interned Serb heavy weapons and ammunition. Back at the residence, the team first noticed a Serb woman standing on the porch, brandishing an AK-47. Their initial thought was that she posed a threat to the IPTF officers, who were looking out the windows. In fact, the woman was the IPTF officers' landlady, and she was protecting her rent-paying boarders. Using the German IPTF officer's radio, the team tried to get the IPTF officers to come out to the van. When this tactic failed, two members of the team left the vehicle and began waving and motioning the officers to leave the residence.[25]

At this point, the helicopter arrived overhead. Again the

team assumed the gunship had moved in to protect them. Instead, the helicopter crew was in radio contact with Camp McGovern, requesting permission to fire on the van if its armed passengers endangered the IPTF officers in the house. Fortunately, the helicopter's noise and downward prop wash created a momentary diversion that enabled the IPTF officers to reach the van, which sped off. At this point, McGovern warned the helicopter to be on the lookout for a U.S. team in a "blue" van. The gunship answered that the van below them was "gray" and was heading toward the U.S. military base. Aboard the van, the U.S. team was joking with the rescued British and Indian policemen when they spotted a heavily armed, rapid reaction force from McGovern that had been sent to intercept them. Having left the base with their weapons but without identification, the team was disarmed and held under guard until their commanding officer was brought to the roadblock to identify them. Once back in uniform, the team received a hero's welcome at the base and military commendations for bravery.[26]

Despite these efforts, seventy-five to eighty IPTF officers remained trapped in the town and at risk of assault by gangs of increasingly intoxicated Serb thugs. Under a plan devised by Chief Grady, the remaining IPTF officers were told to slip away from their residences after dark and make their way to a few predesignated roads, where they would be picked up by SFOR vehicles. The plan misfired when the evacuees were given the wrong time and began arriving at the pickup points before the rescue vehicles had left Camp McGovern. Eventually, the recovery effort went forward, concluding at 3:30 A.M. with the safe recovery of the last IPTF officer from Brcko—twenty-three hours after the rent-a-mob arrived.[27]

THE BRCKO BRIDGE

As various SFOR platoons were attacked and overrun by crowds of up to eight hundred rioters, they fell back toward the SFOR fixed position guarding the bridge across the Sava River. SFOR's principal lifeline to Croatia and its supply base in Hungary, the

Brcko Bridge was regularly guarded by a company of American SFOR troops from the U.S. Army's First Mechanized Infantry Division. The troops were barricaded behind sandbags and supported by an Abrams M-1 tank and two Bradley fighting vehicles. They were armed with M-16 automatic rifles, grenades, and sidearms. Facing them was a hostile mob of civilians, including large numbers of women and children. For nearly twelve hours, hostile Serbs armed with bricks, railroad ties, and Molotov cocktails assaulted the bridge's defenders. The mob made repeated advances, pelting the soldiers with rocks and bricks. Rioters attempted to penetrate the wire barrier and to climb onto and damage military vehicles. As the troops were under orders not to fire, they used their rifles to push back the crowd, but the fighting was often hand-to-hand. There were fistfights. Troops grabbed rioters and pushed them back into the crowd. Serb men used railroad ties to damage vehicles and to injure soldiers, who lost their footing and fell to the ground.[28]

As the day wore on, the U.S. commander, Captain Kevin Hendricks, began to rotate his men to the Croatian side, where they were able to rest, eat, and recuperate out of sight of the struggle for control of the bridge. He also began to use a careful, graduated escalation of warning shots—from pistols to rifles to machine guns—in an attempt to deter the crowd. Specific soldiers were assigned this responsibility, ordered when to fire, and instructed to aim at targets that could be hit without endangering the rioters. This tactic had no apparent effect until the soldiers fired a heavy machine gun that tore away the facade of an abandoned building. This display of firepower dissuaded the crowd, which drew back and limited its further attack to stones and Molotov cocktails.[29] Finally, when a Molotov cocktail was thrown at a military vehicle, the troops lost patience and fired tear gas, the first time this chemical agent was used in Bosnia. Tear gas was also dropped from a hovering helicopter.[30]

At 7:30 P.M., Momcilo Krajisnik, the Serb member of the Bosnian presidency, and Dragan Kalinic, speaker of the RS People's Assembly, arrived in Brcko in an impressive motorcade of black limousines. They stopped at the mayor's office, which was located adjacent to the Brcko Bridge, and went inside for a meeting with local officials.[31] At the conclusion of the meeting, Krajisnik emerged and stood on a vehicle to address the crowd that had been attacking the bridge. Krajisnik praised the demonstrators for their actions and for their sacrifices in defense of the Serbian people. Almost as suddenly as the violence at the bridge started, it was over. Krajisnik's speech, exhaustion, and the coming of darkness quieted the rioters. A few hours later, General Grange convened a meeting at Camp McGovern attended by Colonel James Greer, commander of the "Steel Tigers," Task Force 1-77 Armor; Farrand; Grady; the mayor of Brcko; the new acting police chief; and the local SDS party boss to discuss restoring public order.[32]

In Sarajevo, August 28 was the first day in office for the new United States ambassador to Bosnia, Richard D. Kauzlarich. Having arrived in Sarajevo the previous afternoon, Kauzlarich was informed of the situation in Brcko as he prepared for his first meeting with the Bosnian foreign minister and the formal presentation of his credentials to the Bosnian and Croat members of the tripartite Bosnian presidency. Kauzlarich and his staff were in the process of preparing for a previously scheduled visit on August 30 from the U.S. special Balkan envoy, Ambassador Robert Gelbard, and the NATO Supreme Allied Commander Europe (SACEUR), General Wesley Clark. The new ambassador's immediate concern was for the safety of Americans in Brcko, particularly U.S. military forces and members of the American contingent of the IPTF. Kauzlarich presented his credentials at 11 A.M. The Serb member of the presidency, Momcilo Krajisnik, did not attend the presentation, in keeping with his policy of visiting Sarajevo only for formal meetings of the joint presidency.[33]

In the afternoon, Kauzlarich received a telephone call from Farrand, who briefed the ambassador on the situation in Brcko. Farrand was also concerned about the safety of the Americans, particularly those in the IPTF. By the time of the call, however, Farrand seemed comfortable that most Americans had already arrived safely at Camp McGovern. Farrand told the ambassador he was certain the riot was orchestrated by Serb hard-liners in Pale. Kauzlarich's day concluded with a meeting with a U.S. congressional delegation composed of members of the House of Representatives and led by Missouri Democrat Ike Skelton. In their meeting, the congressional delegation made clear to the ambassador their opposition to continuing U.S. troop presence in Bosnia. They also made clear they did not want U.S. troops placed in dangerous situations, such as pursuing war criminals, or subjected to the kind of risks they were experiencing at that moment in Brcko.[34]

In Washington, the retiring chairman of the Joint Chiefs of Staff, General John Shalikashvili, held his farewell press conference on August 28. The general played down the Brcko incident, telling reporters the police chiefs in four Bosnian Serb towns had changed allegiance to Mrs. Plavsic, and the UN IPTF had gone there to begin the process of police reform. He noted that things had gone smoothly in all the towns but Brcko, "where some hard-liners had resisted, moving in busloads of supporters and agitating." Shalikashvili said, "Some elements (peacekeepers) got caught up in the middle of a demonstration, which got pretty heated."[35] White House Deputy Press Secretary Joe Lockhart took a stronger line. Speaking from the president's vacation retreat at Martha's Vineyard, Lockhart said the U.S. "will hold the parties' leadership responsible for keeping their people under control."[36]

On August 30, Ambassador Gelbard, the U.S. special representative for implementation of the Dayton Accords, arrived in Sarajevo and delivered a blunt warning to Krajisnik and other hard-line Serbs during a visit to their headquarters in nearby Pale. Speaking to a Krajisnik aide, Gelbard accused the hard-liners of instigating the violence in Brcko and of "incredible cowardice in using women and children as shields" during the violence. Gelbard warned that continued opposition of Dayton implementation would not be tolerated, and any repetition of events in Brcko would have "the most serious consequences imaginable."[37] Gelbard's tough message was reinforced by a warning from General Clark: peacekeeping troops in Bosnia would use deadly force, if necessary, to deal with future mob violence and to protect U.S. forces.[38] Clark's statement was made in accordance with guidance received from U.S. Secretary of Defense William Cohen to not "let our troops be forced off the field of battle."[39] On September 3, Defense Department officials announced that an additional eighteen F-16 fighters based in Aviana, Italy would patrol the skies over Bosnia to act as a deterrent to those who might foment violence or attempt to disrupt the September elections.[40]

On September 2 in Brcko, the Principal Deputy High Representative, Ambassador Jacques Klein, and Task Force Eagle's commander, General Grange, appeared with Brcko Supervisor Robert Farrand at a media conference to demonstrate the international community's support for Farrand and the Dayton process. Klein said it was clear that the August 28 riot was "orchestrated from elsewhere." The "conductors," Klein said, were the same leaders who had led the Serbs into "cul-de-sacs" that were not in their interest. He said the international community was evenhanded, but that it would help those who supported democracy and the Dayton process. Klein's remarks were echoed by Farrand, who said the August 28 event was part of a deliberate plan to use violence to discredit the international community, particularly SFOR and the IPTF. As evidence that the violence had been orchestrated, Farrand cited the sirens that signaled the start of the riot and the fact that the mobs at every location made the same demands. Farrand said the citizens of Brcko were ashamed of the violence and embarrassed that Serbs were responsible for the disturbance. He said the international community knew who was responsible and would "keep the spotlight of accountability on those authorities."[41] General Grange condemned the local Brcko police for not attempting to control the riot and said that it appeared that the police, in conjunction with the local radio station, had incited the violence. Grange praised the performance of his soldiers, saying they had shown heroic restraint in the face of "insults and cowardice."[42]

On September 6, U.S. forces withdrew from the Brcko Bridge, believing they could do a better job of providing security

Bosnia and Herzegovina

Source: Perry-Castañeda Library Map Collection, University of Texas

for the town by active patrolling rather than guarding fixed positions. While tactically correct, the withdrawal was a political disaster. It created the impression that the Serb mob had achieved its objective of intimidating and driving away the American soldiers. International civilian administrators in Bosnia and the media criticized SFOR for sending a message of weakness by abandoning its position in the face of Serb pressure just prior to September's municipal elections.[43]

STATUS OF BRCKO

Behind the bold facade of official statements, the Brcko incident left the Clinton administration and U.S. military leaders with a bad case of the jitters. The decision by SFOR to help President Plavsic's supporters seize police stations and television transmitters was the boldest move by NATO in the nineteen months since the beginning of the peace process. The fact that pro-Karadzic forces were able to quickly organize a mob assault on American troops in Brcko sent a political message and raised the specter of U.S. casualties with the attendant possible loss of U.S. congressional and public support. U.S. concerns focused on two principal issues. The first was Brcko.

Prior to the Bosnian conflict, Brcko was one of Yugoslavia's most prosperous communities. Its location near the Zagreb-Belgrade highway and its port on the Sava River, the largest river port in Bosnia, made it an important trading center. The town and its suburbs covered about a fifth of Brcko municipality. It had a multiethnic population of forty-one thousand people, 55 percent Moslem, 19 percent Serb, and 7 percent Croat. In April 1992, a Serb militia had occupied Brcko, killing or driving out the non-Serb inhabitants and destroying their homes. Hundreds of ethnic Croats and Moslems were herded into a bus company barn, where they were systematically tortured and executed. Following the ethnic cleansing, the town was inhabited entirely by Serbs.[44]

At Dayton, the status of Brcko was not resolved. Under the General Framework Agreement for Peace in Bosnia and Herzegovina,[45] the division of territory between the Croat-Moslem Federation and the Republika Srpska made Brcko the geographic lynchpin of the peace process. Brcko's location astride the five-kilometer-wide Posavina Corridor connecting the eastern and western parts of Bosnian Serb territory controlled the road, rail, and river routes linking the RS capital of Banja Luka with the Serb hard-liner's stronghold of Pale. Its position also gave it control of the north-south lines of communication linking the industrial city of Tuzla in the Bosnian Federation with the river port and bridge over the Sava River

to Croatia and the rest of Europe. With all parties demanding
control of this strategic location, a compromise was reached:
Brcko would remain under the control of Serb authorities
while its final status was decided by international binding arbitration. The status of Brcko was to be determined one year
after the signing of the agreement (originally December 1996)
by an arbitration tribunal composed of three members: an ethnic Serb, Dr. Vitomir Popovic; an ethnic Moslem, Professor
Cazim Sadikovic; and the presiding arbitrator, American
lawyer Roberts Owen.[46] The Dayton Accords stated that "the
Parties agree to binding arbitration of the disputed portion of
the Inter-Entity Boundary Line in the Brcko area indicated on
the map attached at the Appendix." In an apparent oversight,
the map was omitted. As a result, not only the status of Brcko
needed to be determined, but also the extent of the area subject
to arbitration.[47]

Throughout the first year after Dayton, the pressure on the
arbitration tribunal mounted. The federation's argument was
that Brcko should be returned to its original Moslem and Croat
inhabitants. The Serbs responded that if Brcko were given to the
federation, the RS would be divided and effectively destroyed.
Brcko's proximity to the "Arizona" market, a flourishing free-
trade zone located in the Zone of Separation between the RS
and the Bosnian Federation, gave it additional postwar prominence. After Dayton, Serb authorities in Pale attempted to reinforce their claim on Brcko by relocating displaced persons to the
town. In March 1996, the Serbs conducted a form of ethnic
"self-cleansing" during the transfer of the Sarajevo suburbs to
control of the federation. Some ten thousand ethnic Serbs were
brought from Sarajevo to Brcko to join other Serbs relocated
during the conflict.[48] Over all, two-thirds of Brcko's Serb population was composed of displaced people from other areas.
Against this background, the arbitration tribunal met in
February 1997, but it was unable to reach a decision. It did,
however, call for the appointment of an International Supervisor
for Brcko and the deployment of a UN IPTF contingent to monitor the local Serb police. As the Bosnian members of the arbi-

tration tribunal would continue to cancel each other's vote, it became clear the decision rested with Owen and, in a larger sense, with the United States.

As the new International Supervisor for Brcko, Farrand was directly subordinate to the High Representative, the senior civilian official responsible for peace implementation in Bosnia. His mandate was to restore the city's pre-war, multiethnic character by facilitating the return of former residents. During the conflict, Brcko's suburbs were reduced to bombed-out houses and mine fields. Starting in the summer of 1997, Farrand began the difficult task of rebuilding houses and encouraging the return of the original residents. Farrand's actions generated high-level attention from the U.S. government. In June 1997, Secretary of State Madeleine Albright visited Brcko to reopen the bridge over the Sava River. In a warning to the hard-line Serbs who still controlled the town's government, Albright said a price would be paid for the atrocities that had been committed. Brcko was a ward of the international community, but it had an American protector. Located in the American sector with its American administrator and American arbitrator, Brcko was seen as an American problem. The Serb mob action in Brcko was a direct challenge to the United States.

The second issue of concern to U.S. policymakers was the American military force structure in Bosnia. Designed to intimidate and, if necessary, quickly defeat Serb military forces, the U.S. contingents in the NATO-led Implementation Force (IFOR) and the follow-on Stability Force were built around heavy armored divisions, supported by helicopter gunships and airpower. Following the entry of IFOR into Bosnia in January 1996, the military tasks assigned in Annex I of the Dayton Accords were quickly accomplished. These tasks included supervising the separation of opposing military forces, cantonment of heavy weapons, monitoring the Zone of Separation between the entities, and assuring a safe and secure environment. To accommodate those who wanted NATO to play a larger role, the Dayton Accords included a formula under which IFOR would have the authority to assist with civilian implementation, but its obligations were limited to the military requirements in the accords. Completion of the assigned military tasks did not lead to a military withdrawal. Instead, NATO was increasingly drawn into assisting with the implementation of the civilian aspects of the peace process.[49]

Under Dayton, the Office of the High Representative was responsible for civilian implementation. Its authority, however, was limited to offering guidance to the various international organizations, nongovernmental organizations (NGOs), and bilateral donors involved in postconflict state building. OHR could coordinate but not direct the reconstruction effort. There also was no requirement in the accords for cooperation between NATO and the High Representative. NATO resisted the pressure to become involved in civilian implementation, particularly the need to perform police functions. In March 1996, during the transfer of the Sarajevo suburbs, NATO troops did not intervene to prevent Serb militants from torching buildings, destroying property, and forcing the evacuation of Serb residents. It was also clearly understood that the primary task for U.S. elements in IFOR was "force protection," or the use of all means necessary to avoid casualties. U.S. military forces generally remained within their fortified bases, venturing out only in armored convoys with troops swathed in Kevlar. This policy severely restricted the ability of American troops to interact with civilians and to engage in activities related to postconflict reconstruction.[50]

In the aftermath of August 28, it was clear that the mob action in Brcko was an asymmetrical response by Serb hard-liners to the heavy armored forces of SFOR. Serb leaders knew they could never challenge SFOR militarily. They also knew SFOR soldiers would not harm civilians. The Serbs had observed the progress of the intifada in Israel and noted the success of mob warfare against conventional forces. The mob in Brcko was not a spontaneous gathering of people with a complaint. In fact, many people subsequently admitted they were paid one hundred deutsche marks to participate. The mob was armed with clubs, stones, and Molotov cocktails that were used to set vehicles on fire. They were highly disciplined and responsive to instructions from demonstration organizers. A group of several hundred would mass and intensively attack a small group of soldiers. They would then fall back, rest, and eat before going back on the offensive in response to new instructions. By attacking in waves over a prolonged period, they were able to wear down the troops and eventually force them off their positions.[51]

For SFOR, the Brcko incident came as a surprise. No pre-planning had been done to deal with such a challenge. After August 28, it was clear to the new SFOR commander, General Eric K. Shinseki, that the U.S. military had faced an enemy in Brcko that it was ill prepared to fight. Tanks, armored personnel carriers, and helicopter gunships were of little use against hostile mobs of women and children providing cover for drunken, club-wielding thugs who threw stones and Molotov cocktails. U.S. military attention focused on the confrontation on the bridge, where American soldiers were pinned down by a hail of rocks and bottles. Although heavily armed, the U.S. troops were not trained or equipped to confront a violent mob. Regular infantry guarding fixed positions with automatic weapons, fixed bayonets, and machine guns were also at a disadvantage against crowds that rampaged at will. Fortunately, the soldiers had performed admirably and had not lost their composure under extreme provocation—despite taking casualties. This was not the enemy U.S. troops had been trained to fight. SFOR command understood the necessity for supporting civilian implementation and the need for continuing to support President Plavsic. Unable to confront the United States with conventional military forces, Serb hard-liners appeared to have found a way to turn American heavy weapons and respect for human rights into liabilities. In pursuit of their goal of obstructing Dayton implementation, they had found a means to embarrass the U.S. and the international community.[52]

THE U.S. REACTION

In response to the incident in Brcko, the Pentagon's first reaction was to look for a quick fix by using new technology. On September 3, the Pentagon announced that U.S. troops in

Bosnia would be equipped with sponge grenades and dye-filled balloons for use against unruly Bosnians. The sponge grenades were 40 mm projectiles fired from grenade launchers that were designed to knock people down but not cause serious injury. The balloons were filled with latex paint and could be thrown by soldiers to mark ringleaders and violent militants for later arrest. Some balloons contained special ink visible only under a black light. According to a Pentagon spokesman, the nonlethal weapons were not intended to move U.S. troops into the role of international police, but to give them a broader range of options.[53]

At the time, the United States was also at work on more esoteric nonlethal weapons. These included special devices that incapacitated rioters with low-frequency sound waves and by covering them with glue. Among the weapons under development was a "net gun" that fired a chemical that turned into a sticky net that entangled human targets. There were stun guns that knocked targets unconscious for several minutes but did not cause serious harm. U.S. forces had experimented with a "slime," or foam, gun that emitted a stream of sticky chemical that would "glue" attackers to the ground. There were also tests of acoustic weapons that made internal organs vibrate, causing disabling diarrhea or vertigo that would render them unable to move.[54]

Simply equipping infantry and armored forces with a range of nonlethal weapons, however, was not the answer. Pentagon officials knew that technology, no matter how imaginative, was no substitute for international security forces with the proper training and equipment to handle civil disorder. Such forces would need to be highly mobile and to have effective communications that would enable them to respond quickly to areas threatened by mob violence. They would require the ability to interact effectively with civilians, especially as they would be dealing with representatives of newly elected municipal governments following the September elections. To avoid exacerbating tensions, these security forces would need to be trained to use the minimum amount of force necessary to achieve their objectives. They would need experience in dealing with civil disorder, especially demonstrations organized by nationalistic, corrupt, political elites and their allies, the organized criminal enterprises that controlled many Bosnian communities. As such groups were supported by the remnants of former secret security services, international forces would also require the capacity to defend themselves against armed groups, if required.

Such highly capable forces existed, but not in the U.S. inventory, and not in Bosnia. So-called "constabulary forces," mobile forces with the capacity to perform both police and military functions, were, however, part of the force structure of many of America's European allies. None had been deployed to Bosnia as part of the NATO military force, but individual gendarmes were serving as unarmed police monitors with the IPTF. Constabulary forces were, however, in short supply. In most European countries, they were assigned civilian police functions in peacetime and were fully engaged with domestic police duties. The challenge facing U.S. officials was to convince European members of NATO of the wisdom and the necessity of assigning such forces to Bosnia, where they would certainly face potentially dangerous confrontations. The United Nations Protection Force (UNPROFOR), which served in Bosnia from 1992 to 1995, included seven hundred UN civilian police monitors with significant contingents from European countries. Some of these European officers were taken hostage and used as human shields or otherwise humiliated by all factions.[55] Europeans clearly recalled these bitter experiences and did not want them repeated. To convince European governments to commit police constabulary units to deal with future mob actions like the incident in Brcko was going to be a hard sell.

Finding European contributors to a new multinational police force was especially difficult because it was generally expected that Bosnia was headed for a time of widespread civil disorder. The September municipal elections allowed minority representatives to seek election to municipal councils regardless of their current residence. Successful candidates would have to return to their hometowns, however, to assume office. This process of seating minority officials in towns across Bosnia was likely to touch off widespread violence that would directly challenge SFOR. The process of political reintegration also was expected to encourage the widespread return of refugees and displaced persons to their home communities. Given the violence that had resulted from relatively limited attempts at refugee return, it was generally believed the spring of 1998 would be a period of renewed ethnic tensions, with the potential of reigniting a general conflict. This period of potential violence was also the period in which NATO would have to implement its decision on whether to extend its presence in Bosnia beyond the June 1998 expiration date for SFOR's mandate—a decision largely dependent upon whether American troops would remain in Bosnia despite President Clinton's repeated statements that they would be out by the June deadline. It was unlikely European governments would volunteer their own forces for hazardous duty in Bosnia if it appeared the United States was preparing to withdraw.

2
CONSTABULARY

✛ ✛ ✛ ✛ ✛ ✛ ✛ ✛ ✛ ✛ ✛ ✛

I F CONSTABULARY FORCES WERE THE SOLUTION to the kinds of problems international peacekeepers encountered in Brcko, there remained some obstacles to embracing the concept—first and foremost, finding a proper definition of the term. What exactly *is* a constabulary? Webster defines it as a "body of peace officers organized on a military basis."[1] The obverse, however, is also true: there are "constabularies" that are military organizations with the characteristics and authority of police forces. Constabulary forces are found in both democratic and authoritarian countries, but there is a widespread and mistaken belief that the United States has never had such forces.

Among academics, there is a range of opinion on what constitutes a constabulary. Some scholars have sought to define constabulary by the nature of its organizational structure, while others have developed definitions based on the functions or the tasks it performs. In the former group, Erwin A. Schmidl defines constabulary as a force that is "organized along military lines, providing basic law enforcement and safety in a not yet fully stabilized environment. Such a force can provide the nucleus for a professional law enforcement or police force," and he points to the Mexican Rurales and the Canadian Mounties as examples.[2] Morris Janowitz, the dean of American sociologists on the military, takes a functional approach: "The military establishment becomes a constabulary force when it is continuously prepared to act, committed to the minimum use of force, and seeks viable international relations rather than victory because it has incorporated a protective military posture."[3] His views are supported by Charles Moskos, Jr., who noted the emergence of a "constabulary ethic" among peacekeeping troops in Cyprus that was based on "behavioral adherence to the minimum-use-of-force

33

concept." In contrast to regular armed forces, Moskos states, constabularies are concerned with attaining viable political compromises rather than with resolving a conflict by force.[4] Other definitions focus on the tasks constabulary forces are expected to perform. Don Snider and Kimberly Field define a constabulary force as "one which provides for public security in a postconflict area of operation after the combat-heavy units have redeployed and before peacebuilding efforts have succeeded in re-establishing local or federal law enforcement agencies."[5]

The search for a definition of constabulary forces is complicated by the common use of the term "paramilitary" to describe a wide range of armed groups that may resemble constabularies. Lumped together under "paramilitary" have been such diverse entities as the Yugoslav Interior Ministry's Special Police Units (or MUP in the Serbo-Croatian acronym), Haiti's Tontons Macoutes, and the Irish Republican Army. The MUP, which perpetrated ethnic cleansing in Bosnia, was comparable to mechanized infantry in Western armies. The Tontons Macoutes, which terrorized Haitians during the regime of "Papa Doc" Duvalier, were neither military nor police but had overlapping functions and common membership. The Irish Republican Army was a secretive terrorist organization that affected military dress and opposed British rule in Northern Ireland.[6] British journalists first used the term "paramilitary" to describe Nazi-sponsored "Brown Shirts" in the 1930s. Paramilitaries are normally nonstate, illegitimate, poorly trained, lightly armed, highly fragmented, and politically motivated. The U.S. Defense Department defines paramilitary forces as "distinct from the armed forces of a country, but resembling them in organization, equipment, training, or mission."[7]

In an effort to lump everything together, Andrew Scobell and Brad Hammit define "paramilitary" as any uniformed group, usually armed, that is neither purely military nor police in form and function. Such a group may or may not serve as an agent of the state, perform international security functions, or have a wartime role as an adjunct of the regular armed forces. Alice Hills counters that "it is impossible to suggest one definition to contain all so-called paramilitary forces, but it is reasonable to suggest that paramilitary forces are forces whose training, organization, equipment, and control suggest they may be used in support, or in lieu, of regular military forces." Hills warns that attempts to fit constabulary forces under an umbrella definition of "paramilitary forces" can erroneously link them to organizations that have historically operated outside of a specific mandate and have used coercion or violence to further political agendas.[8]

In their book, *Policing the New World Disorder: Peace Operations and Public Security*, Robert Oakley, Michael Dziedzic, and Eliot Goldberg identify a specific role for constabulary forces in peace operations. In Dziedzic's conceptual introduction to the volume, international military forces intervening in "failed states" inevitably encounter an atmosphere of complete disorder brought about by the collapse or defeat of indigenous security forces during the conflict. The first responsibility for the military is to restore order and create a stable and secure environment. Military forces are well suited to this task because they can deploy rapidly and employ overwhelming force. The military's role in the initial phase of a peace operation entails separating local armed groups, restricting them to assembly areas, impounding their weapons, and supervising demobilization. While the military's role is critical, Dziedzic points out that the military is a "blunt instrument" capable only of imposing a rigid form of internal order that normally does not extend to dealing with civil disturbances, acts of revenge, and ordinary crime. Military forces are reluctant to engage in confrontations with civilians and are neither trained nor equipped for controlling riots, negotiations, or de-escalation of conflicts. For this reason, military officers do not seek these duties and are often unwilling to perform them.[9]

Normally, military forces rely on the local police to deal with civilians and problems related to domestic law enforcement. In postconflict environments, however, Dziedzic notes that local police forces are incapable of restoring public order, participate in the violence, or threaten the international intervention force. At the same time, international civilian police forces have proven incapable of rapid deployment and are often precluded from helping to restore internal security either by their mandate or because they are unarmed. Dziedzic argues that a "security gap" is created by the absence of a force that can maintain public order and restore the rule of law. Those who oppose peace often take advantage of this gap to engage in politically motivated violence and promote civil unrest.

While restoration of absolute public security is not possible, Dziedzic argues that the security gap can be narrowed by increasing the willingness of international military forces to expand their scope of operations and by deploying international constabulary forces to perform the functions required to restore internal stability. He and his co-editors point out that constabulary forces are capable of restoring public order and are better suited for law enforcement functions and for interacting with local police and civilians than military forces. In Panama in 1990, for example, the task of restoring and maintaining public order was assigned to U.S. military police and U.S. military reservists, many of whom were police officers in civilian life. They were teamed with newly trained members of the Panamanian national police to jointly take on responsibility for providing police services and maintaining internal security.

Even after the military has established effective control and international and local civilian police are in place, Dziedzic notes that there is a continuing need for constabulary forces. Between the "outer shell" of security provided by the military and the "inner shell" of security provided by civilian police, courts, and prisons, an "enforcement gap" may arise. Typically this gap relates to the "basic maintenance of law and order or noncompliance with the peace agreement" and involves serious breakdowns in public order and challenges from spoilers who want to continue the conflict. Even in mature peace operations, Dziedzic points out, the international community can be acutely challenged because the capabilities of the international military and the international and local police may not overlap. Military forces may have only heavy armor units available, while the police may not have the weapons, equipment, or training to handle major confrontations. This has been the case in every instance where international civilian police have been deployed. The experience of international police in peace operations has demonstrated the need for specially trained and equipped constabulary forces to support the police and, if necessary, to intervene directly to restore public order.

CONSTABULARY FORCES IN DEMOCRATIC COUNTRIES

The ambiguous and conflicting definitions of a constabulary can be clarified by looking at the specific organizations and functions of constabulary forces in democratic countries. These forces are highly trained, flexible organizations with distinct histories of civilian and military service to their respective governments. They have a clear command structure and operate under specific guidelines laid out in their individual mandates. Their primary functions center around the protection and well-being of the country and its citizens and the fulfillment of the interests and international obligations of the government. What follows are descriptions of the organization, mission, and international involvement of the constabulary forces of France, Italy, the Netherlands, Spain, and Argentina.

The French Gendarmerie

Organization. Most of the world's paramilitary police forces are modeled on France's Gendarmerie Nationale. This national police force is military in character and answers to the Minister of Defense. The Gendarmerie is divided into two subdivisions: the Departmental Gendarmerie (Gendarmerie Départementale) and the Mobile Gendarmerie (Gendarmerie Mobile).[10] Additionally, there are special formations with about 4,500 personnel, including the Republican Guard, and squads for protection of commercial aviation. With approximately 63,400 personnel, the Departmental Gendarmerie is responsible for law enforcement in towns with fewer than 10,000 inhabitants and in rural areas, and for fulfilling the duties of a military police. Special units of the Departmental Gendarmerie handle investigations for the judicial police, undertake surveillance duties, prevent and research traffic law violations, and protect mountain regions and trails. The Mobile Gendarmerie's 129 companies of 17,025 personnel constitute a reserve force that can be used to maintain public order. It is sent into action on the orders of the municipal authorities of any of France's territorial-administrative *départements* to deal with emergencies or serious civil disturbances.[11] Recruits must have completed military service and meet other standards. Additionally, they must complete basic and specialized training courses. Officer candidates are usually recruited from the army officer corps, and then they must complete a training course at the Gendarmerie officers' school.

Mission and functions. In peacetime, much of the Gendarmerie is engaged in routine domestic police work. In 2000, 53 percent of its mission involved administrative policing, traffic control, and public security.[12] Specialized Maritime Gendarmerie and Air Transport Gendarmerie units are responsible for security of these installations and for investigating accidents.[13] An additional 35 percent of the organization's work in 2000 was in judicial investigation. In times of war, the Gendarmerie comes under the Ministry of Defense and is considered part of the French army. Its duties include protection of domestic territory and military police functions.

International involvement. To meet an increasing international demand for its services, the French Gendarmerie promotes multilateral law enforcement cooperation in Western Europe, provides bilateral police assistance programs in developing countries, and serves in international military and police forces under the auspices of NATO and the United Nations. In Europe, the Gendarmerie is actively involved in Europol—the European Union's (EU) criminal intelligence agency—and other regional organizations that enhance law enforcement cooperation. In this regard, the French Gendarmerie has a special cooperative agreement with other European constabulary forces—specifically, the Spanish Guardia Civil, Italian Carabinieri, and the Portuguese Republic National Guard.[14]

In the field of bilateral cooperation, the French Gendarmerie works with similar forces in the countries of Eastern and Central Europe and also in a number of African countries. Finally, the French Gendarmerie has a long and distinguished record of service in peace operations. Since 1978, the Gendarmerie has served in peacekeeping missions in Haiti, El Salvador, Cambodia, and the former Yugoslavia. It has furnished observers to Western Sahara. The Gendarmerie is also involved in missions where the French army is involved, such as the Persian Gulf, Somalia, Rwanda, and Albania. The organization has an officer in the Organization for Security and Cooperation in Europe's (OSCE) office in Vienna and will participate when the European Union assumes the lead for the operation in Bosnia. It also plans to have an organizational presence in the UN's Department of Peacekeeping Operations.[15]

The Italian Carabinieri

Organization. Formed in 1814 as part of the Army of the States of Savoy, the Carabinieri's authority was extended to all of Italy after reunification in 1861. The Carabinieri are an arm of the Italian armed forces and report to the Ministry of Defense in matters of military pertinence. In matters of domestic public order, including crime and natural disasters, they are subordinate to the Ministry of the Interior. Additionally, specialized units answer to other government ministries including Health, Culture, Labor, Agriculture, and Foreign Affairs.

The Carabinieri are both military police and an internal security force. Duties range from criminal investigation to riot control to border patrol, and they often operate in tandem with regular army units. Like the French Gendarmerie, the Carabinieri are organized along military lines, composed of 5 divisions, 18 regional commands (*comandi di regione*), 102 provincial commands (*comandi provinciali*), 11 groups (*gruppi*), 526 companies (*compagnie*), and 4,663 stations (*stazioni*); the divisions have interregional competence.[16] Recruitment is done mainly among military personnel leaving the service, so most members of the Carabinieri have military experience. Some lower ranking positions may be filled with personnel with no military experience on a contract basis, but candidates for officer and noncommissioned officer (NCO) positions are always military veterans. Recruits complete a nine-month course at one of the Carabinieri academies and then serve nine months in a training unit. NCO and officer candidates receive additional training at specialized schools.[17]

Mission and functions. Each provincial capital has a Comando Provinciale Carabinieri and an operational unit (*reparto operativo*) which, among other duties, deals with civil disturbances. There is also a criminal investigation unit (Nucleo Polizia Guidiziaria or Squada Polizie Giudziaria) and other units as required by local conditions. Mobile units (*Mobile*) operate throughout Italy to protect the national territory and guarantee the maintenance of public order. These mobile units include special police officers and account for approximately 5 percent of the Carabinieri.[18] The Eleventh Brigade of the Carabinieri is responsible for front-line activities in cases of public calamities and provides assistance and material aid to those affected.

International involvement. The Carabinieri have a long tradition of participating in international police missions. Their experience extends from Crimea in the 1850s; to the Persian Gulf, El Salvador, and Cambodia in the 1990s; to present-day missions in Albania, Kosovo, Bosnia, Guatemala, and Eritrea.[19] Italian Carabinieri serve in three forces in Bosnia. As part of SFOR, Italy provides leadership and most of the personnel for the Multinational Specialized Unit, whose mission is to control and manage crisis situations. Carabinieri provide tactical-military assistance and serve as military police in other SFOR units as well as members of the UN IPTF.

The Netherlands Royal Marechaussee

Organization. The Royal Constabulary (Marechaussee) is one of three police forces in the Netherlands. The history of the Marechaussee dates back to 1814, when it was first established by King Wilhelm I as a gendarmerie force with the dual task of maintaining law and order and monitoring the borders and highways. During the years of the First and Second World Wars, the composition and status of the Marechaussee changed frequently, particularly under the orders of occupying forces. After liberation in 1945, the Marechaussee once again returned to its original mandate and duties.[20]

A military police corps, the Marechaussee is subordinate to the Ministry of Defense, but other ministries are closely involved with its duties. Made up of some 4,400 men and women, Marechaussee personnel are assigned to the Ministry of Defense and the Royal Netherlands Navy, Army, and Air Force as a police force. The riot squad unit assists the State Police (Rijkspolitie) and the Municipal Police (Gemeentepolitie).[21] The Marechaussee command is divided into districts, one for each of the Dutch provinces. Each district commands a number of brigades. More important municipalities, such as Amsterdam, and the international airport are assigned a brigade.[22]

The Marechaussee training center in Apeldoorn provides instruction for all ranks from sergeants to officers. Marechaussee personnel receive general military training and are initially offered a short-term contract of service. Upon completion of the short-term contract, candidates are re-evaluated and potentially offered a fixed-term or indefinite contract of service with the corps. Officers appointed to the Marechaussee are required to have served at least three to four years in the military before entering the force. Officers can choose to continue their specialization training in law or military studies at the university level. All attendees at the training center receive instruction on security and service procedures, ethical issues surrounding the use of force, social development, social skills, and marksmanship. Noncommissioned officers who are offered fixed-term contracts also undergo extensive legal and managerial training.[23]

Mission and functions. The mission of the Marechaussee is to uphold the rule of law and provide assistance to civilian police units and the armed forces. As such, the Marechaussee has both civilian and military tasks. The civilian tasks include protecting members of the royal family, assisting the civil police in maintaining order and combating cross-border crime, monitoring of asylum seekers and providing police security for the residence of the prime minister. The Marechaussee also maintains a strong presence at Schiphol Airport, where it is responsible for security, monitoring high-risk flights, and traffic control.[24]

The military tasks of the Marechaussee include the provision of military police for the Royal Armed Forces, the protection of all foreign armed forces stationed in the Netherlands, and the coordination and control of civilian and military traffic. Units also guard Dutch military air bases and naval stations and are stationed wherever Dutch armed forces are serving abroad.[25]

International involvement. The Marechaussee has participated in peacekeeping operations as military police with Dutch troops or as part of civilian police missions. The Marechaussee has taken part in a variety of UN missions, including Namibia, Cambodia, Haiti, Angola, and Bosnia. It also supplied the Military Police Unit for the Multinational Force and Observers in the Sinai from 1982 to 1995. In case of a UN request for a rapid response unit, the Marechaussee can provide a detachment of about fifty, usually within forty-eight hours.[26]

The Spanish Guardia Civil

Organization. One of the three main police forces in Spain, the Guardia Civil was formed in 1940 from a merger of the original Guardia Civil and the Carabineros. The Guardia Civil is an organ of the Ministry of Internal Affairs and is directly under the State Security Secretariat. The Spanish Civil Guard is a constabulary force with both civilian and military capabilities. In times of war, it comes under the authority of the Ministry of Defense. The total complement is around sixty-five thousand with an additional force of nine thousand auxiliary guardsmen performing military service.[27]

The Guardia is organized into seventeen zones that correspond with Spain's provincial boundaries. Each zone is policed by mobile patrols, typically consisting of three or more officers, with a separate traffic division responsible for patrolling main roads.[28] Other units include four companies of the Rural

Antiterrorist Group, stationed in the Basque country and Navarre to handle extremist activities by Basque separatists; helicopter and special intervention units can supplement this force, if necessary. Mountain units are stationed along the Pyrenees frontier to deter smugglers and terrorists, as well as provide routine police and rescue services.[29]

Recruitment, training, and deployment are matters of joint responsibility for the two ministries. The sharing arrangement came as a result of the 1986 Organic Law on the Security Corps and Forces, passed to unify different elements of the National Police Corps and introduce a common ethics code for police practices. Although the Guardia Civil remained separate from the National Police Corps, the new law provided for the appointment of the first civilian director-general of the force.[30] Prior to 1986, the director-general was always an army lieutenant general.[31]

The Guardia Civil has a long tradition of family service. The majority of its recruits are the sons of former or current guardsmen. The 1986 reform laws stipulated that the two-year compulsory military service requirement for men could be performed in the Guardia instead of the army. Recruits entering at the age of sixteen or seventeen undergo a two-year course at one of the Guardia's training colleges prior to service. Entrants that have served the required two-year period in the army can join the force after an eleven-month training course at one of the colleges. After fourteen years of service, guardsmen can be promoted to officer rank. Direct commissions are possible for graduates of the General Military Academy in Zaragoza. Cadets enter the Guardia as lieutenants following an additional three years of training at the Special Academy of the Civil Guard at Aranjuez.[32]

Mission and functions. The primary mission of the Guardia Civil is to provide public order and security within Spain's borders. The civilian functions of the Guardia include rural and traffic patrols. In addition to these tasks, the Guardia Civil is responsible for control of firearms and explosives, policing interurban roads, transportation of prisoners, airport security, and enforcing environmental and conservation laws. They also protect communication routes, coasts, borders, and ports.[33] In times of war, emergency, or as part of peacekeeping missions, the Guardia Civil is attached to the military and functions as military police. They assist the regular armed forces by providing a range of police services, including military traffic control, weapons and customs control, and the protection of high-ranking officials and heads of state. They also conduct criminal investigations in cases involving military personnel.[34]

International involvement. At SFOR headquarters in Sarajevo, the main task of the Guardia Civil is the security and control of restricted areas. They also control the weapons of visitors that enter the Joint Operations Center at headquarters.[35] The Guardia Civil is also attached to the Spanish Task Force in the Multinational Division Southeast where, in cooperation with the UN IPTF, they are responsible for providing traffic and weapons control in the divided community of Mostar. One of their primary activities in the Mostar region is collecting ammunition, explosives, mines, and grenades that are turned into local police stations for destruction.[36]

The Argentine National Gendarmerie

Organization. The Argentine National Gendarmerie (Gendarmeria Nacional Argentina) was formed in 1938 in response to public demand to improve protection of the country's international borders and ensure the safety of Argentine citizens residing in the national territories and in more remote parts of the country. The new gendarmerie replaced the Argentine army regiment that was formerly responsible for border surveillance and national security. Although the organization of the force is military in structure, its primary functions fall within the scope of internal security. During times of peace, its primary tasks involve domestic police functions. In times of war, it can assist with the ground operations of a military campaign. The force also participates in international missions, most notably as members of UN peacekeeping forces.[37]

The Argentine National Gendarmerie is an internal security

force with military capability, reporting to the Department of the Interior. The High Command is responsible for providing overall direction to a force composed of groups, squadrons, mobile units, Special Forces units, and units assigned to specific tasks such as highway security and mountain rescue teams.[38] The group (*grupo*) is the basic unit and is divided into sections (*secciones*); three groups make up a squadron (*escuadron*), and several squadrons constitute a battalion (*agrupacion*). Mobile reserves are based in each regional headquarters. There are also support elements that provide logistical, telecommunication, and medical assistance to the groups.[39]

Training for the Argentine National Gendarmerie seeks to mold recruits into "soldiers of the law" through intense military and police training. The instruction is based on military doctrine and regulations, but it incorporates law enforcement training that is related to the force's domestic security functions. The Gendarmerie has a general staff college as well as training academies for commissioned and noncommissioned officers. There are also centers that provide instruction for members who are going on foreign missions and for specialized activities like mountain rescue.[40]

Mission and functions. The missions and functions of the Argentine National Gendarmerie directly address the needs of the country in regard to domestic and national security and foreign policy. In its role as a domestic security force, the Gendarmerie deals with drug trafficking, terrorism, and organized crime. It also enforces environmental laws, highway safety regulations, and airport security. The Gendarmerie provides customs and immigration police and riot control units when crowd control requirements exceed the abilities of the civil police. The Gendarmerie also provides protection for public officials and visiting foreign dignitaries.[41]

Within the framework of national defense, the Argentine National Gendarmerie works with the army to monitor and control the 9,370 kilometers of international borders Argentina shares with five neighboring countries. This responsibility includes patrolling and maintaining the security of international highways and lakes situated across international borders. The Gendarmerie's other defense functions include joint planning and participation in military missions as mandated by Argentina's National Defense System.[42]

International involvement. The Argentine National Gendarmerie has seen extensive service in a number of international peace operations. Companies from the Argentine Gendarmerie have served in peacekeeping missions in Angola, Guatemala, Lebanon, Rwanda, Haiti, and Bosnia. In these assignments, the companies have served as rapid reaction forces, on international observation teams, and in UN civilian police units. In November 1997, 150 Argentine gendarmes provided a strategic reserve and rapid reaction force for the UN Civilian Police Mission in Haiti (MIPONUH). Additionally, the Gendarmerie provides security for Argentine embassies and consulates, as required by the Ministry of Foreign Affairs.[43]

DEFINITION OF A CONSTABULARY FORCE

For the purpose of this study, the term "constabulary force" will refer to armed forces of the state that have both military capabilities and police powers. Such forces can serve in either a military or civilian capacity and operate independently or in cooperation with other military or civilian police forces. In examining the constabulary forces of France, Italy, the Netherlands, Spain, and Argentina, it is clear these forces fit the definition used in this text in several important ways.

First, constabulary forces in democratic countries are trained and tasked with performing police functions such as traffic control, criminal investigations, and public security. They also serve as border guards and customs officers and as riot squads. Beyond the specific functions outlined in their mandates, constabulary forces assist police forces in times of need. This includes supporting police by patrolling, providing area security, staffing checkpoints, and intervening directly if events go beyond the competency of local authorities.

A second characteristic of constabulary forces is their participation in the activities of the military organizations of their countries. Whether attached to a particular unit in times of war, assisting military planning, or providing military police services, constabulary forces are trained to function as part of the national armed forces in times of war. In many cases, constabulary forces are trained to operate as mobile light infantry and to perform military police duties such as handling prisoners, directing vehicle traffic, and policing the battlefield.

Third, deployed as members of an international peacekeeping force, constabularies perform both military and police functions and can be assigned in either a military or civilian capacity. Constabulary units are currently serving with NATO military forces in Bosnia, in both NATO military and UN civilian police forces in Kosovo, and as UN civilian police in East Timor. The combined training and experience of these units make them ideal for service in "complex contingency operations," where flexibility and adaptability are critical requirements.

HISTORY OF CONSTABULARY FORCES IN THE UNITED STATES

Contrary to popular opinion, constabulary forces have a history in the United States. Constabulary forces in the United States have formal roots in the Second Amendment of the U.S. Constitution, which states, "A well regulated Militia, being necessary to the security of a free State, the right of the people to keep and bear Arms, shall not be infringed." This amendment ensured that the states would have forces to execute laws of the Union and to repel invasion.[44]

The Texas Rangers

The best known historical example of a U.S. constabulary force is the Texas Rangers. During their storied past, the Rangers served as a volunteer frontier defense force, a military unit within the Union and Confederate armies during the Civil War, and as a Texas state constabulary with responsibilities for border control, frontier defense, and law enforcement. The origin of the Texas Rangers is found in the tradition of frontier self-defense forces organized in the original American colonies. Local militias, called "rangers," protected the frontiers of Virginia, the Carolinas, and Georgia.[45] Beginning in the 1820s, when Texas was under Spanish rule, English-speaking settlers from the southern United States requested permission from the Spanish authorities to form militias to preserve local order. The Spanish governor, Colonel José Félix Trespalacios, responded by organizing a volunteer force based on the Spanish militia system that had been transplanted to Mexico. The earliest defenders of Texas were a "hybrid of Hispanic-Mexican traditions," with the Anglo-Saxon concepts brought to Texas from the United States.[46]

Stephen F. Austin, the "Father of Texas," first referred to these citizen militias as "Rangers" in 1823, "because their duties compelled them to 'range' over the entire territory of Texas." These were citizen-soldiers who assembled when necessary and returned to their homes when no longer needed. Their primary role was to protect frontier settlers against attacks by Native American tribes.[47] In 1835, at the outbreak of the Texas war for independence, the Permanent Council of the new Texas Republic created a corps of Rangers with three companies, each with fifty-six men. The Texans' principal adversary was the Mexican army, led by General Antonio López de Santa Anna. The conflict was, however, a two-front war, which also involved fighting against Plains Indians along Texas's northwestern frontier. Ranger companies were assigned the latter mission, while the Texas militia faced the Mexicans. A Ranger company, however, did manage to reach the besieged Alamo prior to the famous battle, and its members died with the other defenders.[48]

After winning freedom from Mexico, Texas entered the Union as the twenty-eighth state. In 1846, the United States declared war on Mexico. Texas Ranger companies were mustered into the U.S. Army and served as scouts. This situation was repeated when Texas seceded from the Union and joined the Confederacy during the American Civil War. A Ranger regiment was formed as part of the Confederate army to protect frontier settlements against marauding Plains tribes and Mexican bandits, while thousands of individual Texans went east to join regular military units.[49] Little fighting related to the Civil War took place on Texas soil, but there were serious clashes with various Native American tribes. During the conflict, the western edge of the frontier retreated nearly 150 miles as outlying settlements were attacked and survivors moved back to more established communities for protection. In the words of one Texan, "It looked as if all the Indians on the Plains had found out there was a good place in Texas for their business and had gathered there."[50]

After the Civil War, the full force of Reconstruction fell on Texas. The state was left in economic and social chaos. Conditions were not unlike those existing in contemporary "failed states" that have experienced civil war resulting from political, ethnic, or religious conflicts. At the time, the justice system in post–Civil War Texas was in shambles. Most counties did not have the money for sheriff's deputies, courthouses, or jails. Such jails as did exist were so flimsy that prisoners could simply walk out. Judges rarely leveled fines because the defendants usually could not afford to pay them, and juries often could not be formed because few qualified males had taken the loyalty oath required of former Confederate citizens. In some areas, outlaws made up such a large percentage of the population that they could operate with impunity.[51] Frontier communities and citizens' groups repeatedly called upon the Radical Republican governor, Edmund Davis, to raise Ranger companies for their defense against Indians and bandits. On September 21, 1866, the Texas legislature passed the first law that explicitly used the designation "Texas Rangers," but the frontier defense force authorized in the bill was never funded.[52] For the next ten years, the Texas Rangers ceased to exist; law enforcement was the responsibility of a highly politicized and widely hated Texas State Police Force, which was eventually disbanded. This force did, however, demonstrate the value of a "permanent constabulary."[53]

In April 1874, the state legislature created the Frontier Battalion—Texas Rangers as a "permanent, professional, statewide

gendarmerie," ending the era of the citizen-ranger. In addition to
the traditional duties of fighting Indians and patrolling the border
with Mexico, the Rangers would also have civil police powers. In
the words of an early historian, "This did not lessen their duties as
soldiers, but greatly widened their field of usefulness and brought
them into closer touch with law-abiding people by giving them
authority to act as peace officers statewide." Although Ranger
companies spent much of the early 1870s fighting Apaches on the
state's western borders, civil police authority was also needed, as
the closing of the frontier coincided with an outbreak of lawlessness from highwaymen, rustlers, and bank robbers. "When a
Ranger was going to meet an outside enemy, for example, the
Indians or the Mexicans, he was very close to being a soldier; however, when he had to turn to the enemies within his own society—
outlaws, train robbers, and highwaymen, he was a detective and
policeman."[54] In the aftermath of the bitter Civil War, the Rangers
also had to deal with revenge killings, blood feuds, and range wars,
which were fought between rival bands and resulted in hundreds
of casualties. One classic feud erupted in 1875 between German
cattle ranchers who had supported the Union and Anglo-Saxon
farmers who had fought with the Confederacy.

During the 1870s, the Texas Rangers were involved in some
shootouts with the most celebrated outlaws in the history of the Old
West. Ranger John B. Armstrong confronted John Wesley Hardin,
an outlaw who reputedly had killed thirty-one men, and three com-
panions on a train. When the smoke from Armstrong's Colt .45
Peacemaker cleared, Hardin had been knocked unconscious, one of
the desperadoes was dead, and the other two were in custody. This
incident helped establish the Rangers' reputation for personal bravery in the face of daunting odds. A similar fate befell notorious train
robber Sam Bass, who was wounded and later died after his gang
engaged in a shootout with four Rangers. The Rangers' legendary
prowess in surmounting overwhelming odds was summed up in the
oft-used phrase, "One riot, One Ranger."[55]

Between 1874 and the early part of the twentieth century,
the mythology of the Texas Rangers grew in dime novels and pulp
magazines. During the Wilson administration, the Rangers' repu-

tation received a boost when they were drawn into the U.S. campaign against the Mexican revolutionary Francisco "Pancho" Villa. Wilson federalized the National Guard, turning the Big Bend area of Rio Grande River country into a virtual war zone. The governor of Texas, James Edward Ferguson, created special units of the Texas Rangers to defend the border. After Villa conducted raids into the United States, Ranger units patrolled the Rio Grande, ensuring that the Mexican combatants stayed on their side.[56]

At the end of the border disturbances, the Rangers became concerned with routine law enforcement. During the 1920s and 1930s, the popular myth and legend of the Texas Rangers virtually replaced the reality. The fictional portrayal of the Rangers took on added dimensions through novels, mass marketing, and the new medium of radio. On January 30, 1933, the "most famous Texas Ranger of all"—the Lone Ranger—made his debut on station WXYZ in Detroit. According to the fictional story line, a young Texas Ranger was the sole survivor of an ambush of his Ranger company by outlaws. Nursed back to health by his "faithful Indian companion," Tonto, he became the Lone Ranger, wearing a black mask to conceal his identity. The Lone Ranger rode his white horse, Silver, through decades of radio shows, television programs, and motion pictures.[57] The theme of all of the Lone Ranger episodes was the same: someone was in trouble and the "Masked Rider of the Plains" came to the rescue.

U.S. Experience with Constabulary Forces Abroad

The American experience with constabulary forces in foreign interventions dates from the era of "gunboat diplomacy" at the turn of the twentieth century. U.S. Marines occupied several Caribbean and Central American countries to protect U.S. investments, enforce internal stability, and foreclose the possibility of foreign encroachments in a region seen as vital to U.S. security. U.S. military authorities sought to restore internal stability by creating native constabularies with U.S. Marine officers to shore up local regimes and safeguard American interests. These forces were military in organization but were vested with police powers and performed police functions. In every case except Cuba, these indigenous constabularies evolved into antidemocratic armies, providing a vehicle for the rapid advancement of local dictators. The first of these constabularies, the Cuban Rural Guard, was created in 1898. Within the next two decades, the United States established the Policia Nacional in Panama (1904), the Guardia Nacional de Nicaragua in Nicaragua (1912), the Garde d'Haiti in Haiti (1915) and the Guardia Nacional Dominicana in the Dominican Republic (1916) following military interventions.[58]

Cuba

In 1898, immediately following the end of the Spanish-American War, the American army's occupation force of forty-five thousand soldiers was inadequate to both conduct military patrols and handle local law enforcement. The issue of how to maintain internal stability in Cuba was particularly challenging, given the breakdown in public order, environmental and health threats to U.S. soldiers, and demands from Congress and the public to bring home the troops after the U.S. victory. In time, this issue took on additional importance as the United States faced a growing insurgency in the Philippines. After the Spanish surrendered in Manila, indigenous rebel groups refused to accept the American occupation and continued their fight for independence. With nearly thirty thousand former members of the Cuban Liberation Army unemployed, the risk of a similar uprising in Cuba was too great to ignore.[59]

The U.S. military governor of Santiago Province, Brigadier General Leonard Wood, formed a Cuban rural constabulary to restore public order in the chaotic region that had been the principal battlefield of the war. The force, which was modeled on Spain's Guardia Civil, was led by American officers and numbered sixteen hundred "constables." The force was dressed and equipped to resemble the U.S. Cavalry, but its duties ranged from suppression of banditry to executing court orders and investigating crimes, accidents, and arson. In 1899, General Wood became the military governor of Cuba, and in April 1901 the constabulary formally became the Cuban Rural Guard.

Under close American supervision, the Rural Guard became, for a time, the most important police force in Cuba.[60]

The War Department liked Wood's experiment because it enabled the Wilson administration to respond to public and congressional pressure to bring home U.S. forces, who were in danger from tropical diseases and armed brigands. The Cuban Rural Guard initially was so successful that Secretary of War Russell Alger recommended the formation of a similar constabulary "sworn in the service of the United States for police duty" for Puerto Rico and the Philippines. His successor, Elihu Root, also endorsed the idea noting that the creation of such a force would absorb potential bandits, "educating them into Americans and making an effective fighting force."[61]

Panama

In November 1903, a group of Panamanian revolutionaries carried out a successful uprising against the Colombian government with the assistance of U.S. naval and marine forces that prevented the Colombians from suppressing the insurrection. On November 6, President Roosevelt recognized the new Republic of Panama. On November 18, 1904, Secretary of State John Hay and Panama's new ambassador to the United States signed the Hay-Bunau-Varilla Treaty. The agreement granted to the United States "in perpetuity the use, occupation, and control of a zone of land . . . for the construction, maintenance, operation, sanitation, and protection" of a canal that would be constructed by the United States linking the Atlantic and Pacific Oceans. Panama became a de facto protectorate of the United States through other provisions of the treaty that guaranteed Panamanian independence in return for the U.S. right to intervene in Panama's domestic affairs.[62]

In 1904, the small Panamanian army was disbanded at the request of the U.S. diplomatic mission and replaced by a constabulary force with police powers. The new Corps of National Police was composed of seven hundred Panamanians with Americans in charge. For the next forty-nine years, the National Police, which increased in strength to about one thousand men, was the country's only armed force. Panama did not need a national army because the United States guaranteed its independence. U.S. leadership of the National Police was intended to impart democratic ideals to and ensure American control of Panamanian affairs, an arrangement that would also result in substantial savings compared to the cost of stationing U.S. troops in Panama. The force received extensive U.S. material assistance and training, increasing its influence. The United States hoped that the presence of a professional constabulary would help shape Panamanian political opinion in favor of continued U.S. presence in the Canal Zone. Unfortunately, the fact that the National Police enjoyed a monopoly on armed force within the country made it an ideal vehicle for a commander with political ambitions and a disregard for democratic principles.[63]

By 1948, the National Police and its commander, José Antonio Remon, were able to install and remove presidents at will. In 1953, Remon transformed the police into a military force with a new name, the National Guard. In the 1970s, President Jimmy Carter negotiated the full transfer of the Panama Canal and the Canal Zone to Panama beginning in the year 2000. The negotiations succeeded in large part because of the cooperation of the head of the National Guard, Panamanian strongman General Omar Torrijos. In 1983, a new law created the Panama Defense Force (PDF) as the successor institution to the National Guard. Critics of the law claimed it "implied the militarization of national life, converted Panama into a police state, made the members of the armed forces privileged citizens, and gave the force commander authoritarian and totalitarian power." Five years later, the PDF and its new commander, General Manuel Noriega Moreno, were targets of a U.S. military invasion of Panama, Operation Just Cause.[64]

Nicaragua

U.S. Marines occupied Nicaragua from 1912 to 1933. Until 1925, internal order was assured by the presence of a one-hundred-member Marine guard at the U.S. legation in Managua. In 1925, public complaints about the Marines' arrogant and abusive behavior led the State Department to submit a detailed plan to the Nicaraguan government for establishing an American-trained constabulary, the Guardia Nacional, with U.S. Marine officers and Nicaraguan personnel.[65] The plan specified that the force eventually was to replace the existing national police, navy, and army of Nicaragua. The force would be divided into a "constabulary proper" and a "training branch," with American officers holding the primary positions in both parts. To head the force, the State Department appointed Marine Major Calvin Carter, who had served in the Philippine constabulary.[66]

Initial efforts to organize the Guardia were overtaken by the country's rapid descent into civil war. In 1927, U.S. Marines intervened en force to bring an end to the conflict. President Coolidge sent former secretary of war Henry Stimson to Nicaragua to dictate the peace. Stimson's terms included (1) a cease-fire and general amnesty; (2) inclusion of the opposition Liberal Party in President Diaz's cabinet; (3) general disarmament; and, (4) creation of a new Guardia, under the command of U.S. Marine officers, accompanied by a drawdown of U.S. military forces. When the rebel commander, General Moncada, and his subordinates presented Stimson with a signed agreement to his terms, one rebel leader refused to go along. His name was Augusto Cesar Sandino, and his followers became known as Sandinistas.[67]

To implement Stimson's proposal, President Diaz issued an emergency decree on July 30, 1927, authorizing a new Guardia, with U.S. Marine Lieutenant Colonel Elias Beadle (promoted to the Nicaraguan rank of brigadier general) as its commanding officer. An initial compliment of 93 officers and 1,136 men was recruited, but the force eventually grew to 2,500. The new constabulary would take over "police functions, control the movement of arms, and manage all buildings and material connected with such functions." Technically the Guardia reported to the president of Nicaragua, but its American officers were responsible for recruitment, training, promotion, discipline, and operations. The United States insisted that the Guardia be the country's sole security force under centralized authority, resisting

local demands for creation of a municipal police force in
Managua until 1931, when such a force was authorized as an
integral part of the Guardia. Beadle made a priority of indoctri-
nating the U.S. norms of political neutrality and national patri-
otism in new recruits. Among the Guardia's first assignments
were disarming rival factions and providing security for presidential elections in 1928 and congressional elections in 1930. In
both elections, the Guardia performed with notable impartiality.[68]

The Guardia's primary preoccupation, however, was the
threat posed by a growing insurgency led by Sandino. By the fall
of 1932, there was almost continuous fighting in all parts of the
country.[69] The Sandinistas' rebellion marked the first time U.S.
Marines, supported by local forces, encountered a national liberation movement led by a modern and charismatic leader with
an international reputation. The Marines and the Guardia
fought bravely and won most of the battles, but Sandino
embodied an appeal to nationalism that could not be defeated
militarily. The Sandinista cause received strong support from the
American left and broad support from governments in Latin
America. Fund raisers were held in New York and Washington;
hundreds of pro-Sandino demonstrators were arrested by police.

Mired in the Great Depression, President Hoover made
American withdrawal a priority. On November 6, a Liberal, Dr.
Juan Sacasa, was elected president of Nicaragua. He appointed a
former provincial governor, Anastasio Somoza, head of the
Guardia Nacional de Nicaragua, which had assumed full respon-
sibility for the war against Sandino. On January 1, 1933, the day
of Sacasa's inauguration, U.S. forces completed their withdrawal.
The Marines had suffered 135 killed and 66 wounded in fighting
against Sandinistas. President Sacasa negotiated a truce with
Sandino, who joined him for dinner at the presidential palace on
February 21, 1934. After dinner, Sandino was kidnapped on
Somoza's orders and killed by a Guardia firing squad.[70] In 1936,
Somoza staged a coup d'état, establishing a family dictatorship
that ruled Nicaragua until it was overthrown by a new generation
of Sandinistas in 1979. By then the Guardia had become a "Mafia
in uniform" that controlled prostitution and gambling, engaged

in smuggling, ran protection rackets, took bribes and kickbacks, and was thoroughly hated by all Nicaraguans.[71]

Dominican Republic

By 1916, the Dominican Republic had established a tradition of politics through revolt and military rule. Civil war had replaced elections as the mechanism for transferring power from one member of the country's landowning, military elite to another. Faced with a situation of continuous instability, U.S. Secretary of State William Jennings Bryan proposed that the United States assist in organizing a nonpartisan constabulary to maintain public order. This suggestion was resisted by President Juan Isidro Jiménez Pereyra, until a major insurrection against his government prompted the landing of U.S. Marines. On November 29, 1916, Rear Admiral H. S. Knapp issued a proclamation declaring the Dominican Republic subject to military administration by the Untied States. In Nicaragua, the U.S. intervention had limited objectives, and national institutions such as the presidency, congress, and the courts continued to function. In the Dominican Republic, the United States established a virtual dictatorship with U.S. military officers in charge of the country's institutions. Admiral Knapp became military governor and ruled by decree after the Dominican legislature was suspended.[72]

The primary result of the U.S. military intervention was the replacement of the traditional warring militias with a modern, unified constabulary, the Guardia Nacional Dominicana. The Guardia was to be commanded by U.S. Marines until local officers could be trained to replace them.[73] In fact, the American intervention led to the alienation of the Dominican upper class, which refused to serve as officers in the constabulary. Since the United States was unable to attract educated Dominicans to take positions of command, this role went by default to members from the lower classes and opportunists who saw service in the Guardia as the road to social and political advancement. The Guardia's enlisted ranks were also drawn largely from the illiterate lower strata of society, including former criminals and men of questionable character. Those who cooperated with the Americans by joining the Guardia were despised and considered traitors by other Dominicans. As the United States entered World War I, there was also a problem providing competent American military officers. Not surprisingly, the constabulary developed a reputation for uncivil and abusive behavior.[74]

With an initial strength of fewer than one thousand officers and enlisted men, the Guardia's first task was pacification of the northern and eastern provinces, a rural area with a long tradition of banditry. In 1922, Brigadier General Harry Lee assumed command of the Marine brigade in the Dominican Republic. Lee organized a special Guardia force composed of Marine officers and enlisted men that had suffered at the hands of the bandits and wanted revenge. In cooperation with the Marine brigade and with the assistance of these special constabulary units, the Guardia pacified the region at a heavy cost to local civilians. The main focus of the Guardia's activities then shifted to the south, and its mission changed from military duties to policing. An academy was also founded to improve the quality of the local officers.[75]

Among the representatives of the lower classes who took advantage of the possibility for advancement offered by serving in the Guardia was a small-town, petty criminal named Rafael Leonidas Trujillo Molina. Trujillo graduated from the military academy and in five years rose to a position in the highest echelons of the constabulary. On June 14, 1921, the U.S. government issued a proclamation for the withdrawal of American forces that called for the dispatch of a U.S. military mission to the Dominican Republic to maintain the political neutrality of the Guardia. The Dominicans resisted this plan, but the constabulary was transferred to civilian control and its title changed to the "Dominican National Police." This change was in keeping with the U.S. conception of the future function of the force. Subsequently, a U.S. decree was issued aimed at ensuring the force's political neutrality by transferring authority for appointments and promotions from the president to the police commander. The American effort backfired. Following the U.S. military withdrawal, Trujillo became commander of the National Police and used his authority over appointments to turn the force into his private army. In 1928, Trujillo was appointed chief of staff of the renamed "National Army." In May 1930, an election was held in which Trujillo ran unopposed and was elected president, beginning the longest period of dictatorial rule in the history of the Dominican Republic.[76]

Haiti

On July 28, 1915, U.S. Marines landed in Port au Prince to restore order on a day when a mob broke into the French legation, seized Haitian president Guillaume Sam, tore his body into pieces, and ran through the streets carrying the parts. The marines departed on August 15, 1934, following a "cordial and dignified ceremony" where a crowd of ten thousand Haitians applauded the lowering of the American flag.[77] During the intervening nineteen years, Marine Corps officers served as Haiti's effective chief executive; commanded its security forces; disbanded its parliament; managed its elections; ran its civil administration and judiciary; developed its transportation, communication, and education systems; controlled its media; and conducted its international relations. Authority for these actions rested on the presence of a marine brigade and the U.S. Marine-led Haitian constabulary, the Garde d'Haiti, which repeatedly was used to crush internal dissent.[78] In 1925, a visiting delegation of the Women's International League for Peace and Freedom concluded that Haiti's problems did not result from "individual instances of misused power, but in the fundamental fact of the armed occupation of the country."[79]

A major goal of the U.S. occupation was the development of an indigenous security force that would put an end to Haiti's history of repeated military insurrections. The history of the Haitian police constabulary is divided into three stages that roughly coincided with outbreaks of rebellion against the U.S. occupation. Haitian dissatisfaction grew out of the revival of a corvée law permitting the use of forced labor in road construction. The Garde d'Haiti was used to force peasants to report to work sites and to donate their labor. This road-building program led to a dramatic increase in anti-Americanism and generated a guerrilla resistance movement that engaged in periodic insurrections. In 1915, a Haitian constabulary was established with Marine Corps officers to perform police duties. From 1922 to 1928, with the consolidation of authority in the hands of a U.S. Marine general who served as High Commissioner, the constabulary became both a military and police force. From 1928 to 1934, following the Haitianization of the officer corps, the Garde became a military force, but it continued to perform police functions, particularly in the capital of Port au Prince.[80]

The Marines divided Haiti into four military departments, with regional headquarters linked to a central command in the capital by a network of newly built roads and a telegraph system. This created a hierarchical military organization for the country to which the Marines added an effective system for intelligence collection and a rural police force. In 1925, the Marines appointed *chefs de section* aided by *gardes-champetres* who were provided with "blue denim uniforms and rifles and ammunition" to maintain order in the countryside.[81] The Marine-led Garde d'Haiti created a model in which U.S. military officers provided guidance to Haitian political leaders. When the Americans left, Haitian military officers continued the practice of military dominance over civil authorities.[82] The Garde evolved into the Forces Armées d'Haiti and the *gardes-champetres* into the *attaches* that were the primary targets of Operation Uphold Democracy, the U.S.-led Multinational Force intervention in Haiti in 1994.

Post–World War II Experience

The U.S. Constabulary in Germany

Throughout most of its history, the U.S. Army has performed constabulary functions, and on several occasions it has organized forces that it formally characterized as "constabularies." In the very early years of its history, the army was frequently called upon to enforce the authority of the new central government. As the need to protect the federal government's authority became paramount during the Civil War, the army's internal policing activity increased to dealing with strikes and other manifestations of civil unrest. Following the Civil War, the army protected settlements and was often the only source of "law and order" on the American frontier. In the opening decades of the twentieth century, the army was called out on numerous occasions to control large-scale civil disturbances. According to the U.S Army's chief historian, General John S. Brown, the army's most successful effort to create a constabulary force was in the Philippines from 1902 to 1935. The army's largest effort occurred immediately after World War II, when several constabulary regiments were formed to police the U.S. Zone of Occupation in Germany.[83]

Following the end of World War II in Europe, the United States faced the problem of providing a permanent occupation force in Germany at the same time it was redeploying forces to the Pacific and demobilizing excess forces on the continent. When Japan surrendered four months later, redeployment ended, and general demobilization began in earnest. The wartime Allies divided Germany into zones with an occupying power responsible in each zone for civil administration, including law enforcement. Germany had no government. Its economy and infrastructure were in ruins. People were hungry. The country was spotted with camps for displaced persons and refugees. In this atmosphere of deprivation and disorder, the U.S. Army began considering plans for the most efficient use of the relatively small forces that would be available, given the public demand for the return of U.S. troops to the United States. In 1945, General George C. Marshall asked General Dwight D. Eisenhower to comment on a plan of occupation for Japan and Korea that envisioned a military police organization composed of local personnel with American officers. Eisenhower thought the plan could also be applied in Europe, but it required modification—specifically, the organization should be composed entirely of American military personnel. He believed the "police-type method of occupation offered the most logical, long-range solution to the problem of security coverage in Germany."[84]

In October 1945, the War Department asked the European Theater Headquarters to consider organizing the majority of the

Figure 1. Hand-Drawn Illustration of a Constabulary Patrol in Postwar Germany from a 1947 U.S. Army Report

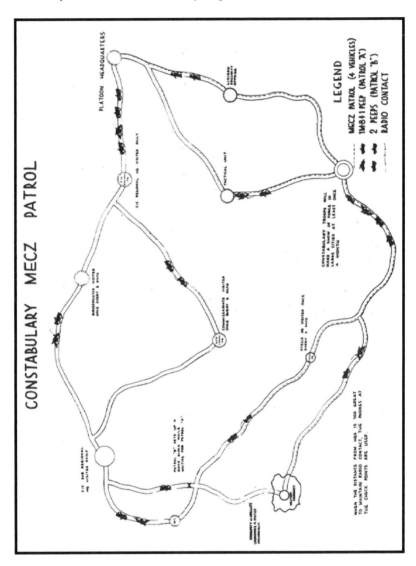

Source: Major James M. Snyder (U.S. Army, Calvary), "The Establishment and Operation of the United States Constabulary, 3 October 1945–30 June 1947" (unclassified report archived at the U.S. Military History Institute available at http://www.carlisle.army.mil/usamhi/ DL/ chron.htm#AworldWarII 19391945).

American occupation force into an efficient military police force
modeled on state police forces in the United States. By the end of
1945, the European Theater Headquarters provided Washington
with a plan for an elite, highly mobile force composed of the best
soldiers available from the voluntary re-enlistment program and
equipped with the most modern weapons, communications, vehicles, and aircraft. It would be organized to coincide with the geographic divisions of German civil administration to facilitate liaison with the German police and the U.S. Office of Military Government. The force would include 3 brigades, 9 regiments, 27
squadrons, and 135 "troops," plus headquarters units. The primary unit, the "troop," would be organized on the pattern of
mechanized ("mecz") cavalry units used during the war (see figure
1). Each "troop" would have three Jeeps and one armored car to
serve as a command vehicle. Each regiment would have a mobile
reserve of one company equipped with light tanks. Horses would
be provided for patrolling in mountainous terrain, motorcycles for
controlling traffic on the Autobahn. Members of the new force
would wear U.S. military uniforms but would be distinguished by
a lightning bolt shoulder patch, bright yellow scarves, and helmet
covers with insignia and yellow and blue stripes. The new force,
which would have an authorized strength of 32,750 personnel,
would be called the "United States Constabulary."[85]

To train the new force, a constabulary school was established at a former Nazi youth training academy in Sonthofen,
Germany, which was located in a winter sports area at the foot
of the Allgau Alps. It offered a curriculum that included courses
in German geography, history, and politics, plus basic police
skills such as criminal investigation; report writing; arrest procedures; self-defense; patrolling; and the role, mission, and
authority of the constabulary. The school received professional
guidance from Colonel J. H. Harwood, a former state police
commissioner of Rhode Island, who also developed a "Trooper's
Handbook." The constabulary drew its personnel from
armored cavalry divisions with some of the most distinguished
combat records in the European theater. Unfortunately, redeployment and demobilization had reduced these units to only

25 percent of their war-time strength, and most combat veterans had returned to the Untied States. The army's goal was to have the organizational structure of the new force in place and twenty thousand personnel trained and ready for duty the following summer.[86]

On July 1, 1946, the U.S. Constabulary in Germany became operational on schedule. Its mission was to maintain general military and civil security and to control the borders of the U.S. Zone of Occupation in Germany. It was responsible for an area that was nearly the size of Pennsylvania, with more than forty thousand square miles of territory and nearly fourteen hundred miles of international borders and occupation zone boundaries. This area was inhabited by sixteen million Germans and more than a half million refugees of many nationalities. It included numerous large cities, most of which had suffered extensive war damage.[87]

Almost before it could begin work, the constabulary was nearly decimated by a sudden speed-up in demobilization that resulted in the loss of fourteen thousand personnel, or nearly 43 percent of its strength, in the first two months of operation. The task of finding and training replacements for those who had just graduated from the constabulary school was staggering. There was also a serious shortage of noncommissioned and junior officers. During the first year of operation, the average stay of a soldier in the constabulary was about eight months. While other army occupation units experienced difficulties in maintaining sufficient personnel, the problem was more acute for the constabulary, given its unique mission. Constabulary officers were required to operate in small groups with limited supervision. They also had to prepare detailed incident and crime reports, interpret military government regulations and U.S. military laws, apply the rules of evidence, and use discerning judgment. Operating in a country where black markets provided the major economic activity, personnel also needed strength of character, discipline, and dedication to duty. Constabulary members were subjected to a broad variety of temptations offered by persons who often faced desperate circumstances.[88]

There was no shortage of challenging assignments for the new force. The largest and most widely publicized operations were conducted by "troop" or larger-size units against black marketing and illicit trafficking of contraband goods across international borders and between zones of occupation. These operations took the form of "search-and-check operations, shows of force, zonewide checks," and operations conducted in conjunction with allied forces against Germans, refugee camps, and, in some cases, U.S. forces. One such effort, Operation Scotch, was conducted on November 22, 1946. It combined a light tank troop, a motorcycle platoon, a horse platoon, and light aircraft, which were used to establish road blocks, inspect traffic, and search an eighteen-square-mile area of mountainous terrain in conjunction with a parallel French operation along the border between the respective zones of occupation. Operation Scotch netted a number of illegal border crossers; large quantities of cigarettes, cloth, weapons, and liquor; and a number of "suspicious characters." Operation Camel, a raid on a refugee camp, occurred seven days later on November 29. A constabulary force of 676 officers and troops searched persons and buildings in a camp housing Polish refugees where black marketing and other types of "nefarious activities" were taking place. The following spring, a large operation, code-named "Traveler," was conducted around U.S. military bases to snare AWOL soldiers and military and civilian personnel engaged in illegal activities.[89]

Within the U.S. Zone of Occupation, the U.S. constabulary had primary responsibility for law enforcement and civil security. This responsibility was exercised through extensive patrolling and through close liaison with the U.S. military government, U.S. military police, the U.S. Counter Intelligence Corps, the Criminal Investigation Division, and the German police. Liaison was conducted with counterpart agencies in the British and French zones and, with frustrating delays and other difficulties, Soviet authorities (see figure 2). The constabulary operated in a postconflict environment of ruined cities; a suspicious, disillusioned, needy, and often nearly starving population; camps of displaced persons and refugees; and political agitation by parties

Figure 2. Hand-drawn Illustration of Constabulary Border Control Points in Postwar Germany from a 1947 U.S. Army Report

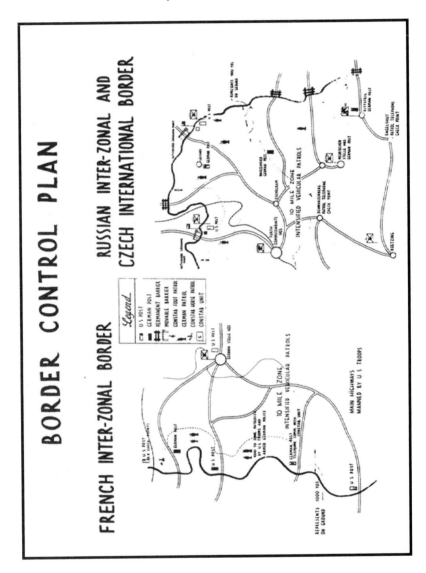

Source: Major James M. Snyder (U.S. Army, Calvary), "The Establishment and Operation of the United States Constabulary, 3 October 1945–30 June 1947" (unclassified report archived at the U.S. Military History Institute available at http://www.carlisle.army.mil/ usamhi/ DL/chron.htm#AworldWarII19391945).

of conflicting ideologies. In a situation in which all goods, including food and daily necessities, were in extremely short supply, black marketing and petty crime flourished. Refugees posed a particular problem, accounting for a disproportionate percentage of violent crimes involving the use of firearms. Camps containing displaced Jews presented special problems, as they could not be resettled and most agitated to leave Germany. During the first six months of their operations, constabulary forces conducted 168,000 patrols in Jeeps, tanks, and armored cars. Over time, an analysis of crime statistics resulted in a higher frequency of patrols in high-crime areas. Constabulary patrols normally included an English-speaking German police officer who made arrests in cases involving local citizens. American constabulary forces handled arrests of Americans or foreign nationals.[90]

In addition to controlling crime, the constabulary was responsible for civil disorder management among the German population and border security. Civil disturbances involving German citizens were few and generally resulted from food shortages, the general scarcity of goods and living quarters, and competition from an influx of refugees. At times, the food situation became so serious that farms were attacked for their crops, and there were armed robberies of U.S. Army facilities to obtain food. In response, the constabulary was deployed in an antipilferage program to provide protection. On the boundary with the Soviet zone and on the Austrian frontier, teams of seven or eight constabulary soldiers manned border-crossing points. Constabulary forces and unarmed German police also patrolled on horseback, on foot, in vehicles, and by air at a depth of ten miles along the borders, turning back twenty-six thousand undocumented travelers and intercepting twenty-two thousand illegal border crossers during one six-month period in 1946.[91]

As Germany recovered during the postwar period and assumed its place in a revitalized Europe, the need for the U.S. constabulary gradually disappeared. By 1948, West German police assumed responsibility for the constabulary's civilian police and border control missions. At the same time, the pressing security needs of the Cold War caused the U.S. Army to strengthen the constabulary regiments for possible combat missions by adding reconnaissance, rifle, and heavy weapons platoons. Eventually the army deactivated the Fifteenth Constabulary Regiment and reorganized three other regiments into armored cavalry units. On November 24, 1950, the headquarters of the U.S. constabulary was deactivated and its remaining elements transferred to the Seventh Army. The last units of the U.S. constabulary were removed from active service in December 1952.[92]

U.S. Constabulary in Japan and Korea

In Germany, the United States shared responsibility for administering the country with three other occupying powers. In Japan, the United States, for all practical purposes, acted alone in establishing a military government. In Germany, the Nazi regime was removed and the Allies governed Germany directly. In the American zone, General Lucius Clay was in charge of a military government that governed German citizens living within its borders. Since Japan surrendered prior to the entry of U.S. forces, the United States established a military administration but left the emperor and the Japanese government in place. As the Supreme Commander for Allied Powers (SCAP), General Douglas MacArthur ruled Japan, but did so indirectly through existing Japanese institutions. At its peak, MacArthur's headquarters consisted of some three thousand Americans and was organized in sections corresponding to the Japanese administration. Edicts were issued in the name of the emperor and carried out by Japanese government departments. For participation in war crimes, more than two thousand Japanese civil servants were purged from public life. Yet most of these positions were in the Internal Affairs Ministry; technical ministries, such as the Ministry of Finance, were hardly affected by the vetting process.[93]

In Japan, General MacArthur initially commanded the American Sixth and Eighth Armies, with a total of 230,000 men. Within the first two months of the occupation, these forces oversaw the disarming and demobilization of the Japanese military, which was accomplished with Japanese cooperation and without resistance. At the end of the first year, the Sixth Army was disbanded. By the end of 1948, U.S. military forces in Japan were reduced to 117,580 personnel. These troops were configured as constabulary and assigned to occupational duties. In contrast to Germany, the Japanese civil police remained in place and were given responsibility for law enforcement. The Japanese Home Ministry controlled the police, which had been responsible for public order, law enforcement, tax collection, customs, census taking, intelligence gathering, and censuring public expressions of dissent. The police enjoyed a positive reputation among the Japanese public, despite their broad and authoritarian powers. How to institute police reform became a sensitive issue within SCAP and with the Japanese government.[94]

During the occupation, SCAP removed senior police leaders, completely separated the police from the military, and reduced their function to law enforcement. Other institutions were created to take on firefighting, customs, intelligence gathering, and other functions. In 1948, SCAP created a Japanese police force of 125,000 personnel divided into two parts: (1) a 30,000-member national rural police that operated in rural areas and small towns, and (2) a 95,000-member force that was divided into 1,600 independent municipal police departments on the American model. In 1954, two years after the end of the occupation, the Japanese government returned the police to central control under a national commission of public safety and a national police agency.[95]

As in Germany, American military units in Japan were downsized and their personnel were trained to perform constabulary functions. Unlike Germany, however, the U.S. Army in Japan did not have time to reorganize, retrain, and re-equip these units to face the new threats of the Cold War. Untrained for combat and equipped with World War II leftovers, U.S. military forces in Japan were rushed to Korea, where they made a heroic attempt to blunt the assault by the North Korean Army at the beginning of the Korean War.[96]

On June 25, 1950, North Korean forces crossed the thirty-eighth parallel, swept through Seoul, and were headed toward the southern coastal city of Pusan and total victory. To stop the advance, President Truman ordered General MacArthur to send American forces from Japan to halt the invasion and make clear that the United States would assist South Korea in resisting aggression. In response, MacArthur ordered the U.S. Army's Twenty-fourth Infantry Division to move immediately from Japan to Korea. In terms of readiness for combat, MacArthur had little choice from among the four U.S. divisions under his command. On May 30, the Twenty-fourth Division was reported to have the lowest combat effectiveness, but it was located closest to Korea and could arrive quickly. To engage the North Koreans as soon as possible, it was decided to send a small task force under the command of Lieutenant Colonel Charles Smith ahead by air. On July 1, Task Force Smith, made up of elements from the First Battalion, Twenty-first Regiment, Twenty-fourth Infantry Division, landed at Pusan Airfield. The task force comprised part of the battalion headquarters' company, two under-strength rifle companies, a recoilless rifle platoon, two mortar platoons, and a medical company—a total of 406 officers and men. In Korea, the task force was joined by part of the Fifty-second Field Artillery Battalion, armed with 105 mm howitzers and 108 additional personnel. Smith immediately moved his force of 514 men north through hordes of fleeing refugees and retreating South Korean army units to Osan, where they engaged the enemy at dawn on July 5. The Americans were vulnerable to flanking attacks and had no reserves, and a steady rain precluded air support.[97]

The North Korean force of two regiments of six thousand men and thirty-three of the latest Soviet-made T-34 tanks rolled over the Americans. Outnumbered 15-to-1, Smith's men watched helplessly as the shells from their antiquated, World War II anti-tank weapons bounced off the North Korean armor. The Americans held their ground until they expended their ammunition and then fell back in disarray, suffering 181 casualties. Describing the engagement years later, Smith said, "After the tanks went through, what I saw was three tanks coming down and then about twenty-five vehicles, loaded, and behind them, North Korean soldiers walking four abreast as far as I could see." Smith said he was "very proud of the fact than not a man left his position until ordered," although everyone knew the odds against them. The enemy advance was delayed by seven hours.[98]

The pattern of the first engagement was repeated in the days that followed as the rest of the Twenty-fourth Division arrived by boat and engaged the North Koreans. The Americans fought bravely, but superior North Korean weaponry and greater strength overwhelmed these units at every stand. In particular, the Thirty-fourth Infantry was "thrown into a fight for which it was unprepared and was cut to pieces. Weak in numbers, completely out-gunned, unable to protect its flanks, and short of ammunition, it retreated in disorder, suffering extremely heavy casualties." In every case the Americans fought bravely, but suffered heavy casualties because they were ill-equipped, untrained, and had never been in combat.[99] So searing was this experience that U.S. military leaders swore that "never again" would U.S. military forces be converted to other purposes that would result in their losing their "readiness" and combat effectiveness.[100] This attitude affected the pace of the drawdown of U.S. military forces after the Gulf War. It also heavily influenced thinking in the U.S. Army concerning the use of U.S. military forces in peace operations. U.S. military officials were extremely wary of committing forces to peacekeeping roles that would blunt their war-fighting effectiveness. They were also strongly resistant to suggestions that the United States create special constabulary-type military units designed specifically for peace operations. The underlying fear was that in a future conflict, such forces might suffer the same fate as Task Force Smith.[101]

The Contemporary U.S. Experience

U.S. National Guard

The modern descendent of the colonial tradition of citizen militias is the U.S. National Guard. A uniquely American institution, the

National Guard is the oldest component of the armed forces of the United States; it celebrated its 365th birthday on December 13, 2001. Under the U.S. Constitution, Congress was empowered to raise a militia, but the appointment of officers and training of the militia was reserved to the states. Today the National Guard continues this historic tradition. The National Guard is composed primarily of civilians who serve their country and state on a part-time basis, reporting for one weekend each month and two weeks during the summer.[102] The National Guard is unique in that it can serve under the authority of both the federal and state governments. Normally, National Guard units are responsible to state governors, who can call the Guard into action during local emergencies such as natural disasters or civil disturbances. In addition, the president of the United States can federalize the National Guard to deal with domestic emergencies or for service abroad. When federalized Guard units are sent abroad, they are led by the commander of the theater in which they operate. National Guard divisions fought in both World Wars, Korea, and Vietnam; seventy-five thousand Army and Air Guard personnel were activated during Operation Desert Storm. More recently, National Guard units have seen extensive service with NATO forces in Bosnia and Kosovo.[103]

In the United States, responsibility for civil disorder management, including riot control, rests with civilian law enforcement. When civil disturbances occur in American cities, specially trained and equipped units of police are the first to respond. Normally this is all that is required. The National Park Police, which provides security for major demonstrations in Washington, D.C., and urban police departments across the country have become expert in deterring potential violence and maintaining public order. In exceptional cases, however, where the magnitude of the disturbance exceeds the capacity of civilian police forces to control the situation, the backup for civilian law enforcement authorities is the National Guard, operating under the authority of the state governor. Historically, federal authorities have been extremely reluctant to allow regular military troops to become involved in confrontations with Americans. Involvement of regular U.S. military forces in aspects of civilian law enforcement is seen as blurring the distinction between military and civilian roles in a democracy, undermining the principle of civilian control of the military, and reducing military readiness. Federal authorities have preferred to have the National Guard's more politically acceptable "citizen-soldiers" handle domestic assignments. National Guard units in all states are specially trained and equipped to deal with major civil disturbances. Instances when the National Guard has been called out have been infrequent, and most Americans can enumerate times when the National Guard has been used in this capacity.[104]

Between the start of the Civil Rights Movement and the end of the Vietnam War, the National Guard was repeatedly forced into service as the country was torn by protests and American cities, including Washington, D.C., were the scene of violent confrontations between demonstrators and police and National Guard troops. The president was also forced to exercise his authority to deploy federal troops in several American cities and to federalize the National Guard to quell civil disturbances. The Department of the Army's civil disturbance plan, nicknamed "Garden Plot," was frequently utilized. During this period, a "landmark tragedy" in the history of the National Guard occurred on the campus of Kent State University. In May 1970, a small unit of the Ohio National Guard panicked when confronted by a group of college students during an antiwar protest. Isolated and fearing their lives were in danger, the Guardsmen fired into the crowd, killing four students and wounding many others. The Guardsmen were officially absolved of primary responsibility, but the incident had a major impact on the national psyche.[105]

In April 1992, large areas of southeast and south central Los Angeles were burned and badly damaged during six days of racial violence following the acquittal of four white Los Angeles Police Department (LAPD) officers accused of beating an African American, Rodney King. The riots, which were the most destructive in U.S. history, resulted in the deaths of fifty-four people and more than $800 million in property damage.

The rampage of violence, arson, looting, and other acts of criminal behavior quickly overwhelmed the LAPD. In response, California Governor Pete Wilson activated a total of four thousand members of the California National Guard. Of those mobilized, the initial two thousand Guardsmen were members of the 3rd Battalion, 160th Infantry (Mechanized), 40th Infantry Division of the California National Guard. This unit was especially well suited for the task, as most of its soldiers lived in the neighborhoods affected by the riots. Many of these citizen-soldiers were police officers or had jobs related to law enforcement in private life. The California Guard had extensive experience in supporting police during natural disasters and some older members of the Guard had been deployed during the Watts neighborhood riots in Los Angeles in 1965. The Guardsmen were armed with M-16 rifles and sidearms, but they were used only to support the police in the performance of their duties. Guardsmen operated traffic control checkpoints, escorted fire trucks, protected buildings, and maintained security in areas that had been cleared by police. When the violence continued, President Bush sent two thousand regular army troops and fifteen hundred Marines with orders to "return fire if fired upon." The president also federalized the National Guard and sent one thousand federal law enforcement officers into the city. Imposition of a dusk-to-dawn curfew; exhaustion of the rioters; and the presence of thirty-five hundred federal troops, four thousand Guardsmen, five thousand LAPD officers, and four thousand other California police officers brought an end to the disturbance.[106]

More recently, some 425 members of Washington State National Guard were activated to assist Seattle police in controlling violent demonstrations that erupted during the meeting of the World Trade Organization (WTO) on December 1–3, 1999. Thousands of demonstrators from around the world gathered to peacefully protest the WTO's policies toward developing nations. Yet several hundred self-styled "anarchists" resorted to violence, rioting, looting, and arson in an attempt to disrupt the meeting. The National Guard's mission was to support the police, who used tear gas, flash bombs, and pepper spray and arrested hundreds of protesters. Guard soldiers who supported the police wore flak jackets and Kevlar helmets with face shields. They carried wooden batons but not firearms. Guardsmen did not engage demonstrators; rather, they were used primarily to patrol sidewalks and keep demonstrators out of a fifty-square-block no-protest zone. In one instance, the Guard closed roads to protect protesters from auto traffic. Guardsmen were used to check identification and perform security duties inside hotels housing WTO delegates and in the Seattle Convention Center. The Guard reinforced the security detail at the hotel used by President Clinton and provided a fifty-soldier reaction force for a precinct where police were forced to disperse demonstrators. In addition to the Washington State Guard, the Wyoming Air National Guard contributed by flying in thirty-three hundred pounds of civilian riot control munitions. Some Guardsmen encountered angry demonstrators, but the Guard suffered no injuries. It was the first time in eighty years, since labor riots in 1919, that the National Guard had been called out to deal with civil disorder in Seattle.[107]

Following the terrorist attacks on September 11, 2001, the National Guard was activated in response to a request from President Bush to upgrade security at airports and other sensitive locations. National Guard troops carrying M-16 rifles and wearing camouflage fatigues were highly visible at airports around the country, assisting local security agents in a variety of tasks. In addition to conducting armed patrols and providing area security, National Guard personnel watched over passenger screening points as private security employees checked baggage and assisted passengers through metal detectors. Guardsmen also assisted with controlling traffic outside terminals at passenger drop-off points and in parking lots. Beyond providing a security presence, National Guard personnel did not, however, engage in law enforcement or replace local police and airport security officers.[108]

In the United States, federal armed forces are generally prohibited from engaging in law enforcement activities by the Posse Comitatus Act of 1878. Congress adopted the law in response to abuses committed by federal military forces in the

South during the Reconstruction Era following the Civil War. The statute, as amended, states, "Whoever, except in cases and under instances expressly authorized by the Constitution or Act of Congress, willfully uses any part of the Army or Air Force as a posse comitatus or otherwise to execute the laws shall be fined under this title or imprisoned not more than two years, or both."[109] The law embodied the historic tradition of military subordination to strong civilian authority and the separation of military and law enforcement functions within the United States. It applied only to forces in federal service, however, not to state militias. As the National Guard is the modern-day state militia, the law did not apply to the Guard when it was in its normal status of state service. The provisions of the act do apply to the National Guard, however, when authorized by the president to perform federal service.[110]

Although the Posse Comitatus Act remains in effect, there has been a blurring of the line between military and police functions, and the 1878 law is no longer the last word. In recent years Congress has enacted laws that provide a number of exemptions to the principle of *posse comitatus* (literally, the power or authority of the county) dealing with civil disturbances and insurrections. These statutes authorize—

> the president to provide military assistance to state governments upon request (section 331) or upon his own initiative to use the armed forces or federalized militia to suppress any rebellion that makes it impracticable to enforce the laws of the United States by the ordinary course of judicial proceedings (section 332). Section 333 also permits military intervention when the constitutional rights of any state's citizens are threatened by insurrection, domestic violence, unlawful combination, or conspiracy. Under section 332, before the militia can be called out, the president must by proclamation immediately order the insurgents to disperse, which is to read them the riot act.[111]

Most of the congressional exemptions to the principle of excluding the armed forces from law enforcement functions have come in the context of the War on Drugs declared by President George H. W. Bush in 1989. In response to this "call to arms," Congress designated the Department of Defense as the lead agency for detecting and monitoring air and marine transport of illegal drugs to the United States. Congress also provided for the integration of U.S. command, control, and intelligence assets for drug interdiction. Finally, Congress approved funding for state governors to expand the use of the National Guard in drug control at state borders.[112] Specifically, Congress further amended Title 10 of the United States Code to provide exceptions to the Posse Comitatus Act that authorized the secretary of defense to provide equipment and personnel to assist civilian agencies in the enforcement of drug, immigration, and tariff laws. However, the statute expressly forbids direct participation by members of the U.S. Army, Navy, Air Force, or Marine Corps in search, seizure, arrest, or other similar activity (section 375). Nevertheless, military personnel can operate equipment to intercept vessels or aircraft outside the land areas of the United States or follow in hot pursuit of such craft inland (section 374b).[113]

National Guard participation in counternarcotics operations is provided for under U.S. Code, Title 32, which states that the Guard may only perform counternarcotics duties that are consistent with state law. The National Guard Bureau has adopted policy guidelines that restrict narcotics-related law enforcement activities by the National Guard to strictly controlled, secondary inspections or search of unattended vehicles or cargo. National Guard forces actively engage in cargo inspection operations at U.S. entry points, but they are always accompanied by a civilian law enforcement agent. If Guardsmen observe drug-related criminal activity, they report it to relevant civilian authorities for appropriate action.[114]

In the spring of 2002, President George W. Bush directed lawyers in the Defense and Justice Departments to review the Posse Comitatus Act and all other laws that restrict the military's ability to participate in domestic law enforcement. White House officials said the review was requested to determine whether domestic preparedness and responsiveness against terrorism would benefit from increased military participation. Officials noted that after September 11, the law prevented President Bush from ordering the National Guard to protect the nation's airports. Instead, the president had to request fifty individual state governors to use their authority to perform the same task. The president's call for a review of the law received an immediate endorsement from General Ralph Eberhart, chief of the new Northern Command, which is responsible for defense of the continental United States. It was also endorsed by Senator Joseph Biden (D–Delaware), chairman of the Senate Foreign Relations Committee at the time, who said the law should be re-examined and updated.[115] The National Guard was not, however, included in President Bush's plan for a new Department of Homeland Security. Homeland Security Secretary Tom Ridge said the military's Northern Command would work with state governors to define suitable missions. Nearly a year after the September terrorist attacks, the National Guard still had eleven hundred troops assisting the Customs and Immigration Service around the nation's borders and eighty troops guarding LaGuardia Airport in New York. There were also five hundred guardsmen stationed at nuclear power plants, reservoirs, landmarks, bridges, tunnels, and other possibly vulnerable sites.[116]

While the National Guard has a number of relevant characteristics, it does not qualify as a "constabulary" under the definition used in this study. The Guard has the capacity to deal with civil disturbances and to perform a number of functions related to restoring and maintaining public order. It does not, however, have police powers and, by directive from the National Guard Bureau, operates only in support of civilian law enforcement. Guardsmen are not trained, nor do they have "executive authority," to perform police functions such as conducting criminal investigations and arresting (as opposed to detaining) offenders. In addition, when National Guard divisions are federalized for service abroad, they become subject to the limitations of the Posse Comitatus Act. This is the case of the National Guard divisions that have served in peacekeeping operations in the Balkans. There is, however, a modern-day U.S. organization that has both military capabilities and police powers and that does fit this study's definition of a constabulary. That organization is the U.S. Army Military Police.

U.S. Military Police

Following the end of the Cold War, the U.S. Army Military Police Corps undertook a review of its doctrine to determine if it "was properly articulating its multiple performance capabilities in support of U.S. forces deployed worldwide." The result of this review was a revision that was shaped by recognition that the following factors would influence future operations:

✦ The need to participate in "stability" and peace support operations in which "joint military, multinational, and interagency" cooperation would be common.

✦ The impact of asymmetrical threats (such as narcotics trafficking, organized crime, and terrorism) and the need to deal with humanitarian emergencies and natural disasters.

✦ Advances in information and communication technologies and the threats they may pose.

✦ The probable disappearance of traditional linear battlefields and subsequent requirements for forces that can perform specialized functions to accomplish operational requirements.[117]

The new doctrine that emerged from this review increased the four traditional military police (MP) battlefield missions to five and modified several of the missions to include tasks commonly performed in peace operations. Under the revised doctrine, which continues in force, U.S. Army Military Police have the following responsibilities:

✦ Area security: MP companies are equipped to conduct mobile patrols and to provide security to sensitive locations, such as ports, airports, bridges, and border control points.

✦ Maneuver and mobility support: On the battlefield, this involves conducting reconnaissance, keeping supply lines open, and regulating the flow of vehicles and units. In both war and peace operations, it also involves directing refugees and displaced persons and providing protection and humanitarian assistance.

+ Internment and resettlement: On the battlefield, this involves taking custody of prisoners of war and civilians displaced by the conflict. It can also involve arresting military criminals and detaining civilians who commit crimes.

+ Law enforcement: On U.S. military installations, MP units are responsible for the full spectrum of police functions, from traffic control to criminal investigations. In peace operations, they can perform public order and law enforcement functions, ranging from civil disorder management to detaining lawbreakers.

+ Information gathering: Like military scouts, military police conduct mounted reconnaissance patrols and are trained to find and fix the positions of enemy forces. Like civilian police, military police collect information related to civil disorder and criminal activity.[118]

U.S. Army Military Police undergo the same basic training given to light infantry. MP companies are trained to operate much like military scouts, to conduct reconnaissance and find and engage enemy forces. After completing basic training, MPs receive ten weeks of advanced individual training at the U.S. Army Military Police School at Fort Leonard Wood, Missouri, where they are introduced to basic police skills and law enforcement. MP recruits receive instruction in patrol, traffic control, crime scene protection, criminal investigation, community policing, use of force, nonviolent dispute resolution, relevant laws and codes of criminal procedures, first aid, and driver education. Once assigned to their units, MPs are trained to operate in three-man teams. The basic MP unit is a Humvee vehicle with a three-person crew under the command of a noncommissioned officer. The vehicle is mounted with a "crew-served" weapon (an integrated machine gun system) and the individual soldiers have automatic weapons, a grenade launcher, and sidearms. The units are trained to operate independently (for example, controlling a checkpoint) and to coordinate with other units or quickly combine into a larger force. Two of these three-person teams make a squad; ten make a platoon. As a result of its training, armaments, and mobility, an MP company has greater versatility and more firepower than a regular light infantry company.[119]

What sets military police apart from other soldiers is that they are trained to interact with civilians. MP recruits are generally selected from inductees who score above average on army intelligence tests. In their law enforcement training, MPs are taught interpersonal skills, how to establish trust, and how to use mediation and other conflict resolution techniques to resolve disputes. They are trained to make individual decisions and to be comfortable in ambiguous situations. MPs are trained to use only the minimum amount of force necessary to control the situation. They are also trained to handle victims. This is important in peace operations, particularly in dealing with victims of sexual assault and people with medical problems.[120]

The ability to deal with civilians was evident in the performance of the U.S. Military Police who are part of the U.S. military contingent of NATO's Kosovo Force (KFOR). About five hundred of the fifty-six hundred U.S. troops in Kosovo are MPs. They have been at the center of efforts to maintain public order in the U.S. area of responsibility. While regular troops chafe under the requirement to handle unruly crowds and resolve interpersonal disputes, the military police have taken these aspects of daily operations in stride; trained as police/soldiers, they have proven adept at interacting with civilians. Of particular importance is the fact that MPs, like civilian police officers, operate on a "force continuum," using only the minimum amount of force necessary. For the MPs in Kosovo, this approach to dealing with unruly citizens comes down to the "five S's," which stands for "shout, show your weapon, shoot to wound, shoot to kill, but shoot only at the instigator." Overall, MPs also appear more comfortable with a military mission where the goal is not victory but stability.[121]

3
CIVPOL
✛ ✛ ✛ ✛ ✛ ✛
Police in Peacekeeping
✛ ✛ ✛ ✛ ✛ ✛ ✛ ✛ ✛ ✛ ✛ ✛ ✛

INTERNATIONAL CIVILIAN POLICE FORCES have become an essential element in peace operations. They have also become a component with its own identity and status within the peacekeeping community. United Nations civilian police are referred to as CIVPOL. Their authorized number reached a high point of 8,696 in 1999, with an increase of nearly 300 percent from the previous year.[1] As of April 2002, there were 7,517 CIVPOL serving in eight missions. The majority of these police officers were in Kosovo (4,515), Bosnia-Herzegovina (1,553), and East Timor (1,278). There also were smaller UN police missions in Western Sahara (24), Guatemala (9), Sierra Leone (89), Democratic Republic of the Congo (14), and Cyprus (35). CIVPOL constituted 16 percent of the total number of 46,784 UN peacekeepers deployed.[2] In addition to UN police missions, international police officers from the Organization for Security and Cooperation in Europe and the European Union had taken part in monitoring local police in postconflict environments in Eastern Slavonia, Albania, and Macedonia. The United States was among the largest contributors of personnel to international police missions. American police officers have served in Haiti, Bosnia, Kosovo, and East Timor.[3]

Civilian police were first included in UN peace operations in 1960 in the Congo when a Ghanaian unit was attached to the UN military force to assist the remnants of the Congolese colonial police with maintaining order. The Ghanaians were forced to withdraw because they became involved in local politics. They

83

were replaced by four hundred Nigerian police provided by the UN Technical Assistance Program. The Nigerians served with distinction, staying in the Congo to protect UN personnel and property after UN military forces withdrew. The term "CIVPOL" for "United Nations civilian police" originated when the UN Peacekeeping Force in Cyprus was established in 1964. The UN secretary-general's special representative suggested including a military police unit in the peacekeeping force. The UN military force commander proposed adding a civilian police unit instead, thus the term "CIVPOL" to differentiate civilian from military police.[4]

MILITARY AND POLICE IN PEACE OPERATIONS

The history of the post–Cold War period has witnessed the transformation of wars between states to intrastate conflicts. The collapse of the Soviet Union and Yugoslavia unleashed ethnic tensions long repressed by the heavy-handed tactics of communist regimes. From 1990 to 1997, there were forty-nine wars involving at least one thousand battle deaths. Only seven of these conflicts were between countries; the remaining forty-two were between political, ethnic, or religious groups within a single nation.[5] These wars within states required military intervention by the international community to end the fighting so humanitarian assistance, refugee return, economic reconstruction, and political reconciliation could occur.[6]

  The problem of how to re-establish internal order and develop effective local security forces capable of maintaining a just peace has proven difficult to resolve. In peace operations, military leaders have considered police duties a distraction from their primary responsibilities. Some of this concern arises from the belief that serving in peace operations and, particularly, performing nonmilitary functions will negatively affect "readiness" and "dull the warrior edge" of the armed forces. Other critics have worried about the military becoming a "cash cow" for civilian agencies that are unwilling to pay for activities related to peace operations from their own budgets. The most sustained opposition, however, results not from concern about budgets or resources; it comes from an institutional view of the proper role of the military that is strongly opposed to activities that are not related to "war fighting," which is viewed as the soldier's proper role.[7] Traditionally, military officers have looked upon police-related duties as "undignified." According to Morris Janowitz, "The professional soldier resists identifying himself with the 'police' and the military profession has struggled to distinguish itself from the internal police force. . . . The military tends to think of police activities as less prestigious and less honorable tasks, and within the military establishment, the military police have had relatively low status."[8]

In fact, without appropriate training and equipment, international military forces have often proven ineffective in performing police functions. NATO's Supreme Allied Commander Europe, General Wesley Clark, made this point at the beginning of the Kosovo mission. Clark said, "Experience in peace operations has proven that good soldiers, no matter how well equipped, trained, and led, cannot fully perform police duties among local populations."[9] The tragic death of eighteen U.S. Army Rangers in Mogadishu during a failed "police action" to arrest a Somali warlord reinforced the U.S. military's fears of the dangers of "mission creep" away from strictly military operations.[10]

There are also significant differences in organizational structure and culture between military and police forces. In democratic countries, military forces are organized and trained to defend the nation against external attack. Military forces are heavily armed and trained to operate in units, to concentrate mass and firepower, and to destroy the enemy and its property. Military units live in isolation on military bases. They are self-contained, with their own communications, logistics, and transport capability. In contrast, civilian police are not kept in a state of readiness for deployment abroad. Instead, they are employed in daily service in a profession that suffers from a chronic shortage of personnel. Police training and practice is rooted in the culture of local communities. It is rare to find police with international experience. The role of police is to maintain public order under the rule of law. The use of force by police is severely circumscribed. Police are unarmed in many countries or carry only light weapons. Police operate individually, live in the community, and are trained to "preserve and protect" local citizens and their property. They rely on the community infrastructure for communications and logistics; regular police vehicles are inappropriate for peace operations.[11]

When civilian police serve in peace operations, the United Nations or other sponsoring organization must provide them with appropriate clothing, equipment, communications, and transport. Civilian police must find and pay for their own lodging in the local community and must assume responsibility for their own security, even if they are unarmed. If the international police have executive authority, they must know the laws they enforce.[12] Police arrive in national contingents, but they are assigned by the United Nations as individuals in CIVPOL missions. Often CIVPOL stations are staffed by an international mix of officers from widely varied cultures and traditions and with vastly different views on how to perform police functions. One can imagine the initial conversations between a London bobbie, an American highway patrol officer, and a Rwandan gendarme on how to organize their police station, conduct patrols, or make arrests.

These differences between soldiers and police officers can create problems when they try to work together. The distinction between military and police training in the use of force and the language used to describe it was evident in an incident that occurred during the Rodney King riots in Los Angeles. During the disturbances, LAPD operated in joint patrols with federal troops and the California National Guard. A mixed team of U.S. Marines and LAPD officers went to an apartment building in response to a call concerning a domestic dispute. Outside the building, the patrol took cover and discussed how they would enter the building. The senior police officer told his military counterpart that he would go in first. He then said, "Cover me!" On receiving this order from the police officer, the Marines fired more than two hundred rounds into the building, where there were children.[13] The Marines' reaction was the result of training and vocabulary: In police parlance, "cover me" means be prepared to fire your weapon if I am in danger. This defini-tion follows the police principle of using only the minimum force necessary to accomplish the mission. For the Marines, "cover me," means open fire at once to suppress anyone who might try to impede my advance.

CIVPOL ROLES AND MISSIONS

The increased use of international police in peace operations results from their ability to contribute to public security in the short term, while helping to build law-enforcement and judicial institutions that are critical for long-term stability. During the process of state fragmentation, the police may be swept away, or they may mutate into predators that engage in extrajudicial killings, kidnappings, robberies, and other criminal activities. Police are likely to identify with the existing regime and to per-form an increasingly politicized role, leading to abuse of power and the brutalizing of regime opponents. When the international community intervenes in states in crisis, it is critical that the inter-vention force is capable of effectively performing police functions. In peace operations, international civilian police have proven bet-ter trained and more able than the military to handle such essen-tial functions as monitoring local police forces, controlling crime, handling demonstrations and civil disorder, escorting refugees, and providing election security. CIVPOL missions are much less expensive than military operations. The long-term presence of foreign police is often more acceptable to host governments and citizens than foreign military forces. There is an emerging con-sensus that international police forces offer an effective solution in financial and political terms to the problems of rebuilding post-conflict societies.[14]

The growth in the number of UN police missions has been accompanied by an expansion in the roles and missions CIVPOL are asked to perform. At the core of CIVPOL duties has been the monitoring of local police and the supervision of efforts related to public safety and maintaining public order. These tasks were summarized in the "SMART" concept, which was introduced in

A Trainer's Guide on Human Rights for CIVPOL Monitors, a handbook issued in 1995 by the UN Center for Human Rights. The acronym describes the basic responsibilities that are typically found in all CIVPOL mandates:

+ Supporting human rights;

+ Monitoring the performance of local law enforcement;

+ Advising indigenous police;

+ Reporting on the situation; and

+ Training local police officers.[15]

Traditionally, the UN Department of Peacekeeping Operations (DPKO) believed the primary purpose of UN police was to monitor local police to ensure they acted in accordance with international human rights standards and the rule of law. The UN police monitor's responsibility was to "observe and report" infringements to higher levels in the UN mission. These reports were brought to the attention of local government officials with a request to correct the behavior. Monitoring involved (1) accompanying local police in performing their duties, (2) receiving and investigating public complaints about the police, and (3) supervising investigations conducted by the police.[16]

In addition to monitoring local police, CIVPOL conducted foot and vehicle patrols, acted as the eyes and ears of the intervention force, and cooperated closely with international military personnel to ensure security in the area of operations. In some peace missions, international police were co-located with local police in police stations. In other missions, they maintained their own stations. As part of their responsibility for public order, international police helped identify weapons caches and assisted international military forces with the confiscation of illegal weapons. In all cases, they provided citizens a sense of increased confidence and security by their presence.[17] International police forces also played an important role in the safe return of refugees and displaced persons. This involved escorting such persons, dispersing roadblocks, and preventing harassment. Often it involved ensuring that the local police met their responsibility for preserving public order and protecting the rights of all citizens.[18]

During many peace operations, international police played an important role by assisting with the conduct of free and fair elections. This involved helping to guarantee a neutral and secure environment and to guard against intimidation and interference in the electoral process. International police escorted candidates, supervised election rallies, accompanied election monitors, protected polling stations, and ensured the integrity of ballot boxes. These tasks were performed in support of UN election officials and representatives of nongovernmental organizations.[19]

While international police have been responsible for monitoring the way local police perform their duties, they traditionally have not had executive authority, or full police powers to conduct investigations and to arrest and detain local citizens. Speaking to the UN seminar on "The Role of Police in Peacekeeping" in March 1998, the UN senior police adviser explained the United Nations' traditional view that "security must be maintained by the society's own police. For this purpose, the assistance of the international community is needed to improve local law enforcement mechanisms." The role of CIVPOL is to improve the performance of local police forces through positive example, technical assistance, training, and other types of support. The goal is to strengthen local police, not to replace them.[20]

This situation changed in 1999 when the UN Security Council authorized the creation of UN transitional administrations in Kosovo and East Timor that were empowered to exercise all executive and legislative authority, including the administration of justice and law enforcement. UN civilian police in these peace operations are armed and have full police powers to enforce the law, conduct criminal investigations, and arrest offenders. Assumption of such far-reaching authority was necessitated by the withdrawal of Yugoslav police from Kosovo and Indonesian police from East Timor under the terms of the respective peace agreements. In another departure, UN police forces in Kosovo and East Timor also included "formed Special Police Units" provided by member states with constabulary forces. These integrated units arrive complete with transport, communications, weapons, and an internal chain of command. Their primary mission is crowd control, but they are used for a variety of other purposes.

PROBLEMS IN ORGANIZING CIVILIAN POLICE MISSIONS

While the number of international civilian police and their roles in peace operations have expanded, CIVPOL missions have been deeply troubled by problems, ranging from failures in recruiting and training to controversies over roles, weapons, and responsibilities. The problems in organizing international police missions begin with recruiting adequate numbers of appropriately trained personnel. Unlike military forces, which are maintained in a state of readiness to respond to emergencies, police are employed in daily operations. Politicians and senior police officials are reluctant to release officers for international service, especially in the face of rising crime rates and increased demand from citizens for police services. Police forces find it particularly difficult to part with their best and most experienced officers and those with special skills like narcotics investigators or Special Weapons and Tactics (SWAT) team members.[21]

Recruiting

The United Nations' efforts to recruit civilian police for CIVPOL missions are based on the principle of universality. At the beginning of a peace operation, the DPKO sends letters to the permanent missions of member states in New York, requesting that they contribute police officers to staff the new mission.[22] The UN has faced significant difficulties in simply finding enough police officers to fill the positions authorized by the Security Council. The problem has been one of unwillingness of member states to make available sufficient numbers of civilian police for UN duty. For example, in February 2000, member states had made available only 5,122 police officers to fill the nearly 9,000 positions authorized by the Security Council in the previous two years.[23]

Finding police to serve in international police missions is a particular problem for the United States. Unlike Europe, Canada, and Mexico, the United States has no national police force. Instead, there are nearly eighteen thousand independent state, county, and municipal police forces and more than a dozen federal law enforcement agencies, such as the Federal Bureau of Investigation, the Drug Enforcement Agency, and the United States Secret Service. No U.S. law enforcement agency (including the Justice Department) has legislative authority to recruit Americans for service in UN or other international police missions. The United States Civilian Police Program has no statutory authority and receives its funding from annual appropriations. Responsibility for fielding U.S. contingents for international police missions rests with the U.S. State Department's Bureau of International Narcotics and Law Enforcement Affairs. The State Department, in turn, has contracted out responsibility for the recruiting, training, and logistical support of U.S. CIVPOL contingents to the DynCorp Corporation, a commercial, government-services firm based in San Antonio, Texas. Police officers participating in U.S. CIVPOL contingents are independent subcontractors of DynCorp who receive a fee for service. This arrangement allows the federal government to avoid a myriad of political, administrative, financial, and liability issues that would arise from temporarily placing state and local police in federal service.[24]

The United States is the only country to use contractors of a commercial firm as police officers for CIVPOL contingents. It is also the only country to provide logistics support to its police officers in the field. For all other countries, police participating in CIVPOL missions are in national service and the United Nations provides administrative support. DynCorp provides U.S. police with travel and administrative support and a compensation package that can amount to more than $85,000 a year, plus a substantial completion-of-contract bonus. DynCorp also offers a nine-day, predeparture Police Assessment Selection and Training Process that includes a battery of psychological, medical, and firearms tests; training in police skills and defensive tactics; and training modules on the United Nations, peacekeeping, human rights, living abroad, and the history and culture of the country to which the officers will be assigned. During their orientation, U.S. CIVPOL also receive training in negotiation, mediation, and conflict resolution from the U.S. Institute of Peace.[25]

As personnel shortages in U.S. police departments are common, police chiefs and local politicians are reluctant to let qualified officers take a one-year leave of absence to serve in a UN mission. Active duty officers have had to resign, and it has been difficult for them to find appropriate domestic assignments after returning from abroad. Historically, the majority of U.S. CIVPOL have been retired officers, although the number of active duty officers is increasing. U.S. police officers come from state and local law enforcement agencies of widely varied size and character and from unique regional law enforcement subcultures around the country. There are marked differences between police officers from large urban departments with as many as forty thousand officers and those from small sheriff's offices in rural areas. The result of using retirees and active duty officers from a broad range of police backgrounds is that U.S. CIVPOL contingents are experienced but of highly mixed quality.[26] Using a commercial contractor also limits U.S. government oversight of the conduct of U.S. personnel in the field.

Despite these obstacles, American CIVPOL officers have compiled a record of distinguished service. American police are well educated, trained, and experienced. Among their UN colleagues, they enjoy a reputation for professionalism and are looked to for leadership and technical expertise. There have been cases, however, where the United States has sent officers who were less than fit for strenuous duty. There have also been incidents of American officers returned to the United States for various types of misconduct. Three American CIVPOL officers were killed in the line of duty. All three died in a helicopter accident in Bosnia in 1997 that was the result of poor weather conditions.[27]

Training and Standards

The official policy of the United Nations is that training police for participation in international civilian police missions is the responsibility of member states. Police officers are expected to arrive in the mission area fully qualified to perform their assigned tasks. The report of the UN secretary-general's Panel on Peace Operations (the "Brahimi Report") encourages each member state to establish a national pool of civilian police officers that would be ready for deployment to UN peace operations on short notice. The report further encourages member states to enter into regional training partnerships to promote a common level of preparedness in accordance with the guidelines, operating procedures, and performance standards promulgated by the United Nations. To assist member states, the DPKO issued a number of publications, including *Selection Standards and Training Guidelines for United Nations Civilian Police*.[28] It has also developed the outline for a standard United Nations police officers course.[29] Beyond a basic framework of encouragement, principles, and guidelines, member states must devise their own curricula based on their individual assessment of the requirements for international police service.

Because responsibility for training is left to the more than seventy donor countries, it is not surprising that there are extreme variations in the type of preparation provided to those participating in international civilian police missions. CIVPOL officers are supposed to arrive fully qualified, trained, and equipped to perform their assigned duties. Unfortunately, even western European countries continue to provide training based on the 1995 UN training guidelines and the "SMART" concept, which presumes CIVPOL will be unarmed, serve as police monitors, and will not have executive authority. This type of training does little to prepare police officers for assignments to UN missions in Kosovo and East Timor, where CIVPOL has executive authority and the mandate to provide comprehensive law enforcement services. In general, training by donor countries is overly simplistic and does not sufficiently address the variety of tasks CIVPOL are currently required to perform. In addition, the training often lacks sufficient emphasis on cultural, social, legal, political, and personal issues CIVPOL are likely to encounter working in a postconflict environment. Training should help provide CIVPOL officers with professional and practical skills plus a moral compass to guide their behavior. While the UN CIVPOL Division is fully aware that UN police officers now face new and growing challenges, the development of UN training materials and the training provided by member states have yet to catch up.[30]

Starting with the earliest CIVPOL missions, inadequate training has been one of the primary factors contributing to the difficulties encountered by the United Nations in providing competent international police forces. Until the establishment of the UN Transitional Authority in Cambodia in March 1992, the United Nations had virtually no recruitment standards and, therefore, no standards for what constituted adequate training for police officers participating in international civilian police missions. In Cambodia, many CIVPOL officers arrived with no police experience, no ability to drive, and no ability to speak the mission language. These police were either trained by the United Nations in Cambodia or returned home. When a similar situation occurred during UNPROFOR's mission in the former Yugoslavia, the United Nations established a simple list of recruitment standards: (1) a minimum five years of police experience; (2) ability to drive four-wheel-drive vehicles; and (3) oral and written fluency in English, the working language of the mission. Donor countries ignored even these minimal standards.[31]

The fact that significant numbers of arriving CIVPOL failed to meet even these limited requirements resulted in a series of UN-sponsored conferences to study the problem. In 1996, the UN's DPKO and the Lester B. Pearson International Peacekeeping Training Center in Canada conducted a seminar on CIVPOL qualifications. The seminar addressed generic, mission-specific, and in-theater training guidelines for member states and established additional selection standards for CIVPOL service. These criteria included—

1. Citizenship of the sending country.
2. Sworn member of the police force.
3. Five and preferably eight years of active community policing experience.
4. Ability to meet the UN health standards.
5. A valid 4 x 4 driving license.
6. Speaking and writing ability in their native language and the mission language.
7. Competence in the use of firearms.
8. Impeccable personal and professional integrity.[32]

This effort to establish standards also led to the creation of the CIVPOL Support Unit in Zagreb that tested potential CIVPOL officers on arrival for service in Bosnia. To assist member states in meeting these criteria, the United Nations organized Selection Assistance Teams that traveled to donor countries and pretested recruits for the CIVPOL mission in Bosnia. The first such team saved the United Nations an estimated $527,360, based on what it would have cost for travel, subsistence, testing, and repatriation of police who could not have passed the tests on arrival in country. In addition to testing new arrivals, the UN instituted a one-week CIVPOL orientation course in Zagreb for all police officers who passed the test for new arrivals. The orientation program, which subsequently was moved to Sarajevo, included brief presentations on the history of the conflict, human rights, local language and culture, CIVPOL roles and missions, relations with SFOR, security procedures, land-mine awareness, first aid, election monitoring, report writing, vehicle safety, radio communications, computer skills, and emergency and administrative procedures. Eventually, the UN also developed job descriptions and began recruiting CIVPOL based on specific skills such as criminal investigation, traffic control, management and administration, and police instruction. These efforts produced a higher quality of recruits and brought greater stability to the UN police force.[33]

Logistics

Logistics are the Achilles' heel of international police missions. Military forces arrive with their own equipment and transport; CIVPOL must be provided with everything but their uniforms. Former UN CIVPOL commissioners who attended a 1995 "lessons learned" conference in Singapore listed lack of logistical support as their biggest problem. They reported they had no financial authority for even routine or local purchases and that their recommendations concerning the material needs of the mission often were ignored. Field missions were reliant upon UN headquarters for administrative support, which was often delayed or simply not forthcoming. The commissioners also complained about a lack of dialogue between headquarters and the field and headquarters' lack of awareness of changes in requirements over the life of the mission.[34]

Unfortunately, the United Nations has done little to address the problem, and UN "blue tape" continues to snarl operations. The UN has a logistics base in Brindisi, Italy, but its shelves are often bare and equipment and vehicles often are not in serviceable condition. There is also a problem with procurement and replenishing supplies: The UN budget process is complex and does not readily provide for spending on contingencies. Normally the Security Council must authorize a peacekeeping mission before DPKO can begin procurement. The UN has made an effort to stockpile mission start-up kits, but these are quickly depleted and difficult to replace. There is a need for improvements in warehouse management and inventory control. There is also a need for preplanning and for rosters of administrative personnel who understand the UN system and can deploy with the mission to ensure a smooth start-up.[35]

In April 1996, Commissioner Peter Fitzgerald told a Washington audience that the IPTF had opened thirty-four stations in Bosnia but that he could communicate with only three of them because the rest did not have radios.[36] Snow tires ordered for UN police vehicles in the summer of 1996 did not arrive in Bosnia until the summer of 1997. Individual IPTF officers did not have flashlights, although they were ordered to conduct night patrols. In East Timor, the CIVPOL commissioner was not allowed to purchase equipment locally or in Australia if it was available from the UN supply depot in Italy, resulting in delays of several months in obtaining essential equipment such as generators. Without electricity, radios, office equipment, refrigerators, and air conditioners sat idle, waiting for the UN procurement system to supply a power source.[37]

Weapons

Despite the fact that CIVPOL are performing full police duties in Kosovo and East Timor, there is still a debate within the United Nations over whether future CIVPOL missions should have weapons and executive authority. Historically, the UN has argued against arming CIVPOL because many countries have a tradition of unarmed police; traditional police weapons are no match for heavily armed populations; police should create confidence in the rule of law, not in the resort to violence; and requiring weapons would indicate an unacceptable security risk.[38]

As the United Kingdom, Norway, and many other countries have a tradition of unarmed police, arming CIVPOL also creates a range of practical problems. National contingents may arrive without weapons or with a range of weapons requiring different types of ammunition and spare parts. There are also no UN standards for police weapons, weapons training, certification, or accountability. Critics argue that setting such standards and providing weapons and ammunition is difficult, expensive, and a major logistics problem.[39]

CASE STUDIES

The evolution in the role of international civilian police and the problems inherent in staging CIVPOL missions are evident in a review of peacekeeping missions. The following is a description of the role played by international civilian police in three pivotal operations—Cambodia, Somalia, and Haiti—that influenced the conduct of future police missions.

Cambodia

International peacemaking for Cambodia resulted in the signing of the Paris Peace Accords on October 23, 1991. The Comprehensive Political Settlement of the Cambodia Conflict provided for a total transformation of Cambodia's political system and a transition to democratic elections under United Nations supervision. The UN Security Council expressed its support for the Cambodian settlement in Resolution 745 that created the UN Transitional Authority in Cambodia (UNTAC) with a mandate not to exceed eighteen months. Under the Paris Accords, UNTAC was required to establish a safe and secure environment by disarming and demobilizing local forces. It was also to ensure political neutrality by supervising the key areas of national and local government administration, conducting an election for a constituent assembly, and developing a national constitution. To support this effort, UNTAC had a peacekeeping force of sixteen thousand troops, thirty-six hundred civilian police, and twelve thousand civil and military support personnel. It was the largest operation the United Nations had ever undertaken and the most complex. The United States played a critical role in achieving the peace agreement but did not provide troops or police for the UNTAC mission.[40]

Maintaining internal security was the key to creating a neutral political environment for democratic elections and for the effective implementation of all aspects of UNTAC's mandate. The principal obstacle was the proclivity in former one-party states for the security apparatus to support the existing leadership, which used the old instruments of power for political and criminal gain. Under the accords, each faction was allowed to retain control of local police in the areas under its control. CIVPOL's role was limited to monitoring the local police to ensure the maintenance of public order and effective law enforcement. Given its limited mandate and the highly uneven quality of its personnel, CIVPOL was unable to exert control over the Cambodian police, which remained loyal to the Phnom Penh regime. The Paris Accords did not provide for disarming the Cambodian police, nor did they provide for a new national police force or a judiciary that was free from the control of the former communist parties. Faced with a situation that was beyond its capacity, CIVPOL reverted to "veneer tasks of regimentation, traffic management, and process."[41]

Organizationally, CIVPOL had a policy and management unit in the capital, twenty-one provincial police units, and two hundred police stations. CIVPOL's mandate was to monitor and train local police, assist with resettling refugees, investigate cases of human rights abuse, and assist with staging the elections. As the mission progressed and security conditions seriously deteriorated, CIVPOL received limited executive authority and joined the UN military in providing local security, including the confiscation of arms caches. Despite the danger to all UN personnel, only some CIVPOL were armed during the operation.[42]

The Paris Accords assumed that all three political factions employed police forces. This proved true only in areas controlled by Phnom Penh, and CIVPOL concentrated its monitoring efforts in areas controlled by the government. In other areas, there were no police to supervise. CIVPOL began providing police services directly and built a police training school to provide basic police training for some ten thousand local recruits, including those from the Khmer Rouge. As the elections approached, all factions engaged in politically motivated violence and there was a breakdown in public order. CIVPOL was called upon to investigate complaints of human rights abuse and political intimidation and to conduct security operations. CIVPOL provided security for UNTAC's electoral component and helped safeguard political parties and candidates.[43]

That UNTAC successfully fulfilled its mandate to supervise Cambodia's transition to democratic elections and the installation of a new government is a tribute to all members of the UNTAC mission, including those in CIVPOL. Many CIVPOL officers performed under extremely adverse circumstances with remarkable determination and courage.[44] Despite the heroic efforts of some officers, CIVPOL in Cambodia was plagued with problems. The UN advance mission in Cambodia that deployed in November 1991 to plan the UNTAC operation did not include a police element. Planning for the largest UN CIVPOL mission at that time began only with the appointment of the CIVPOL commissioner in March 1992. Deployment of CIVPOL contingents was extremely slow. The force did not reach full strength until November 1992, six months before the election. While some national contingents were well trained, highly professional, and served with distinction, others were of widely varied quality. Significant numbers of CIVPOL arrived without knowledge of English, French, or Khmer; were unable to drive; and had only limited or no police experience. At least forty CIVPOL were repatriated for unacceptable behavior. Some units engaged in abusing the local population, black marketing, illicit trafficking, and prostitution. CIVPOL's record among UNTAC's components was one of the poorest.[45]

Somalia

In January 1991, following the overthrow of President Mohamed Siad Barre, Somalia was engulfed in civil war. Two clan warlords, Ali Mahdi Mohamed and General Mohamed Farah Hassan Aideed, fought an inconclusive battle for control of Mogadishu, Somalia's capital. By late 1991, government institutions had ceased to function. The civil war had disrupted the country's food production. More than a million Somalis were displaced. Disturbing televised images of starving children coupled with reports of diversion of international relief supplies by armed factions generated public pressure for action by the international community. The unfolding catastrophe of armed conflict, drought, massive refugee migration, and pandemic starvation compelled the United Nations to intervene.[46]

In April 1992, the UN Security Council adopted Resolution 751, establishing the UN Operation in Somalia (UNOSOM I) to monitor a cease-fire between the factions and support a ninety-day plan for emergency humanitarian assistance. The United Nations sent fifty unarmed observers to Mogadishu and agreed to deploy a peacekeeping force to escort relief deliveries. In September 1992, a lightly armed force of five hundred Pakistani troops arrived in Somalia. The force operated under a traditional UN mandate that required strict neutrality and consent of the local parties before deployment. UN peacekeepers were never able to move beyond their initial encampment at the airport. The Pakistanis had neither the mandate nor the strength in numbers and weapons to challenge the warlords and were unable to carry out their mission of safeguarding food depots and escorting relief convoys to feeding stations.[47]

The failure of UNOSOM I prompted calls for direct U.S. intervention. On November 25, 1992, the United States informed the UN secretary-general of its willingness to lead a humanitarian assistance mission to Somalia. On December 3, the UN Security Council adopted Resolution 794, authorizing the use of all necessary means to establish a secure environment for humanitarian relief operations in Somalia. The next day, in a speech from the Oval Office, President Bush explained his reasons for sending twenty-eight thousand American troops to end the humanitarian crisis. Operation Restore Hope lasted from December 9, 1992, to March 26, 1993. Its core was a U.S.-led multinational coalition known as the United Task Force (UNITAF) that consisted of more than thirty-eight thousand troops from more than twenty countries. Its three-part mission was to: secure the Mogadishu airfield, seaport, and areas within the city; secure towns identified as relief centers; and provide for the transfer of responsibility for maintaining a secure environment to a follow-on UN peacekeeping force. UNITAF was the first "peace enforcement mission" authorized under the relevant provisions of the UN Charter's Chapter VII.[48]

UNITAF did not include a UN civilian police mission, but it did become deeply involved in creating an indigenous internal security force, using former members of the Somali National Police (SNP). In January 1991, at the end of the Siad Barre regime, the SNP had numbered fifteen thousand officers with two hundred police stations located in eighteen regional districts. The SNP had a reputation for professionalism, fairness, and clan neutrality; it had not been co-opted by Siad Barre. During the civil war, the SNP—as was the case with all government institutions—ceased to function. Police returned to their homes and stopped performing their duties for their own safety. Most police officers avoided taking sides in the civil conflict, some at great personal risk.[49]

As UNITAF forces deployed, former members of the SNP reappeared in their tattered uniforms and, voluntarily, began assisting UNITAF troops by performing traffic control and other police functions. UNITAF forces had arrested criminals, developed a civilian detainee policy, and established a temporary holding facility. The U.S. military, however, was uncomfortable performing police functions. When U.S. Marines began suffering casualties patrolling the streets of Mogadishu, the hazards of U.S. forces performing police duties became clear. The United States originally expected to leave the task of reorganizing the Somali police to the follow-on UN mission. A growing list of American casualties convinced U.S. special envoy, Ambassador Robert Oakley, that efforts to organize a Somali police force could not wait.[50]

Oakley knew that establishing a Somali police force was the key to improving security in Mogadishu. Indigenous police would eliminate the need for UNITAF to perform police functions. This would free UNITAF troops for other duties and reduce friction with the local population. Local police would allow the Somalis themselves to deal with ordinary criminal behavior such as petty theft; it would also create jobs for several thousand people who would otherwise be unemployed. It was clear that enough former police personnel were available, if funding for salaries, uniforms, food, communications equipment, and vehicles could be located.[51]

Initially, Oakley was opposed by the United Nations, which argued that formation of an internal security force should await the "top-down" creation of a Ministry of Justice and a national police force. The Clinton administration, U.S. Central Command, and the Joint Chiefs of Staff initially were also cool to the idea, fearing "mission creep" and possible violation of congressional prohibitions on U.S. military assistance to foreign police forces. Undeterred, Oakley began talks with the two major Somali warlords, Generals Aideed and Ali Mahdi, on organizing a joint police force. He also requested approval from Washington and New York.[52]

In response to Oakley's request, the Defense Department and the National Security Council authorized UNITAF to help organize an interim Auxiliary Security Force (ASF) composed of former SNP members. The ASF operated under the direction of a nonpartisan police committee whose members were approved by the Joint Security Committee (composed of Aideed and Ali Mahdi representatives) and by the Islamic Higher Council. UNITAF provost marshal, Lieutenant Colonel Steven Spataro, and twenty-two U.S. Marine and Army Military Police provided assistance but no training. Members of the ASF were vetted based on the following qualifications: Somali citizen, no criminal record, police officer with two years' experience prior to January 1991, no physical handicap, and willingness to maintain prior rank. Old training manuals and law books were reproduced. The police committee approved written agreements on procedures and policies. UNITAF wrote an ASF handbook with administrative, training, and operational guidelines. The police were assigned to such basic functions as traffic and crowd control, neighborhood patrol, security of food distribution sites, and security of airfields and seaports. Police were unarmed, but weapons were provided for the protection of police stations and use in joint patrols with UNITAF.[53]

The authority to create the ASF was questionable; there was no UN mandate. The United Nations Development Program (UNDP) paid salaries and operating expenses, provided equipment and office furnishings, and refurbished police stations. Italian, Dutch, and German police experts arrived under UNDP auspices to work with the new force. The United States appealed to other governments to provide assistance it could not provide because of legal or political constraints. The Italians provided uniforms, nightsticks, and whistles. UNITAF provided surplus vehicles and radios brought from Saudi Arabia after

Operation Desert Storm. UNITAF military forces, particularly contingents from Morocco, Botswana, and the United Arab Emirates, provided training and weapons and conducted joint patrols in their sectors. The World Food Program provided rations for ASF members and their families.[54]

By mid-January 1993, the first ASF patrols were on the streets in Mogadishu. UNITAF military advisers were able to use the ASF to perform difficult missions that might have resulted in casualties to the intervention force. By May 4, when UNITAF handed over to UNOSOM II, the ASF numbered three thousand members in Mogadishu. They were organized into four patrol divisions and three special divisions (criminal investigation, traffic, and customs) and occupied refurbished police stations in eighteen districts. An additional two thousand ASF officers were on duty in seventeen other cities and towns in the southern part of the country. The beginnings of a court and prison system were in place in Mogadishu and Baidoa. Islamic courts were operating in many localities.[55]

In May 1993, with relief supplies flowing, famine on the wane, and the country at relative peace, UNITAF withdrew, transferring operations to a significantly less capable UN mission, UNOSOM II. Troop strength was reduced to twenty-eight thousand; only forty-five hundred U.S. troops remained (a fifteen hundred–man rapid reaction unit and three thousand logistics personnel). With almost no planning, the UN Security Council broadened the mandate for UNOSOM II from providing security for relief operations to rehabilitation of political institutions and economic reconstruction of Somalia.[56] Under the enforcement provisions contained in Chapter VII of the UN Charter, Security Council Resolution 814 directed UNOSOM II to establish a secure environment, re-establish national and regional institutions and civil administration, advance political reconciliation, disarm Somali factions, and hold accountable Somalis who breached international law.[57]

The Clinton administration strongly supported the more aggressive policy. From the start, UNOSOM II suffered from a failure of the U.S. government and the UN Security Council to appreciate the resources required to execute the mandate and the time it would take for the new UN mission to deploy. The psychological impact of the May 4, 1993 departure of U.S. combat forces, armed with tanks and helicopter gunships, and their replacement with lightly armed Pakistani forces emboldened General Aideed. The Pakistani units not only were weaker militarily, but they also stopped night patrolling and other aggressive tactics used by U.S. Marines to establish dominance. They also failed to continue the daily meetings with Aideed's commander that had effectively reduced tensions.[58]

UNOSOM II experienced command, control, and communications problems resulting from inadequate planning, absence of clear doctrine, and inadequate liaison among units. UN officials failed to appreciate that the combination of the UN's new, intrusive mandate and the Somalis' perception of UN military weakness would cause the Somalis to return to urban guerrilla warfare. Attempts by UNOSOM II personnel to disarm Somali militia immediately created an impression that the United Nations had abandoned its neutral position among rival factions. General Aideed turned against the United Nations and began a radio campaign characterizing UN soldiers as an occupation force.[59]

Realizing the UN peacekeepers were a far weaker opponent than the U.S. Marines, Aideed immediately increased his armed presence in Mogadishu. His anger at the United Nations was fueled by his antipathy for Egypt and Egyptian-born UN secretary-general Boutros Boutros-Ghali for their previous support for President Barre. On June 5, Aideed's forces ambushed and killed twenty-four UN Pakistani troops who were conducting a previously announced inspection of a UN-sanctioned arms depot that shared a compound with Aideed's radio station. The Security Council strongly condemned the attack. On July 17, the head of the UN mission in Somalia, Admiral Jonathan Howe, issued an arrest warrant for Aideed for the murder of the Pakistanis and announced a $25,000 reward for his capture. The United Nations launched military attacks against Aideed's home and command center. Aideed escaped with his top lieutenants and went into hiding.[60]

On October 3, approximately one hundred U.S. Army Rangers executed a raid to capture some of Aideed's closest supporters. Two Blackhawk helicopters supporting the raid were shot down and militia gunmen and hostile mobs surrounded the U.S. troops. In a fifteen-hour firefight, eighteen Rangers were killed, eighty-four other U.S. soldiers were wounded, and an American helicopter pilot was captured. Americans were stunned by these losses and by televised images of Somalis dragging the naked body of a U.S. soldier through the streets of Mogadishu.

In response to an outcry from the American public and Congress, President Clinton announced on October 7, 1993, that U.S. military forces would complete the withdrawal from Somalia begun in the transition from UNITAF to UNOSOM II, but "on our own terms and without destroying all that two administrations had accomplished." In a subsequent message to Congress, the president outlined a series of steps the United States would take before leaving, but he pledged that U.S. military forces would withdraw from Somalia no later than March 31, 1994. The president noted the United Nations was working to reconstitute a Somali police force that "gradually could assume the security role in some areas" and that five thousand Somali police had returned to their jobs. The president indicated that the United States had offered "$25 million in [Department of Defense] equipment, $2 million for police salaries, and $6 million for a judicial program" to assist the United Nations in this effort.[61]

In fact, creating a Somali national police force capable of assuming responsibility for internal security was already an important part of the UN's "exit strategy" for UNOSOM II. Ali Mahdi and Aideed agreed to this approach, believing a neutral police force capable of dealing with crime and bandit groups was in everyone's best interest.[62] UN Security Council Resolution 814 authorized a fifty-four-member CIVPOL mission whose mandate was to reorganize the Somalia National Police so it could take over general security functions. UN Security Council Resolution 794 created a voluntary trust fund for international contributions to the police program.[63]

The United Nations had made a major effort to plan the UNOSOM II police program. In February 1993, the UN conducted a two-week evaluation of the requirements for a comprehensive police and judicial development effort. The UNOSOM II Justice Division developed a $45-million plan to rebuild a national justice system—police, courts, and prisons—under a Ministry of Justice. The UN plan envisioned a ten thousand–member Somali national police force (a two thousand–man mobile quick reaction force and eight thousand regular police), ninety-four district police stations, and five police academies. The plan called for a judicial system composed of twenty-one district courts, seven regional courts, and two courts of appeal. It also provided for rehabilitation of the existing prisons in Mogadishu and Hargeisa. UN military commanders would have operational control of the indigenous police until a 152-man CIVPOL force arrived. Operational control of the police would pass to the Somali government when it was constituted and could handle the responsibility.[64]

Despite the impressive planning effort and repeated UN statements about the importance of the police and justice program, the Justice Division plan never was funded and the personnel resources were never provided. The special representative of the UN secretary-general (SRSG), Admiral Howe, believed he had obtained support for the plan during a May 1993 meeting in Mogadishu with the head of the DPKO, Kofi Annan. UN headquarters, however, never requested donor contributions for funding, police instructors, or equipment, believing that implementation of the plan should wait until the Somalis had established local, district, and regional councils to supervise the police and judiciary.[65]

After UNITAF departed in May 1993, the Auxiliary Security Force floundered. UN military liaison officers were removed from ASF stations and joint patrols ceased. The United Nations stopped paying salaries. ASF discipline and morale declined sharply after the UN denied military support and protection. As heavily armed bandit groups and clan militia re-emerged to fight each other and the United Nations for control of Mogadishu, the ASF was left virtuously defenseless.[66] Meanwhile, the first members of the UN CIVPOL mission took nearly a year to reach Mogadishu. The CIVPOL commissioner, Chief Superintendent Mike Murphy (of Ireland), did not arrive until April 1994. The fifty-four–man CIVPOL contingent representing fourteen countries did not reach full strength until July 1994, some fourteen months after the departure of UNITAF.[67]

Somalia represented a new departure for UN civilian police missions. All previous CIVPOL missions had been assigned to security functions and to monitoring the performance of local police. This was the first UN CIVPOL mission whose mandate was limited to training and institutional development. Five CIVPOL officers were assigned to organize the ten thousand–member Somali national police force called for in the UNOSOM II Justice Division's plan, but their number was clearly inadequate for such a monumental task. UN CIVPOL officers had no funds, no blueprint for building a national police force, no training curriculum, no classroom facility, and, in many cases, no common language. There were also wide differences in policing philosophies and operating styles between officers from constabulary units like the Italian Carabinieri and unarmed civil police officers from the United Kingdom and Zambia. CIVPOL officers apparently had little contact with the remnants of the ASF or the Somali Police Committee. More than a year after the departure of UNITAF, it was doubtful that much remained of the ASF in areas that were contested between rival militias.[68]

By early 1994, frustration among UNOSOM II military commanders with the UN Justice Division's failure to implement an effective police development program resulted in the creation of a military police liaison cell commanded by a Canadian officer, Major Thomas Haney. UNOSOM II military units developed a series of basic courses for the police in marching, weapons handling, and patrol. Unfortunately, this effort was too little and too late. The failure of Somali leaders to achieve political reconciliation meant that Somali police forces were functioning in the absence of a national government and were supervised only by weak local councils.[69]

Under the leadership of Commissioner Selwyn Mettle (of Ghana), the UNOSOM II CIVPOL mission remained in Somalia until the end of its mandate in March 1995. The failure of the Somalis to implement UN-brokered agreements for national reconciliation, and a further deterioration in the security situation (including attacks on UN forces), led the Security Council to conclude that the continuation of UNOSOM II could no longer be justified. At that time, the Somali National Police consisted of eight thousand officers deployed in eighty-two district stations; of those officers, 2,179 had undergone some UN training. The UN had begun to pay police salaries and had provided 206 vehicles (transferred from UNTAC in Cambodia).[70]

The international intervention in Somalia is said to have failed because a political settlement was not achieved and the United Nations decided to withdraw. This occurred primarily because of the UN's decision to have the military take on police functions (mission creep) and the inability to develop an effective Somali police force, which was the key to the UN's exit strategy. U.S. military involvement in Somalia began as a humanitarian relief operation, but it became a police action to arrest General Aideed. The United States left Somalia after taking unacceptable casualties, with the political situation unresolved and the level of violence much as it was at the beginning of the intervention.

Haiti

Planning for the U.S.-led intervention in Haiti was influenced by the perceived failure of the UN peace operation in Somalia. The U.S. Department of Defense (DOD) was determined to prevent the type of mission creep that had occurred in Somalia and to have an exit strategy in place that would permit an early U.S. withdrawal. DOD made clear that U.S. military forces would not perform police functions and that an effective indigenous security force had to be created to maintain public order. The goal was to recruit and train a Haitian police force that could provide internal security and permit the departure of U.S.

forces. The problem was that Haiti had never had civilian police.[71]

The only security force on the island was the Forces Armées d'Haiti (FAd'H), which performed both military and police duties. In a September 1991 coup, the FAd'H had overthrown Haiti's first democratically elected president, Jean-Bertrand Aristide, and established a military dictatorship under Lieutenant General Raoul Cedras. The FAd'H was an untrained and ill-equipped force of seven thousand men supported by uncounted numbers of thugs called *attaches*. Members of the FAd'H were guilty of gross human rights abuses, murder, torture, and other criminal activities. During the planning for the Haiti mission, it appeared the FAd'H would resist international intervention.[72] The question was how to destroy the FAd'H as a fighting force and still utilize some of its members as an interim security force while a new civilian police force was trained.

The answer was the creation of a force of 920 international police monitors (IPMs) from twenty-six countries, primarily Europe, the Middle East, and Latin America. Under the 1993 Governor's Island Accord signed by Haitian strongman General Cedras and President Aristide, the IPMs carried sidearms, had arrest powers, and could use deadly force in self-defense or to prevent Haitian-on-Haitian violence. The IPMs' initial mission was to supervise an Interim Public Security Force (IPSF) of three thousand former members of the FAd'H. After vetting to remove criminals and human rights offenders, IPSF members received a one-week orientation course in democratic policing. They were given new uniforms and sent back to areas where they had served previously under the watchful eye of the IPMs. This interim force subsequently was reduced in stages that coincided with the deployment of a new, U.S.-trained, indigenous police force, the Haitian National Police (HNP).[73]

Applying lessons learned from previous operations, the IPM commissioner, former New York City Police Department Commissioner Ray Kelly, reported directly to the commanding officer of the Multinational Force (MNF) as part of a unified chain of command. IPM national contingents were assigned as units to geographic sectors or to perform specific functional responsibilities. For example, an elite Israeli police unit was given responsibility for the poorest and most dangerous slum in Port au Prince. IPMs were located in Haitian police stations along with U.S. military police. Patrols were conducted by "four men in a Jeep." This concept brought together an MNF vehicle with a military police driver, an IPM officer, an IPSF officer and an interpreter, so that all police elements with full police powers were present.[74]

From the MNF's first day in Haiti, representatives of the U.S. Department of Justice began working with French and Canadian counterparts to establish Haiti's first national police academy and to train Haiti's first civilian police force. At its peak, the Haiti police training effort employed more than three hundred trainers and interpreters with three thousand cadets in training. When the Haitian government increased the number of HNP required from thirty-five hundred to five thousand, a second campus was opened at Fort Leonard Wood, Missouri. By February 1996, a total of 5,243 new Haitian police officers had completed training. As new recruits graduated from the academy, they were placed under the supervision of IPMs, who acted as field training officers for the rookie cops. As new groups of HNP deployed, corresponding groups of the IPSF were demobilized and assigned to job-training programs or returned to private life.[75] In the view of most observers, Operation Uphold Democracy successfully achieved its objectives, which included removing the Cedras regime, restoring President Aristide to power, and handing off to the United Nations in six months.

In accordance with UN Security Council Resolution 975 (1995), the MNF was replaced by the UN Mission in Haiti (UNMIH). On March 31, 1995, the IPMs were replaced by a force of 870 UN CIVPOL, which was also armed and had executive authority. Its mandate was to provide training and monitor the HNP and to assist in establishing a secure and stable environment. Planning for the transition began in October 1994. The CIVPOL advance team participated in the selection of HNP cadets, determined the personnel and matériel requirements for the follow-on mission, worked out concepts of operation, and developed the mission's mandate in cooperation with MNF counterparts. CIVPOL were encouraged to live in the communities where they were stationed and to use the principles of community policing to engage local citizens. CIVPOL also served as field training officers for the new HNP, reporting back to the police academy on shortfalls that were discovered in the cadets' training. In addition to CIVPOL, two hundred U.S. Military Police remained in Port au Prince, reinforced by a 120-man MP company from India and a company of Guatemalan MPs stationed in the country's second largest city, Cap-Haïtien.[76]

In addition to helping to restore public order and perform other security-related functions, CIVPOL proved an effective part of the exit strategy for the UN military force that departed once the peace operation had achieved sustainable security. In all, the Security Council authorized four peacekeeping missions in Haiti. The final one, the UN Civilian Police Mission in Haiti—La Mission de Police Civile des Nations Unies en Haïti (MIPONUH)—was composed exclusively of three hundred police from eleven, primarily French-speaking countries (including a 150-man Argentine SWAT team) that remained until February 2000. Its mandate was to contribute to the professionalism of the HNP, which was fully responsible for maintaining internal security. The long-term presence of international civilian police proved acceptable to both the Haitian government and critics in the UN Security Council. MIPONUH not only assisted the HNP, but also enabled the UN secretary-general's special representative to remain in Port au Prince and the Security Council to formally monitor events in Haiti.[77]

Cambodia, Somalia, and Haiti provided instructive experiences in the use of police in peace operations. Unfortunately, the lessons learned in these missions were ignored by those responsible for "peacemaking" in Bosnia. The result was a painful process of rediscovery that continues to this day.

4

TEST CASE

✢ ✢ ✢ ✢ ✢ ✢ ✢ ✢ ✢

Creating Postconflict

✢ ✢ ✢ ✢ ✢ ✢ ✢ ✢ ✢ ✢ ✢ ✢

Security in Bosnia

✢ ✢ ✢ ✢ ✢ ✢ ✢ ✢ ✢ ✢ ✢

A FTER THREE WEEKS OF NEGOTIATIONS at Wright-Patterson Air Force Base in Dayton, Ohio, the Bosnian war ended with the initialing of the General Framework Agreement for Peace in Bosnia and Herzegovina on November 21, 1995. Issues relating to the role of police were contained in Annex 11, entitled, "International Police Task Force." The Dayton Accords provided that the Bosnian entities would be responsible for creating a safe and secure environment for all persons in their jurisdictions by maintaining civilian law enforcement agencies, which would operate in accordance with respect for human rights and fundamental freedoms. The parties to the agreement requested that the UN Security Council establish a UN International Police Task Force to assist Bosnian law enforcement agencies in this effort.[1]

The mandate and organization of the IPTF was the result of a compromise between American and European diplomats and not the product of negotiations with the parties to the peace agreement. It was also not the work of the police experts, as there were no police officers or law enforcement specialists at Dayton. In fact, the most important negotiations concerning the creation of the IPTF took place in Washington on the weekend before the final negotiations convened in Ohio. In a Saturday meeting at the State Department, representatives of the Contact

Group (United Kingdom, France, Russia, Germany, and the United States) met to work out differences on military issues, constitutional questions, and the nature of the international police force.[2]

In the discussion of police, the United States presented the Contact Group with three models for an international police force for Bosnia: (1) a "traditional" UN CIVPOL model of unarmed civilian police monitors with no executive authority, (2) a "Cambodia model" of a UN CIVPOL force with limited executive authority and some arms, and (3) a highly capable police force, including a Rapid Reaction Unit. The United States preferred the third model, which would be composed of western European civilian police and gendarmes with some participation by the United States and Canada. The entire force would be well trained, fully equipped, highly mobile, armed, and have executive authority. The Rapid Reaction Unit would have helicopters and armored fighting vehicles. There would be no UN participation. The force would be recruited, equipped, and funded by Europe. As the United States had primary responsibility for IFOR, policing would be left to the allies.[3]

The European members of the Contact Group were opposed to a strong international police force for Bosnia. They were afraid that a strong force with an aggressive mandate would be drawn into dangerous confrontations and would suffer casualties, a scenario that would be unacceptable to European publics. They questioned the appropriateness of foreign police taking responsibility for civilian policing in a third country—even a European one that was still being ravaged by violent ethnic conflict—and had strong doubts concerning the international community's ability to recruit, train, and deploy such a force in the short period between signature and implementation of the agreement.[4] And they were firmly, even angrily, opposed to the model preferred by the United States. The UK representative, Pauline Neville-Jones, said she could not accept, support, or even allow such a proposal. She maintained that British tradition and the legacy of Northern Ireland made it impossible for London to approve arming British police officers and authorizing them to make arrests on foreign soil. She argued that European police might have to enforce laws their governments found unacceptable. Local judges might throw out cases because they did not accept foreign police intervention. The European Union's representative, Carl Bildt, offered that a strong international police force would suggest an "occupation regime" rather than institution building.[5] The Europeans were determined to assign responsibility for the international police force to the United Nations. The U.S. representatives argued for a more capable force, but the Europeans rejected anything beyond a force of unarmed UN police monitors.[6]

At Dayton, the Europeans' preference for a weak IPTF mandate was shared by the U.S. Defense Department.[7] American military officials wanted to ensure that IFOR was the only legitimate armed force in Bosnia, and they were afraid that an armed international police force might be preyed upon for its weapons. They also feared an armed IPTF with an aggressive mandate would create problems and additional responsibilities for IFOR. If IPTF got into trouble, IFOR would have to rescue the police and take over performing police functions. U.S. military officials argued that performing police functions would constitute "mission creep," a politically potent term the U.S. military used when arguing against assignments it felt were counter to its interests. U.S. military leaders feared another imprecise mission like Somalia and did not really want American troops in Bosnia. Beyond the "hangover" from Vietnam, the U.S. military remained deeply troubled by the loss of the Army Rangers in Somalia. The result was the creation of what Ambassador Richard Holbrooke described as a "'Vietmalia' syndrome," a Washington phobia against the U.S. military's involvement in peace operations.[8]

Once the talks convened at Dayton, U.S. diplomats who favored a strong international police mandate faced the combined opposition of the U.S. military and the European members of the Contact Group. They also had to address a myriad of other issues, many of which were far more critical to reaching a settlement of the conflict. The major issues of concern to Ambassador Holbrooke and the Balkan presidents were IFOR's mandate, the division of territory between the Bosnian Federation and the Republika Srpska, and whether the High Representative would have authority over IFOR as well as civilian implementation. The three-week deadline set by Holbrooke for concluding the negotiations placed a premium on the time allotted to the consideration of any part of the agreement. Those issues that were critical to ending the conflict received first priority. Issues (like police) that related to peace implementation and nation building received less attention. Among the "civilian questions," humanitarian assistance, return of refugees, and elections were viewed as more important than the role of the IPTF.[9]

In the closing days of the Dayton talks, Ambassador Holbrooke made a final effort to rescue a robust police mandate by getting agreement from Washington to pay the cost of organizing and arming a strong IPTF. Unfortunately, Holbrooke's appeal came at a time when the Clinton administration was locked in a bitter budget fight with Congress that eventually led to a temporary shutdown of the government. Without hope of obtaining adequate financial support, Holbrooke concluded that the United States could not "write the rules." The IPTF was given a weak mandate and assigned to the United Nations. As General Wesley Clark observed to Holbrooke, this "left a huge gap in the Bosnia food chain," with the UN and the IPTF at the bottom.[10]

Under the agreement, the IPTF would be headed by a commissioner who would "receive guidance" from the High Representative; the latter would be given overall responsibility for coordinating peace implementation. The IPTF was responsible for the following functions:

- ✦ Monitoring, observing, and inspecting law enforcement activities and facilities, "including associated judicial organizations, structures, and proceedings."
- ✦ Advising law enforcement personnel and forces.
- ✦ Training law enforcement personnel.

✦ Facilitating the parties' law enforcement activities within IPTF's mission of assistance.

✦ Assessing threats to public order and advising on the capability of law enforcement agencies to deal with such threats.

✦ Advising Bosnian government authorities on organizing effective civilian law enforcement agencies.

✦ Accompanying Bosnian law enforcement personnel in the performance of their duties, as the IPTF deemed appropriate.[11]

Missing from the list of IPTF functions was executive authority—the authority to enforce the law, conduct investigations, make arrests, and perform other crucial police duties. The IPTF was envisioned as an international civilian police force that would monitor, mentor, and train Bosnian police, who would be responsible for law enforcement and citizen protection. The IPTF would be unarmed and would rely on the local police and IFOR for protection. The IPTF's mandate was to provide advice and encouragement to the Bosnian police. If that advice was ignored or rejected, the IPTF's recourse (Annex 11, Article V) was to notify either the High Representative or the IFOR commander, who could bring such failures to cooperate with the IPTF to the attention of the local authorities, the United Nations, the Joint Civilian Commission, or relevant states. In cases involving human rights violations, the IPTF could inform the Human Rights Commission established under Annex 6 of the Framework Agreement. Given this weak mandate (to advise, assist, monitor, observe, and report), it was clear the IPTF would have to interpret its mission flexibly and be prepared to push the limits of its authority. The IPTF would also need the cooperation of Bosnian law enforcement authorities to achieve Dayton's objectives of providing for the restoration of law and public order, freedom of movement, and justice as the basis for a lasting peace.[12]

The prospect for the IPTF receiving such cooperation from the Bosnian police was highly problematic. What the drafters at

Dayton failed to appreciate was that the nature of the Bosnian conflict meant that the police forces of the three rival parties were ethnically based. This meant local law enforcement authorities were unlikely to provide protection or police services to minorities, particularly given the history of the involvement of police in the conflict. Further, because the IPTF was unarmed and had no police powers, it meant there would be no police force in Bosnia to protect minorities nor any means beyond persuasion for the IPTF to compel compliance with the Dayton Accords. While IFOR could provide area security and reinforce patrolling to deter lawlessness, its forces would not be trained or equipped to control demonstrations or perform routine law enforcement functions. Appeals to the High Representative would be of limited utility as that office had little authority and few resources. IPTF could function effectively only with the consent of those it was assigned to monitor and advise.[13]

Signing the Dayton Agreement

Immediately following the initialing of the Dayton Accords in late November, the UN Security Council authorized under Resolution 1026 the dispatch of a UN assessment mission to determine requirements for the IPTF. The team found that Bosnia's three ethnic-based police forces had expanded greatly during the conflict to a total of 44,750, including large numbers of former soldiers with no police experience. The team determined the IPTF should number 1,721 officers, using a ratio of 1 IPTF member for every 30 local police with an additional 229 officers to compensate for routine absences.[14] Completion of the assessment was followed by a month of frenzied diplomatic activity that culminated with the arrival of IFOR in Bosnia in January 1996.

On December 8 and 9, 1995, a Peace Implementation Conference convened in London to mobilize international support for the Dayton Accords. The conference endorsed the agreement, including creation of the IPTF. It also established the

Peace Implementation Council (PIC) composed of concerned states and relevant international organizations to oversee the peace process in Bosnia.[15] Less than a week later, the three Balkan presidents, Alija Izetbegovic, Franjo Tudjman, and Slobodan Milosevic, met in Paris to sign the General Framework Agreement on December 14. The Bosnian Serbs and Croats had not been invited to Dayton. Milosevic and Tudjman signed the accords on their behalf. On December 15, the UN Security Council adopted Resolution 1031, authorizing member states to establish IFOR under unified command, with ground, air, and maritime units from NATO and non-NATO countries. The Security Council authorized member states to take all necessary measures under the peace enforcement provisions in Chapter VII of the UN Charter to implement the Dayton agreement. On December 21, the Security Council adopted Resolution 1035, which created the United Nations Mission in Bosnia and Herzegovina (UNMIBH) and established the IPTF with an authorized strength of 1,721 international police monitors, 254 international staff, and 811 local personnel. On December 22, 1995, the UN Department of Peacekeeping Operations issued a *note verbale* to forty-five UN permanent missions in New York, inviting their governments to contribute civilian police to the new Bosnian mission. Eventually, forty-three countries responded, but the IPTF was extremely slow to deploy and did not reach its full compliment until August 1996.[16]

IMPLEMENTING THE DAYTON ACCORDS

The IPTF faced its first test early in 1996, when the seven Bosnian Serb–controlled municipalities surrounding Sarajevo were transferred to the control of the federation. Under the Dayton Accords, the seven Serb-held "suburbs," which were located on the high ground surrounding the city, were to transfer to federation control to make Sarajevo less vulnerable to attacks by artillery. More than one hundred thousand ethnic Serbs inhabited these areas; many were long-time residents. As the deadline for the transfer approached, hard-line Serb leaders in Pale ordered Serb residents to evacuate and to destroy everything they could not carry. Departing Serbs were ordered to thoroughly ransack, burn and destroy buildings so incoming federation authorities would find a wasteland. The Office of the High Representative allowed Serb police to remain in the municipalities on the assumption they would protect Serb residents. Instead, Serb police and groups of young Serb thugs engaged in "ethnic self-cleansing," forcing as many as thirty thousand Serb residents that might have stayed to withdraw. From late February to mid-March, all Serb residents were either evacuated or were forced to leave for the Republika Srpska, taking the wiring, windows, and pipes from their apartments and destroying or booby-trapping what could not be removed. Some families exhumed the bodies of their relatives and carried them to the RS. Television pictures of burning buildings and fleeing refugees gave the world an image of general lawlessness that IFOR was unable to control.[17]

As the February 23 start date for the transfer approached, the IPTF was not yet operational. The first IPTF commissioner, Peter Fitzgerald, had not arrived in country, and only 230 of the 1,721 IPTF monitors had been deployed.[18] With a mass exodus of Serb residents already in progress, the transfer of the first municipality, Vogosca, "went wrong from the start." Federation police ordered the Serb mayor to leave and then ransacked his office under the pretense of looking for concealed bombs. This action violated an agreement with the federation that civilian administration in the suburbs was to remain untouched. As word of this incident spread, panic followed. IFOR gave permission for the Serb army to send trucks to complete the evacuation, ending any hope that a portion of the Serb population might be convinced to stay. Events on the first day in Vogosca made the subsequent transfers of the other municipalities more difficult. In Hadzici, Serb arsonists burned the town's municipal offices on the evening before the transfer. In Ilidza, gangs of hooligans ran through the streets terrorizing the remaining three or four thousand Serbs just before the transfer of authority took place.[19]

As the forced evacuation proceeded, IFOR, which was present in force, did nothing to stop it. Admiral Leighton Smith, the first U.S. commander of IFOR, smartly executed the military aspects of the Dayton agreement but considered civilian aspects of the implementation process, including police functions, outside of his responsibility. As the destruction of infrastructure and attacks on civilians proceeded, IFOR troops stood by and watched, refusing requests for protection from civilians who wished to remain and appeals from the OHR to intervene and arrest marauding arsonists. IFOR even kept its firefighting equipment locked inside IFOR compounds. An IFOR spokesman stated that while the burning of buildings was "unfortunate," the Serbs had the right to burn their own houses. As the violence increased, General Michael Walker, IFOR's second in command, rejected a personal appeal for military intervention from his civilian counterpart, Deputy High Representative Michael Steiner. IFOR had the capacity to prevent the destruction of property and the violent expulsion of thousands of residents, but it refused to do so because police functions were not in its mandate. A NATO spokesman put it bluntly: "IFOR is not a police force and will not undertake police functions." Failure to prevent the violence was a defining moment for the IPTF, setting the tone for the initial phase of the peace operation.[20]

In addition to its problems with deployment and initial failure to maintain public order, the IPTF suffered from the poor quality of CIVPOL personnel. Although IPTF members were required to demonstrate a working knowledge of English and the ability to drive a four-wheel-drive vehicle, many failed the test on arrival and were repatriated.[21] IPTF also faced major logistics problems. Equipment left behind by UNPROFOR was transferred to IFOR. IPTF was the first CIVPOL mission to operate without a companion UN military force, which would have provided logistical support, including a medical unit. Instead, the IPTF had to rely on the UN's inadequate procurement system and thus experienced extreme shortfalls in vehicles, communications, and other types of equipment. IPTF was forced to turn to IFOR for such essentials as medical care, vehicle maintenance, access to food stores, and mail delivery. IPTF did not co-locate with local police; instead, it built separate police stations, a process that took time and further delayed effective operations.[22]

While the IPTF struggled operationally, it succeeded in its mission to downsize and restructure the Bosnian police and to develop and introduce principles of democratic policing. During the conflict, three ethnic-based police forces developed. After the conflict, each ethnic group sought to maximize its security by transferring combatants into police units to avoid demobilization. When the IPTF arrived in Bosnia, the standard police uniform was military fatigues and the standard police weapon was the AK-47.[23]

One of the IPTF's initial tasks was to downsize the Bosnian police by removing nonpolice personnel. The goal was to create a police force with a police-officer-to-population ratio consistent with European standards.[24] This effort was complicated by the Dayton agreement's confirmation of the wartime division of Bosnia into two separately controlled entities, the Bosnian Federation and the RS. Within the federation, internal security was the responsibility of a federation police force and independent police forces in each of the ten cantons. In the RS, there was another police force under tight central control of ethnic Serb authorities. In the initial stages of the peace operation, the various Bosnian police forces cooperated poorly with the IPTF—when they cooperated at all. Matters began to improve in April 1996, when the IPTF convened an international conference on police restructuring in the German town of Petersberg, a suburb of Bonn. Federation officials, UN representatives, and senior IPTF officers attended the meeting along with delegations from donor countries, including the United States. RS officials and police were invited but did not come.[25]

The so-called Petersberg Declaration, signed on April 25, 1996, provided for a two-thirds reduction in the size of the federation police forces to 11,500. Restructuring would be accomplished through a vetting process by screening applicants against standards established by the IPTF (graduation from a police academy, professional police experience, and a good record) to remove imposters, criminals, and human rights offenders. Applicants' names were checked against the database of the International Criminal Tribunal for the Former Yugoslavia (ICTY) in The Hague. They were also published in local newspapers with an invitation for persons with negative information to come forward. Candidates who met the criteria and survived the vetting process would take a written examination and physical and psychological tests. Any police officer not certified by this process would be dismissed from the force. Any person who was armed but not a certified police officer would be handled by IFOR.[26]

The IPTF's goal was to reorient the Bosnian police from their previous role of protecting the state to protecting the rights of citizens, regardless of ethnicity, and to adopting the international standards of democratic policing. During 1997, IPTF completed the provisional certification of Bosniak (Bosnian Muslim) police officers in the federation and started to work on certifying the Croats. It also assisted in reopening the police academy in Sarajevo and enrolling the first multiethnic class. The academy's curriculum reflected a commitment by the local police to respect human rights and protect democracy. Such a commitment was also important for the orientation of the IPTF itself, which was composed of police officers from a broad range of countries with a diverse understanding of how police should function in a democratic society.[27]

At the March 6–7, 1997 meeting of the Brcko Implementation Conference in Vienna, the United Nations proposed enlarging the IPTF to provide a special unit to monitor the RS police in Brcko. The primary objectives of the new unit would be to ensure freedom of movement, the return of refugees, and the restructuring and training of the local police. The goal was to reshape the local police force so it would represent the interests of all the people in the area, regardless of ethnicity. As the IPTF unit would consist of unarmed personnel without executive authority, the UN secretary-general requested that it receive the support of the international community and the close cooperation of SFOR in performing its duties.[28] On March 31, 1997, the Security Council authorized an additional 186 IPTF monitors and 11 civilian personnel for Brcko and called upon member states to contribute police personnel to staff the new mission.[29]

The expansion of the IPTF force in Brcko was among the steps taken to implement the February 14, 1997 interim decision of the Brcko arbitration tribunal. Unable to reach a final decision on the future of Brcko, the arbitration panel decided to retain jurisdiction for another year and to establish the Office of the International Supervisor of Brcko. It also set requirements for the RS authorities, including the return and resettlement of displaced persons and the creation of a multiethnic administration in Brcko, including the local police. Creation of a reinforced IPTF unit for Brcko was among the steps taken by the international community to ensure the instructions of the arbitration panel were carried out.[30]

In the aftermath of the Brcko incident and the September 1997 elections in Bosnia, attention in Washington and Brussels turned to the future of SFOR. At the halfway point in the eighteen-month SFOR mandate, it was evident that the decision on whether to renew the mandate must be made by December 1997, so it could be implemented before the June 1998 deadline for SFOR's withdrawal. While the tasks enumerated in the military annex of the Dayton Accords had been accomplished quickly, the failure to make similar progress in civilian implementation required a continued military presence. From the outset of discussions on the future of SFOR, two things were clear: (1) the Clinton administration and Congress favored transferring responsibility for peacekeeping in Bosnia to the Europeans, and (2) the Europeans would not remain in Bosnia without the United States.[31]

The prospects for resolving this dilemma and retaining an effective NATO presence were not promising. In December 1995, congressional support for a one-year deployment of twenty thousand American troops to Bosnia was unenthusiastic. It disappeared almost entirely when President Clinton decided in December 1996 that eighty-five hundred troops would remain for an additional eighteen months. In June 1997, the

House of Representatives passed the FY 1998 Defense appropriations bill, which barred funding for the deployment of U.S.
ground troops in Bosnia after June 1998. The Senate version of
the bill did not include a ban on funding; instead, it adopted a
nonbinding resolution calling for a U.S. troop withdrawal at the
end of the SFOR mandate. The Senate resolution also called for
the European allies to supply all the combat troops for the
follow-on force in Bosnia. Senate action came in the aftermath
of a raid by British SFOR that resulted in the capture of one
accused war criminal and the death of another. The Senate
urged that U.S. troops not take part in arrests of war criminals
on grounds that such efforts could result in American casualties.
In the end, the two houses adopted and President Clinton
accepted a provision that barred funds for U.S. troops in Bosnia
after June 1998 but allowed the president to waive the provision
if he provided a strategic rationale for the extension and a
detailed exit strategy.[32]

By fall 1997, it was clear that a substantial majority of both
houses were opposed to an extension of the U.S. troop presence
in Bosnia and wanted any follow-on force to be provided by the
Europeans. In the conference report on the FY 1998 Defense
authorization bill, Congress repeated the negative provisions in
the FY 1998 appropriations law and added a few more. This legislation (PL 105-85), which was signed by the president on
November 18, 1997, stated that it was "the sense of Congress
that U.S. ground forces should not participate in the Bosnian
follow-on force, except to provide command and control, intelligence, and logistic support for European forces." Any presidential waiver that extended the U.S. troop presence would have to
include assurances that U.S. forces would not be used as civil
police in Bosnia. Other sections required the administration to
report on the activities of U.S. troops to show what steps had been
taken to transfer responsibility to a European-led peacekeeping
force. It was going to be a hard sell if the administration was
going to get Congress to acquiesce to U.S. troops remaining in
Bosnia. At the same time, the administration was going to have to
convince the Europeans that they would have to do more.[33]

There was no indication, however, that any European country was interested in leading or even participating in a post-SFOR force without the United States. European efforts to deal with the dissolution of Yugoslavia had ended in disaster. The end of the Bosnian conflict at Dayton re-established U.S. leadership in NATO, a reassertion of authority that was warmly welcomed in Europe. The issue was not whether European countries could provide the required number of soldiers. Rather, European insistence on U.S. participation reflected concern about the credibility of an all-European force and about the need for continued U.S. leadership within the alliance. U.S. intervention in Bosnia had revitalized NATO and was responsible for securing Russian participation in SFOR. It had also encouraged participation by NATO Partnership for Peace countries, such as Poland and the Czech Republic, that promised to create the basis for NATO enlargement. Awareness that these gains were at risk was the basis of the European "in together, out together" refrain in discussions on the future of SFOR.[34]

SUPPORT OF THE POLICE IN BOSNIA

There was also little evidence of European interest in supporting the police program in Bosnia, either by providing assistance to the indigenous police or by contributing forces to an armed constabulary. U.S. efforts to support the Bosnian police had begun a year earlier. On September 29, 1996, a UN-sponsored donors' conference was held at Dublin Castle in Ireland to raise money for reforming and retraining the Bosnian police. UN undersecretary-general for peacekeeping affairs Kofi Annan opened the conference, which was co-chaired by the High Representative, Carl Bildt, and attended by the Irish prime minister and representatives of thirty-four countries that contributed police officers to the IPTF. IPTF commissioner Peter Fitzgerald presented an elaborate program for equipping the Bosnian police, including provision of vehicles, communications equipment, uniforms, and forensics laboratories. Annan called on UN member states to review the extensive materials prepared by the IPTF on the needs of the Bosnian police and to make contributions so the United Nations could purchase the $100 million worth of equipment and training required.[35]

In response to the UN's appeal, the United States spoke first by prearrangement with the conference organizers. The leader of the U.S. delegation, Assistant Secretary of State for International Narcotics and Law Enforcement Affairs Robert Gelbard, said the United States was committed to the success of the IPTF and the police assistance program in Bosnia. Gelbard said the U.S. had 225 civilian police officers serving in the IPTF and would donate $19 million in equipment and training for local police. A series of European representatives followed Gelbard to the podium. Most said they would first have to study the UN documents before deciding if contributions might be possible. A few countries offered to make slots available for Bosnians in their own national police academies or to make donations of small amounts of equipment. The Irish government offered to train eighteen Bosnian police officers at the Irish police college. Germany offered fifty Volkswagen vans for police transport. Most delegates said that beyond contributing police officers to the IPTF, it was unlikely they would make other contributions. Excluding the U.S. contribution, total pledges at the conference were not more than a few hundred thousand dollars. The French delegate began his remarks by asking in what language did the alphabetical order allow the United States to speak first.[36]

In the year following the conference, Europeans contributed little to the UN police training effort in Bosnia, while the United States provided substantial technical assistance and training through the U.S. Department of Justice International Criminal Investigative Training Assistance Program (ICITAP). At the same time, Assistant Secretary Gelbard began a campaign for the creation of an armed, international police force for Bosnia. In March 1996, Gelbard had "watched in disgust" as the IPTF and IFOR stood by and refused to apprehend marauding Serb thugs and arsonists during the transfer of the Sarajevo suburbs. As buildings burned, small groups of unarmed IPTF

officers watched, apparently afraid to intervene. Armed units
from various IFOR contingents also stood by and did nothing.
When Gelbard asked IPTF officers or IFOR soldiers to take
action, they explained they could do nothing because it was not
part of their mandate. In one case, Gelbard appealed directly to
a group of Italian soldiers manning a checkpoint to assist an
injured Serb couple whose car had been stoned and flipped over
by a mob. The soldiers looked up from their chess game and
said they were sorry, but assisting civilians was not in their mandate. Appalled by this behavior, Gelbard protested directly to
Iqbal Riza, the senior UN official in Sarajevo. Riza claimed the
United Nations could do nothing because the IPTF was
unarmed and its mandate was limited to monitoring the local
police. Gelbard also raised the issue with IFOR commander
Admiral Leighton Smith, who said IFOR could not intervene
because its mandate excluded police functions.[37]

In Washington, Gelbard appealed directly to the secretary of
state, the White House, and the Pentagon for a change in the IPTF
and IFOR mandates. Gelbard explained that there was a serious
gap in the "spectrum of response" of the security forces in Bosnia
between IFOR and the IPTF, which meant there was no one who
could deal with civil disorder. After his appointment as U.S. special representative for the implementation of the Dayton Accords
in April 1997, Gelbard met repeatedly with Defense Department
officials at the Pentagon and with the European allies on the need
for NATO to create an international constabulary to handle the
kind of violence he had witnessed in Sarajevo. At the Pentagon,
Gelbard encountered resistance from the chairman of the Joint
Chiefs of Staff, General John Shalikashvili, who opposed U.S. military forces performing police functions and the creation of an
armed police element within SFOR. General "Shali's" position
was understandable: he had assumed office a few days before the
failed attempt to arrest Somali warlord Mohamed Farah Hassan
Aideed in Mogadishu that resulted in the death of eighteen U.S.
Army Rangers, an incident that was gruesomely portrayed in the
popular motion picture *Black Hawk Down*. Gelbard also met
with UN secretary-general Boutros Boutros-Ghali and undersec-

retary-general Kofi Annan in New York to discuss expanding the IPTF to include an armed constabulary. The United Nations proved unwilling to amend the IPTF mandate and Gelbard returned to his preferred option of creating the constabulary unit within SFOR.[38]

On July 11, 1997, General Wesley Clark became NATO's Supreme Allied Commander Europe. Clark was intimately familiar with Bosnia, having served on Ambassador Richard Holbrooke's negotiating team and as Holbrooke's senior military advisor at Dayton. Clark's arrival in Brussels followed the June 12, 1997 meeting of NATO's North Atlantic Council defense ministers, which endorsed a more aggressive strategy of providing military support for civilian implementation in Bosnia. At their first meeting, NATO secretary-general Javier Solana informed Clark that SFOR "must actively help the civilians to succeed" if the entire international mission in Bosnia was to achieve its objectives. Solana told the new NATO commander that his mission was "not simply a matter of protecting your forces."[39]

NATO's more aggressive policy toward assisting civilian implementation in Bosnia reflected a growing frustration and a change of attitudes within the Clinton administration. General Clark's assumption of command coincided with SFOR's first arrest of a war criminal indicted by the ICTY. This action followed a high-level and extremely contentious policy debate in Washington and a subsequent U.S. effort to organize a NATO working group in The Hague to direct such operations. Clark's arrival accompanied a new activism on the part of SFOR in the Republika Srpska. In late summer 1997, SFOR took control of the RS police antiterrorist brigade, a Serb military police unit that had conducted ethnic cleansing and continued to perform clandestine duties for Serb hard-liners in Pale. Clark approved SFOR's active support for RS president Biljana Plavsic in her struggle against Radovan Karadzic. In mid-August, British SFOR troops intervened to thwart a coup attempt against Plavsic, seizing weapons caches, rounding up plotters, and surrounding the antiterrorist brigade's station in Banja Luka with armored

vehicles. SFOR's support for Plavsic involved a series of operations to take control of police stations around Banja Luka from
RS police who were loyal to Karadzic. In late August, General
Eric Shinseki, the new U.S. commander in Bosnia, called Clark to
report that a pro-Plavsic police captain was poised to attempt to
take over the police station in Brcko.[40]

THE U.S. DEBATE ON EXTENDING SFOR

Despite opposition from Congress and dissent from senior
administration officials, the White House began laying the
groundwork for an extension of the U.S. military commitment
in Bosnia in the fall of 1997. In late September, the national
security adviser, Samuel R. "Sandy" Berger, began providing a
rationale for continuing U.S. presence in Bosnia while stressing
that the president had not made a decision. Berger publicly reiterated that the United States maintained a significant stake in
the success of the Dayton peace implementation process and left
open the possibility of longer-term U.S. involvement in Bosnia.
This effort followed a meeting of the National Security Council
on the future of SFOR in Bosnia. After the meeting, administration officials began an extensive round of consultations with
members of Congress, explaining the rationale for extending the
SFOR mandate and for American troops remaining in Bonsia.[41]

On November 4, 1997, President Clinton held a White
House meeting with more than a hundred members of Congress
to discuss Bosnia. Invitations went to the leadership of both houses, committee chairmen, and key members of both political parties. The president, Secretary of State Albright, and Ambassador
Gelbard made the case for renewing the SFOR mandate and continuing the U.S. troop presence. Attendees asked questions but did
not challenge the president's apparent intention to commit the
United States to a long-term engagement in Bosnia. After the
meeting, Secretary Albright told the press that a "consensus was
emerging" between the administration and Congress on the need
to maintain a robust peacekeeping force in Bosnia, including a
contingent of American ground troops.[42]

Albright's optimistic statement was challenged immediately by Secretary of Defense William Cohen. On November 6, Cohen denied that a consensus had emerged. He said the president would not make a decision until he had reviewed all the options, which ranged from complete withdrawal to extending the existing force. Beyond the expenses and the negative impact on troop morale, Cohen said the United States must weigh its global commitments and determine if the Europeans could play a larger role. Secretary Cohen's statement was consistent with his long-standing opposition to retaining U.S. troops in Bosnia. As a former Republican senator, Cohen was well aware of the anger and frustration expressed by many lawmakers over President Clinton's decision to extend the original December 1996 deadline by eighteen months to June 1998. At his confirmation hearing, Cohen stated emphatically that U.S. troops would leave Bosnia as scheduled. Cohen warned his administration colleagues that congressional support was eroding and that the Pentagon could not continue to spend $2 billion annually to keep U.S. forces in Bosnia. He also believed the Europeans should be forced to do more. As a U.S. pullout appeared increasingly unlikely, Cohen attempted to use his position as the administration's chief critic on Bosnia to leverage a larger European contribution, particularly in assisting the Bosnian police and providing constabulary forces.[43]

In early November, the U.S. proposal for an international police force for Bosnia received qualified support from NATO secretary-general Javier Solana. Speaking in Berlin at a European forum on "Pan-European Peacekeeping" on November 8, He said successful peace support operations required NATO to adapt to new demands in the security environment by creating new political and military structures. Among the lessons learned from Bosnia, he said, was that appropriately armed and trained forces were essential in effecting the transition from hostilities to peace. He said experience in Bosnia had revealed a gap between the ability of SFOR and the local police to provide a secure environment and that creating an international police force or gendarmerie to manage crises in Bosnia would help restore civil order because some situations were too difficult for the IPTF but were not appropriate for the military.[44]

A DECISIVE DECEMBER

The role of civilian police in Bosnia emerged as the major point of contention between the United States and its European allies at the meeting of NATO defense ministers in Brussels on December 2, 1997. In discussions on the follow-on force to SFOR, Cohen recommended the creation of a deterrent force ("DFOR") that would be based on both a reduction in the number of NATO troops and the transfer of responsibility for maintaining public order to a multinational police force. Cohen made clear that the United States wanted a reduction in the overall size of the NATO presence from thirty-four thousand troops and a drawdown in the eight thousand American personnel. He suggested that U.S. participation in the follow-on force should be limited to providing logistics and intelligence support and supplying "over the horizon" protection from air power based in other countries.[45]

Cohen also called for a substantial increase in European assistance to the Bosnian police. The U.S. defense secretary pointed out that the United States had contributed $30 million toward police reform in Bosnia, while European countries had contributed only $5 million. Cohen said the Bosnian police remained short of personnel and equipment because much of their $100-million budget had not been funded. He warned that President Clinton would have trouble persuading Congress to support continued American troop presence in Bosnia unless he could demonstrate that the Europeans were prepared to carry a larger share of the peacekeeping burden and contribute more resources. Cohen said there was a "serious deficiency" in European commitment to building a well-trained local police force that was not under the control of the obstructionists who were attempting to frustrate the Dayton peace process.[46]

Cohen's most controversial proposal, however, was for the creation of an international police force drawn from the constabulary forces of the European allies. Cohen noted that SFOR was not trained or equipped to do policing, which created a security gap that was exploited by local politicians, including suspected war criminals. He said there was a need for a specially trained international police force that could take over such tasks as crowd control, election security, and protecting returning refugees. Creating such a force would reduce the need for the United States and NATO to maintain large numbers of troops in Bosnia. Cohen did not specify which countries the United States wanted to contribute to such a force, but it was clear that the Italians, the French, and the Spanish were the most likely candidates. According to a senior Pentagon official, this could be done by "building a public security force that could take over the kinds of responsibilities that were in the hands of the international military presence."[47]

Cohen's message was reinforced by General Clark, who told the defense ministers that a substantial follow-on force would be needed to sustain the progress achieved in implementing the Dayton Accords. Clark warned that without a robust NATO presence, reconstruction efforts could collapse and war could resume in Bosnia. Clark said the military challenge remained formidable, as SFOR conducted more than 150 patrols a day to maintain a fragile truce between the former warring parties. In addition, NATO peacekeepers were overwhelmed by civilian tasks such as supervising elections and resettling refugees because the United Nations was unable to handle such responsibilities. Clark made a particular point of the need for an international police force that could stop the political corruption and rampant smuggling that undermined Bosnia's economic recovery and subsidized the "Mafia-type" activities of ethnic Serb hard-liners like Radovan Karadic.[48]

At the defense ministers' conference, the Europeans pressed Secretary Cohen to continue the American military presence while resisting U.S. pressure to create an international police force in Bosnia. British defense minster George Robertson "chided" the Clinton administration for refusing to renew the commitment of American forces, claiming an American withdrawal could undermine the tenuous peace that had existed since IFOR arrived in January 1996.[49] The Europeans countered American requests for a constabulary by claiming they would be hard pressed to find the kind of highly trained police that could handle such a sensitive mission. Only a small number of countries in NATO—France, Italy, Spain, Portugal, and the Netherlands—had such forces. To take police from only a few countries to perform dangerous tasks would represent an unfair burden and violate the NATO principle of sharing risks equally. The Europeans also claimed there were legal issues associated with the use of international police in a peace operation. Among these were questions about whether they would have law enforcement authority and under what conditions could they use deadly force. There were also objections to sending an international force that might substitute for the local police. An international police force, some argued, would lack the kind of firepower that deterred the former belligerents from attacking NATO peacekeepers. Yet Cohen's recommendation for an international constabulary was included in the instructions given to the alliance's military planners to develop a set of options for a follow-on force to replace SFOR.[50]

On December 8, 1997, Secretary Cohen received explicit support for his position from two influential dailies. In an editorial, the *New York Times* noted that the Clinton administration was "sidling toward" a positive decision on maintaining troops past the June deadline. The editorial claimed that Secretary Cohen had "chosen his words more wisely" than Secretary Albright, placing two important conditions for a continued U.S. presence in Bosnia. According to the *Times*, Cohen wanted a shift of security responsibilities from soldiers to a stronger international police force and greater European participation to meet congressional concerns. Noting that the IPTF was composed of police monitors "hemmed in by a weak mandate and faulty UN recruiting procedures," the *Times* counseled that what was needed was a new armed international police force to fill the gap between heavily armed NATO soldiers and unarmed UN police trainers. Such a force could come from the large, armed "paramilitary police forces" in many western European countries.

Sending European constabularies to Bosnia would not only relieve the burden on NATO but would also "be a good way to increase Europe's share of the overall security burden." The editorial concluded that the United States should not stay in Bosnia unless a compelling need for U.S. troops had been established and "a clear strategy leading to their early replacement by an armed police force had been put in place."[51]

On the same day, *Newsday* said Secretary Cohen's plan for the NATO allies to form an international police force to take over from military peacekeepers in Bosnia made sense. "A police force," the newspaper stated, "in credible numbers and with appropriate powers and jurisdiction, can do what military peacekeepers cannot do without distorting their role: live among the population, cultivate informants, arrest suspects, quell civil disorder, and handle routine disputes." According to the editorial, NATO provided little more than a "wet blanket dampening down smoldering resentments that could flare up at any time." An international police force would be better suited to the long-term mission of maintaining civil order with the provision that NATO troops could return if war erupted.[52]

In fact, the editorials foreshadowed actions the United States and Europe would take to resolve their differences over the future of NATO's presence in Bosnia. Under arrangements that would emerge from high-level political decisions and NATO military planning, the United States would agree to keep a smaller number of American troops in Bosnia and the Europeans would commit to provide a constabulary force that would be armed and experienced in dealing with civil disorder. The European contribution of such a force would be presented to Congress as proof that the NATO allies were prepared to shoulder more of the burden in Bosnia. As a consequence, U.S. military forces would be less likely to face hostile mobs and risk suffering casualties.

On December 9 and 10, the Peace Implementation Council convened in Bonn to review progress on civilian implementation of the Dayton Accords. The PIC stated that considerable progress had been achieved in improving security and addressing the prerequisites for reconciliation, such as freedom of movement and improvement of the economy. It also noted that "much more could have been achieved if the Bosnian authorities contributed their full share to the construction of a civil and democratic society." As for the IPTF, the council endorsed the progress made in reforming and restructuring the local police. It also called for the creation of new IPTF units that would specialize in "key public security issues," including managing civil disorder.[53]

While the creation of a constabulary force for Bosnia was not on the PIC agenda, it was the subject of a meeting "on the margins" between NATO secretary-general Javier Solana; Gregory Schulte, the director of NATO's Bosnia Task Force; and a senior U.S. military officer. During the discussion, Schulte took out a piece of paper and drew two circles, marking one "SFOR" and the other "UN IPTF." A discussion then proceeded on the respective merits of locating the proposed constabulary unit in one or the other circle. The trio agreed that the United Nations was unwilling to arm the IPTF or expand its mandate. The senior U.S. military officer expressed concern about SFOR's performing police functions. He was more concerned, however, about the proliferation of armed groups outside of SFOR. At the end of the discussion, Schulte placed the letters "MSU" for "Multinational Specialized Unit" within the circle marked "SFOR." None of the three liked the name, but they could not think of another. Having privately reached agreement in principle, there still remained the difficult task of achieving formal agreement on the renewal of the mandate and the inclusion of a constabulary unit within the follow-on force to SFOR.[54]

At the December 16, 1997 meeting of NATO foreign ministers in Brussels, the United States and its allies moved closer to endorsing publicly the extension of the SFOR mandate beyond the June 1998 deadline. Emerging from the first day's session, French foreign minister Hubert Vedrine told the press that his colleagues had reached consensus on retaining a reduced NATO military presence in Bosnia, although a formal decision including numbers would have to await the report of the military planners. NATO officials attending the conference were quoted as stating that the new "slim-line" unit, tentatively named "DFOR," would be reduced to between fifteen thousand and twenty thousand troops, or roughly half the size of the existing force of thirty thousand soldiers. American troops would be included, but their number would be reduced to eighty-five hundred. There would also be a contingent of constabulary police to deal with crowd control and refugee return. The new force would not have an exit date, but its mandate would be reviewed every six months. The ministers said a final decision on the composition of the new force was required by March 1, 1998 to allow adequate time for redeployments.[55]

At the conference, Secretary of State Madeleine Albright reiterated that the Europeans must contribute more toward police if the U.S. Congress was to support a continued American military presence in Bosnia. Albright said it was unacceptable for the United States to provide 90 percent of the funding for training and equipping the Bosnian police when creating law and order was critical to "a sensible exit strategy" for all NATO countries. Albright also reaffirmed the need to strengthen the international police in Bosnia to take responsibility for civilian reconstruction tasks that a smaller SFOR would be unable to perform. She suggested that NATO should support the IPTF by providing the "capabilities that are found in many countries in the form of Gendarmes and Carabinieri." Albright said such forces could increase SFOR's flexibility, enhance force protection, and promote Dayton implementation. Secretary Albright had no problem praising the Europeans for their efforts but said they "must do much, much more."[56] To drive home the secretary's point about the need for constabulary forces, the NATO ministers were shown a video of the August 28 riot in Brcko. They were told that if the soldiers had been unable to hold their position on the bridge, the only fallback available was the helicopter gunship overhead—obviously, not a desirable option. Instead, SFOR required constabulary forces that were trained and equipped for crowd control.[57]

Two days later, on December 18, 1997, President Clinton announced his decision to retain U.S. troops in Bosnia. At a White House news conference, the president announced the U.S.

"commitment in principle" to extend the presence of American troops in Bosnia beyond the June 1998 deadline. In his opening statement, Clinton noted that progress had been achieved toward a lasting peace in Bonsia, but that challenges still had to be faced in order to finish the job. Clinton said the international community had helped Bosnia create democratic institutions, improved the lives of the Bosnian people, and provided for their security by training ethnically integrated police forces in the Bosnian Federation and "taking the first step toward a professional, democratic police force" in the Republika Srpska. He said progress was "unmistakable, but not yet irreversible." The Bosnians still needed the "safety net and helping hand that only the international community, including the United States, could provide."[58]

To finish the work, the president said the international community must continue to provide an international military presence to enable economic reconstruction and the return of refugees to proceed in an atmosphere of confidence. For this reason, the president said, he had instructed the U.S. representative to NATO to inform our allies that "in principle, the U.S. will take part in a security presence in Bosnia when SFOR withdraws this summer." The agreement in principle would become a commitment only when the president approved the action plan NATO military authorities would present early the following year. While not wanting to prejudge the details of the plan, Clinton listed several criteria the plan would have to meet, including the ability of the follow-on force to protect itself. Although the force would be smaller, he would insist that it be of sufficient size and have the capability to achieve its mission and defend itself. In addition, the European allies would have to assume their share of responsibility. He noted the Europeans had done a great deal but said they could do more. Finally, he said the new force would have to enjoy the support of Congress and the American people. With that in mind, he announced that members of Congress from both parties had accepted his invitation to accompany him on a forthcoming visit to Bosnia.[59]

On December 22, 1997, the president and Mrs. Clinton,

along with daughter Chelsea, spent twelve hours in Bosnia delivering a political message to Bosnian leaders in Sarajevo and yuletide cheer to American troops at Eagle Base in Tuzla. The president was accompanied by former senator Robert Dole, his Republican opponent for the White House, Mrs. Dole, and eleven members of Congress, including Senator Ted Stevens, chairman of the Senate Appropriations Committee, and Representative John Kasich, chairman of the House Budget Committee. Clinton met with the Serb, Croat, and Bosniak members of Bosnia's collective presidency and had a private meeting with Biljana Plavsic. In a twenty-minute speech delivered to four hundred religious and political leaders crowded into Sarajevo's small National Theater, Clinton praised Bosnian leaders for the progress they had achieved but then went down a checklist of things they still had to do. The president's list included sharing power, returning refugees, ending corruption, freeing the media, and capturing war criminals. President Clinton said they must also "take the police out of the hands of the warlords" and "reform, retrain, and re-equip a democratic police force that would foster security, not fear." At Club 21, a large shed with a sheet-metal roof at Eagle Base, Clinton told several hundred cheering GIs that the United States was determined to do its part in Bosnia but rightly expected Bosnians to do theirs.[60]

Clinton's Christmas visit was a defining moment in the Bosnian peace process. Until that time, hard-line Serbs and other opponents of the Dayton agreement believed they could simply wait until the United States and the international community left in June 1998. Clinton's decision that U.S. troops would remain indefinitely nullified that option. Clinton's visit to Bosnia convinced the Europeans and the Bosnians that the U.S. was committed for the long term.[61] Once it was certain the U.S. would remain, the pace of the peace implementation process began to accelerate. Within the first two months of 1998, there was more progress toward national integration than in the previous two years. In rapid succession, a flag, a common currency, a unified telephone system, and common license plates were adopted; limited air, rail, and truck traffic began to operate.[62]

PLANNING FOR THE "DETERRENT FORCE"

NATO planning for the SFOR follow-on force accelerated in January 1998. At Supreme Headquarters Allied Powers Europe (SHAPE), four options for the "Deterrent Force" were under consideration: (1) complete withdrawal, (2) continuation of the current force levels, (3) a smaller force with a broad military and civilian-assistance mandate, or (4) an even smaller force limited to military tasks.[63] The first two options were "throwaways"; only the last two were serious. Under option three, an international constabulary force would be included. The new Multinational Specialized Unit would fill the security gap between SFOR and the IPTF and would be used primarily for crowd control. Its mission would be to protect returning refugees, ensuring the "right of return" provided for in the Dayton Accords. It would also assist with the installation of minority mayors and municipal council members who had been elected in absentia in the fall of 1997 but had been unable to return to their hometowns to assume office. It was widely predicted that international efforts to return refugees and seat minority politicians would be met with a wave of ethnic-related violence. The UN High Commissioner for Refugees, Sadako Ogata, urged NATO to include rapid reaction police units in its plans for the follow-on military force for Bosnia. Ogata said a strong international police force was important to successfully completing the refugee resettlement program in Bosnia.[64]

On February 20, 1998, the North Atlantic Council, composed of ambassadors from the sixteen NATO member states, agreed to continue the NATO military presence in Bosnia indefinitely beyond June 1998. The council's decision was subject only to approval by the UN Security Council, which was a formality. The NATO-led force would retain the name SFOR, primarily to avoid the $1 million cost of repainting signs and vehicles and issuing new identification cards. The mission of the new version of SFOR would be to deter the renewal of hostilities and create an environment conducive to successful implementation of civilian aspects of the Dayton peace process. In this regard, the new force would have "enhanced capability to help promote public security" in close cooperation with the OHR, the IPTF, and the Bosnian authorities. The council instructed NATO military authorities to prepare a final operations plan for the new force that could be reviewed with non-NATO contributors.[65]

Included in the new, smaller version of SFOR would be "tough new police units" capable of dealing with ethnic-related civil disturbances that regular soldiers were not trained or equipped to handle. According to a senior Clinton administration official, the new multinational police unit would be drawn from European constabulary forces and would have "more balanced capabilities and training than just retreating or killing." The new force would be well armed and would be supported by regular SFOR troops, if necessary. The senior official noted that all three ethnic groups supported by local police were guilty of preventing the return of refugees of different ethnicity. The NATO police force would "try to coax local law enforcement to act," the official stated, but if it failed to respond the international police would take responsibility.[66] NATO commander General Wesley Clark expressed a somewhat different view. According to Clark, the new force was a "step toward adapting the capability of SFOR to meet new requirements on the ground." Clark said it was "not a police force," but a force that would provide "tangible assistance" to the local police, filling the gap between them and the IPTF. It was unclear, he said, if the new force would arrest war criminals. Italy, Argentina, and Hungary, Clark said, had volunteered to provide personnel.[67]

CREATING THE MSU

Recruiting

Recruiting constabulary units for the new Multinational Specialized Unit was not easy. Despite appeals from the United States, European donor countries proved unwilling to participate.

After a prolonged recruiting effort, only Italy stepped forward to volunteer three companies of Carabinieri. Additional platoons had to be recruited from non-NATO states to form the first battalion. The process of raising, training, and deploying the first MSU battalion took nearly eight months, so the first SFOR constabulary unit did not reach Sarajevo until August 1998. A second battalion was scheduled to arrive in Bosnia in November 1998. Efforts to recruit personnel from Spain, Poland, the Czech Republic, Hungary, and the Netherlands failed to result in contributions, and the second unit was never deployed.

For Italy, assisting with planning for the MSU and providing most of the personnel was part of a larger effort to increase its status in NATO. It was also part of a defensive strategy to exert greater influence in the Balkans, a region that was vital to Italian national interests. Sharing the Adriatic Sea coastline with Albania, Croatia, Bosnia, Montenegro, and Slovenia, Italy was a magnet for refugees and a target for Balkan organized crime. In 1994, when the European Union assumed responsibility for policing the southern Bosnian city of Mostar, Italy sent forty Carabinieri as part of the international police force organized by the Western European Union. In January 1996, some thirty-two hundred Italian troops were part of IFOR when NATO troops arrived in Bosnia. In 1997, Italy took the lead in organizing Operation Alba, an eight-country, seven-thousand-member intervention force that restored order in Albania after the collapse of a series of pyramid investment schemes led to a situation of total anarchy. A "coalition of the willing" authorized by the UN Security Council, Operation Alba was the first peace enforcement mission composed entirely of Europeans.[68]

For the Italian press, it was the Italian Carabinieri's performance in Operation Alba that brought Italy the honor of leading the MSU. In January 1998, Italian newspapers reported that General Clark had been so impressed with the Carabinieri's operation in Albania that he personally asked the chief of the Carabinieri if Italy would take the lead in organizing the MSU for Bosnia. On January 20, 1998, the Carabinieri established an MSU working group in Rome to plan and initiate formation of the MSU. At the same time, a Carabinieri officer was assigned to the MSU working group at NATO headquarters in Brussels. A month later, on February 27, 1998, the Carabinieri established the MSU training base at Gorizia, Italy, and began preparations for deploying to Bosnia.[69]

The reaction to NATO's call for contributions to the MSU from the other two most likely NATO contributors—France and Spain—was less than forthcoming. The French were strongly opposed to the MSU from the start. For Paris, the U.S. proposal for creating a European-led constabulary force for Bosnia was simply a means for Washington to pass the buck to the Europeans. Because the United States did not have forces similar to the French Gendarmerie or the Italian Carabinieri, the Americans could not be expected to participate. This left the responsibility for filling the ranks of the new multinational police force solely to the few countries in Europe that had such forces. The French saw the role envisioned for the new specialized unit as highly risky and likely to set a negative precedent for future operations. To ensure proper burden sharing, the French argued that crowd control and refugee return should be handled by regular infantry trained to perform those functions. This attitude was shared by the United Kingdom, which reported having no problem dealing with mob violence in its sector. With their experience in Northern Ireland, British troops were accustomed to dealing with civil disturbance and saw no need for a specialized police force to handle such contingencies.[70]

In Madrid, the plan to include an MSU within SFOR was greeted with initial enthusiasm. On the eve of Ambassador Robert Gelbard's visit to Spain in January 1997, the Spanish press announced the Guardia Civil was preparing to send between 300 and 500 men to Bosnia as part of the new multinational police force. Reports noted there were already 144 members of the Guardia Civil in Bosnia: 68 were serving as military police with Spanish forces, 56 were in the IPTF, and 20 were providing close protection for High Representative Carlos Westendorp, a Spaniard. As the new multinational police force would be armed and part of NATO, the press stated that U.S.

attention had been attracted to the Spanish Guard because of its discipline and its distinguished service in Bosnia.[71] The results of Gelbard's visit were positive and the Spanish seemed genuinely interested in participating. In the final analysis, however, the Spanish government decided not to join, despite the personal appeals from another Spaniard, NATO secretary-general Javier Solana. The primary reason was that the Guardia Civil was engaged in an intensive struggle against Basque separatists that badly stretched its limited resources. In May, the Spanish defense minister announced that his country would "remain on the sidelines" and not participate in the MSU. Instead, Spain preferred to retain its military police in regular SFOR units and would not reduce or reconfigure its military presence in Bosnia.[72]

Roles and Missions

On March 4, 1998, President Clinton certified to Congress that the presence of U.S. forces was required in Bosnia after June 1998. The president stated that it was in the interest of U.S. national security for the Dayton agreement to be implemented rapidly, which required the continued participation of the U.S. military in the NATO-led peacekeeping force. He called for a reduction in the number of U.S. troops from 8,500 to 6,900, but he proposed that no end-date or "arbitrary deadline" should be established for their withdrawal. The president asserted that the deployment would not be open-ended; rather, the United States would substitute an "end state" for an "end date." He outlined ten conditions to be met that would permit a NATO-led withdrawal. These included creating a restructured, retrained, and reintegrated police force; judicial reform; arrest of war criminals; press freedom; democratic elections; refugee returns; and a multiethnic administration in Brcko. The president asked Congress to provide $2.35 billion in 1998–99 to support this effort.[73]

In explaining the president's decision, Ambassador Robert Gelbard told the press that SFOR would retain its name and would not see a reduction in troop levels until after the

September 1998 elections. The size of the U.S. combat force would remain at three battalions, but the number of other U.S. troops would decline as the Europeans took over logistics and other support functions. What was new, Gelbard said, was that NATO was organizing specialized units composed of European military police that would handle the expected increase in civil unrest generated by increased refugee returns and the seating of minority municipal officials. Gelbard said these international police units would respond in cases where the local police were unable to control the situation. They would also train local police and support the IPTF.[74]

In March 1998, NATO planners at SHAPE were focused on the issues related to the role and mission of the new specialized unit in SFOR. As this was a totally new concept, planners had to determine what duties the new unit would perform, its rules of engagement, and the nature of its relationships with the IPTF and local police. To assist in this effort, General Clark invited Ambassador Robert Oakley and Colonel Michael Dziedzic to Brussels to brief NATO leaders and planners on their theory concerning the use of constabulary forces in peace operations. At the time, Oakley and Dziedzic were staff members of the National Defense University's Institute for National Strategic Studies in Washington, D.C. They were accompanied by a military officer from the Joint Chiefs of Staff to emphasize the importance the Pentagon attached to their views.[75] In their book, *Policing the New World Disorder,* Oakley and Dziedzic had identified the "security gap" that existed between military forces that were reluctant to engage in confrontations with civilians, and international police monitors and local police that were unable or unwilling to do crowd control. To fill this gap the authors recommended the use of constabulary forces that were trained and equipped to handle public disorder and better suited than the military to perform law enforcement functions. They argued that in circumstances in which the likelihood of military conflict had been reduced substantially, constabulary forces could substitute for regular military forces in peace operations and, ultimately, replace them altogether.[76]

On March 4, 1998, the day of President Clinton's congressional certification, Oakley and Dziedzic briefed General Clark's deputy and senior SHAPE planners on the possible roles and missions of a constabulary force in Bosnia. In their briefing, Oakley and Dziedzic stressed the importance of recruiting formed and fully integrated forces from only a limited number of countries with similar policing traditions and philosophies. They stressed the necessity of providing the specialized unit with clear rules of engagement and of clearly defining its relationships with SFOR, OHR, and the IPTF. They envisioned that the new unit would be deployed in a central location and would use nonlethal means to deter and contain politically motivated unrest, to assist the IPTF and local police in handling spontaneous civil disorder, and to promote Dayton implementation in general. The unit would also assist the IPTF in training local police to perform crowd control functions. They cautioned that the new unit should not be used for arresting war criminals, local law enforcement, or as part of an American "exit strategy."[77]

Three weeks later, Oakley and Dziedzic returned to Brussels on March 25, 1998, this time at Solana's invitation, to chair a workshop at SHAPE on the roles constabulary forces could play in a range of future NATO contingencies—from preventing state collapse and facilitating humanitarian relief to providing postconflict security. The workshop was unofficial, but the attendees included field grade officers from the French Gendarmerie, the Italian Carabinieri, the Spanish Guardia Civil, the Dutch Marechaussee, U.S. Military Police, and the Royal Canadian Mounted Police. The Swedish deputy foreign minister and an UNMIBH representative also attended. Participants agreed that constabulary forces provided a valuable mix of capabilities, but that the mission and mandate must be clear and resources must be adequate. There was uniform opposition to constabulary forces exercising executive authority (arrest and detention). The preferred role, the meeting concluded, was for the constabulary to support the local police and hold them accountable to international standards. During the discussion, Solana was particularly concerned about the limited pool of qualified source countries, the need for an adequate mandate, command and control arrangements, and the development of common tactics and doctrine. At the end of the meeting, the Swedish representative offered to host a field exercise involving NATO military forces, the MSU, and UN IPTF personnel as a means of addressing the issues Solana raised. Unfortunately, the proposed Swedish exercise was never held, and these issues would bedevil the MSU long after its arrival in Bosnia.[78]

Riot in Drvar

On April 24, 1998, an incident occurred in the Bosnian municipality of Drvar that reaffirmed the need for an international constabulary force in Bosnia. Once again, opponents of the peace process used a "rent-a-mob" to engage international peacekeepers. Once again, IPTF officers were forced to flee after their police station and vehicles were burned by the mob. Once again, SFOR was forced to engage civilian demonstrators. This time, however, the antagonists were ethnic Croats, not ethnic Serbs.

Prior to the war, the town of Drvar had a population of seventeen thousand, of which 97 percent were ethnic Serbs. During the conflict, the combined Croat and Bosniak armies broke through Serb lines near Drvar, sending the population fleeing to Banja Luka. Surprisingly, the town suffered almost no damage. After the war, the Croatian Democratic Union (HDZ) party took advantage of this situation to resettle six thousand Croat refugees and former soldiers and their families in Drvar. The HDZ also began a campaign of violence and intimidation to discourage Serb returns. On April 16, an elderly Serb couple that had just returned were murdered and their house burned. The next day, the High Representative, the UN's SRSG, and the IPTF commissioner sent a joint letter to the authorities in Canton Ten (Livno) calling for the resignation of the cantonal interior minister and the deputy mayor of Drvar and the decertification of the town's police chief. The letter accused local authorities of failing over a period of several months to investigate and take action in dozens of incidents of assault, harassment, and arson against returning Serbs.[79]

On April 24, a highly disciplined mob of two to three hundred Croats attacked the municipal office building and assaulted the ethnic Serb mayor, who had been elected by absentee voting in September 1997. The mob then attacked and destroyed nearby offices of nongovernmental organizations and the IPTF station, assaulting and seriously injuring several IPTF officers and international NGO staff. Seven UN vehicles were destroyed and others were damaged. Finally, the rioters burned an apartment complex housing Serb returnees, leaving 160 people homeless and injuring SFOR soldiers that tried to protect the building and its residents. The Canadian SFOR troops, which were responsible for Drvar, operated under rules of engagement from Ottawa that prohibited them from performing police duties and engaging the rioters. The Canadian ROEs were different from those of SFOR, but the Canadians followed their national guidance. In the end, SFOR evacuated the IPTF, the mayor, and all the Serbs who wanted to leave for the safety of Banja Luka. During the chaos, the local police refused to intervene and were seen openly fraternizing with the rioters. It was clear from the mob's behavior that the day's events were orchestrated by Croat authorities.[80]

In the aftermath of the violence, a number of senior international officials visited Drvar. High Representative Carlos Westendorp, NATO commander General Wesley Clark, SFOR commander General Eric Shinseki, OSCE head of mission Robert Barry, and several congressmen arrived within weeks of the violence. They stated that the international community was not going to be intimidated, nor were Serbs going to be denied their right of return. General Clark was accompanied by tanks and helicopter gunships to make the point. In fact, Serb returns stopped for two months, and the Serb population did not reach its pre-riot level for six months.[81]

The MSU Advance Team

On April 24, 1998, the day of the Drvar riot, the MSU advance team of the Italian Carabinieri arrived in Sarajevo. In addition to his other duties, the MSU executive officer, Colonel Vincenzo

Coppola, began an extensive round of briefings at SFOR head-quarters and at the headquarters of each of the Multinational Divisions. In these meetings, Coppola sought to introduce the con-cept of a constabulary force and discuss its capabilities, and he quickly discovered a general absence of familiarity with constabu-lary forces and a lack of understanding of their potential role and mission in a peace operation. This was particularly true among military officers from the United States and northern Europe. Coppola also encountered a general reluctance to accept the idea that the MSU would operate like "a police force with military characteristics." In the Italian's concept of operations, the MSU's primary mission would be to serve as a deterrent force. The unit would patrol widely, constantly interact with civilians, and spot and defuse trouble before it could start. This contrasted markedly with the general understanding of senior SFOR officers, particu-larly the MND commanders. In their view, the MSU should per-form like a "riot squad" or "strategic reserve" that would remain in its barracks in Sarajevo and would enter its areas of responsi-bility only when needed. Once the initial round of briefings was concluded, Coppola found that summer transfers and the influx of new officers required that he repeat his briefings for a new cast of characters.[82]

In addition to briefing SFOR, Colonel Coppola met with the leadership of the IPTF to discuss possible areas of coopera-tion. Here again, Coppola found a general lack of familiarity with constabulary forces among the British, American, and German police officers who held the most senior positions in the IPTF. There was a general wariness on the part of the IPTF that the MSU would become a competitor and would attempt to take over some of its functions. There was also a fear that the Bosnians would not be able to distinguish between the members of the MSU and their IPTF counterparts. In these meetings, Coppola sought to reassure the IPTF leadership that the MSU, in its distinctive blue uniforms with red berets and red arm-bands, would be easily identifiable from other SFOR units and the IPTF, which wore national police uniforms and blue UN berets. MSU vehicles would be painted blue with SFOR markings, in contrast to the IPTF vehicles that were painted white with the letters "UN" in black on the side. Coppola also sought to reassure the IPTF that the MSU intended to cooperate fully and to coordinate its operations with the United Nations through the SFOR commander. Yet he made it clear that, to be effective, the MSU would have to engage in information gathering and that once an intervention was ordered, the MSU would have responsibility for determining the force level, tactics, and timing of the operation. Coppola left his meetings with the IPTF officials feeling he had been less than fully successful in allaying their concerns.[83]

Final Approval

On May 28, 1998, the NATO foreign ministers met in Luxembourg and adopted the operations plan prepared by the alliance's Military Committee for extending SFOR beyond the June deadline. The plan, code-named Operation Joint Forge, called for a reduction in military force levels after the September elections. It also called for creating an MSU in SFOR of six hundred men with the same mandate as other SFOR elements. The new unit would enhance "SFOR's ability to support local authorities in responding to civil disorder without engaging in police functions so as to assist the return of refugees and displaced persons and the installation of elected officials."[84] According to General Wesley Clark, the specialized police unit would be composed of police from the Italian Carabinieri and the Argentine National Gendarmerie. The MSU, Clark said, would be based at a central location and would be dispatched as needed. It would operate under NATO rules of engagement, but it would not have responsibility for arresting war criminals. It also would not replace the local police or have responsibility for local law enforcement. Clark noted that in the future, NATO would review the SFOR mandate every six months but that there would be benchmarks to be met rather than an arbitrary end date for the mission.[85]

In recruiting for the MSU, General Clark was forced to turn to Buenos Aires after France, the Netherlands, Spain, and

Portugal refused to participate. Like Italy, Argentina saw participation in NATO-led peace operations as a means of burnishing its international image. It also saw responding to the request from General Clark as a way of improving its ties with the United States. In December 1997, Argentina had provided 140 gendarmes as part of the United Nations Civilian Police Mission in Haiti. The Argentine mission was to provide for the security of UN personnel, including thirty-one American CIVPOL officers. The provision of a similar number of gendarmes for the MSU in Bosnia was part of this larger effort to gain positive international recognition after a series of repressive regimes and the debacle of the Falkland Islands war.[86]

On June 11, 1998, the NATO defense ministers agreed to the activation order required to continue SFOR beyond the June deadline, subject to the resolution of the UN Security Council. SFOR's mission would be to continue to deter renewed hostilities and to contribute to a secure environment. The NATO-led force would include an MSU, which would assist in the transition from military to civil implementation.[87] On June 15, 1998, UN Security Council Resolution 1171 formally authorized the extension of SFOR's mandate an additional twelve months. It also extended the mandate of UNMIBH and the IPTF for the same period.[88] On June 20, 1998, the NATO-led international military force in Bosnia became the "new" SFOR. Speaking at a NATO information seminar in Sarajevo a few weeks later, Gregory Schulte told the audience of local leaders that they "probably did not notice much of a change." In fact, after all the meetings, speeches, and planning, SFOR remained much as it had been the previous summer. What was new, Schulte said, was the addition of the Multinational Specialized Unit that would be trained to deal with violent demonstrations, such as the one that had occurred recently in Drvar. The unit would also assist SFOR in countering those who use thugs and criminals to prevent the return of refugees and the seating of elected officials. By introducing such a force, Schulte said, "We want to promote public security, which is a key to a lasting peace."[89]

5

BLUE BOX

The Multinational

Specialized Unit in Bosnia

O N August 2, 1998, Colonel Leonardo Leso, the Italian commander of the Multinational Specialized Unit, arrived in Ploce, Croatia, with "350 well-equipped soldiers and 100 vehicles" en route to his headquarters at Camp Butmir, Sarajevo.[1] Despite the efforts of Colonel Coppola and the MSU advance team, opinions in Sarajevo on the new unit's role and mission varied widely. Senior U.S. military officers in SFOR viewed the MSU as simply another military unit that would be subject to the same command structure and rules of engagement as all other units in SFOR. The MSU would be part of the SFOR strategic reserve and would be deployed *in extremis* if the IPTF and the local police were unable to handle the situation. In the view of one American general, the MSU was "one more club in the SFOR bag." Another U.S. general described the MSU as "just another bunch of guys in tree suits," a reference to the camouflage uniforms worn by SFOR troops.[2]

Colonel Leso's view could not have been more different. He conceived the MSU as a "police force with military status" and believed it would give priority to providing services, including patrol and community policing to prevent friction among ethnic groups. The MSU would also have (1) credible military capabilities, (2) the capacity to control territory, (3) the ability to collect human intelligence, and (4) if necessary, the ability to provide a rapid response to control riots and other types of civil disorder. The MSU would close the operational gap between SFOR and the local police and work in perfect harmony with IPTF in the areas of public security and public order management. Preparation of the new unit, which was conducted in Italy, included training in firearms, combat techniques, riot control, martial arts, intelligence gathering, principles of international law, use of communications equipment, and spoken English. While the MSU was trained to handle worst-case scenarios, its primary goal would be conflict prevention through its professionalism and the use of basic police skills to defuse potentially violent situations.[3]

For its part, the United Nations had already taken steps within the limited IPTF mandate to meet the need for police, who were capable of civil disorder management. At its December 9–10, 1997 meeting in Bonn, the Peace Implementation Council called for modifications of the IPTF structure to provide maximum support for "the most pressing needs of civilian implementation" and recommended the creation of a special ten-member IPTF "Public Order and Major Incident Management Unit" made up of gendarmes serving in an individual capacity as UN civilian police monitors. The unit was tasked with organizing and training crowd control units among the Bosnian police. Creation of similar specialized IPTF units was also recommended to deal with refugee returns, organized crime, and terrorism.[4]

The PIC recommendations were subsequently endorsed in UN Security Council Resolution 1144, which extended the IPTF mandate until June 21, 1998, unless there were "significant changes in the security arrangements provided by SFOR." The PIC "encouraged" the secretary-general to implement the its recommendations, particularly the creation of specialized IPTF units to address "key public security issues." It also encouraged member states to increase their contributions of training and equipment for the local police.[5]

During the summer of 1998, IPTF worked with the U.S. Department of Justice's International Criminal Investigative Training Assistance Program to organize, train, and equip a 350-

man, multiethnic Civil Disorder Management Unit in the Bosnian Federation. Officers were provided by nine of the ten cantons and the federation police. Canton Ten (Livno) was excluded because ethnic Croat authorities refused to remove an offensive nationalist shoulder patch from police uniforms. Units from canton police forces were brought together in Sarajevo and trained to operate in integrated formations. The goal was to encourage cantons and the federation to work together and to call upon each other for assistance. Subsequently, canton-level crisis management operations centers were established in each canton to coordinate emergency response, including police, fire, and rescue services. A similar program to create riot control units in the RS was subsequently carried out by the IPTF.[6]

Meanwhile, the UN leadership in Sarajevo saw the decision by NATO to deploy the MSU as the international community's vote of no confidence in the IPTF. Senior UN officials believed NATO's decision to create an armed constabulary showed SFOR lacked confidence in the unarmed IPTF and its ability to properly train and motivate local law enforcement authorities. UN officials believed it was a mistake for the international community to assume a larger role in peace implementation rather than place increasing responsibility on the Bosnians. There was also a strong feeling that it was counterproductive to turn over responsibility for civil disorder management to the military while the international community was attempting to build democratic institutions and introduce community-oriented policing based on democratic principles.[7]

For its part, the IPTF saw the deployment of the MSU as a potential threat to relationships painstakingly developed with local authorities. Senior UN police officials were wary that the MSU might try to assume responsibility for training, reforming, and advising local police, particularly in the area of civil disorder management. Bosnia's ethnic-based police forces had demonstrated a strong disinclination to protect returning refugees and a general unwillingness to confront demonstrations against refugee resettlement. IPTF officers were afraid reliance on the MSU would provide local police with an excuse to avoid responsibility for protecting minorities. IPTF leaders also feared MSU involvement in violent clashes with Bosnians might spell danger for IPTF officers. MSU personnel would wear their national police uniforms rather than military attire, which might make them indistinguishable from members of the IPTF. Senior IPTF officers feared that Bosnians would take revenge on unarmed CIVPOL officers for actions of their armed counterparts in the MSU.[8] As a result, the IPTF leadership ordered the IPTF Public Order and Major Incident Management Unit to avoid contact with the MSU. The MSU would have no role in training the local police. Liaison between the MSU and the IPTF would be limited to a single officer assigned to their respective headquarters. Neither SFOR nor the IPTF briefed the Bosnian police and their newly created civil disorder management units on the role and mission of the MSU. This angered the Bosnians, who felt that IPTF and SFOR should have sought their cooperation and held joint exercises.[9]

MSU MANDATE AND ORGANIZATION

The lead elements of the MSU arrived in Sarajevo in July 1998. As stated in Annex JJ of SHAPE Operation Plan 10407 and later in SFOR's operations plan, the mission of the MSU was to—

+ Promote public security by utilizing the unit's ability to serve as a strategic reserve force and to operate throughout the theater.

+ Assist with refugee return by establishing local area security and ensuring freedom of movement across the Inter-Entity Boundary Line (IEBL) and within the Bosnian Federation.

+ Support installation of elected minority government officials.

+ Perform crisis management to maintain public order, including the use of force in riot and crowd control.

+ Collect intelligence and process information for operational purposes.

✦ Enforce directives of the Office of the High Representative related to public security.

Under these guidelines, the MSU would operate primarily as police rather than as a military force. It would engage in gathering police-related information as a prerequisite for conducting operations. For this purpose, the MSU would make contact with the local population to establish confidence and develop sources. The MSU would conduct patrols to provide area security and conduct surveillance. It would engage in crisis management. It would use persuasion and other nonviolent means to prevent or defuse conflicts. It would rely on nonlethal force for riot and crowd control to restore public order. If necessary, it would have the capacity to use lethal force, including snipers, to suppress armed instigators.[10]

While this description of the prospective duties of the MSU was important, there was an equally long list of operations the MSU would not undertake and tasks it would not perform. The MSU would intervene to maintain public order, but it would not engage in law enforcement. Under its restricted mandate, the MSU would not—

✦ Act as an international police force by conducting routine police operations such as traffic control or escorting convoys.

✦ Replace the IPTF, which would remain responsible for monitoring, reforming, and retraining the local police.

✦ Replace the local police, which would retain primary responsibility for law enforcement and maintaining public order.

✦ Conduct criminal investigations unless directed by the SFOR commander.

✦ Make arrests or detain suspects longer than the time required to turn offenders over to IPTF or the local police.

✦ Engage in war crimes investigations.

✦ Deal with official corruption.

+ Conduct hostage rescues, although it maintained a special weapons and tactics capability to intervene in such situations.

+ Engage in counterterrorism operations.

+ Train local police—not even in the MSU's specialty, crowd control.[11]

As the only NATO member willing to contribute forces, Italy was given the lead in organizing and commanding the MSU. The Italians contributed 386 Carabinieri, or 75 percent of the MSU's personnel. Argentina was the second largest donor, contributing 76 members of its Gendarmeria Nacional. The remainder of the force was composed of a platoon of 24 Romanian Politia Militari and a platoon of 23 Slovenian military police, plus 3 American and 2 Dutch liaison officers. The MSU's organization was based on a regimental headquarters with an operational battalion, a support company, and a maneuver unit. The MSU commander reported directly to the commander of SFOR. The unit was structured so that up to three additional battalions could be added. The first operational battalion was made up of four companies. Alpha Company was composed of three Italian and one Romanian platoon. Bravo and Charlie Companies each comprised three Italian platoons. Delta Company had three Argentine platoons and the Slovenians.[12]

The MSU maneuver unit was made up entirely of Carabinieri and included a SWAT team, an intelligence unit, snipers, and a K-9 unit. The dog team had three "Italian speaking" German shepherds trained in riot control techniques and their Carabinieri handlers.[13] The MSU support company performed standard logistics, personnel, and administrative duties. All units in the operational battalion were equipped with flak jackets, leg and arm protection, shields, batons, tear gas grenade launchers, pistols, submachine guns, assault rifles, and machine guns; they could quickly convert to light infantry, if required. The MSU was logistically autonomous. Housed originally in tents at Camp Butmir, in early 1999 it occupied a new compound next door called Butmir II. The cost of constructing the camp was paid almost entirely by Italy, which also provided logistical support for the entire MSU in return for a per-person, per-day fee paid by the other participating countries for their units.[14]

The Italians chose officers with broad experience in a wide range of police disciplines and in previous peace operations. Many of the Italians had already served a tour of duty as members of the IPTF. The Argentines were veterans of the mobile battalions of the Gendarmeria Nacional, antiriot forces with specialized training in maintaining public order. To enhance prospects for cooperation with the Italians, the Argentines chose officers with Italian or Spanish ancestry. Argentine MSU members joked that the official language of the unit was "Italo-Espanol," although their officers also spoke English, the official language of the Bosnian mission. Prior to departing for training with the Carabinieri in Italy, the Argentines underwent a month's training at the Training Center for Missions Abroad in Argentina on the specifics of serving in Bosnia.[15]

The MSU arrived in Bosnia as an integrated unit, having received classroom instruction and participated in field exercises prior to deployment. The Italians and Argentines received six weeks of training in Gorizia, Italy, at the headquarters of the Thirteenth Friuli-Venezia Giulia Battalion of the Carabinieri, using the standard Carabinieri curricula, procedures, vehicles, and equipment. At the conclusion of the training, senior officials from NATO, the UN, and the IPTF—including SACEUR General Wesley Clark and IPTF deputy commissioner Mark Kroeker—attended a demonstration of riot control tactics, during which Clark asked Kroeker, who was deputy chief of police in Los Angeles during the 1992 Rodney King riots, for his evaluation of the MSU. Kroeker said the MSU appeared to be a highly professional and well-trained force. Its tactics and formations for crowd control were consistent with international standards and were those utilized by all major civilian police forces. Kroeker questioned the effectiveness of their use of voice commands rather than hand signals during noisy street confrontations, but otherwise he believed they would make a positive contribution and looked forward to working with the Italians.[16] After the Italians and Argentines arrived in August, units from non-NATO countries where added. They received in-country training and were certified as meeting NATO standards on September 11, 1998, after participating in a thirty-hour field exercise held in Doboj, Bosnia. The exercise culminated in a military parade and ceremony attended by the commander of MND-North, U.S. Major General Larry Ellis.[17]

COMMAND AND CONTROL

The Italians arrived in Sarajevo full of positive expectations that they could contribute in numerous ways to the peace implementation process. They believed the MSU would have full freedom of movement and unlimited access to all areas in Bosnia. They believed it was essential that the MSU become thoroughly familiar with the territory, major roads, and urban centers through frequent patrolling and reconnaissance operations and by mixing with local officials, police, and citizens. To do this, the MSU would have operational autonomy in the choice of routes, timing, and forces. By employing this approach, they believed the MSU could develop a detailed knowledge of the country, particularly those areas where there was refugee resettlement. The Italians believed the MSU's most important contribution would be its ability to provide early warning of potential threats to public order and to gather and analyze information on criminal activities, particularly organized crime. This information would be provided to the SFOR commander on a daily basis. It would then be disseminated widely throughout the command. This concept of operations was based on normal police practices and on the manner in which the Carabinieri conducted its operation in Italy.[18]

Unfortunately, little had been done to prepare SFOR for the arrival of the MSU. Created as the successor to IFOR, the NATO Stabilization Force (Operation Joint Guard/Operation Joint Forge) was established on December 20, 1996. Its primary missions were to prevent a resumption of hostilities or new threats to peace, to promote the peace process, and to support civilian organizations selectively—"within its capabilities." SFOR was composed of troops from NATO members and fifteen other countries.[19] By the time the MSU arrived, the three Multinational Divisions—MND-North (United States), MND-Southwest (United Kingdom) and MND-Southeast (France)—had developed substantial autonomy. Known popularly as "The Three Kingdoms," they were large organizations with multinational headquarters, complex commands, complicated procedures, and thousands of troops wearing an array of national uniforms. Fortunately, the entire MSU was quartered in a compound adjoining SFOR headquarters at Camp Butmir in Sarajevo. Just getting the attention of SFOR, however, was an initial challenge for the MSU battalion.

From the outset, the MSU had to cope with unfamiliarity, misunderstandings, and outright prejudices within SFOR. Beyond determining what tasks the MSU would perform (and what it would not do), no doctrine had been developed concerning its relationship to the SFOR command structure or the conduct of SFOR operations. Acting on preconceived notions or their own national doctrine concerning military police, the SFOR commander and the MND commanders initially regarded the MSU as simply another infantry unit, subject to the same tactics, techniques, and procedures as all other military units under their command. As MND commanders were responsible for all activities conducted in their sectors, they were initially unwilling to allow the MSU to enter, to move freely between sectors, or to conduct operations within their sectors without express prior permission. As such permission was not readily forthcoming, this restriction made it difficult for the MSU to utilize its capacity to conduct mobile patrols, provide a security presence, or gather information. The MSU requests to conduct operations across MND boundaries were often misdirected or lost in the SFOR chain of command. The MSU was generally seen as a "strategic reserve," a force that should remain in its barracks until it was called out in response to an emergency.[20]

Under these restrictions, MSU operations initially were confined to patrolling and information gathering. From August 7,

1998, to January 25, 1999, the MSU conducted 243 reconnaissance missions, 87 information-gathering operations, and 33 public order interventions, of which only a small number involved crowd control. Procedures were developed under which security patrols and information-gathering missions were planned by the MSU, coordinated with the MND, and approved by SFOR. In such operations, the MSU reported to the commander of SFOR, which allowed it to move between MND sectors and operate throughout the country. In practice, the MSU did have contact with local civilians and established relations with local police. Under its mandate for information collection, the MSU gathered information on local political and social conditions and on the activities of organized crime by following the normal police practice of engaging in informal conversations in roadside markets, bars, and restaurants. The MSU made it a practice to visit local officials and police stations during vehicle patrols. The MSU viewed this as following standard police procedures and essential to its function of serving as the eyes and ears of SFOR. Information concerning local conditions was collected according to a weekly plan. It was processed by fifteen experienced Carabinieri analysts assigned to the MSU headquarters and disseminated within the MSU and through the SFOR commander to the MND commanders. Apparently unaware that the MSU had this capability, SFOR initially made few requests to the MSU for information, which further restricted its utility.[21]

PUBLIC ORDER AND REFUGEE RETURNS

While SFOR restrictions on routine operations were frustrating for the MSU, procedures and command relationships established by SFOR for dealing with civil disturbances were nearly disastrous. While three MSU platoons engaged in daily operations, one platoon was kept in reserve to serve as a rapid reaction force for unexpected contingencies. In case of a potential threat to public order, the MND would submit a request for MSU assistance to the SFOR commander, who, in turn, would task the MSU to provide a mission analysis and operational plan, which the SFOR commander would pass back to the MND. SFOR would task the MSU for the operation, transferring tactical command of the MSU to the MND. In emergencies where the MSU was used as a rapid reaction force, the same procedures were followed, except the MSU would deploy without doing a mission analysis or operations plan. Instead, it would rely on its advance units to conduct on-site surveillance and to report to the most senior MND officer available. In both scenarios, the leader of the MSU detachment would be under the command of the senior MND officer present. The MSU commander would not control his own forces, nor would he be able to direct the operation based on his experience and standard operating procedures.[22]

On October 1, 1998, the MSU faced its first test when demonstrators blocked the road between Sarajevo and Ploce near Capljina in southern Bosnia. This was the first time the MSU was used for crowd control and to assist with the return of displaced persons and refugees. The incident occurred during an attempt by OHR to return internally displaced persons to their original homes. The demonstrators were ethnic Croats who had been displaced from central Bosnia and had resettled in Tasovcici. They were protesting the return of fifty Bosniak families to houses in Tasovcici they now occupied. Croatian television's news coverage of the incident showed "Italian policemen" with helmets, shields, batons, and firearms charging a group of mostly women and children. The broadcast also showed "the Italians" using their shields to protect themselves from stones and bottles thrown by the crowd. Three MSU officers received superficial wounds. A grenade thrown from a vehicle killed one returnee and wounded three others.[23] A similar attack on returnees also occurred in the nearby town of Stolac. An SFOR spokesman stated that the MSU had been used as a "last resort" because the local police failed in their duty to protect minorities.[24]

When the MSU platoon reached the roadblock, it found an SFOR contingent facing a growing crowd of hostile demonstrators. The MSU platoon commander, an Italian captain, requested permission to conduct his own reconnaissance and to talk with the protesters to determine the reasons for the demonstration. He was overruled by the senior SFOR officer present, a Spanish major, who ordered the captain to attack the roadblock and clear the area of protesters. The MSU carried out the order, using force to break through the barrier and disperse the crowd. The MSU officer then requested permission to remain in Capljina overnight to ensure that the protesters would not reassemble. At sundown, however, the Spanish major ordered the MSU to return to its barracks. During the night, widespread violence erupted in the town. Without the MSU, SFOR was forced to deploy armored vehicles to quell the disturbance.[25]

The arbitrary misuse of the MSU, the resulting violence, and Italian protests caused SFOR to re-evaluate its procedures for using the MSU to control civil disturbances. The outcome of this review was a new doctrine governing the use of the MSU in crowd-control situations. In dealing with civil disorder, the senior MSU officer present would not only command his own unit, but all other forces within the immediate Area of Responsibility (AOR) during the operation (see figure 3). The AOR or "Blue Box" (for the color of the Italian Carabinieri uniforms) was established in both space and time. Once the operation began, any forces coming into the "Blue Box" were under MSU command until the operation was completed. All other SFOR troops in the surrounding AOR or "Green Box" would remain under the command of the senior MND officer present and provide support for the MSU. Under this arrangement, the MSU officer would be able to decide whether to use nonviolent tactics to attempt to defuse the situation or to use force, if necessary. This allowed the MSU to operate like a police force, utilizing persuasion followed by ascending levels of nonlethal force to control the situation.[26]

This revised doctrine was tested in early November 1998 in Mrkonjic Grad in the Republika Sprska. Nearly two hundred former workers at Udarnik, the state transport company, protested in front of their former factory, which had been appropriated by the British SFOR contingent as the MND-Southwest headquarters. The protesters demanded either the return of their factory and

Figure 3. The "Blue Box"

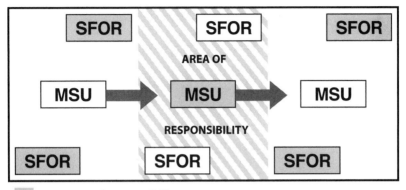

= command responsibility

reinstatement of their jobs or compensation for the use of the building. Previous efforts to resolve the problem had been met by statements from the British that they were there under orders from the SFOR Central Command, so the problem had to be resolved in Sarajevo. The British requested MSU assistance to remove the crowd that was blocking the road in front of one of the buildings.[27]

Operating under the new guidelines, the MSU officer in charge, a Carabinieri captain, positioned his forces out of sight. He then approached the barricade the Bosnians had erected across the road, accompanied by his interpreter. The officer discovered from talking with the demonstration's leaders that when the workers had lost their jobs, they were promised compensation that had not been forthcoming. Repeated appeals to SFOR and RS authorities had produced nothing. The people had erected the roadblock because they had expended their savings and had no food or oil to heat their homes. With winter approaching, they were now desperate. In response, the Italian captain offered the protesters a deal: If they would remove the roadblock and disperse peacefully, he would invite the leaders to a nearby coffeehouse to discuss their grievances. If they could prove their case, he would intervene with the authorities to see they received the compensation to which they were entitled. The roadblock disappeared and the crowd returned to their homes.

After the conversation in a nearby café, the MSU officer intervened on behalf of the community.[28] On November 10, the RS Ministry of Transport and Communication informed the workers that until the future of the factory was resolved, they would receive 200,000 dinars in place of their salaries for October and thirty metric tons of oil to meet the needs of the community.[29] Using standard police tactics, the MSU had defused a potentially explosive situation through negotiation, without resort to a show of force or the use of violence.

In early 1999, events in Brcko came full circle. On Friday, March 5, High Representative Carlos Westendorp announced the final award of the arbitral tribunal for the dispute over the Inter-Entity Boundary in the Brcko area. Under the arbitration panel's ruling, Brcko was not awarded to either entity but, instead, was made a self-governing neutral district under international supervision. Administration was placed in the hands of an elected, multiethnic district government, which would operate under the supervision of the Brcko Supervisor. In the language of the final award document, Brcko would be governed by a "new institution, a new multiethnic democratic government to be known as the Brcko District of Bosnia and Herzegovina." The new municipal authority would be composed of an elected district assembly, an executive board selected by the assembly, an independent judiciary, and a "unified police force under a single command structure with one uniform and badge and complete independence from the police establishments of the two entities." The entire territory within the boundaries of the prewar Brcko municipality (*opstina*) would be "held in condominium by both entities simultaneously: The territory of the RS will encompass the entire opstina, and so also will the territory of the Federation. Neither entity, however, will exercise any authority within the boundaries of the district, which will administer the area as one unitary government."[30]

On the day the arbitral award was announced, two other unrelated events combined with news of the Brcko decree to produce an angry Serb response. Westendorp announced his decision to sack the Bosnian Serb president, Nikola Poplasen, for obstructing the peace process. On the same evening, a Serb ultranationalist was shot dead by an American Special Forces sergeant in a town near Brcko. In what was apparently a pre-meditated attack, a group of Serbs accosted four U.S. Special Forces soldiers having dinner at a café. When one of the Serbs struck the sergeant with a club, the soldier shot his assailant. Reaction to these events from political hard-liners in the Republika Srpska was virulent. Zivko Radisic, the Serb representative in Bosnia's joint presidency, suspended his participation. The RS prime minister, Milorad Dodik, announced his intention to resign, and the republic's parliament passed a law withdrawing all Serb representatives from Bosnian state institutions and barring Serb officials from speaking to representatives of the international community. Demonstrations were staged in the RS and in Brcko; UN vehicles were attacked and destroyed. Tensions were further heightened by the breakdown of the Rambouillet peace talks in late February and the beginning of the NATO bombing campaign against Yugoslavia on March 24, 1999. During the air campaign, NATO jets on their way to attack targets in Belgrade and Pristina overflew Brcko several times a day, raising anti-American sentiment among Serbs to a fever pitch.[31]

Unlike the Brcko riot in 1997, this time SFOR had the proper mix of forces to deal with any eventuality. The MSU battalion headquarters, together with two companies and part of the maneuver unit, was deployed to Brcko before the announcement and remained until after tensions had eased. The center of town was declared a "Blue Box," and the MSU prevented demonstrations while SFOR provided security around the town perimeter and the IPTF contingent was reinforced. With professional riot control units in place, regular SFOR troops were not called upon to confront civilian demonstrators.[32] Within a week, the protests over the decision had died away. In the words of one reporter, "Less than a hundred people showed up. Waving banners and posters of their president, marching behind a battered car with loudspeakers mounted on the roof. It was a poor turnout for the disciples of hate."[33]

Although the MSU's primary mission was crowd control,

its primary contribution was its apparent ability to deter civil disorder. The announcement of the arbitration award in Brcko was only one of numerous incidents where the deployment of the MSU was enough to dissuade would-be troublemakers. Over time, MSU deployments became a routine part of SFOR operations for public events and ceremonies. During the Israeli army's incursion into the West Bank and Gaza in the spring of 2002, the Israeli national soccer team played against the Bosnian team in Zenitsa, which is in a Moslem area. The MSU deployed en force, including stationing officers in plain clothes inside the stadium. SFOR troops also were present to support the MSU and there were no incidents. The MSU was also deployed for the annual July 11, 2001 return of the "Women of Srebrenica" to the town in the RS to commemorate the wartime massacre. The MSU collected information on public attitudes and provided highly visible support for the RS police. The event was held without incident. While it is impossible to say with certainty that deploying the MSU deterred violence, senior SFOR officers believed the presence of professional, armed police in full riot gear had a salutary effect.[34]

While civil disorder management remained a primary MSU mission, the potential for widespread violence caused by the massive return of displaced persons and refugees did not materialize. This was due to both the pace and the volume of returns, which was slower and smaller than international experts had predicted. The fact that the process was prolonged meant that returnees faced decreasing antagonism over time as communities resolved to overcome wartime differences. By summer 2002, SFOR relied primarily on regular military units to provide security for returning refugees. The MSU contribution was limited to routine patrolling and information collection.[35]

COMBATING ORGANIZED CRIME

Increased SFOR confidence in the MSU coincided with the appearance of the next "problem set" to confront the international community in Bosnia: the emergence of organized crime

and official corruption as major impediments to Dayton implementation. During the conflict, international sanctions and the
exigencies of war forced the political leadership of all three ethnic
groups to rely on the criminal underworld to perform essential
services. Faced with an international arms embargo, the Bosniak
leadership in Sarajevo was dependent on military weapons and
equipment smuggled by criminal groups to provision its military
forces. For the Serbs, smuggling and black marketing of consumer
goods and primary products generated the revenue to fund the
war effort and enabled hard-liners like Radovan Karadzic to
retain their hold on power. All sides relied on armed gangs and
paramilitary groups that engaged in illicit trafficking. Groups
with names like "Arkan's Tigers" and "White Eagles" profiteered
from the war and were used to create terror and conduct ethnic
cleansing. While the leaders of some of the groups involved were
subsequently indicted as war criminals, many people continued to
regard them as war heroes.[36]

	After the conflict, these groups allied with extreme national-
ists and corrupt politicians and continued their criminal activities
under various kinds of commercial or quasi-official front organizations. All three ethnic communities remained under the control
of autocratic elites who relied on extralegal intelligence, police
and security services and organized criminal syndicates to retain
power and obstruct Dayton implementation. In addition, Serb
hard-liners continued to receive political and financial support
from the Milosevic regime in Belgrade, while Croat extremists
received assistance from the Croatian Democratic Union party in
Croatia. Members of these unholy alliances exercised control
through intimidation and violence and their ability to make
appointments and set salaries for judges, prosecutors, and police
officers. They cooperated across ethnic boundaries for personal
profit, even when such cooperation was against the best interest
of their communities. By 1999, organized criminal elements
began to play an increasingly central role in the Bosnian power
structure. From 40 to 60 percent of Bosnia's economy was based
on black-market commerce. A wealthy criminal class allied with
extremist politicians diverted public revenues, ensuring the

country's continued dependence upon outside assistance. It became apparent that organized crime and official corruption posed a greater threat to security and stability than the increasingly unlikely possibility of renewed military conflict. Unless this situation was rectified, the international community's efforts to empower Bosnians would do little more than further consolidate power in the wrong hands.[37]

For the United States, a particularly embarrassing manifestation of the emergence of organized crime was the Arizona Market. Established by SFOR in 1996 with $40,000 in U.S. funds, the market was named after the NATO designation for the adjacent highway and was located near Brcko in the NATO-enforced Zone of Separation between the RS and the Bosnian Federation. The market was envisioned as an area where "free enterprise would flourish." Within three years, the sprawling complex of stalls, shacks, and temporary structures employed more than twenty-five hundred people and attracted ten times as many customers on an average weekend. Located in a kind of "no man's land," the market's operations were easily taken over by criminal gangs, and it soon became a center for tax cheats, prostitutes, and sellers of contraband cigarettes, counterfeit CDs, narcotics, and stolen vehicles. The Bosnian government lost an estimated $30 million a year from untaxed sales of goods at the market. Much of the illegal activity occurred with the complicity or active participation of local police. The Brcko Supervisor, Robert Farrand, viewed the market as a potential source of revenue for the municipality, if properly regulated. The senior UN official in Bosnia, Jacques Klein, disagreed; he saw it as a center for organized crime and said the site should be reclaimed by SFOR and bulldozed.[38]

Given the IPTF's limited mandate and the timidity of local judges and police, only SFOR had the intelligence assets and coercive capacity to confront organized crime in Bosnia. In this regard, the MSU, with its hybrid military and police capabilities, appeared particularly suited for operations that were conducted by SFOR but required law enforcement skills. The prominence of the Italian Carabinieri in the MSU also seemed particularly fortunate. The Italians were highly experienced in dealing with organized crime as a result of their experience in fighting the Italian Mafia. They were also extremely professional in analyzing criminal data and utilizing highly sophisticated information technology such as crime mapping and link analysis. Unfortunately, under Italian law, the Carabinieri could not perform criminal investigations or engage in law enforcement unless they were under the authority of the Italian Ministry of the Interior. In Bosnia, the Carabinieri assigned to the MSU were under the authority of the Ministry of Defense and, in any case, law enforcement was outside of the MSU's mandate.[39]

Within those limitations, however, the ability of the MSU to conduct patrols, collect and analyze information on criminal activity, and conduct covert surveillance contributed substantially to SFOR efforts to counter organized crime. With the exception of U.S. Special Forces, the MSU was the only element in SFOR whose members could wear civilian clothes and conduct operations out of uniform. This gave the MSU the ability to engage in plainclothes surveillance and to obtain information from informants without attracting attention. In addition, the MSU's ability to provide armed escorts for prisoners and assist with witness protection proved extremely useful to SFOR in its efforts to counter organized crime.[40]

In 1999, the evident weakness of the local judicial system resulted in a NATO decision for SFOR to become directly involved in the fight against organized crime and other illegal activities aimed at obstructing implementation of the Dayton peace process. On January 18, 1999, Herzegovina-Neretva Canton police arrested Jozo Peric, the local organized crime boss and owner of the infamous Renner Transport Company, which was a front for a number of illegal operations. A number of Peric's criminal associates were also arrested.[41] The local police acted with the support of the MSU, which deployed to the town and carried out surveillance and information gathering over an extended period. While the arrests temporarily disrupted the group's illegal operations, Peric received advance warning and was able to remove incriminating documents and material before the police arrived. After spending six months in jail, he was released for lack of evidence.

On October 14, 1999, SFOR raided the Mostar headquarters of the National Security Service (SNS), a covert Bosnian-Croat intelligence agency with links to its Croatian counterpart and the nationalistic HDZ party. Dubbed Operation Westar, the SFOR action netted computers, databases, encryption software, and equipment for producing forged credit cards and bankcards and for distributing pornographic materials throughout Europe. Troops discovered a cache of illegal weapons and ammunition. The raid also found substantial evidence that the SNS was engaged in four separate intelligence operations aimed at disrupting the work of the ICTY and the Dayton peace process. Although SFOR troops seized substantial amounts of illegal property, they found the SNS offices empty. There were no arrests and no injuries.[42]

From an analysis of the materials seized in the raid, it was evident that the SNS had engaged in financial crimes to fund its activities. The four intelligence operations—code-named *Puma*, *Grom* (Thunder), *Munja* (Lightning) and *Panter* (Panther)—were aimed at monitoring the activities of the OHR and other international organizations, compromising and recruiting their local staff, and gaining access to OHR, SFOR, and UN facilities. Operation Puma involved photographic surveillance, wiretapping of ICTY personnel, and monitoring of their investigations. The operation included the collection of information on local citizens who contacted ICTY representatives and the recruitment of ICTY local interpreters. Operation Munja involved surveillance of OHR, international military and civilian humanitarian organizations, and the Agency of Investigation and Documentation, the Bosniak security service. The operation focused on collecting embarrassing or damaging personal information on international and local employees. Included in the materials seized were reports on the sexual preferences of shadowed persons and photos of international representatives in compromising positions. Operation Panter was directed toward collecting information on individuals and international organizations outside the ethnic Croat regions of Bosnia. This operation was designed to counter alleged efforts by the international community to destabilize the Bosnian Croat leadership and to place responsibility for the failure of Croat-Bosniak cooperation on the Croats. Operation Grom was aimed at countering the alleged activities of foreign intelligence agencies, whose agents SNS believed made up the vast majority of the foreign personnel assigned to international organizations in Bosnia. Here again, the goal was to collect information on and to recruit ethnic Croats who worked for international organizations as informants and operatives.[43] Under the limitations of its mandate, the MSU's role was restricted to surveillance, information collection, and supporting the SFOR units that conducted the raid.

In the spring of 2001, pressure from OHR and SFOR on nationalist politicians and organized crime in ethnic Croat areas of Bosnia produced political insurrection and an explosion of violence against the international community. In March, Ante Jelavic, the Croat member of Bosnia's tripartite presidency, and local officials of the HDZ party announced they were withdrawing from the Bosnian Federation and establishing Croat self-government in parts of Herzegovina. A new Croat National Assembly began to set up self-rule in five Croat-dominated cantons. It appealed to ethnic Croat military forces to withdraw from the federation army and to ethnic Croat police to defect to the new regime. On March 3, High Representative Wolfgang Petritsch dismissed Jelavic from the presidency and banned him and his followers from engaging in future political activity. SFOR's deputy commander, Major General Robert Connatt of the United Kingdom, made clear that SFOR would prevent any attempt by Croat military units to withdraw from the federation's army. IPTF Commissioner Vincent Coeurderoy warned canton police chiefs that police officers would be dismissed if they engaged in political activity. Despite these actions, substantial numbers of Croat military and police personnel left their posts and identified themselves with the new regime. The new Croat "government" raised prices on public utilities, levied taxes, and used intimidation to force local businesses to provide financial support.[44]

Faced with a growing insurrection, SFOR struck against the financial underpinnings of the illegal Croat ministate. On April 6, 2001, SFOR troops, including elements of the MSU, attempted to seize records and audit the accounts of the Herzegovacka Bank in Mostar and other cities. The bank was controlled by a group of ethnic Croats known locally as the "Young Generals," men who made fortunes smuggling arms and food and were rewarded with military rank during the conflict. Many of these individuals held senior positions in the Bosnian branch of the hard-line nationalist HDZ party. They were also the leaders or close allies of local organized crime. These Croat extremists used the bank to launder profits from an illegal trade in oil, cigarettes, liquor, and stolen vehicles. They also used the bank to divert contributions from international organizations that were supposed to be distributed to veterans' organizations and local charities. The bank was the financial citadel of organized crime and Croat political extremists in Mostar who were engaged in establishing the independent Croat political entity. HDZ party officials used the bank to enforce discipline through payments to police and local politicians and to control public information through cash transfers to local newspapers and radio stations.[45]

To take down the Croats' illegal financial empire and undermine the foundations of the Croat insurrection, OHR launched Operation Athena, the forcible seizure by SFOR of the headquarters and branch offices of the Herzegovacka Bank so that accountants from the U.S. firm of Kroll–O'Gara could audit its accounts. Under the plan for inspecting the records of the bank's main headquarters in Mostar, a small number of MSU officers would escort teams of American auditors into the building. They would order the employees to leave and then provide security while the auditors collected incriminating information. Boxes of bank records would be removed in SFOR vehicles. If the "Blue Box" contingent required backup, MSU officers inside the bank would radio for assistance from the "Green Box," regular SFOR troops positioned outside of town.[46]

Unfortunately, the plan to seize the bank headquarters was compromised from the start. The audit teams and their MSU escorts entered the bank's modern, highrise office building in downtown Mostar in late morning and ordered the employees to depart. Once the MSU officers and the auditors entered the bank offices, groups of tough looking men with shaved heads appeared outside the bank and began pelting the building with eggs and rocks. Organized groups of Croat school children were placed at the front of a growing crowd of protesters who threw objects and shouted abuse at the MSU officers. Groups of armed thugs then rushed the main door of the bank, closing off any possibility of escape and pushing their way inside. Croat thugs grabbed, beat, and threatened to kill the auditors. They also attacked and beat the MSU guards. Under death threats from the mob, the auditors were forced to return all the records they had collected.[47]

During the mob's assault, MSU calls for assistance from SFOR troops stationed outside the town went unanswered. Although equipped with armored vehicles, the SFOR reaction force was deterred by the prospect of threading its way through roadblocks of trucks and burning trash cans and the possibility that the incident might become more violent if they intervened. This scenario was repeated at several branch offices where there was similar mob violence with serious consequences. At one branch, an American auditor suffered serious eye damage from broken glass, while a European Union monitor from Ireland was beaten unconscious and suffered permanent brain damage. The most dangerous standoff occurred in the town of Grude, where the auditors and their escorts were held for twelve hours at gunpoint. Mob leaders refused to release their hostages until all the seized bank records that had been taken away in a truck were returned. During the entire operation, twenty-nine internationals and Bosnians were injured, several seriously. Eleven of the injured were members of the MSU. Ten days later, SFOR returned to the bank headquarters in Mostar. Armored personnel carriers were parked bumper to bumper to "ring the building in steel," and heavily armed troops entered the bank's offices. They found the files empty and the computerized records they had seen previously had disappeared.[48]

In addition to dealing with organized crime, the MSU's purview was expanded to include supporting SFOR efforts to conduct investigations and arrest persons indicted for war crimes by the ICTY. MSU platoons were trained in both seizing war criminals and dealing with the possibility of adverse public reaction to such operations. In these exercises the main force of the MSU provided area security and crowd control, while the MSU SWAT team actually made the arrests.[49]

In the spring of 2002, SFOR was asked to assist investigators from ICTY with collecting information in Bosnia. One hundred ICTY investigators were sent to search eight sites in MND-North, including four local police stations. This was the first time ICTY had attempted to enter Bosnian police stations, and there was concern about the reaction. On the day of the operation, SFOR placed two MSU platoons on standby to serve as a rapid intervention force. MSU officers in civilian attire were assigned to "drink coffee" at cafés near the targeted police stations, where they could report developments by cell phone. Their reports provided the SFOR commander with situation awareness that he could not have obtained in any other manner. The operation was conducted without incident.[50]

COUNTERTERRORISM

The events of September 11, 2001 resulted in a change in the original MSU mandate and the addition of counterterrorism to the list of its assigned responsibilities. The MSU was instructed to carry out antiterrorism operations as a special mission under the direction of the SFOR commander.[51] The involvement of SFOR and the MSU in the War on Terrorism resulted from NATO's decision on September 11 to invoke Article 5 of the North Atlantic Treaty. This action triggered the collective defense arrangements—this time, to protect the United States—that European countries had relied upon during the Cold War. Seven NATO Airborne Warning and Control System (AWACS) aircraft were deployed to watch the skies over the eastern United States in Operation Eagle Assist, which freed U.S. aircraft for service in Afghanistan. This unprecedented use of NATO assets to protect the United States ended when the planes returned to Europe on May 16, 2002.[52]

The MSU's involvement also resulted from threats posed by Islamic extremists in Bosnia to American diplomatic facilities and to American and western European military units in SFOR. During the war in Bosnia, hundreds of Arab fighters came to Bosnia to fight alongside Bosniak forces. These *mujahideen* displayed great courage and were held in high esteem by their fellow Muslims. After the war, most returned home; but some remained, married local women, and acquired Bosnian citizenship. These "stay behinds" were joined by Arab nationals who came after the war to work for international humanitarian organizations. Together, these two groups provided financial aid and other types of support to Islamic extremist organizations. They operated undisturbed until American and European intelligence agencies began to investigate al Qaeda's activities in Europe following September 11.[53]

Involvement in the War on Terrorism changed the focus of the MSU's surveillance, information collection, and analysis functions to a concentration on Islamic organizations that might pose a direct security threat to SFOR. It also involved the MSU in take-down operations against terrorist cells in Bosnia. On September 25, 2001, in the immediate aftermath of the attacks on New York and Washington, SFOR stormed the Saudi High Commission for Assistance to Bosnia in Sarajevo. Code-named Operation Hollywood Hotel, the operation netted computers, documents on how to fly crop-dusting aircraft, large amounts of cash, and fake American embassy identification badges. The raid resulted in the arrest of four men, two of whom were Egyptians.[54] The MSU provided area security and support for the raid that was executed by U.S. Special Forces.

Over the next month, Bosnian police, working with the MSU and SFOR, conducted a number of operations under the supervision of the Joint Coordination Committee for the Fight Against Terrorism in Bosnia, a group that brought SFOR together with U.S., international, and Bosnian intelligence and law enforcement agencies. The raids resulted in the arrest of some twenty persons suspected of belonging to a terrorist cell that planned attacks on American facilities in Bosnia. Among those taken into custody was Densayah Belkacem, who worked for a humanitarian assistance agency in the town of Zenica. Investigators obtained telephone records showing that Belkacem was in frequent contact with Abu Zubaydah, one of Osama bin Laden's senior lieutenants. On October 16, the American and British embassies in Sarajevo closed when a plot was discovered against both installations and Eagle Base, the main U.S. military facility located in Tuzla. The discovery resulted in the arrest of six suspected terrorists for plotting to bomb the embassies. On December 15, Bosnian federal police staged raids against two Arab humanitarian agencies, Taibah International and the Global Relief Foundation, that were suspected of fund-raising and providing logistical support for al Qaeda.[55]

On January 18, 2002, U.S. forces in Sarajevo took custody of the six suspected terrorists—five Algerians and one Yemeni— who had been arrested by Bosnian police in October. As the United States was unwilling to release intelligence reports for use in a trial, the Bosnian supreme court ruled that there was insufficient evidence against the suspects. The Bosnian government then agreed to allow American SFOR troops to seize the men as they were released from detention. To prevent the handover, nearly four hundred family members, friends, and supporters attempted to disrupt the operation by surrounding the SFOR vehicles to prevent their departure. American-trained Bosnian riot-control police were called in and were able to control the situation. The MSU was positioned to provide backup for the local police to ensure success of the operation. According to a U.S. embassy statement, the men posed a credible security threat to U.S. personnel and facilities. U.S. Army General John Sylvester, the American SFOR commander in Bosnia, said they were part of a group with direct links to al Qaeda. The men, five of whom were Bosnian citizens, were transported to the U.S. military's terrorist internment facility in Guantanamo Bay, Cuba.[56]

TRAINING BOSNIAN POLICE

On May 7, 2001, a mob of ethnic Serb nationalists attacked a group of international officials and Bosnian Muslims during a ceremony to mark the start of reconstruction of the sixteenth century Ferhadija Mosque in the RS capital of Banja Luka.

The mosque had been destroyed in 1992 by Serb forces. In 1999, the Human Rights Chamber, an international human rights commission, ordered its reconstruction. The ceremony to lay a new cornerstone was attended by nearly three hundred Muslims and was intended to demonstrate that it was safe to return to the city, which had a large prewar Muslim population. As the ceremony began, a crowd of two thousand protesters attacked the visitors, severely beating ten people, overturning vehicles, and setting buses on fire. Muslim clergy and a group of international dignitaries—including the senior UN official in Bosnia, Jacques Klein, and the ambassadors from the United States, the United Kingdom, Sweden, and Pakistan—were forced to take refuge in the Islamic Community Center, where they were trapped during the rampage. A riot squad of IPTF-trained RS police was present but was seen shaking hands and joking with the demonstrators. After several hours, RS authorities responded to threats from Klein to call in SFOR and ordered the police to create a cordon so that the dignitaries and the visiting Muslims could be evacuated.[57]

This incident left the international community in Bonsia badly shaken. Klein remarked that it was "a sad day when brave Serb men throw stones at old Muslim women." High Representative Wolfgang Petritsch said he was "shocked that the RS still appeared to be a place with no rule of law, no civilized behavior, and no religious freedom." U.S. ambassador Tom Miller condemned the riots and called on Bosnian Serb officials to punish the perpetrators. In the riot's aftermath, the United Nations and several Western governments expressed renewed interest in providing civil disorder management training and equipment to the Bosnian police.[58]

As a result, the IPTF overcame its reluctance to work with

the MSU on police training. Representatives from the IPTF Public Order and Major Incident Management Unit sought MSU assistance to update and refurbish the training of the Bosnian crowd-control units that had been created by the IPTF and ICITAP in 1998. The program, which started in January 2002, brought together one platoon of police from each ethnic area for two weeks of intensive training at Camp Butmir. Units were housed together in the MSU compound and participated in a series of joint planning and operational exercises. Trainers from the IPTF, MSU, and ICITAP provided instruction. The first three units to receive training were from Brcko, Banja Luka, and Sarajevo. The course covered such topics as strategic planning, civil disorder management, crowd control, vehicle searches, identification checks, and arrest procedures. To encourage participation, the IPTF and MSU provided transportation and paid for meals and lodging. The goal was to train a group of three platoons each month for nine months with the program ending in September, just prior to the general elections that were scheduled for October. As the elections might be the first in which the old guard of nationalist politicians was seriously challenged, there was the possibility that these newly retrained units would be needed to deal with campaign-related violence.[59]

The MSU was also used to train Bosnian Special Police Units for an April 8, 2002 raid on a brothel suspected of employing women who had been brought to Bosnia against their will and forced to engage in prostitution. The brothel, which was located on top of a hill at the end of a long road, could be approached successfully only by helicopter. To prevent compromise, the Bosnian police were told only that they were being trained to conduct helicopter assaults. Their "graduation exercise," however, was an actual night assault on the brothel that succeeded in liberating several captive women.[60]

MSU EXPANSION

With the addition of counterterrorism and training to MSU's mandate and the continuing drawdown of SFOR military forces, the overall personnel strength of the MSU increased from 550 to 750 in the fall of 2002. On December 2, the Argentine contingent concluded its assignment in Bosnia and returned to Buenos Aires. The Argentines would have preferred to continue their participation, but deteriorating economic conditions at home made it impossible for them to continue the mission. Their place was scheduled to be taken by 150 police from Hungary. The Hungarians underwent training by the Italian Carabinieri in Hungary during the spring and early summer of 2002 and were scheduled to arrive in Bosnia in August. At the same time, NATO headquarters in Brussels began efforts to recruit the second MSU battalion that had been part of the original plan. Italian participation in the new battalion was questionable, as the Carabinieri's participation in constabulary forces in Bosnia, Kosovo, and Albania was already stretching the organization's budget and material resources.[61]

Despite their expanded mandate and new resources, the MSU leadership remained frustrated by the restraints placed on its operations by its location in SFOR. The Italian Carabinieri had the capacity to play a larger role in the fight against organized crime; they also could assist local police with civil disorder management, the MSU's primary mission. Following the Herzegovacka Bank debacle, the MSU was used sparingly and, during the first six months of 2002, did not undertake crowd-control operations. This was due in part to the generally peaceful environment in Bosnia, but it was also the result of SFOR wariness about deploying the MSU. Despite the development and further refinement of MSU doctrine, there remained considerable misunderstanding within SFOR over the MSU's role and mission. The entire MSU battalion was quartered in Sarajevo and made at least one platoon available each week to every MND. The Americans in MND-North were the largest consumers of MSU services. French and Italian forces in MND-South routinely declined the offer. Even in the American sector, problems with language and terminology precluded the MSU from playing a more prominent role. Few members of the Carabinieri spoke English, which made it impossible for them to undertake high-risk arrests and other missions in which real-time communication was vital. Over time, the MSU mandate had grown from crowd control and refugee return to include organized crime, counterterrorism, and training local police. The unit had established itself as an integral part of SFOR, and American commanders were grateful for its presence and its service.[62]

6

ODD JOBS

✦ ✦ ✦ ✦ ✦ ✦ ✦ ✦ ✦

Constabulary Forces

✦ ✦ ✦ ✦ ✦ ✦ ✦ ✦ ✦ ✦ ✦ ✦

in Kosovo

✦ ✦ ✦ ✦ ✦ ✦ ✦

HE UNITED NATIONS HAD LITTLE TIME to prepare to provide civil administration and the rule of law in Kosovo. During the conflict, it appeared these responsibilities would be assigned to the Organization for Security and Cooperation in Europe. Prior to the beginning of the NATO bombing campaign, OSCE provided the Kosovo Verification Mission (KVM), a force of two thousand unarmed monitors that included five hundred police officers. The broad KVM mandate included verifying an agreed-upon reduction of Yugoslav security forces and the training of a new ethnic Albanian communal police.[1] After the bombing ended, the OSCE option proved unacceptable to Moscow and Belgrade. Responsibility for the administration of Kosovo was given to the United Nations. Security Council Resolution 1244 created the UN Interim Administration Mission in Kosovo (UNMIK).[2]

The United Nations was responsible for the entire spectrum of civil administrative functions, from health and education, to finance and telecommunications, to police, courts, and prisons. At the same time, the UN was tasked to create democratic self-government institutions that would ensure a peaceful life and prosperous future for Kosovo's inhabitants. There was, however, a critical contradiction in the UN's mandate. While UNMIK was supposed to develop the institutions of self-government, Security

Council Resolution 1244 did not define a specific end state. Instead, it left to future deliberations whether Kosovo should be prepared for eventual independence, reintegration in the Republic of Serbia, or some other final status.

UNMIK was unprecedented not only for its scope, but also for the fact that no previous peacekeeping mission had been designed with multilateral organizations as partners under UN leadership. The mission was composed of four "pillars" with an international or regional organization as the lead agency for each component. The Special Representative of the UN Secretary-General led the mission assisted by a principal deputy SRSG. The UN High Commissioner for Refugees was responsible for humanitarian assistance (Pillar I), the UN for civil administration and law enforcement (Pillar II), the OSCE for democratization and institution building (Pillar III), and the EU for reconstruction and economic development (Pillar IV). The senior official for each pillar had the rank of the deputy SRSG and reported through the senior deputy SRSG to the chief of mission. The first SRSG was Dr. Bernard Kouchner, the former French health minister.[3]

KFOR

On June 9, NATO Lieutenant General Mike Jackson (UK) and Yugoslav General Svetozar Marjanovic signed the military technical agreement that provided for the withdrawal of all Serb security forces and the entry of peacekeeping forces into Kosovo. The Kosovo Force, a NATO-led military force of fifty thousand troops from thirty countries, was responsible for creating a safe and secure environment and for ensuring that conditions would permit the safe return of refugees and the implementation of the UN's mandate. KFOR entered the province on June 12, 1999, two days after the adoption of UN Security Council Resolution 1244. In accordance with the military technical agreement, KFOR's deployment was synchronized with the withdrawal of Yugoslav military and police, which was completed without incident. Responsibility for security in

KFOR Multinational Brigade Sectors

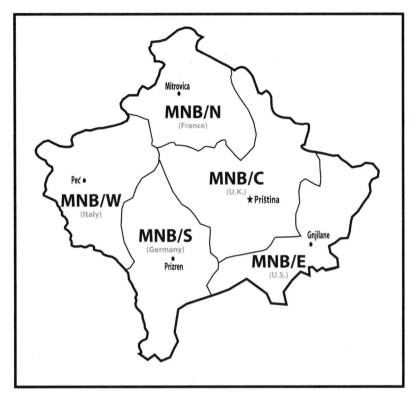

Source: Adapted from NATO Allied Forces Southern Europe web site, available at http://www.afsouth.nato.int/operations/kfor/sects.gif.

Kosovo was divided among five Multinational Brigades (MNBs) with a major NATO partner in charge in each sector. The United Kingdom was the lead country in MNB-Center (Pristina), France in MNB-North (Mitrovica), Germany in MNB-South (Prizren), the United States in MNB-East (Urosevac), and Italy in MNB-West (Pec). Twelve non-NATO countries, including Russia, contributed forces. The MNB-East included military units from Russia, Ukraine, Lithuania, Poland, and Greece, in addition to U.S. forces. KFOR's initial challenge was to ensure the safe return of more than eight hundred thousand ethnic Albanian refugees. Once this reverse migration was completed, KFOR was forced to deal with a fury of vengeful attacks by ethnic Albanians against Serbs and other minorities and an ensuing period of general lawlessness.[4]

Benefiting from the lessons learned in Bosnia, NATO had prepared for handling widespread civil disorder by including constabulary units in KFOR. Four of the five NATO nations commanding the Multinational Brigades deployed with military police units as an integral part of their military contingents. In addition, KFOR included a stand-alone Multinational Specialized Unit modeled on the MSU in Bosnia. For its part, the United Nations included ten Special Police Units (SPUs) in the civilian UNMIK police force. For NATO, the inclusion of constabulary forces was also a reflection of the fact that KFOR's mandate was broader than SFOR's in Bosnia. Under UN Security Council Resolution 1244, KFOR was responsible not only for establishing a safe and secure environment but also for ensuring freedom of movement, conducting border patrols and demining operations, and supporting and cooperating closely with UNMIK.

In MNB-North, French KFOR included 140 gendarmes that were an integral part of the French brigade. In MNB-Central, the British contingent included 140 Royal Military Police and 13 military investigators from the Special Investigation Branch. In MNB-East, the U.S. military brought along a company of U.S. Army Military Police that performed constabulary functions. In MNB-West, the Italians could call upon the Carabinieri and Spanish Guardia Civil. These units were under the command of the NATO general in charge of each sector. They also had the same rules of engagement as other KFOR units. This meant they could perform public order functions such as conducting patrols, detaining people they witnessed committing crimes, weapons searches, disarmament, and riot control. The presence of these units gave each MNB its own capacity to handle situations with appropriately trained and equipped military police units instead of having to rely on regular infantry and armored forces.[5]

In addition to military police units, KFOR's "force package" included an MSU, which reported directly to the KFOR commander and conducted operations in all five MNB areas of responsibility. This stand-alone constabulary force was composed of 277 Italian Carabinieri, 51 French Gendarmes, and 23 Estonian military police. As in Bosnia, the Italian Carabinieri was assigned the lead and provided the unit's commanding officer. The MSU's primary function was to provide a security presence by conducting patrols in all MNB areas; it was also assigned the tasks of maintaining public order, crowd control, information gathering, antiterrorism activities, and obtaining intelligence on organized crime. The MSU maintained one company full time in Pristina, with four operative detachments composed of at least one platoon allocated to each MNB and located in the towns of Mitrovica, Djakovica, Prizren, and Silovo. Specific assignments and the strength of these MSU detachments fluctuated, based on of the specific needs of each MNB commander.[6]

With its Italian and French components, the MSU brought substantial capacity and experience in the areas of criminal investigation, civil disorder management, and the maintenance of public order. As a part of KFOR, however, the MSU operated under the same rules of engagement and was subject to the same restrictions as NATO military forces. The MSU did not have executive authority to engage in law enforcement. It could collect intelligence on organized crime, and many observers believed the MSU was concerned with targets more of interest to Rome than to Pristina. The MSU could not, however, conduct criminal investigations or legally collect evidence that could be submitted directly to court. This mismatch between capability and mandate resulted in misunderstandings between the MSU and other elements in KFOR; and there were clashes over authority, roles, and missions between the MSU and the UNMIK police, which included Special Police Units. The presence in Kosovo of highly capable, international military and civilian constabulary forces with different mandates, authorities, and chains of command caused confusion. As part of KFOR, the MSU was reluctant to acknowledge UNMIK regulations or to comply with the criminal procedure code used by the UNMIK police in Kosovo. This resulted in situations in which the MSU would turn over suspects and contraband to the UNMIK police but not detain the individuals or collect evidence in a manner that could be admitted in court to obtain convictions. For their part, the UNMIK police, particularly the Special Police Units, had little incentive to cooperate with the MSU, considering their redundant capability and the difficulty of communicating via KFOR's chain of command.[7]

In MNB-East, the American sector, the MSU was given the mission of collecting criminal intelligence on organized crime and detaining perpetrators. Many historic smuggling routes lie across the Macedonia-Kosovo border, and the MSU was assigned the task of conducting reconnaissance on potential drug and weapons routes and storage areas; it also monitored crossborder trafficking in women for prostitution. Yet the U.S. KFOR contingent's lack of familiarity with constabulary forces, as well as the problems of different languages and professional cultures, limited the MSU's effectiveness. Without a clear understanding of MSU capabilities, U.S. commanders often had false expectations concerning the contribution the MSU could make to joint operations. This confusion led to an underutilization of the true strengths of the MSU as a peacekeeping force. Additional problems between the MSU and American forces arose because of problems with communication. In June 2000, an MSU team of between fifteen and twenty personnel was deployed to MNB-East to assist in riot control and counterinsurgency efforts. Unfortunately, only two members of the unit spoke English. Although they were adequately equipped with weapons and secure communications, the Italians found they could not communicate effectively with U.S. forces and, therefore, could not conduct joint operations.

Both the MSU's accomplishments and its frustrations were captured in the following description of its achievements provided by a senior Carabinieri officer.

> We charged one thousand persons with violations, of which five hundred were arrested [by UNMIK police]. We seized thirty-five thousand items, including mortars, bullets, grenades, and other explosives. We seized over a hundred

tons of contraband cigarettes. We freed fifty young women who had been forced into prostitution. We identified thirty-five criminal groups and compiled criminal records on ten thousand individuals. We achieved this through the use of the Ulysses computer system, which allowed us to make real-time connections between incidents and criminal groups. Moreover, we did this in Kosovo, where there was no local police force and we had to start from zero.[8]

As in Bosnia, the Italian-led MSU chafed under its restrictive mandate. Its leadership recognized the contribution the MSU could make to local law enforcement. In Kosovo, however, this responsibility rested with the civilian UNMIK police and a new institution, the Kosovo Police Service.

THE KOSOVO POLICE SERVICE

Unlike Bosnia, there were no local police in Kosovo. During the conflict, Yugoslav Interior Ministry's Special Police Units (MUP) were responsible for the some of the worst incidents of ethnic cleansing. Under the terms of the military technical agreement signed between NATO and the Federal Republic of Yugoslavia, Yugoslav security forces, including the civilian police, were withdrawn from Kosovo. The resulting vacuum was filled initially by a force of 3,155 UNMIK police that would have full executive authority, including the right to make arrests, detain suspects, and use deadly force. Paragraph 11(i) of UN Security Council Resolution 1244 provided that the principal responsibilities of the international civil presence would include: "maintaining civil law and order, including establishing local police forces and meanwhile through the deployment of international police personnel to Kosovo." This was the first time the United Nations provided an armed, executive police mission in a situation where there was no host government. In addition, UNMIK was responsible for supervising the establishment of the new, multiethnic Kosovo Police Service (KPS). This meant the United Nations was faced with the dual challenge of creating two police forces at the same time.[9]

Under the international division of labor in Kosovo, training for the KPS was provided by the OSCE. This involved establishing the Kosovo Police Service School (KPSS) and training a cadre of police officers with proportional representation of all ethnic groups, including Serbs. The KPSS was located in the town of Vucitrn, twenty-five kilometers north of Pristina, on the fully remodeled campus of a former MUP training center. It opened on September 7, 1999 with an initial class of 200 multiethnic students selected from more than 19,500 applicants. When fully operational in March 2000, the KPSS was staffed by 200 international police instructors from twenty-two OSCE member states with a complement of 600 cadets in training at any time. The director, a quarter of the school's training staff, and the basic curriculum were provided by the U.S. Department of Justice's ICITAP program. The newly renovated facility had the residential capacity to house up to 705 students with separate quarters for men and women. The school also had two gyms, a weight room, a mess hall, a laundry, warehouse, armory, medical and administrative offices, and twenty-eight classrooms. The KPSS was the only multiethnic institution functioning in Kosovo.[10]

The OSCE's mandate was to provide "democratically oriented police training" for 5,300 KPS officers by December 21, 2002. At the KPSS, students undergo twelve weeks of basic police instruction under the guidance of OSCE international police instructors. Lessons are delivered in English and translated by local language assistants into both Serbian and Albanian. The core curriculum emphasizes community service and respect for human rights. Courses include patrol duties, use of force, basic criminal investigation, forensics, traffic control, defensive tactics, first aid, applicable laws, interviewing techniques, and report writing. Following graduation, officers are assigned to fifteen weeks of structured field training under the supervision of UNMIK police and KPS field training officers, who are also trained by the international staff of the KPSS. Trainees spend nine weeks of this time in the field and six weeks at the KPSS or a regional training center in the classroom. After completing a total of twenty-seven weeks of classroom and field instruction, the new KPS officers are eligible for certification and independent assignment. In addition to basic training, the KPSS offers a first-line supervisors course, training for senior police managers, and advanced courses in a number of specialized police skills such as criminal and accident investigation. It also offers a trainer certification program for KPS instructors, who are taking increasing responsibility for teaching at the school.[11]

The KPS was created as a multiethnic, community-oriented police organization that would eventually replace the UNMIK police. To ensure that all ethnic groups were represented, recruiting quotas were established for women (20 percent) and minorities (15 percent), including Serbs. The United Nations agreed that half of the original cadre of four thousand officers would be former members of the Kosovo Liberation Army (KLA). To ensure a leavening of experience, the UN also agreed that 25 percent would be drawn from the ranks of those who previously had served as police officers in Kosovo during the period of provincial autonomy that ended in 1989. Unfortunately, this left little room for unaffiliated, ethnic Albanian men who were otherwise qualified. Recruits were required to be between twenty-one and fifty-five years old, have a secondary education, good health, and strong moral character. Applicants had to pass a UN-administered interview, a written examination, a psychological test, a medical exam, and a physical agility test. They were also required to undergo a background investigation, including a vetting process to remove anyone who had committed human rights abuses or engaged in criminal activities. The screening process had an 80-percent failure rate, primarily from educational deficiencies and failure to pass the written examination.[12]

After graduating from the KPSS and completing field training, KPS officers were assigned to UNMIK police stations with ethnic Serb police, serving only in areas where Serbs were a majority. The KPS operated under the UNMIK police Planning and Development Department and the watchful eye of its international counterparts. KPS officers were co-located in UNMIK police stations and functioned as auxiliaries of the UNMIK police because the United Nations was unwilling to create a separate institution pending a decision on Kosovo's final status. In its first months on the job, the KPS made a positive impression. Despite problems of low pay (380 DM per month), ill-fitting Norwegian uniforms, and inadequate vehicles and equipment, KPS members took their responsibilities seriously. KPS officers initially worked unarmed, as it took the UN four months to resolve the problem of how to provide them with sidearms. On several occasions, they came face-to-face with armed criminals; fortunately, there were no casualties. KPS officers had to deal with public distrust of the police, a leftover from the days of communist rule. There was also the problem of inadequate judicial and penal systems, which took much longer to begin functioning.[13]

UNMIK POLICE

Within UNMIK, the interim civil administration pillar included a police component under the command of the UNMIK police commissioner assisted by two deputy commissioners responsible for operations and administration (see figure 4). The UNMIK police had three separate but coordinated components: the UN Civil Police Unit, a UN Border Police Unit, and a UN Special Police Unit.

The Civil Police Unit was responsible for routine police functions such as patrol, criminal investigation, and traffic control. It was also responsible for more specialized police functions such as narcotics trafficking and organized crime. The civil police were divided among five regional commands and maintained forty-five police stations. The unit's goal was to assume "primacy" for law enforcement and maintenance of public security from KFOR in each of the five regions. It also had responsibility for establishing and monitoring the KPS, including providing field training officers. Practically every member of the UN Border Police Unit came from the Bundesgrenzschutz, the Federal Republic of Germany's border guards and customs service. They provided a police presence on Kosovo's international borders with Albania and Macedonia, but not on the internal boundary with Serbia. While KFOR had

Figure 4. UNMIK Police Organization Chart

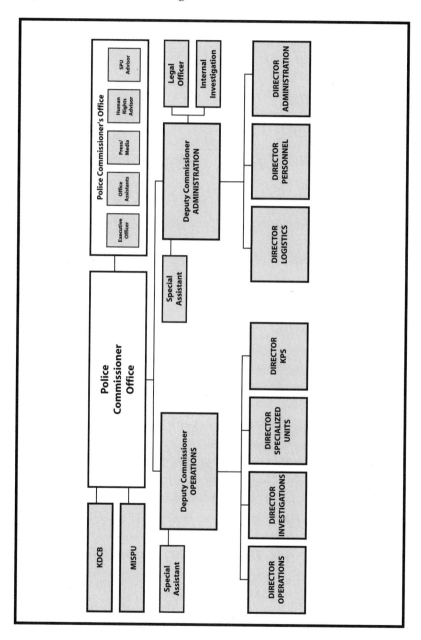

Source: UN Mission in Kosovo web site, available at http://www.
unmikonline.org/civpol/structure.htm.

primary responsibility for border control, the UNMIK border police advised KFOR on managing border traffic and controlling the transit of goods and people. When KPS border police were trained and deployed, the UNMIK police monitored their performance.[14]

SPECIAL POLICE UNIT

The Special Police Unit was responsible for crowd control and other special police functions related to maintaining public order. This was the first time a UN CIVPOL mission included constabulary forces that were armed and had executive authority. Ten "formed" Special Police Units were drawn from the constabulary forces of member states. The SPUs were fully integrated, national units with internal discipline and their own weapons, equipment, transport, and communications. Their mission was to assist the regular UNMIK police, including the Border Police Unit, and KFOR with maintaining internal stability.[15]

Planning for the SPU was done by the Civilian Police Division of the Department of Peacekeeping Operations at UN headquarters in New York. As the United Nations had no previous experience in fielding constabulary forces, the task was assigned to the only staff member with relevant experience, a French gendarme. Not surprisingly, in concept and organization, the SPUs were modeled on France's national Gendarmerie. France was a founding member of an association of European countries with constabulary forces, and most countries were familiar with the French model. Many countries had adopted the French model in creating their own forces and had received French security assistance. The training and operational procedures of constabulary forces from most prospective donors were also consistent with those used in France. This was fortuitous because the SPUs were recruited from a wide range of countries.[16]

In its initial contacts with potential donor countries, the United Nations did not request that member states simply contribute existing constabulary units. Instead, the UN Civilian Police Division developed a concept of operations for the Special Police

Figure 5. Special Police Unit Organization Chart

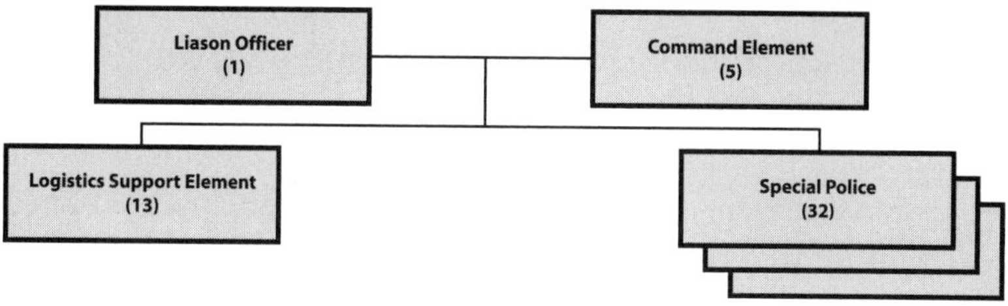

Unit	Element	Total
Special Police Unit	Command	6
	Special Police Platoons	96
	Support and Services	13
		115

Source: UN Mission in Kosovo

Units that called for creating ten identical, independent, and self-sustaining units, each with 115 officers. Personnel for these units could come from existing constabulary forces or from regular police units. Organizationally, each SPU had a command element; three operational platoons with thirty-two officers each; and a thirteen-member logistical support element made up of a medical team, mechanics, armorers, and technicians capable of maintaining the unit's vehicles, weapons, and communications equipment (see figure 5). The UN ensured that each SPU had the same complement of vehicles, weapons, and equipment. It also made certain that personnel joining these units received common training and deployed with their equipment to Kosovo.[17]

In recruiting for these new SPUs, the UN allowed member states to ignore the usual requirement that CIVPOL personnel must individually meet certain standards for serving in an international civilian police mission. These selection criteria were established at the beginning of the Bosnian mission and included at least five years of professional experience, proficiency in the mission language, familiarity with driving a police vehicle, and ability to use firearms. Instead, in the Kosovo mission, the SPUs were accepted as "formed units" without regard to the qualifications of every participant (the approach used in recruiting UN military forces). The rationale for this decision was that the units would be used primarily for crowd control and would deploy in force, at the platoon level or higher. In theory, this meant that only commanding officers needed to speak the mission language and professional drivers would take care of troop transport. In practice, it meant that the units could not be expected to break down below the level of a ten-man group, and most preferred to operate at the platoon or company level. Other CIVPOL officers who were required to speak English could be given individual assignments or dispatched in two-person teams to perform specific duties. The SPU had to move in strength and could undertake only certain specific functions.[18]

As with other CIVPOL missions, contributing nations were responsible for the preparation and training of police officers serving in Special Police Units. The CIVPOL Division, however, specified the training that the SPU should receive. It also sent out Special Police Assessment Teams to pre-test the SPU officers to assure they had received the proper training and had achieved an acceptable level of competence. The UN-prescribed regime included training in the following elements:

+ Individual and collective crowd-control techniques and procedures up to the company level, with special attention to negotiation, maneuver, and weapons.

+ Individual and collective area security and patrol procedures in urban areas, including the use of night vision and global positioning systems.

+ Rules of Engagement observed by UNMIK.

+ Organization and mandate of UNMIK and its area of operations.

+ Map reading and communications.

+ Geographic, historic, and cultural background of Kosovo, including the origins of the conflict.

+ Mine awareness.[19]

COMMAND AND CONTROL

The SPUs were under the overall command and control of the UNMIK police commissioner and his deputy for operations, but they reported to the UNMIK police regional commanders for day-to-day operations. The SPUs were also responsible to the office of the SPU special adviser to the UNMIK police commissioner, which advised on SPU operations and supervised the administrative aspects of SPU participation in the UN mission. The special adviser's office was responsible for the management and coordination of SPU operations, including preparation of orders and mission assignments. It conducted inspections of SPUs on arrival and at five-month intervals to ensure operational readiness and effective maintenance. It handled administrative matters, such as leave and equipment acquisition, and was responsible for coordinating unit rotations. In addition, the SPU adviser or his staff were present when SPU elements deployed en force to ensure that such operations were properly coordinated with the UNMIK police and KFOR. Once all ten of the SPUs were in place, the special adviser's office began working on developing joint training programs to ensure that the various national contingents could work together effectively.[20]

As a component of the UNMIK police, the SPUs were subject to the same rules of engagement and UN rules for the use of force and firearms as the rest of CIVPOL in Kosovo. Under the UN CIVPOL Division's concept of operations, each SPU was able to function independently and to perform the same functions, which included—

+ Managing civil disorder during violent demonstrations through the use of nonlethal weapons and the minimum amount of force (to include firearms) needed to control the situation.

+ Providing a rapid reaction capability to deal with emergencies and unforeseen threats to public order.

+ Providing operational support and backup for the UNMIK police, KPS, and KFOR.

+ Providing area security and collecting information through the conduct of preventive vehicle patrols, including light armored vehicles.

+ Providing protection and security for UN officials and UN border police in the performance of their duties.

+ Assisting humanitarian organizations, UN agencies, and the ICTY.

+ Providing radio communication and liaison in the working language (English) for units in the field and international authorities.[21]

FINANCIAL ARRANGEMENTS

Under the Memoranda of Understanding with contributing countries, the UN agreed to pay the standard UN financial reimbursement for every officer in each of the Special Police Units. Under the UN schedule for personnel expenses, members of an SPU received the following payments each month in addition to their regular salary, which was paid in national currency by the contributing country:

+ "Troop cost" at the rate of $988 per month per unit member.

+ Daily allowance at the rate of $1.28, plus a recreational leave allowance of $10.50 per day for up to seven days of leave during each six-month period.

+ Personal equipment allowance at the rate of $65.00 per month per unit member.

+ Weapon and ammunition allowance at the rate of $5.00 per month per member.

+ "Specialist's allowance" at a rate of $291.00 per month per unit member for up to 10 percent of the contingent.[22]

Under this payment schedule, the monthly personnel costs to the United Nations for the standard SPU of 115 members was $131,987. On an annual basis, the cost for one SPU was $1,583,844, plus an additional $16,905 in vacation allowances.

At this rate, the total annual personnel cost to the UN for all ten of the SPUs in Kosovo was in excess of $16,007,490.

In addition to personnel costs, the UN agreed to reimburse contributing countries for the equipment they provided according to standard UN rates. This reimbursement was done under terms of a "wet lease" arrangement that provided contributing countries with financial compensation for the use of the equipment brought by their units to Kosovo. For a representative SPU vehicle package of three unarmed armored personnel carriers, twelve Jeeps, and eleven trucks and other support vehicles, the monthly compensation was $40,500. The UN provided monthly compensation payments for weapons, ammunition, generators, containers, and other types of equipment from loudspeakers to tear gas launchers brought by each SPU from its own national inventories. The type and condition of the equipment, performance standards, maintenance requirements, provisions for replacement in case of damage or loss, and ultimate disposition were spelled out in each Memorandum of Understanding. These agreements also specified the financial compensation and performance standards for SPU "self-sustainment." These provisions covered catering, communications, medical and dental care, and office equipment. Each SPU received compensation for bringing its own cooks and doctors as well as nuclear, biological, and chemical weapons protection. Interestingly, the agreements specified the telephone as the primary means of communication and required that SPU kitchens have "hot dish-washing capabilities."[23]

SPU "PERSONALITIES"

The goal of the UN CIVPOL Division's concept of operations was to make various SPUs virtually interchangeable. Each SPU had the same number of personnel, organization chart, and equipment package. They underwent similar training, met the same performance criteria, and were sent to Kosovo to perform the same mission. Yet, beyond organization uniformity and professional similarities, each SPU retained its distinct national character. Like other CIVPOL, members of the SPU wore their national uniforms with the blue UN beret and UN shoulder patch. They brought with them to Kosovo the traditions and culture of their national police organizations and their own customs, procedures, and practices for relating to the general community and conducting operations. The following is a description of the SPUs provided by three of the seven contributing countries that highlights their unique "personalities."

Pakistan

The first SPU to arrive in Kosovo, the Pakistanis were assigned to Mitrovica, where they subsequently were joined by units from Spain and Poland. The camps of the three units are located side-by-side along a dusty road that runs parallel to the banks of the Ibar River, which divides the town into ethnic Serb and Albanian sectors. All three camps are within a few hundred yards of the main bridge, which has been the flashpoint for frequent clashes between the two ethnic groups. For the Pakistanis, serving in a hot spot is routine. The unit's commander, Colonel Hameed Iqbal Khaled, is an army officer on loan to the Ministry of the Interior. The unit's personnel are Pakistani Rangers who would otherwise be engaged in tracking Taliban remnants and al Qaeda operatives in the mountains of Pakistan's tribal area bordering Afghanistan or confronting separatists in Kashmir. Having deployed in April 2000, the Pakistani SPU was on its third complete rotation of personnel a little more than two years later.[24]

Yet by July 2002, the Pakistani SPU had yet to engage in riot control—despite its location in a town that had witnessed some of the region's most intense ethnic conflict. Instead, the unit had performed a variety of other missions involving escort and security functions. Since arriving, the current unit conducted 303 operations in its first sixty-eight days in country, an operations tempo similar to other SPUs and one that was well within its capabilities. In one notable case, the Pakistani's Muslim faith proved an advantage when they were called to confront an unruly crowd of three to four hundred ethnic Albanians that had collected following a soccer match. Arriving during the evening call to prayer, the Pakistanis were able to appeal to their fellow Muslims to join them in praying at the local mosque. In another unique assignment, the Pakistani SPU was responsible for providing security at the railroad station and along the tracks of the train that operated twice daily from Zvecan to Kosovo Polje through Mitrovica. The Pakistani unit also routinely contributed personnel to the joint force of SPU officers that provided security at the Dubrava prison, shift work that required a daily commitment of thirty of its personnel.[25]

Three years into their Kosovo assignment, the Pakistanis' problems had more to do with the condition of their compound, lack of UN administrative support, and difficulties with their own government than with their location in the most sensitive area of Kosovo. After three years of effort, the Pakistanis had yet to convince the UNMIK administration to provide asphalt covering for the roads and parking areas of their compound. This situation resulted in clouds of dust in summer and mud in the winter. UNMIK had also failed to install security lights or provide gutters and drains to prevent water from seeping through the floors of their living quarters. The Pakistanis had an ongoing pay dispute with their government. Officers reported no problem receiving their normal salaries, which were paid in rupees directly to their families, or their monthly allowance of about $40 that was paid to them in Kosovo by the UN. They did have a problem obtaining the $988 per month for "meals and incidental expenses" that was paid to them by the UN through the government of Pakistan. Members of the unit said the Pakistani government was normally four to five months behind in its payments. As a result, the current group of Rangers had yet to receive any money despite having been in Kosovo for more than three months.[26]

Despite these administrative frustrations, the members of the Pakistani SPU were glad to be in Kosovo. They were proud that their unit was well organized and had carried out its mission effectively. They were also proud of their relationship with the local community. The unit had held a "field day" for Mitrovica school children from both ethnic groups—featuring food, games, and dancing—and was planning to hold another. Members of the unit were allowed to go into Mitrovica in small groups to shop, have coffee, and get their hair cut. They reported that normally they were well received by the locals. The Pakistanis also enjoyed the pleasures of home cooking in their compound's cafeteria, which offered excellent Pakistani cuisine prepared by cooks brought from Pakistan.[27]

India

The Indian Special Police Unit was formed from members of the Rapid Reaction Force, an elite unit of the Indian Central Reserve Police Force. The force's primary mission is riot control, but its members are also trained in firefighting, first aid, and disaster management. In India, the Rapid Reaction Force also assists communities to recover from man-made or natural calamities. Prior to arriving in Kosovo, the Indian SPU received familiarization training concerning the local language, customs, and traditions. Training was also provided about the terrain, the politics of the region, and the origins of the conflict in Kosovo.

At the end of its first year in Kosovo, the Indian SPU took pride in having brought the approach and skills of the Rapid Reaction Force to Kosovo. It was proud of the social and religious diversity within its own ranks. The fact that the Indian SPU was a secular and multiethnic organization was considered a plus in promoting good relations with Kosovars who recently had suffered from ethnic and religious-based violence. The Indian SPU conducted a number of activities that were aimed at fostering a closer relationship with the local community. Doctors assigned to the SPU regularly held clinics to treat Kosovo citizens. The Indian SPU also organized and participated in a host of sporting events designed to bring the local community and the UNMIK police into closer contact. The unit was proud of the number of championships it had won in these friendly competitions. Establishing trust and maintaining a positive public image was important to the Indian SPU.

Romania

The last of the SPUs to arrive in Kosovo, the Romanians reached their base in Ferizaj in February 2002. The unit was drawn from the ranks of the Special Intervention Brigade of the Romanian Gendarmerie, which is subordinate to the country's Ministry of Interior. This was the first time a Romanian gendarme unit had served in a UN mission, and the Romanians intended to make a good first impression. For the Romanians, serving in Kosovo was part of a multiphased effort to obtain membership in NATO and integration into Europe. The Romanians already had joined France, Italy, Spain, Portugal, and the Netherlands as members of the association of European countries with constabulary forces. They viewed serving in UNMIK as an opportunity to demonstrate that their gendarmes met international standards. To this end, the Romanian SPU was given three months of intensive training before departing for Kosovo.[28]

The Romanians' effort to put their best foot forward was personified by their commander, Lieutenant Colonel Ioan Ovidiu Bratulescu, a veteran of recent NATO exercises, a highly professional officer, and a born diplomat. Able to converse comfortably in English, French, and Russian, Bratulescu worked easily with his international counterparts and with the U.S. military officers who were his "hosts" in MNB-East. According to the commander, all members of the Romanian SPU had at least a working knowledge of English and other languages, particularly French and Russian. The Romanians had an additional linguistic advantage in that some of the unit's members were from a region that bordered on Serbia, while others had family ties that gave them the ability to converse in Albanian. Unit personnel were allowed to spend their leisure time in town and were encouraged to interact with the locals.[29]

The Romanian SPU was a highly professional, "spit and polish" organization with a complete complement of vehicles, communications, weapons, and equipment of the latest design and Romanian manufacture. It was housed in a spotless compound of new, prefabricated, air-conditioned buildings with a fully equipped vehicle maintenance facility and cafeteria. The compound boasted a supply room bulging with extra uniforms, cold weather gear, riot-control equipment, and a range of

expertly maintained weapons. It also had a fully equipped, mul-
tiroom infirmary with a full-time Romanian doctor, medical
technician, and two corpsmen. The unit's vehicles were new, of
advanced design, and in some cases equipped with external television cameras that provided their occupants with a 360-
degree view of their surroundings.[30]

If the Romanians had a problem in July 2002, it was staying busy. Their location in the U.S. sector, their presence nearby
the Ukrainian SPU, and the general peacefulness of the region
resulted in an operations tempo of fewer than five missions per
day, which required only a portion of the force. The Romanians
were proud of their cooperation with the U.S. military. They
were also proud of their participation in UNMIK's crackdown
on organized crime and their role in recent high-risk arrest
cases. Based on their professionalism, training, and experience,
the Romanian gendarmes felt they "belonged" on the international stage. For the Romanian SPU and its commander, Kosovo
presented a "not-to-be-missed" opportunity to demonstrate
that Romania can contribute effectively to international peace
operations.[31]

DEPLOYMENT

With almost no time for advance preparation, the various elements of UNMIK were very slow to deploy; this was particularly
true of the UNMIK police. Kosovo was the first UN experience
with fielding a police organization that required the capacity to
perform all police functions from traffic control to fighting organized crime. An initial component of 169 members of the UN
International Police Task Force was immediately transferred from
Bosnia, but this group of officers was unarmed and did
little more than try to establish a headquarters operation.[32]
Logistics were also a problem, as the United Nations was unprepared to equip a substantial force of police officers with all the
equipment required to provide comprehensive police services.
The UNMIK police arrived in a "blank-slate situation" with none

of the facilities and materials used by police departments—no police stations, desks, radios, telephones, office furniture, stationery, heat, water, mail—and few vehicles.[33]

From the point of view of the UN CIVPOL Division, however, the deployment of the SPU to Kosovo was one time when the UN system worked more quickly than might reasonably have been expected. That the first SPU arrived in Kosovo in April 2000, ten months after the start of the UN mission, was viewed as an achievement by the CIVPOL Division. This was the first instance in which the United Nations had deployed "formed" constabulary units in a police mission, and time was required for conceptualizing and planning the creation of the force. Since the UN did not simply take existing units, potential donors had to wait until planning for the force structure and the concept of operations was completed before determining whether they could participate in the mission. Those countries that decided to go forward then engaged in negotiations with the UN and ultimately signed agreements covering the terms for participation, including a specific list of duties their forces would perform. At the same time, the CIVPOL Division had to obtain funding through the complicated UN budget process to lease or purchase the equipment needed to outfit ten units. Donor countries also had to recruit, organize, and train the new forces.[34]

Another reason for the delay in deploying the SPU was the need to locate and refurbish suitable facilities to house the units before their arrival. While these formed units came equipped with their own vehicles and communications, they were not outfitted like military units and were unprepared to live in the field. They could not set up camp and operate independently of the local infrastructure. Instead, they required the elements associated with a police headquarters—offices, barracks, and garages—plus electricity, heat, and water. Each unit required a kitchen and dining facility capable of feeding 120 people twice a day with food service available for duty personnel around the clock. All units brought along medical personnel, requiring an infirmary.[35]

In searching for suitable facilities, UNMIK officials responsible for finding housing for the SPU were competing with their UN counterparts and representatives from other international agencies in a postconflict environment where undamaged buildings were at a premium. Representatives of donor countries also had to approve the sites and their preparation. In one celebrated case, the Spanish government refused to allow its SPU to be quartered in a new, unoccupied, and only slightly damaged prison facility because they considered it inappropriate for their police to be housed in a jail. For most of the SPUs, the United Nations resolved the housing problem by refurbishing war-damaged buildings and by constructing camps using containers and prefabricated buildings erected on concrete slabs. In some cases, the availability of housing actually determined where the SPU was stationed. The tenth SPU, the Romanian unit, arrived on February 22, 2002, and was quartered in Ferizaj because suitable buildings were available. The Romanians were a late selection by the UN CIVPOL Division. They responded quickly after several other countries turned down UN requests to provide the final unit.[36] With the arrival of the Romanians, the ten SPUs were deployed in the locations shown in table 1.[37]

As police units, the SPUs could not deploy without military support and could not operate in areas where KFOR had yet to establish a level of reasonable security. The SPUs were more capable of operating independently than the UNMIK police,

Table 1. Deployment of Special Police Units in Kosovo

Location	Number of Units	National Composition
Pristina	3	India (2), Jordan
Pec	1	Argentina, Spain
Mitrovica	3	Pakistan, Jordan, Poland
Prizren	1	Argentina
Gnjilane	1	Ukraine
Ferizaj	1	Romania

Source: United Nations, CIVPOL Division

but they required military backup in order to conduct operations. The rapid escalation of ethnic violence and criminal activity that greeted the arrival of UNMIK provided additional disincentives for donor countries to rush their newly created constabulary units to Kosovo.

CRIME AND ETHNIC CONFLICT

Short of personnel and resources, the United Nations was unable to manage the wave of violence that swept Kosovo following the mass return of ethnic Albanian refugees from camps in Albania and Macedonia. Returning Kosovars took revenge on the Serbs, the Roma, and other minorities that were accused of looting and pillaging following the ethnic cleansing of Albanian villages by Serb security forces. In the absence of international and local police, KFOR was forced to intervene to stem the violence and attempt to restore public order. In mid-July 1999, within six weeks of the start of the UNMIK mission, KFOR commanders were already beginning to chafe under the responsibility of performing police functions. In Washington, Defense Department and U.S. military officials went before Congress to criticize the slowness of UN efforts to deploy international police and to relieve the military of the responsibility for arresting and detaining local citizens.[38]

There was also confusion within the United Nations about what law the UNMIK police should enforce. Initially, the UN declared the laws of the Federal Republic of Yugoslavia and the Republic of Serbia would continue to apply insofar as they did not conflict with international human rights standards and the UN mandate.[39] Local judges and prosecutors, who associated Yugoslav law with Serb oppression, challenged this decision. Kosovo Albanians advocated using the legal code from the period prior to 1989, when the province enjoyed substantial autonomy. Under pressure to re-establish the Kosovo criminal justice system, the UN agreed in December 1999 to base the legal system in Kosovo on the legal code that had been in force before March 22, 1989. Thereafter, the applicable law in Kosovo became an almost unfathomable combination of old law, international and European human rights conventions, UNMIK regulations, and police directives. According to an UNMIK publication, the applicable law in Kosovo was literally "the regulations promulgated by the Special Representative of the Secretary-General and subsidiary instruments issued thereunder, and the law in force in Kosovo on March 22, 1989, according to UNMIK Regulation 1999/24 ("On the Law Applicable in Kosovo"), as amended by UNMIK Regulation 2000/59."[40]

In September, UN secretary-general Kofi Annan informed the Security Council that "the level of violence in Kosovo, especially against vulnerable minorities, remained a major concern."[41] With only 1,100 officers, the UNMIK police were struggling to control the re-emergence of Albanian organized crime; massive smuggling of cars, cigarettes, narcotics, fuel, and general contraband; and exploding street violence. UNMIK police commissioner Sven Frederiksen acknowledged the growing magnitude of crime and attacks on minorities but said he did not have the police personnel to stop it.[42] In December 1999, with serious security incidents on the rise, the murder of a newly arrived UNMIK international staff member, and the first assassination of an ethnic Albanian political leader, the Security Council acted on the secretary-general's recommendation and increased the authorized strength of the UNMIK police to 4,718 personnel. Unfortunately, only 1,817 CIVPOL had arrived in country, including 78 IPTF members who were transferred from Bosnia and authorized to carry weapons and exercise executive authority by their governments.[43]

The senior UN official in Kosovo, Bernard Kouchner, called the failure of UN member states to honor their commitments to supply personnel a "scandal" that was contributing to general lawlessness.[44] The new NATO commander, German General Klaus Reinhardt, reversed the policy of his predecessor and ordered his troops back onto the streets to assist the UNMIK police to restore order.[45] In his December 1999 report to the Security Council, Secretary-General Annan noted the deteriorating security situation in Kosovo. He also pointed out that six months after the start of the UN mission, none of the Special Police Units that had been expected to spearhead the effort to control civil unrest had reached Kosovo. Annan blamed the problem on "logistical and other constraints" that delayed their arrival.[46]

MITROVICA

In early 2000, the full fury of ethnic hatred in Kosovo was felt in Mitrovica. Located in the northern part of the province, Mitrovica was situated astride the Ibar River just south of Kosovo's only major industrial center, the Trepca mining and smelter complex. The Ibar's meandering course marked an informal boundary between ethnic Serb areas extending northward forty kilometers to the border with the Republic of Serbia and areas occupied by ethnic Albanians to the south. "North of Mitrovica, civil servants were paid by Serbia, newsstands sold only Belgrade papers, prices were quoted in dinars, and schools used the Serbian curriculum." Initial NATO reluctance to establish control over Mitrovica's northern section resulted in a de facto division of the region. A short bridge in the center of town became the principal crossing point between the Serb and Albanian sectors. When French KFOR troops stationed tanks behind tumbles of razor wire and established an armed checkpoint on the bridge, Mitrovica became a divided city.[47] This division was perpetuated when KFOR failed to protect ethnic Albanians living north of the bridge or stop a similar process of ethnic cleansing of Serbs in the southern part of the city. As tensions escalated and clashes became more frequent, a group of several hundred young Serbs organized to control the north end of the bridge and prevent an influx of ethnic Albanians into the northern part of the city.[48]

These so-called "Bridge Watchers" gradually became more organized as they rallied behind a leader, Oliver Ivanovic, and equipped themselves with Motorola radios, sirens, and truncheons. Formally identified as the Citizen's Association of Bridge St. Demetrios, the group claimed to be a community self-defense and philanthropic organization. According to an

Mitrovica, Kosovo (March 2000)

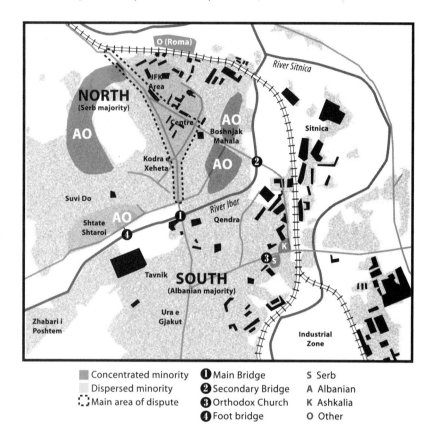

▦ Concentrated minority	❶ Main Bridge	S Serb
▨ Dispersed minority	❷ Secondary Bridge	A Albanian
⬚ Main area of dispute	❸ Orthodox Church	K Ashkalia
	❹ Foot bridge	O Other

Source: Humanitarian Community Information Center, United Nations Office for the Coordination of Humanitarian Affairs, 22 March 2000; modified and reprinted with permission.

International Crisis Group report, the Bridge Watchers were in fact paid operatives of the Serbian Ministry of the Interior in Belgrade whose mission was to incite violence against ethnic Albanians and the international community. Bridge watching became a regular job with wages and shifts. Some members were "employed" as hospital security staff and were paid by the Serbian Ministry of Health, supplementing their incomes through "donations" from local citizens. Others enriched themselves by engaging in intimidation and protection rackets, illicit trafficking, and other forms of organized crime. In time, the Bridge Watchers became a parallel security force that checked identification, responded to complaints, and detained petty criminals. This security function was bolstered by the presence of plainclothes officers from the Serb Ministry of Interior who were former police officers in Mitrovica.[49]

Belgrade's maintenance of parallel administrative and security structures in Mitrovica and the rest of northern Kosovo was in direct violation of UN Security Council Resolution 1244. It was also a direct challenge that UNMIK and NATO seemed powerless or unwilling to counter. Given the continuing violence, north Mitrovica and neighboring Zvencan were the only Kosovo municipalities where it was too dangerous to station KPS officers. Mitrovica was the only place in Kosovo where Albanian confidence in KFOR was in doubt, given the seemingly pro-Serb attitude of French troops. It was also the only place in Kosovo where local residents repeatedly demonstrated their willingness to use violence against the international community. UNMIK police conducted daily weapons searches in Albanian areas but could not conduct similar operations in the north. The Serbs seemed intent on defying UNMIK in order to establish self-rule. The Albanians seemed equally determined to prevent Kosovo's de facto partition.

In February 2000, a series of violent clashes occurred in Mitrovica between crowds of ethnic Albanians and Serbs. On February 2, a UN High Commissioner for Refugees bus carrying 49 Serbs was bombed, leaving two dead and three injured. In Mitrovica, the two days of rioting that followed severely tested relations between KFOR and the UNMIK police. Primacy for maintaining public order in Mitrovica rested with the 250-man infantry battalion of French KFOR troops. The UNMIK police had an understrength detachment of 65 officers that attempted to patrol on both sides of the Ibar. During the riots, there were numerous occasions when French KFOR troops failed to respond to requests from the UNMIK police for support. In one incident, an American CIVPOL officer and a detachment of French paratroops were attempting to reach a small group of Albanians that was trapped by a Serb mob. When the UNMIK police officer was knocked to the ground, he expected the French to come to his rescue. Instead the French soldiers retreated to the protection of their armored personnel carriers. Eventually, a company of Danish KFOR troops responded and rescued the Albanians. Such incidents created bad blood between the French KFOR contingent and the UNMIK police and between KFOR and local Albanians, who felt the French were acting on their historic affinity for the Serbs.[50] On February 13, a grenade attack on a Serb café in northern Mitrovica was followed by sniper attacks on French KFOR positions that wounded two soldiers. In an exchange of gunfire, one sniper was killed and another wounded; both were Kosovo Albanians.[51]

In March, Secretary-General Annan informed the Security Council that the deteriorating security situation in Mitrovica highlighted the "policing gap" that existed in Kosovo because of the failure of member states to contribute police personnel. He also noted that the continued absence of the ten Special Police Units meant that responsibility of maintaining public order necessarily continued to rest with KFOR.[52] In April 2000, the first SPU, a unit from Pakistan, arrived in Kosovo and was assigned to Mitrovica. In areas where UNMIK police did not have primacy, KFOR retained responsibility for law enforcement and maintaining public order. This was the case in Mitrovica.[53] In repeated incidents requiring riot control and civil disorder management, the French KFOR contingent relied on its own resources and the Pakistani SPU was not used. This was true even though French troops suffered casualties in violent clashes with local Serbs.

One particularly glaring example of the French unwillingness to allow contact between the Pakistanis and Serbs occurred on June 21, 2000, when a group of Serb Bridge Watchers clashed with UNMIK police, leaving twenty Serbs wounded and thirteen UN police and other international vehicles burned or damaged. The incident occurred when a group of Serbs began throwing rocks and breaking windows in three eleven-story apartment buildings located in a UN "zone of confidence" near the north end of the bridge. Three-quarters of the buildings' inhabitants were ethnic Albanians, but one-quarter were ethnic Serbs. UNMIK police responded to complaints about the rock throwing from building residents and seized one of the vandals. A crowd of Bridge Watchers quickly surrounded the police to prevent his arrest.[54] Some of the UNMIK police wanted to release the suspect, but the American officer in charge placed the Serb under arrest and radioed for the Pakistani SPU to provide backup. After a considerable delay, the Pakistani SPU arrived at the southern end of bridge. Standing in formation, the Pakistanis were pelted with rocks but were prevented by French KFOR troops and armored vehicles on the bridge from going across.[55]

Why French FKOR troops refused to allow the Pakistani SPU to assist in controlling mob violence in Mitrovica perplexed observers and was never officially explained. The French apparently did not trust the Pakistanis, who had a reputation for using violence against demonstrators and were untested in riot-control situations in Kosovo. The French also seemed concerned about the appearance of Pakistani Muslims clashing with Orthodox Christian Serbs. French motives may have derived from a perception of France's long-term commercial interests in Serbia and a belief that the region's future stability required an ethnic Serb presence in Kosovo. The French seemed to feel morally responsible for preventing the numerically superior Albanians from expelling the Serb minority.[56] As a practical matter, the presence of a force of French gendarmes within the French KFOR contingent gave French commanders an option for dealing with crowd-control situations that did not require going outside their own force or command structure. French gendarmes were co-located with the French military forces, immediately available, fully trained and equipped, and totally compatible in terms of language, communications gear, and doctrine. In contrast, radios used by the English-speaking Pakistani SPU were not compatible, so the two forces could not communicate during an operation. There was also at least the possibility of problems arising because of differences in doctrine and tactics. For some or all of these reasons, the French chose to rely on their own forces in dealing with civil disorder management in Mitrovica.[57]

The only exception to the general practice of not using the SPU for security functions in Mitrovica was Operation Vulcan, the UNMIK takeover of the Trepca mining and industrial facility. Located just north of Mitrovica, Trepca was a complex of forty mines and processing plants that produced a range of metals and employed two thousand Serbs. Trepca was the last major industrial unit operating in Kosovo and the primary source of employment for Serbs in Mitrovica. More than a year after the arrival of the United Nations in Kosovo, Trepca remained under the control of Serb engineers who took orders from Belgrade and exported the plant's entire production to Serbia. On August 14, 2000, a force of five hundred British, French, and Danish KFOR troops supported by helicopters and armored vehicles seized control of the facility. According to a KFOR spokesman, the action was taken to force closure of the Zvecan lead smelter, which was pumping more than two hundred times the safe level of lead fumes into the atmosphere. The UN's Kouchner, a physician and former French health minister, called Trepca an environmental disaster and said its continued operation was hazardous to public health. He noted the plant's management repeatedly refused requests to close the smelter and rejected the right of the United Nations under various Security Council resolutions to manage former Yugoslav state factories for the general good of Kosovo. Kouchner said the UN was prepared to invest $16 million to renovate the plant's buildings and outdated equipment. He also guaranteed that workers would continue to receive their salaries while the facility was undergoing renovation. The plant's managers called the UNMIK takeover "a classic case of robbery."[58]

Arriving before dawn, the first British KFOR elements clashed with workers protecting the front gate of the complex. As more employees arrived for work, the level of violence increased with the crowd throwing rocks and pieces of wood at the soldiers. At the Zvecan smelter, a group of thirty to forty Serb engineers locked themselves in the building and refused to shut down the furnace. By afternoon, resistance was overcome and UN experts closed down the facility. Meanwhile, in Mitrovica, a Serb mob clashed with British soldiers, who retaliated by firing rubber bullets. In a related incident, UNMIK police closed down a nearby Serb radio station that had been used to broadcast anti-UN and anti-KFOR propaganda.[59] Following the takeover in Trepca, the Pakistani SPU was brought from Mitrovica to provide area security and guard the Zvecan smelter. The SPU established two guard posts and conducted area patrols, but the very size of the facility defeated efforts to provide truly effective security. Given the high levels of environmental pollution in the area, the UN was acutely aware of the dangers to its personnel. During the brief period of their deployment to Trepca, SPU personnel were subject to weekly blood tests, and their uniforms were cleaned every day to prevent contamination.[60]

Two Years of Violence

Throughout the winter of 2000 and spring of 2001, continued high levels of politically motivated violence, illicit trafficking, organized crime, and street crime in Kosovo reflected the generally unsettled conditions in the region. During January 2001, a series of attacks on ethnic Serbs was followed by a major incident on February 16, when a bus loaded with Serbs in the weekly KFOR-escorted convoy from Nis in Serbia to Gracanica near Pristina was bombed, resulting in ten deaths and injuries to forty others. Demonstrations were staged in more than fifteen Serb enclaves, often involving up to sixty-five hundred people. This incident led to a general increase in tensions in the Mitrovica, Gnjilane, and Prisitina regions and imposed severe limitations on freedom of movement for ethnic Serbs. During this period there was a shift of criminal behavior, with an increase of violence against the international community. There was also a trend toward increased aggression against UNMIK law enforcement and KFOR personnel, including the killing of a Russian KFOR soldier.[61]

Mitrovica remained the focal point for ethnic violence and civil disobedience. On March 14, 2001, a Serb crowd surrounded an UNMIK police station, trapping police officers inside. The crowd demanded the release of three Serbs who had been detained for assaulting UNMIK police officers. The crowd caused extensive damage to the station and burned or damaged seven police vehicles. In the melee, twenty-one UNMIK police were injured. The crowd was dispersed by KFOR troops, who fired tear gas and stun grenades at the rioters and blocked the bridge across the Ibar.[62] As a result of this incident, UNMIK police temporarily suspended patrols in northern Mitrovica, resuming them only in late May with KFOR assistance. The incident appeared to be part of an orchestrated effort to drive UNMIK out of northern Mitrovica.[63] On April 19, a similar clash occurred when KFOR attempted to remove roadblocks established by Serbs protesting UN efforts to collect taxes on goods arriving from Serbia, a means of controlling the black market. Ten Serbs where injured when KFOR fired tear gas to disperse the demonstration.[64]

On May 21, 2001, UNMIK established a new "Pillar I" in the UN administrative structure, which realigned UNMIK's police and Department of Judicial Affairs into one structure headed by a newly arrived deputy SRSG, Ambassador Gary Matthews (see figures 6 and 7). This replaced the previous humanitarian assistance pillar, whose residual functions were assumed by the UN's civil administration (Pillar II). Creation of the new pillar brought the police, security, and justice structures under common management. It also brought greater coherence and centralized control of countercrime efforts and improved UNMIK's ability to deal with street violence and organized crime. Matthews, a former U.S. State Department Foreign Service Officer, had served previously as Deputy High Representative in Bosnia and was an auxiliary police officer in his hometown in Virginia. In organizing the new structure, Matthews sought to better focus UN law enforcement efforts, while promoting judicial system reform through increasing the number and quality of judges and improving penal facilities. He

Figure 6. UN Civil Administration in Kosovo: The Four Pillars

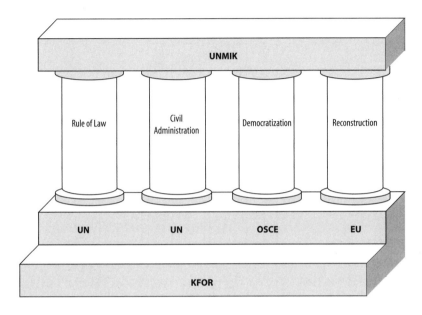

Source: UN Mission in Kosovo

also sought to take advantage of new UN legislation providing heavier penalties for illegal weapons possession, weapons trafficking, and illegal border crossing. The new pillar provided a single point of contact for cooperative efforts with KFOR, which continued to play a major role in ensuring public order.[65]

By June 2001, nine of the ten SPUs had arrived in Kosovo. The units were from India (two), Jordan (two), Spain, Pakistan, Poland, Ukraine, and Argentina. Their 1,089 personnel brought the total number of UNMIK police to 4,378, or better than 90 percent of the authorized force strength. The addition of the nine SPUs provided the UNMIK police with substantially increased capacity to engage in civil disorder management and to perform tactical police functions.[66] Despite repeated incidents of civil disorder and ethnic violence, none of the SPUs was used for crowd control, which was their primary function; rather, they were put to use in a hodgepodge of security-related tasks.

Figure 7. Organization Chart of UNMIK's New Pillar I

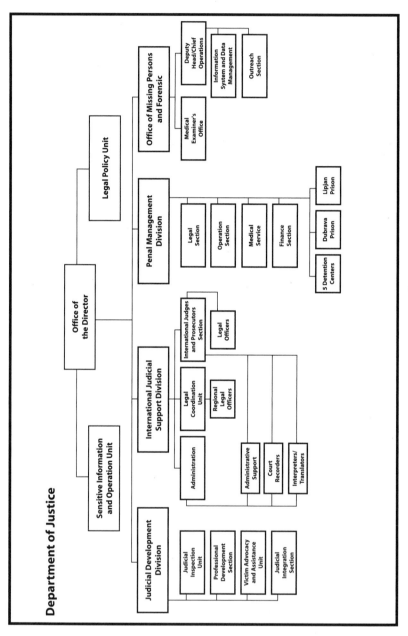

Source: UN Mission in Kosovo, available at http://www.unmikonline.
org/justice/organigram_justice.htm.

THE "ODD JOBS" UNIT

The reasons the SPUs were not used for civil disorder management and riot control but instead were used for a variety of "odd jobs" were many and varied. First, the senior leadership of the UNMIK police was drawn from police forces in northern Europe and North America. These police officers came from policing traditions that did not include constabularies. The officers were therefore unfamiliar with how to use these resources, and there was a natural reluctance to deploy them in sensitive situations.[67] At the same time, between 15 and 20 percent of the duties assigned to the UNMIK police were not related to law enforcement but were requests from various sources for police services.[68] As the arriving SPUs did not have assigned duties, UNMIK police officials saw them as an available labor pool that could perform a variety of necessary tasks and free regular UNMIK CIVPOL for duties related to law enforcement. SPUs had their own vehicles, communications, and weapons, which made them natural candidates for escort duty, close protection work, and other police services that required mobility. As they were trained to deploy in strength, they had a natural comparative advantage over regular UNMIK police in handling assignments that required large numbers of personnel. SPUs were called upon to serve as static guards for buildings, provide security for events, and handle other situations that required a large-scale security presence. As one senior UNMIK police official said, "In the beginning, UN commanders did not know what to do with the SPU. Now they cannot do without them."[69]

Second, the United Nations had expected that most of the SPUs would come from countries in western Europe. In fact, European countries, which were also members of NATO, preferred to have their gendarmes serve as members of KFOR and not in the UNMIK police. After efforts to recruit European units were largely unsuccessful, the UN turned to countries in the Middle East, South Asia, Latin America, and the former Soviet republics. This meant dealing with donor countries that represented a broad range of military and police traditions and cultures.[70] It also meant accepting some forces that were more military in character and others that were an unknown quantity in terms of how they might react if they became involved in a violent confrontation. UNMIK officials were leery of employing the SPUs in situations where they might use tactics that would cause civilian casualties. Following their arrival, several of the SPUs received additional training in civil disorder management with an emphasis on nonviolent means of maintaining public order. In sectors where KFOR maintained primacy for law enforcement and public order, military commanders preferred to rely on constabulary units that were part of their own commands rather than cross jurisdictional boundaries and use forces that had a different chain of command and rules of engagement. At the same time, senior UN officials were reluctant to press KFOR to utilize the SPUs, particularly in Mitrovica, fearing KFOR might seize the opportunity to shed responsibility for what were frustrating and dangerous assignments.[71]

Third, what one UNMIK police official described as the "European cultural context" for using gendarmes in civil disorder management was also missing in Kosovo. In western Europe, there was a tacit understanding between police and demonstrators about how demonstrations should be conducted and the limits of acceptable behavior for both parties. In democratic countries, riot control forces were trained to regard protesters as fellow citizens and not as "the enemy." At the same time, protesters knew the arrival of constabulary forces meant the demonstration had reached the limits of official tolerance and that further escalation would result in a violent response from the authorities. With its history of communist rule, Kosovo lacked such traditions and understandings. Demonstrations were most often staged not by citizens with a complaint or legitimate problem, but by a "rent-a-mob" of paid and disciplined partisans with a specific political objective. Groups such as the Mitrovica Bridge Watchers used civil disorder and violence as a means of continuing the original conflict. In such circumstances, provoking violence was the aim of civil action rather than an unfortunate by-product of a situation that inadvertently got out of control.[72]

Finally, the gradual passing of the immediate postconflict environment, the growing number of UN and indigenous police, and the assertive presence of KFOR brought an eventual decline in the number of violent crimes and the restoration of more normal conditions. During 2001, the number of murders declined by 50 percent from the previous year, incidents of arson fell by 58 percent, and looting by 73 percent. Only the number of sexual assaults increased, which probably was the result of an increased willingness to report such crimes. This decline in violence was likely assisted by the departure of large numbers of Serbs and the retreat of those remaining into enclaves guarded by KFOR. With the exception of Mitrovica, which remained a flashpoint and center of interethnic violence, tensions in the remainder of the country began to relax. At the start of the Kosovo mission, a climate of impunity prevailed. There were too few UNMIK police to provide security, no judicial system, and no prisons. By December 2001, trained KPS officers patrolled the streets, a judiciary was hearing cases, and the penal system was functioning. The UNMIK police had primacy for law enforcement for all areas except Mitrovica. Cities in Kosovo had crime rates that would be envied by most communities in the United States.[73]

In such a relaxed environment, there were almost no demonstrations and little call for formed police units to control civil disorder. Instead, UNMIK officials used the SPUs for a wide variety of duties.

Static guard duty. SPUs were used to guard UNMIK facilities, courthouses, and other sensitive facilities such as the Trepca industrial complex. A platoon of the Indian SPU plus a Ukrainian K-9 unit provided airport security. These officers were present at the airport to provide perimeter control and to observe operations. The Indian SPU also provided security for the minor offenses court in Pristina. Near Mitrovica, eighteen officers from five Special Police Units and two K-9 teams from the Ukrainian SPU were assigned full-time to guard the exterior of the Dubrava prison. A similar detachment of eighteen members of the Indian SPU was stationed at a detention center in Pristina. Five-member SPU teams provided backup at road-blocks for UNMIK civil administrative officers, checking licenses, registration, and ethnic ridership levels of buses in Pristina.

Protecting minority communities. SPUs manned check-points, conducted patrols, and took other security measures to protect minority communities, cultural sites, and people in the witness protection program. In Obilic, the Indian SPU conduct-ed routine foot and vehicle patrols to protect Serb residences. In Dubrava, the Spanish SPU provided a group of ten officers to guard the residence of a family of a witness in a trial.

Major events. SPUs provided security at major public events, such as political ceremonies, soccer matches, and gradu-ations. In February 2002, five platoons from three SPUs were deployed in connection with the annual ceremony commemo-rating the massacre of Adam Jashari, a Kosovo Liberation Army leader, and his family by Serb forces in February 1999. One Jordanian platoon and two Polish platoons were assigned as a rapid intervention force at three pedestrian checkpoints, while three Pakistani platoons were on standby at the local police station. Some thirty thousand people attended the cere-mony, which proceeded without incident. On March 9, three platoons from the Argentine SPU were dispatched to deal with a gang fight and riot following a basketball game in Prizren. Hooligans threw rocks and bottles at the SPU officers, who responded with tear gas to control the situation. Following this incident, SPU platoons were routinely deployed at sporting events where violence might occur.

Border patrol. SPUs assisted the UNMIK border police at checkpoints on the border with Albania and Macedonia. The SPUs conducted vehicle searches, including the use of K-9 teams to identify drugs and weapons, and provided security and armed support. Under an agreement reached in the spring of 2002, the SPUs conduct joint patrols with the border police along the frontier and provide a rapid reaction force to inter-cept illegal crossings discovered by foot patrols and helicopters.

High-risk arrests. SPUs provided support for the UNMIK

Special Operations Unit during the conduct of high-risk arrests. The SPUs provided backup teams for the UNMIK police and, in cases where forced entry was required, actually made arrests. They were also deployed en force in situations where it appeared the arrest might spark public demonstrations. On February 21, 2002, seven platoons of SPU were placed on standby and later deployed to the UNMIK police station in north Mitrovica in connection with the arrest of two ethnic Serbs. The deployment was later reduced to one platoon that remained in place for several days. No incidents were reported.

Close protection. SPUs provided close protection for high-risk persons, including visiting dignitaries, international judges and prosecutors, UN personages, and local government officials. SPU officers were routinely assigned to escort provisional government officials and assembly members, particularly ethnic Serbs, from their homes to meetings in Pristina. This was a major commitment for the SPU, requiring up to one hundred officers and dozens of armored vehicles two or three times a week. A platoon of the Indian SPU conducted routine patrols within Pristina to protect UN buildings and the residences of senior international officials. SPUs also provided support for the close protection unit of the UNMIK police for particularly sensitive missions.

Election security. SPUs provided election security by protecting polling stations and escorting candidates. In November 2001, elections were held for a 120-member Kosovo assembly that would in turn select a president and provisional government. Three ethnic Albanian parties contested the election. Serbs participated by voting for seats reserved for minorities. Voter turnout was high (63 percent) and there were few incidents and disruptions. During election campaigns, the SPUs provided escorts for candidates and security at election rallies. During the voting, the SPU secured voting stations, protected ballot boxes, and ensured that voters of all ethnicities could reach the polls.

Providing escort service. SPUs provided security for payrolls and the transfer of large amounts of currency. Between December 15, 2001 and early February 2002, SPUs were continually involved in escorting shipments of up to $100 million worth of currency in the change from the deutsche mark to the euro. Units also secured roads, the Bank of Kosovo, and the airport during the arrival and departure of special chartered aircraft. Between ten to thirty officers were assigned to convoy duty with every shipment of currency. The Pakistani SPU routinely provided escorts for the transfer of prisoners from Dubrava prison to the courthouse in Mitrovica. Two SPUs provided an escort and rapid reaction force during the politically sensitive return of one hundred and twenty ethnic Albanian prisoners that had been held in Serbia since the end of the NATO bombing campaign in June 1999.

Joint operations with KFOR. It was envisioned that the SPUs would work closely with KFOR in conducting joint security operations. In fact this did not happen, and joint operations were the exception rather than the rule. In MNB-East, the Romanian SPU and U.S. KFOR troops have conducted joint training exercises and conducted joint operations in manning checkpoints. Also in MNB-East near Gjilane, the Ukrainian SPU worked with KFOR to provide security for shipments of explosives used in commercial mining operations. KFOR developed the schedule and provided a liaison officer, while the SPU provided the security escort.[74]

A CAMPAIGN FOR LAW AND ORDER

In January 2002, UNMIK began a concerted effort to crack down on organized criminal activity within Kosovo. The primary targets of this campaign were a small number of ethnic Albanians who were formerly members of the Kosovo Liberation Army and current members of its successor organization, the Kosovo Protection Corps (KPC). Some were also leading members of the Democratic Party of Kosovo, led by former KLA commander Hashim Thaci. UNMIK believed these persons were guilty of wartime atrocities and postwar involvement in organized crime. They were also suspected of engaging in the harassment, intimidation, and assassination of members of Ibrahim Rugova's more moderate political party, the Democratic

League of Kosovo. Many of these individuals were regarded by the public as war heroes and were thought by many people to enjoy a privileged status. UNMIK's intention was to remove these negative elements from society and to demonstrate that in a democratic society, no one is above the law. While this operation was fully consistent with UNMIK's rule-of-law mandate, it was not without risks for the UN interim administration. The KPC was composed of five thousand combat veterans who wore military uniforms, were authorized access to weapons, and were formally tasked by UNMIK with a number of functions, including search and rescue operations and responding to natural disasters. It was uncertain how the general public would react to arrests of KPC members or if criminal elements could whip up public demonstrations in support of their comrades. It was also not certain how the UNMIK police, the KPS, and the SPU would handle the kind of widespread civil disorder that might result from a province-wide law enforcement effort against a number of well-known and presumably popular individuals.[75]

The answers to these questions were not long in coming. On January 28, UNMIK police arrested three ethnic Albanians suspected of wartime atrocities and postwar criminal activities. The three were former KLA members and current members of the KPC. They were also identified with former KLA commander Thaci's political party and with the National Intelligence Service, a shadowy organization formed by Thaci following the conflict. One of those arrested was also a member of the Kosovo Police Service. The arrests resulted in a series of public demonstrations in Pristina by KPC members and KLA veterans' organizations. These were the first public demonstrations in the provincial capital since the arrival of KFOR. On February 8, the third such demonstration in a week turned violent when three thousand demonstrators attacked UNMIK police, broke windows, and then attacked bystanders sitting at a nearby café for failing to join the demonstration.[76] In response, one platoon of the Jordanian SPU and two platoons of the Indian SPU were deployed to control the protesters and prevent them from reaching UNMIK headquarters. This was the first time the SPU had faced rioters in the capital. There was a tense standoff, but, when confronted by trained riot control police in full riot gear, the crowds dispersed without incident. Following the arrests on January 28, an SPU platoon was assigned to protect the UNMIK police station in Lipjan, where there were also demonstrations. In addition, a group of ten officers from the Indian SPU was assigned to protect the UNMIK police commissioner's residence in Pristina for fifteen days, but no incidents were reported.[77]

While the appearance of trained and properly equipped riot control police was enough to dissuade the demonstrators, this first use of the SPU for crowd control brought out several of its shortcomings. The first difficulty involved communication, as individual members of the SPUs were not required to demonstrate proficiency in English, the mission language. The first members of the Jordanian SPU to arrive on the scene could not speak English and could not communicate with other UNMIK police who were attempting to control the situation. To address the problem, UNMIK police had to find Arabic-speaking CIVPOL who also spoke English to act as liaison officers and interpreters for the SPU officers. The second problem involved command and control of the elements below the company level. The first SPU element on the scene arrived by armored vehicle without a senior officer present. As there was no one to command them to deploy, the officers stayed in their vehicle, ignoring the mayhem that was taking place around them, until a sufficiently senior officer arrived to order them to disembark.[78]

A second attempt in early 2002 to deploy the SPU to deal with civil disturbances also encountered difficulties. Three years after the start of the UN mission, Mitrovica remained a divided city with no meaningful UN law enforcement or administrative presence north of the Ibar. On April 8, an incident occurred that involved the most violent attack against UNMIK personnel since the inception of the UN presence. At 2:00 P.M., UNMIK police established a traffic inspection checkpoint at the north end of the main bridge that links the two parts of the city. The checkpoint was in front of the La Dolce Vita Café, a well-known Bridge Watcher hangout. The action was part of a new program to ensure that vehicles were registered and that motorists had proper documentation. At 4:30 P.M., the UNMIK police stopped what they thought was a stolen car and arrested the driver, an ethnic Serb member of the Bridge Watchers. Word of the arrest spread quickly, and a group of about forty Bridge Watchers gathered, supported by a crowd of about three hundred other Serbs. The arresting officers called for backup. A platoon of the Polish SPU responded but found the main bridge was closed by a company of gendarmes from the French KFOR contingent that was observing the confrontation. The Poles were delayed for a time but were finally allowed to cross.[79]

The mob threw stones at the SPU, which responded with tear gas. Slavoljub "Pagi" Jovic, a leader of the Bridge Watchers, was arrested for throwing rocks and inciting the crowd against the police. When Jovic tried to resist arrest and threatened the UN police officers with a switchblade knife, the confrontation escalated sharply. This was the first time the SPU had engaged in crowd control in Mitrovica. It was also the first time the Polish SPU was called out to deal with a riot. Instead of accompanying the prisoner through the French lines and across the bridge to safety, the UNMIK police and the Polish SPU held their positions and then attempted to break up the crowd. The Serb rioters responded by throwing two fragmentation grenades into the Polish ranks. The Poles retreated behind their vehicles but came under fire from Serb snipers. The SPU returned fire against the snipers and used rubber bullets and tear gas to disperse the crowd.[80]

The grenade blasts injured nineteen SPU members, who were hospitalized with shrapnel wounds. One critically injured officer was treated by KFOR medical officers and evacuated to Poland. Seven UNMIK civilian police (five Americans and two Germans) also received injuries. According to a local Serb leader, twelve Serbs were injured. At least two Serbs received bullet wounds; one was in critical condition. With the Polish SPU out of action, the UNMIK police commissioner turned responsibility for controlling the situation over to French KFOR soldiers. Units from the Spanish and Romanian SPUs also were deployed but were not involved in the violence.[81]

Immediately after the incident, UNMIK and KFOR officials claimed that the injuries had occurred because of a poorly organized police action and a breakdown of communication between the UN police and KFOR. A more thorough internal investigation discovered that the incident occurred because of the type of confusion and miscommunication between organizations and nationalities that often occurs in peace operations. In fact, the traffic inspection checkpoint was a cover for a "snatch operation" to arrest Jovic, the leader of the Bridge Watchers, who was wanted for previous crimes. It was orchestrated by Team Six, a Special Operations Unit of the UNMIK civil police, composed mainly of Americans. Team Six established the checkpoint in front of the café, knowing Jovic was likely to be there. To ensure that he would come out, the first motorist arrested was Jovic's brother.

Team Six ran its operation without informing UNMIK police headquarters or the regional UNMIK police commander. It also failed to inform the Polish SPU and the French KFOR contingent in advance of the operation. Once Jovic was arrested and transported across the bridge to the UNMIK police station in south Mitrovica, the Team Six commander on the scene had neither the experience nor the authority to handle the mob action that ensued. At the time, the regional commander was attending a meeting in Pristina and his deputy was away on leave. The Polish SPU responded to the call for backup without knowing the true purpose of the arrest operation or that its target was already in custody. Rather than escorting the UNMIK police across the bridge to safety, however, the Polish SPU attempted to ease the pressure on the UNMIK police checkpoint by forcing the rock-throwing mob backward, away from the bridge and deeper into the ethnic Serb stronghold. As the Poles engaged the mob, they were attacked with grenades and automatic weapons fire. Throughout the incident, French KFOR gendarmes in full riot gear stood within a few feet of the Bridge

Watchers, who were throwing rocks and grenades at the SPU, but they did not intervene.[82]

The injury of twenty-six UN police in a single incident sent shock waves across Europe. On the day following the incident, Polish prime minister Leszek Miller traveled to Pristina accompanied by Poland's interior minister and the head of the Polish police. Miller visited the wounded Polish police officers in the hospital and met with the newly arrived head of UNMIK, Michael Steiner, to discuss the situation in Kosovo. During a visit to the hospital with the prime minister, Steiner strongly condemned the violence that, he said, not only injured the police who were performing their duties under difficult circumstances, but also "hurt the legitimate interests of Serbs in Kosovo." The SRSG said the United Nations would not be "bullied" into leaving Mitrovica. The next day, thousands of Serbs returned to the streets of Mitrovica to protest the imprisonment of their leader, but they dispersed without violence. As a precaution, UNMIK police were withdrawn from patrolling the northern parts of the city and were confined to their fortified compound.[83]

In any case, the fact that UNMIK police could not stop vehicles without fear of armed attack argued that something needed to be done by the United Nations to reclaim north Mitrovica and to make it a suitable environment for civilian police.[84] On July 2, 2002, an agreement was signed between UNMIK and French KFOR commander General Yves De Kerambon to ensure improved cooperation and coordination in Mitrovica. The agreement coincided with a major change in attitude on the part of French KFOR. The new MND-North commander arrived with apparent instructions from Paris to cooperate with UNMIK in extending the UN's writ beyond the Ibar. UNMIK officials were grateful for the change in the French attitude, which made real cooperation between the two parts of the international mission possible. In addition to improved cooperation between KFOR and UNMIK, the security situation in Mitrovica was enhanced as a result of renewed dialogue between UNMIK and Belgrade. On May 31, UNMIK, the Federal Republic of Yugoslavia, and the Republic of Serbia signed a protocol on police cooperation that provided for increased exchanges of information on terrorism and organized crime. This understanding was followed on July 9, with the signing of an agreement between the Serbian Justice Minister, Vladan Batic, and the chief of the UNMIK justice system, Jean Christian Cady, providing for the return of forty Serb judges and attorneys to work in Kosovo courts. This agreement was reached in the context of an understanding that Serbia would take steps to eliminate parallel security and judicial structures in Mitrovica and northern Kosovo. Pristina and Belgrade also agreed to encourage Serbs in northern Kosovo to apply for admission to the Kosovo Police Service School as a means of increasing the number of Serbs in the Kosovo Police Service.[85]

Finally, the UNMIK campaign to crack down on organized crime met with increasing public acceptance. On June 18, 2002, UNMIK police arrested six members of the KPC for alleged involvement in the killing of four ethnic Albanians from a rival faction immediately after the war. One of those taken into custody was Daut Haradinaj, a former commander of the KPC Third Zone and war hero. Haradinaj was arrested in Peja by a team from the Romanian SPU when he walked into a trap set by UN authorities. Following the arrests, demonstrations occurred in the towns of Decani and Djakovica, and two thousand protesters from the KLA heartland in western Kosovo marched to Pristina to demand their release. In the capital, local residents failed to join the protest, indicating growing support for UNMIK's effort to demonstrate that no one is above the law. On July 6, 2002, eleven members of the Kosovo Guard, an elite unit within the KPC, were arrested in connection with the postwar murder of Hamze Hajraj, a former Yugoslav police officer and suspected "collaborator" with Yugoslav authorities, and his family. The response from the KPC was muted in the face of public indifference to the operation. Commenting on the arrests, the UNMIK police spokesman stressed that action was taken against the individuals involved and not against their organization. SRSG Michael Steiner pledged that the campaign would continue and that those who had committed crimes would be brought to justice.[86]

On July 30, 2002, Steiner reported to the Security Council on the status of Kosovo. He said Kosovo had made progress, but there was much to be done before determining final status. "Our message," Steiner said, "is standards before status." Kosovo had yet to achieve the standards set by the international community, and its people were tired of lawlessness. Kosovo had not yet become "democratic, safe, and respectable" and clearly was not on the path to integration in Europe. Steiner insisted that UNMIK's policy was "zero tolerance for crime and corruption." The UNMIK and Kosovo police had cracked down on organized crime and illicit trafficking, confiscating cigarettes, gasoline, and alcohol. UNMIK was also intent on establishing its authority in Mitrovica and northern Kosovo. As for ethnic relations, Steiner noted that the number of minority returns now exceeded the outflow, but that the pace of returns was too slow. In response to Steiner's statement, the American representative, James Cunningham, said the United States applauded the increase in the number of Serb judges and prosecutors. He also said the Kosovo Police Service had "been a success far beyond what anyone had expected."[87]

THE FUTURE OF THE KOSOVO POLICE SERVICE

Coincident with the campaign against organized crime and the arrest of major offenders, UNMIK turned its attention to planning for the future of the Kosovo Police Service. By July 2002, there were more KPS officers than there were UNMIK police. Some 4,770 KPS officers had completed training and entered active service, compared to 4,524 "internationals" in UNMIK. KPS officers also made up between 65 and 75 percent of the police serving in four of five police regions and had taken over responsibility for most routine operations. The exception to this general takeover of routine duties by local officers was Mitrovica and northern Kosovo, where only a limited number of ethnic Serb KPS officers were deployed. With the change in the numerical balance between international and local police, UNMIK began implementing its plan for an orderly transition of responsibility for law enforcement to the KPS. A senior rank structure was introduced and the first 203 sergeants and 20 lieutenants were appointed. By the end of 2002, the UNMIK police would transfer full responsibility for patrol duties to the KPS, with UN police in a monitoring capacity. UNMIK also hoped to transfer responsibility for one of the five regional police headquarters at about the same time. Over the next two years, the KPS will increase in personnel strength to 6,300, while gradually assuming responsibility for more functions and the management of more regional centers. By 2006, the leadership, management, operation, and "the keys to the main police headquarters" would be in the hands of the KPS.[88]

As part of the planning for the transfer of responsibility to the KPS, UNMIK began working with the OSCE and the Kosovo Police Service School to develop a concept of operations and a training program for the creation of an indigenous police constabulary. UNMIK police officials envisioned training the first of three KPS Special Operations Units (SPOs) in 2002, with the second and third units coming on line in 2003 and 2004. Each unit would have 115 officers trained in civil disorder management, riot control, hostage negotiations, close protection, high-risk arrest techniques, use of police dogs, and other types of special police operations. Members of the new unit would be selected from the ranks of experienced officers in the KPS. They would receive eleven weeks of intensive instruction at the KPSS and training in highly specialized skills in other countries. The U.S. State Department had provided riot control gear for the first unit and the UN had set aside 1.3 million euros to purchase armored vehicles and other types of equipment. SPU officers would provide field training and supervision, but the new SPO units would not adopt the SPU model. Instead, the UNMIK police commissioner decided that their organization should reflect a composite of the best aspects of U.S. and European police practice and structures.[89]

UNMIK's unwillingness to replicate the model adopted by the United Nations in creating the SPU reflected the continued ambiguity concerning these units on the part of the senior

UNMIK police leadership. While the SPU special adviser's office was asked by the commissioner to submit a draft concept of operations covering the mission, organization, equipment, and logistics for the new KPS units, its recommendations were apparently factored in with submissions from the OSCE and other sources. The European gendarmes who composed the SPU special adviser's senior staff felt strongly that a constabulary force modeled on those of Kosovo's southern European neighbors was most appropriate. In the view of these officers, the traditions, politics, culture, and "passion" of the Kosovars required a "Latin solution" to what they believed would be a continual problem with mob violence.

This view was not shared by police officers from Northern Europe and north America who composed the leadership of the UNMIK police and the Kosovo Police Service School. In the view of these officers, the appropriate model for Kosovo was closer to the approach for special police operations used in many American cities and in northern Europe. Under this concept, members of special operations units are trained together to perform specialized functions, but they do not serve in separate units. Instead, they are assigned to regular police operations and come together only in an emergency or when their services are required. This approach maximizes the utility of individual officers, avoids the creation of underutilized "strategic reserves," and, for small police forces with limited resources, is most cost-effective.[90]

UNMIK's reluctance to embrace the UN's own model of constabulary forces also reflected a general uneasiness on the part of the UNMIK police leadership concerning the use of the SPUs in crowd control, high-risk arrests, and other sensitive situations. In part, this reflected a simple lack of familiarity with the SPU on the part of some headquarters staff and regional commanders. In many cases, the SPUs were considered a "strategic reserve" and left alone unless required to handle an emergency. Located in their separate compounds, SPU commanders were often not invited to routine staff meetings and were not always included in planning for operations. This situation fed a belief in some quarters that the SPUs spent their tours in comfortable camps, relaxing, eating well, and enjoying their recreation facilities. (It was said the Indians spent more time on the tennis court than on patrol.) This misperception was exacerbated by the UN's leave and rotation schedule, which often meant that acquaintances were barely made before officers were on their way to new assignments.[91]

More seriously, it reflected problems in the command and control relationship concerning the SPU. The SPU tripartite command structure meant that SPU commanders were responsible to the commissioner, the regional commander, and the SPU special adviser. These three frequently competing authorities often failed to communicate with one another before tasking unit commanders. This meant that the SPU could not always respond or would have to delay while requesting clarification of priorities. SPU commanders were frustrated by instructions from the commissioner or regional commanders that failed to recognize the complex nature of their organizations. Instructions to "make ten men available on a certain date" begged the question of what type of personnel, weapons, equipment, and vehicles for what mission?[92]

There was also the unresolved question of who was in charge once the SPUs were called out and ordered to conduct a specific operation. SPU commanders strongly believed that they should be told what to do, but that, as professionals, they should decide how to do it. Senior SPU officers felt they were best qualified to command their men once an operation started. This troubled the UNMIK police leadership, which was unwilling to simply turn things over to generally more junior SPU officers and hope for the best. As during the early days of the MSU in Bosnia, the problem resulted from a lack of agreed-upon doctrine for the use of SPUs in peace operations. The SPU special adviser's office was the first to recognize the impact of the absence of common understandings and agreed-upon operating procedures on SPU operations. In the spring of 2002, it began drafting a common doctrine regarding command and control functions and the techniques employed in crowd control and other missions. Included in this task was the compilation of a glossary of frequently used terms, because the absence of common meanings even for such words as "group" and "team" resulted in confusion.[93]

Two years after the arrival of the first SPU in Kosovo, the ten Special Police Units were, at best, underutilized and, at worst, misunderstood or ignored. This was not completely surprising, given the fact that their core mission was envisioned as crowd control in a generally lawless environment. Had the SPU been present at the start of the Kosovo mission, circumstances would have ensured their use to control ethnic violence. By the summer of 2002, the situation had changed dramatically. According to the UN secretary-general's report to the Security Council, the number of cases of murder, kidnapping, arson, and looting continued to decline, while most crime appeared to be economically motivated. With the exception of the protests over the arrests of former KLA leaders, demonstrations concerned economic issues, such as teachers' salaries, and were peaceful. Incidents of ethnically motivated assaults and intimidation decreased to the point where they were no longer systematic.[94]

The United States also seemed to have lost interest in whether the SPUs were used effectively. At the onset of the mission, President Clinton and Secretary of State Albright personally lobbied Spain's King Juan Carlos and other leaders to donate constabulary units for service in Kosovo. When the number of SPU personnel climbed above nine hundred and conditions quieted, the U.S. moved on to other priorities.[95] One exception to the general trend toward greater ethnic harmony was a series of explosions that damaged Serb houses in the ethnically mixed village of Klokot in MNB-East. The explosions injured two U.S. soldiers on the day after American troops were told they could stop wearing flak jackets and helmets because security conditions had improved.[96] As UNMIK entered its third year, it seemed fair to ask whether Kosovo required the services of ten Special Police Units, particularly since plans were underway to train three additional units of local police. The answer to that question hopefully would be decided in the context of considerations related to the overall international force structure and the need to shift responsibilities for public security from KFOR to civilian authorities.

7

POLICEKEEPING

+ + + + + + + + + + + +

U.S. Policy

+ + + + + + + +

on Peace Operations

+ + + + + + + + + + + + +

N 1997, THE CLINTON ADMINISTRATION BEGAN what stretched
into a three-year interagency effort to analyze and learn from
the experiences of the peace operations in Bosnia and
Kosovo. The interagency review began with a request from the
National Security Council (NSC) staff to the Office of the
Secretary of Defense to prepare the first draft of a Presidential
Decision Directive on international police and judicial assistance
in countries emerging from ethnic conflict. Images of American
soldiers standing aside while Serb thugs burned buildings and
wreaked havoc during the transfer of the Sarajevo suburbs had
endured. There was also continued unhappiness in Washington
with the performance of the IPTF. This concern was amplified
when deploying the MSU failed to have a noticeable impact.
After NATO forces entered Pristina in July 1999, the drafting
process was updated to reflect the difficulties encountered by
the United Nations in recruiting the UNMIK police and in dealing with ethnic violence and explosive street crime in Kosovo.

The goal of the interagency process was to find ways in
which the United States could improve its capacity and that of
the United Nations to rapidly deploy effective civilian police
forces and rebuild criminal justice systems during peace operations. Normally, the assignment to prepare such a presidential
directive would have gone to either the Department of State or

the Department of Justice. The NSC staff understood, however, that the primary problem was the unwillingness of the Defense Department and the Joint Chiefs of Staff to allow U.S. military forces to perform police functions. Absent a willingness to allow U.S. military forces to handle lawlessness and civil disorder during future peace operations, it was clear that little would be gained from going any further. Thus, the assignment went to the Office of Peacekeeping and Humanitarian Affairs in the Office of the Secretary of Defense at the Pentagon.

Within both the Office of the Secretary of Defense and the U.S. military there was a general distaste for participating in peace operations and for performing police functions. U.S. military leaders believed their job was to "fight and win the nation's wars." Participation in peace operations dulled combat skills, expended resources, exhausted troops and equipment, and reduced readiness. In addition, soldiers were neither trained nor equipped to deal with civilians and to handle tasks related to fighting crime and maintaining public order. This predilection to avoid "nation building" was reinforced by the traumatic experience of Somalia. At the Pentagon, the majority view was that discussions on this topic were to be avoided. Once opened, this "can of worms" would be impossible to close, and the military would be stuck performing functions that were outside of and detrimental to its primary mission. Representatives of this group were quick to point out a myriad of problems and uncertainties involving legal authority, funding, administrative restrictions, and interagency differences as reasons why the U.S. military should avoid peacekeeping and could not perform police functions.

A minority, however, believed that future peacekeeping missions were inevitable. If U.S. troops were going to participate, DOD had a responsibility to develop policy and doctrine and to think through contingencies before American soldiers encountered them in the field. For the drafters of the presidential directive, this minority view provided the opening they required. The drafters believed the problems raised by the opponents of peacekeeping were simply excuses that could be overcome. If U.S. troops were going to be handed this responsibility, they argued, the Pentagon had a duty to provide clear guidance and the authority to perform what were described in the directive as "constabulary" functions. For a year, the drafters worked with both military and civilian defense officials to find acceptable language and to clear their draft through the Pentagon's bureaucracy. The process became one of adding caveats and exceptions in exchange for approvals at various levels. Ultimately, the draft, which was only half of the final document, was approved by the secretary of defense.[1]

The next year was spent sorting out differences between other relevant agencies. Issues arose between the Departments of State and Justice over roles, missions, and the future of ICITAP. There were also differences between Justice and the Agency for International Development (AID) over rule of law, judicial, and funding issues. Resolving these interagency differences required major additions to the text until the document grew to twice its original length. In all cases, the DOD drafters had to protect the understandings that had been reached within the Defense Department and get agreement from other agencies not to try for additional concessions from DOD and the military. Finally, with all agencies in accord, the draft presidential decision directive was sent to the White House. There it languished throughout 1999 while the NSC staff focused its attention on the actual emergency that was occurring in Kosovo.[2]

PRESIDENTIAL DECISION DIRECTIVE 71

On February 24, 2000, Presidential Decision Directive 71 (PDD-71) on "Strengthening Criminal Justice Systems in Support of Peace Operations" was unveiled.[3] The rollout did not occur at the White House, but at the Department of State. Senior State Department officials who were deeply concerned about the UN's inability to stem the violence in Kosovo discovered that the draft PDD had been sitting in various in-boxes at the NSC for a year, and they issued a virtual ultimatum to the NSC staff to get the directive signed by the president because it was going to be announced by the secretary of state.

At the State Department's regular noon press briefing, Secretary of State Madeleine Albright told reporters the president's directive was aimed at improving interagency coordination of U.S. efforts to maintain order and establish effective judicial systems in societies emerging from conflict. Albright said the directive was also aimed at enhancing the ability of other countries, the United Nations, and regional organizations to plan, mount, and sustain operations in support of the rule of law. "The slowness in deploying desperately needed civilian police to Kosovo," the secretary noted, "provided only the latest evidence that present international capabilities are not adequate." The directive, Albright said, instructed the State Department to create "a lead office" that would be responsible for developing policies, setting priorities, and coordinating U.S. agencies' efforts to improve U.S. participation in the criminal justice components of peace operations. Giving the State Department a leadership role, the secretary said, recognized the importance to U.S. foreign policy of preventing a security vacuum from arising in postconflict situations. PDD-71 would improve U.S. ability to provide civilian police for current peace operations. It would also enhance U.S. ability to train indigenous police. Albright said she would work with the attorney general to prepare a plan for improving the effectiveness of U.S. training programs for the local police during peace operations.[4]

On the issue of constabulary forces, Secretary Albright said, "Old models of peacekeeping did not meet current challenges." Modern peace operations required skills that were neither strictly military nor police, but a combination of both. From her days as U.S. ambassador to the United Nations when she had visited peace operations, Secretary Albright said she felt a "piece was missing somewhere between those who go in full armor and those who are just cops on the beat." The international community needed to create units that could control crowds, deter vigilantes, prevent looting, and disarm civilian agitators, while winning the trust of local communities. The problem, the secretary noted, was that constabulary forces were in short supply and that there were not enough trained units to perform these functions. Albright said the shortage of such personnel was discussed the previous day in her meeting with King Juan Carlos, when she asked whether the Spanish Guardia Civil could help close the security gap in Kosovo.[5]

While the presidential directive extensively addressed the role of civilian police and other issues related to the criminal justice system, it also elaborated the understandings reached within the Defense Department on the need for U.S. military forces to perform police functions during peace operations. These understandings had been reached during the initial stage of the drafting process nearly two years earlier and were reflected in the inclusion of U.S. military police in the American KFOR contingent in Kosovo. According to the directive, in cases where indigenous police were unable to provide adequate public safety, "outsiders" (read "U.S. military forces") could undertake a "narrow range of activities" to "maintain a reasonable measure of public safety." Such actions would include regulating movements, stopping civil violence, and deterring or stopping widespread looting, vandalism, riots, and other types of civil disturbance.

For the purposes of the directive, such tasks were categorized as "constabulary" functions which "the United States shall prefer be conducted by paramilitary forces that exist in other countries." The directive acknowledged, however, that suitable international partners might not be available or that there may be delays in coalition forces becoming operational. In such cases, the U.S. military, "if necessary, shall carry out constabulary functions." The directive contained the caution, however, that having the capacity to conduct constabulary functions would in no way obligate the U.S. military to conduct such activities in any particular mission, nor to develop specialized constabulary units dedicated to that mission. The directive also noted that "outsiders" should normally not engage in law enforcement, nor should they replace local police, who should have ultimate responsibility.[6]

In addition to the agreement to perform constabulary functions, the directive also provided a list of areas in which the U.S. military agreed it would cooperate and coordinate its activities with international civilian police forces. The directive stated that military peacekeepers and CIVPOL should coordinate activities to ensure maximum support of the overall objectives of the operation. Among the potential areas for cooperation between international military and police units were—

+ Conducting joint or parallel patrols including military peacekeepers, CIVPOL, and indigenous police.

+ Providing military communications, logistics, and intelligence support to CIVPOL commanders.

+ Offering technical assistance from military civil affairs and military police officers with expertise in local government, psychological operations, and intelligence.

While this willingness to cooperate was subject to extensive caveats, including that any assistance be provided on a reimbursable basis, the willingness of DOD and the Joint Chiefs of Staff to consider performing such functions and extending such assistance to international civilian police marked an important breakthrough.[7]

On the civilian side, PDD-71 recognized the State Department as the lead agency for implementing the directive. It instructed State to enhance U.S. capability to provide civilian police and improve the capabilities of the United Nations and other countries to support CIVPOL missions. The directive spelled out a number of other steps to be taken, including (1) increasing the speed with which the United States is able to recruit, train, and deploy American civilian police abroad; (2) improving the discipline and accountability of U.S. police personnel; and (3) requesting the required legislative authority and $10 million in new funding from Congress. The U.S. Secret Service and the U.S. Park Police were designated to provide the State Department with law enforcement expertise, as required.[8]

To improve the capacity of international organizations and donor countries, the State Department was instructed to seek the cooperation of like-minded states and international organizations in a concerted effort to improve the capacity of the United Nations to conduct police operations. This was to be done by increasing the number and quality of staff in the CIVPOL unit, improving the capacity of DPKO to plan police operations, and enhancing the UN's standby arrangements to make them an effective means of rapidly recruiting CIVPOL forces. State was also instructed to find the means to enhance the preparedness of foreign civilian police to enable them to more effectively participate in future CIVPOL missions. In this regard, the United States was to develop, in concert with other countries, job descriptions and standard operating procedures for CIVPOL missions and training programs to introduce these new measures to foreign police forces. In cooperation with the U.S. Department of Justice, the directive instructed State to improve U.S. capacity to train indigenous police in peace operations so that local police forces could more readily assume responsibility for ensuring internal security. This would shorten the duration of peace operations and enable foreign military and police forces to withdraw.[9]

Work on implementing PDD-71 began slowly. During the summer of 2000, the State Department created three interagency working groups to address the following subjects: (1) U.S. and foreign CIVPOL; (2) indigenous police development; and (3) rule of law, courts, and prisons. In State's view, the directive identified the immediate need for the United States to provide better-qualified civilian police through an improved selection process with better pre-mission training and preparation. The department's immediate goals were to—

+ Establish an advisory group of police professionals and a "ready roster" of two thousand American police officers who would be available for participation in future CIVPOL missions.

+ Continue the practice of using contractors and of relying on a commercial firm to recruit, train, and provide logistical support for U.S. CIVPOL officers. The State Department would, however, improve its oversight of officer selection and performance.

✦ Improve interagency coordination between State, Justice, and AID on CIVPOL and criminal justice programs.

✦ Expand cooperation with Latin America on CIVPOL training.

✦ Seek an initial budget of $10 million from Congress for FY 2001, as instructed by the directive.[10]

In adopting this approach, the State Department made a conscious decision not to seek new legislative authority or to try to federalize American police who were recruited for international civilian police missions. Instead, State continued to recruit, train, and provide administrative support for American CIVPOL through a commercial contractor. By outsourcing, the State Department was able to manage a large field program with a minimum number of departmental staff. State was able to avoid dealing directly with the chaos of the decentralized U.S. policing system, with its eighteen thousand law enforcement organizations; nearly seven hundred thousand police officers; and a myriad of federal, state, and local laws and regulations, authorities, standards, pay and benefit scales, and so forth. It also allowed State to skirt potential liability issues that might arise from attempting to temporarily assign state and local police officers to national service.[11]

Unfortunately, efforts to implement PDD-71 coincided with the intensely contested 2000 presidential election, the recount and legal challenges that followed, and the chaotic final months of the Clinton administration. The NSC's decision to assign the leadership role for implementing the directive to a single agency, the Department of State, proved ill advised. Without White House oversight and close supervision by the National Security Council staff, inevitable differences arose between agencies with conflicting organizational cultures and institutional priorities. Efforts to draft a plan for implementing the directive became snarled in a dispute between State and the Department of Justice over jurisdictional and bureaucratic issues. These interagency differences delayed the required reports to the president on implementation and impeded State's ability to provide leadership. With the NSC preoccupied with Kosovo and East Timor and the country distracted by ballot counting in Florida, it was an open question whether any single department could have effectively managed the multiagency effort required. At the time President Clinton left office, the State Department's efforts to implement PDD-71 had made little progress.[12]

THE BRAHIMI REPORT

For its part, the United Nations also took a serious look at the manner in which it conducted peace operations. On March 7, 2000, UN secretary-general Kofi Annan convened a high-level panel on United Nations peace operations to review UN peace and security activities and make recommendations for improving the future conduct of such operations. Former Algerian foreign minister Lakhdar Brahimi chaired the panel, whose report was submitted to the Security Council and the General Assembly on August 21, 2000. In requesting the report, Annan was motivated by earlier UN reports that documented the failure of UN peacekeeping forces to prevent the massacre of Muslims in Srebrenica, Bosnia, and the genocide in Rwanda. The report was given added urgency by the initial failure of the UN peacekeeping mission in Sierra Leone, where UN troops were taken hostage. During the year preceding the report, the number of UN troops, observers, and civilian police in peace operations had increased from thirteen thousand to thirty-five thousand in fourteen operations. The panel noted, however, that despite the increase there were still only thirty-two military officers and nine police officers in DPKO responsible for twenty-seven thousand soldiers and nearly nine thousand police in the field. The release of the Brahimi Report was timed to make it available for consideration by world leaders attending the Millennium Summit held at UN headquarters on September 6–8, 2000. The report was approved in principle and all relevant UN bodies were requested to give it every consideration.[13]

In regard to the UN civilian police program, the Brahimi Report recommended a "doctrinal shift" in the use of civilian police in peacekeeping missions. The panel noted that in recent missions, CIVPOL had been required to do more than simply set a good example and report on any unacceptable behavior by the local police. Instead, they were required to reform, train, and restructure local police according to international standards. They were also required to effectively handle civil disorder and to assure their own security. The panel noted the need for strengthening the rule of law and respect for human rights in postconflict environments. It advocated that CIVPOL work closely with judicial and human rights experts. The panel recommended that beyond setting a good example for local police, CIVPOL officers needed to be actively involved in the policing activities of the mission. To achieve this goal, they needed to be clearly informed on which laws to enforce and the appropriate actions to take when confronted with civilian unrest and human rights violations. The report pointed out that it was useless to give CIVPOL officers authority without providing the other elements of a functioning criminal justice system—courts and prisons—with which to operate.[14]

In terms of structural reforms, the panel recommended reorganizing DPKO to (1) remove the CIVPOL unit from the military chain of command and elevate it to division status, (2) upgrade the senior police adviser to the same rank as the military adviser, and (3) increase the CIVPOL Division staff from nine to twenty-three police officers. To improve CIVPOL deployment, the panel recommended creating an on-call rapid response unit composed of one hundred pretrained police executives and related experts that could conduct assessments, establish an in-country headquarters, and do the strategic planning for a new police mission. The panel also recommended establishing a new unit within DPKO staffed with judicial, penal, and human rights specialists to advise CIVPOL on criminal justice issues and to compose rule-of-law teams for deployment in future UN missions.[15]

THE BUSH ADMINISTRATION

Even before President Bush took office, spokespersons for the incoming administration were critical of what they characterized as the Clinton administration's overreliance on the military and its willingness to commit U.S. forces to peace operations in areas where the United States had no strategic national interests. Conservative critics attacked President Clinton for using "democratic enlargement" to justify eight years of global activism, Cold War–era defense spending, and an interventionist foreign policy. The conservatives' criticism focused extensively on the Clinton administration's experiments with nation building in Haiti, Bosnia, and Kosovo. Nation building was described as an intrusive form of foreign intervention in chaotic states that attempted to replace local institutions with those preferred by the intervening powers. Under the banner of multilateralism, nation building was seen simply as an attempt at "social engineering" and "global do-goodism" masquerading as foreign and national security policy.[16]

During the campaign, candidate George W. Bush spoke forcefully against continued U.S. involvement in nation building. In early January 2000, Bush told an event sponsored by ABC News that the president must clearly delineate those areas of the world that are relevant to U.S. national interests. U.S. troops, Bush said, should not be sent to areas that are irrelevant to America's national strategic interests, even to stop ethnic cleansing or prevent genocide.[17] A month later, Bush told a campaign rally in Kansas City that "I'm going to clearly say to our friends, if there's a conflict in your area, America will be the peacemaker; you can put the troops on the ground to be the peacekeepers."[18] During the second nationally televised presidential debate on October 11, 2000 in Winston-Salem, North Carolina, Bush criticized the Clinton administration's involvement in nation building in Somalia, Haiti, and Bosnia. The Republican nominee said, "I do not think our troops ought to be used for what is called nation building. . . . I hope our European friends become peacekeepers in the Balkans. I hope they put their troops on the ground so we can withdraw our troops and focus our military on fighting and winning wars."[19]

In fact, the Bush administration took office at a time when the United States faced a broad range of new and unconventional challenges. In the first decade of the new millennium, the United States was confronted by international threats posed by globalization, failed states, humanitarian and environmental crises, organized crime, terrorist organizations, and the proliferation of weapons of mass destruction. To those assuming office, it appeared the U.S. needed to take better advantage of its considerable diplomatic, economic, and political resources to develop new ways of managing international conflicts. During the campaign, Bush stressed the need for the U.S. to demonstrate humility in its dealings with other countries and the need to build effective coalitions to deal with threats to international security. In asserting that "the U.S. could not be the world's 911," Bush implicitly pointed away from reliance on military forces and toward the need to better utilize America's civilian capacities and its membership in international and regional organizations.[20]

Following the election, National Security Adviser–designate Condoleezza Rice told a conference sponsored by the U.S. Army that "it might be necessary to set up international police forces to perform peacekeeping roles that are now the responsibility of soldiers." Rice said the new administration needed to "think hard" about developing forces to perform police functions, because combat forces performing police duties was not the best answer. In a speech to a largely military audience, Rice tried to offer reassurances that the new administration would not precipitously withdraw U.S. troops from the Balkans. She also sought to identify the Bush administration's perceived need to look at the potential for using armed international police forces instead of military troops in peace operations. Following the speech, Rice told a reporter she was not trying to propose a solution, but only attempting to identify a gap in current capabilities. She also acknowledged the difficulties of substituting police for soldiers in peace operations by saying that those who have tried it in the Balkans "are having a hard time."[21]

The incoming administration's interest in finding alternatives to using U.S. troops for peacekeeping assignments was also evident in remarks made by General Colin Powell at a press conference in Crawford, Texas, called by President-elect Bush to announce Powell's selection as secretary of state. In response to a question concerning U.S. military deployments in the Balkans, Powell said,

> We are going to make on-the-ground assessments of what we are doing now, what is needed now, but also, what is really going to be needed in the future and see if we can find ways that are less of a burden on our armed forces, not as a way of running out, but as a way of substituting others or substituting other kinds of organizations and units and perhaps police organizations to handle the remaining missions.[22]

During the administration's first months in office, Washington agencies began an internal debate over the propriety of U.S. involvement in what were called "complex contingency operations," "stability and support operations," or "multidimensional peace operations." While agency positions were still being formulated, it appeared that those who believed U.S. traditional national interests were unlikely to motivate American involvement in peace operations had a valid point. U.S. military forces primarily existed to defend against threats to the territorial integrity and vital supply lines of the U.S. and its traditional allies. As the world's sole superpower, it seemed unlikely the United States would face the need to defend its homeland or those of its allies from a direct attack. To many, it appeared the U.S. could afford a definition of its national interests that stopped at the water's edge and at the frontier posts of those America was sworn by treaty to defend. It also seemed safer and intellectually more comfortable to retain the U.S. military's Cold War mission of preparing to fight two major theater wars and to leave responsibility for peacekeeping to others.

At the same time, it also seemed clear that traditional American values would not permit the United States to stand idle in the face of genocide, famine, or other large-scale humanitarian crises. A survey of the most senior U.S. military officers found surprising support for participation in peace operations. While acknowledging that peacekeeping was difficult and expensive, those interviewed believed U.S. participation was essential for promoting regional stability, strengthening alliances, demonstrating U.S. leadership, promoting economic development, and improving military efficiency and morale. Those military leaders who advocated participation in peace-keeping were quick to caution that this did not mean the U.S. would become the world's policeman, nor that it should take on every fight. The United States did stand alone, however, in its ability to provide global leadership, which was essential to maintaining international stability.[23]

In public, Powell echoed Rice's earlier comments concerning the administration's interest in replacing U.S. troops in the Balkans with police—specifically, constabulary forces provided by the European allies. In April 2001, Powell visited Europe at a time when ethnic Albanian insurgents were conducting a violent campaign against Macedonian security forces and nationalist Croats were threatening the stability of Bosnia. During a meeting of NATO foreign ministers in Paris, Powell said the Bush administration would not withdraw unilaterally from the Balkans but was considering ways to reduce U.S. deployments, "possibly by replacing soldiers with police officers." The United States, Powell said, was "looking for opportunities to draw down, but not for opportunities to bail out."[24]

At a subsequent NATO foreign ministers meeting on May 29, 2001 in Budapest, Secretary Powell and his counterparts ruled out an immediate reduction of SFOR in light of the fighting in Macedonia and violent clashes between SFOR and Serb and Croat nationalists in Bosnia. The ministers did, however, agree that moderate reductions might be possible if conditions warranted. At the meeting, Powell reiterated his earlier promise that the U.S. would withdraw from the Balkans only when its European allies were able to do so as well. As the nature of NATO's mission was evolving, Powell said what was needed was more manpower for NATO's constabulary units in the Balkans.[25] In a statement to the press following the meeting, Powell said,

> I did encourage my colleagues this morning to be more aggressive in shifting the burden to those kinds of units that are better able to deal with the emerging environment.

For example, NATO has committed nineteen MSU's, . . .
consisting of gendarmerie and Carabinieri, and only eleven
of those are now in place. . . . So, let's get the other nine
[sic] in place because the mission is shifting, it's more of
crowd-control and protection of civilians and other kinds
of missions that could be handled by noncombat troops.
And so we're putting pressure on our colleagues to provide
more of these kinds of units, but it's all within the context
of good dialogue.[26]

Differences between the United States and its European
NATO allies over the importance of involvement in peace opera-
tions and the maintenance of NATO forces in the Balkans were
not the only problems troubling the Atlantic Alliance. A series of
U.S. foreign policy decisions alarmed European leaders that the
Bush administration was intent on abandoning multilateral
engagement in favor of pursuing U.S. interests unilaterally.
Beginning with the administration's blunt rejection of the Kyoto
Protocol on global warming on the eve of German chancellor
Gerhard Schroeder's visit to Washington, U.S. actions created the
impression that Washington was no longer concerned about
European sensibilities.[27] The subsequent U.S. decision to scrap the
1972 Antiballistic Missile Treaty with the Soviet Union and to
begin work on constructing an antiballistic missile defense reinforced this impression. Europeans saw the treaty as the cornerstone of the strategic nuclear balance. Its removal without an
equivalent or better method for assuring strategic stability was
deeply unsettling.[28] There was also concern about U.S. reluctance
to engage on regional issues such as the Middle East, Macedonia,
and Northern Ireland, despite escalating violence. The growing
list of disagreements raised fears that this was more than the typical European nightmare that occurs before every new American
administration ultimately awakens to global realities.[29]

THE WAR ON TERRORISM

The growing U.S. estrangement with Europe was abruptly halted
by the traumatic events of September 11, 2001. On a brilliant

fall morning, nineteen Islamic terrorists hijacked four commercial airliners in flight. The hijackers crashed two of the aircraft into the World Trade Center towers in New York City, destroying both buildings and killing nearly three thousand occupants and emergency personnel. After circling over the White House and the Capitol Building in Washington, D.C., the third aircraft destroyed a major portion of the Pentagon, claiming another three hundred victims. The fourth aircraft crashed into an open field in Pennsylvania during a struggle between the hijackers and the passengers. The hijackers were followers of Osama bin Laden and members of his al Qaeda organization, which had its headquarters in Afghanistan and operated under the protection of the leaders of the country's extremist Islamic regime, the Taliban.

In response, President Bush, with the full and formal support of Congress, declared a War on Terrorism. U.S. diplomats quickly forged an international coalition, dividing the world between those that supported freedom and those that supported evil.[30] U.S. forces deployed to countries surrounding Afghanistan, as flotillas of U.S. warships collected offshore. In Afghanistan, U.S. Special Forces and operatives of the Central Intelligence Agency made common cause with leaders of the Northern Alliance, a loose confederation of ethnic groups opposed to the Taliban. They also formed alliances with and provided aid to disgruntled ethnic Pashtuns who rallied in opposition to the Taliban in the south. In a lightning-fast military campaign that featured precision U.S. bombing and missile strikes on Taliban forces and ground assaults by Afghan fighters, the Taliban was routed. In its place, an interim government, created under UN auspices at a conference of Afghan parties in Bonn, Germany, took power in Kabul. The new government was supported by the five thousand peacekeepers of the International Security Assistance Force and by U.S. military forces that continued, with the support of local Afghan warlords, to pursue remnants of the Taliban and al Qaeda. On October 11, President Bush stated in a nationally televised press conference that the United States would remain to help stabilize post-Taliban Afghanistan once the military mission had been completed. The president's statement appeared to some to mark a departure from the negative position he had taken on nation building during the campaign.[31]

Within hours after the September 11 attacks, NATO, in an unprecedented action, formally invoked Article 5 of the Alliance Charter, triggering collective defense arrangements that resulted in NATO Airborne Warning and Control System aircraft patrolling the coast of the United States. The opportunity to join with the United States in a broad-based coalition against terrorism produced a reshuffling of alliances and a rush by a disparate group of nations to join with Washington to oppose Islamic extremists and international terrorism. Former Cold War opponents Russia and China, former Middle East adversaries Syria and Iran, and even "lost causes" like Sudan sought to join forces and offered assistance in tracking down al Qaeda operatives. There was a rethinking of traditional alliances and a re-evaluation of U.S. involvement in areas that previously were seen as irrelevant to U.S. national interests. Now, these relationships and geographic areas related directly to the two primary objectives of U.S. policy, pursuit of the war against terrorism and homeland defense. This restructuring of the world order and rethinking of the U.S. role had broad ramifications, including the course of the debate over whether the United States should engage in postconflict nation building and, specifically, whether U.S. forces should remain in Bosnia and Kosovo.

The president's statement about the need for the United States to remain engaged in postconflict Afghanistan immediately rekindled the argument over whether peacekeeping was relevant to U.S. strategic interests. In dueling op-ed pieces in the pages of the *Washington Post,* advocates from the "Democratic Left" took on opponents from the "Republican Right." Those in favor of U.S. participation in peacekeeping and postconflict reconstruction argued that claims by the Bush administration that peace operations in Bosnia and Kosovo had failed were simply not true. They pointed out that under the Dayton Accords, Bosnia had enjoyed six years of peace without a single

American or allied death from hostile action. Totaling the results of peacekeeping in the Balkans—two wars ended, most of the NATO force withdrawn, and progress toward peace in sight—these writers said the U.S. should hope for a similar "failure" in Afghanistan. Advocates were critical of the Bush administration's reluctance to engage in postconflict reconstruction in Afghanistan. Administration critics stated bluntly that President Bush would win the military engagement in Afghanistan but would lose the peace because he was unwilling to commit American peacekeepers and engage in nation building. If Afghanistan was worth Americans waging war, it was also in America's national interest to stabilize and rebuild the country. U.S. offers to train a new Afghan army and provide economic incentives were disingenuous if the United States refused to participate in the international peacekeeping force and engage in reconstruction. In the view of these writers, providing security and rebuilding Afghanistan were necessary not only for humanitarian reasons, but also as an integral part of the War on Terrorism.[32]

Conservatives who were opposed to U.S. involvement in peacekeeping and nation building shot back—

> The world's sole superpower has no business squandering its resources and diluting its military doing police work and hand-holding in places like Bosnia and Kosovo. . . . Reconstructing countries in our own image is a huge, decades-long undertaking. Half a century later, we still have troops in Germany and Japan. It is precisely because the task is so formidable that we do it only when the stakes are high and the countries in question are crucial to the security of the United States. Germany and Japan count, Bosnia and Kosovo—the archipelago of Clintonian do-goodism—don't. The American military is the world's premier fighting force and ought to husband its resources. There are dozens of countries that are never going to fight a real war, but whose armed forces are perfectly suited for peacekeeping. We fight the wars. Our friends should patrol the peace.[33]

The conservative critique of peacekeeping was grounded in an analysis of the relative strengths of U.S. and European armed forces and the belief that a natural division of labor could be achieved in dealing with postconflict environments. For conservatives, the test case for this analysis was Bosnia and Kosovo. Conservatives saw the Balkans as an area that was outside the national strategic interests of the United States but not outside those of its NATO allies. For Europe, the Balkans was an area of at least secondary, if not primary, strategic importance. As the United States was engaged in a war against global terrorism, American troops and resources in the Balkans were needed elsewhere. The U.S. should not just walk out, but should signal that it intended to leave and then begin a dialogue with the Europeans on filling in behind. While European military forces might not have the airlift, high-tech weapons, or specialized combat forces to help in Afghanistan or future war zones, their armed forces were more than adequate for peace operations. Moreover, in the critical area of constabulary forces, they enjoyed a comparative advantage. Constabulary forces were ideally suited to dealing with current conditions in Bosnia and Kosovo, where a re-evaluation of the international military force structure was overdue. In the conservative view, by providing constabulary forces to replace departing U.S. forces, the Europeans could demonstrate their value and silence any doubts about the utility of the NATO alliance to the United States. From the conservative perspective, European provision of constabulary forces in the Balkans worked on three levels: operationally, geopolitically, and from the perspective of unity and burden sharing within the alliance.[34]

The conservatives' advocacy of a division of labor between the United States and Europe was reflected in questions raised by U.S. officials about whether the Europeans would fulfill their obligations under the Defense Capabilities Initiative (DCI), which was endorsed at the Washington NATO Summit in 1999. The DCI was developed to close the widening technology gap between American and European militaries that led to problems in alliance interoperability and burden sharing. The gap became evident during NATO operations in Kosovo and loomed even larger in Afghanistan. Joint military operations in Kosovo and Afghanistan exposed shortfalls among Europe's underfunded militaries in such critical areas as strategic lift, secure communications, precision-guided munitions, missile defenses, and Special Forces. In Kosovo, lack of interoperability in communications made it difficult for Americans and Europeans to coordinate operations. In Afghanistan, Germany had to rent transports from Ukraine to airlift a small number of troops to the fighting. Following the defeat of the Taliban, the gap threatened to widen as the United States increased its defense budget to pursue the War on Terrorism, while European defense budgets continued to decline. Absent a major increase in European defense spending, NATO was in fact in jeopardy of becoming a two-tiered alliance, in which the U.S. fought the wars and the Europeans were limited to low-intensity conflict and peacekeeping.[35]

While the conservatives' argument in favor of the Europeans' taking on responsibility for peacekeeping was relevant to Kosovo, it was applied explicitly to Bosnia. In a meeting of defense ministers at NATO headquarters in Brussels on December 18, 2001, U.S. secretary of defense Donald Rumsfeld formally proposed reducing NATO peacekeeping forces in Bosnia by one-third over the coming year. Rumsfeld told his European counterparts that the Bosnian mission was straining the capacity of the United States and NATO at a time when the alliance "faced growing demands from critical missions in the War on Terrorism." Noting that SFOR had kept the peace in Bosnia since the signing of the Dayton Accords in 1995, Rumsfeld said "NATO publics" had a right to expect that peacekeeping commitments would not be open-ended. He called for reducing the eighteen thousand NATO troops in Bosnia by six thousand, with a one thousand–troop reduction of U.S. forces to twenty-one hundred. He called for NATO military authorities to develop options so that the next meeting of defense ministers could decide on a smaller and restructured force that was capable of taking on new tasks. One option Rumsfeld offered was for the European Union to provide an armed police force that could relieve SFOR of its responsibilities for civilian policing. He suggested this could be part of the EU effort to create a crisis management capability including a European rapid reaction military force by 2003. Press reports of the secretary's remarks

noted that the EU rapid reaction force was to include a five thousand–member police unit, including a significant component of
European gendarmes.[36]

In a communiqué issued at the close of the meeting, the
defense ministers reaffirmed NATO's commitment to "security,
stability, peace, and democracy" in the Balkans and to supporting
the work of international organizations in civilian implementation in Bosnia. The ministers instructed NATO military planners
to produce a "force-transition concept" that would preserve the
peace but result in a smaller force presence. They recognized "the
need to improve the capability, confidence, training, and equipment of the local police in Bosnia to deal with civil disorder and
the continuing need for close coordination between the local
police, IPTF, and SFOR." The communiqué concluded that it was
particularly important to accelerate the development of the local
police so that they could assume responsibility for public security
and the rule of law. The ministers noted that the IPTF mandate
expired in 2002 and "welcomed efforts to identify a follow-on
capability as a matter of urgency."[37]

During preparations for the defense ministerial, Secretary
Rumsfeld had made clear to his staff that he wanted to accelerate the drawdown of U.S. and NATO forces in the Balkans. He
believed this was necessary to meet the demands of the War on
Terrorism and because peacekeeping functions in the region
should be shifted to civilians. This issue was also topical because
the meeting coincided with EU efforts to organize the police
component of the European rapid reaction force and initial consideration of which European organization should provide the
follow-on police force for Bosnia. U.S. defense planners were
looking for ways that NATO could expand security cooperation with the EU, and they saw the creation of an armed
European civilian police constabulary in Bosnia as a way that
the EU could assume a mission currently performed by SFOR.
In their view, the MSU eventually could be incorporated into the
European constabulary, since its major contributor, Italy, was an
EU member. For their part, U.S. military commanders in Bosnia
had made their support for the secretary's position conditional

on assurances that a new police mission would improve police capacity in Bosnia and avoid the potential for "mission creep."[38]

In formulating its position in favor of the EU, the Defense Department encountered resistance from the State Department, which wanted the OSCE to provide the follow-on police force because of its previous success in replacing the UN police mission in Croatia. The issue of which European regional organization would receive U.S. support was decided at a meeting of the Deputies Committee, the most senior subcabinet level in the interagency process. Appropriate talking points were included in Secretary Rumsfeld's presentation to the plenary session and for use in bilateral meetings with his counterparts. Rumsfeld encouraged the defense ministers from EU member states to assume responsibility for providing the follow-on police force for Bosnia, which would include an armed constabulary unit that would handle crowd control and crack down on organized crime. Reaction to the secretary's proposal was positive in the sense that the Europeans were pleased by U.S. support for an EU police mission in Bosnia. Reaction was mixed, however, to the proposal for the armed constabulary unit. After consultations, the EU ministers reached consensus on supporting the police mission but opposing the inclusion of an armed unit.[39]

Undeterred, senior Bush administration officials continued to lobby for an armed constabulary in their private conversations with senior members of the EU Council Secretariat. White House officials made clear the United States wanted the EU to replace the IPTF with a follow-on force that included an armed, integrated unit composed of Italian Carabinieri or French Gendarmes. This new police unit would have full executive authority and serve as a civilian counterpart to the Multinational Specialized Unit in SFOR. The unit would have three functions: It would help train local police in public order and crowd control. It would back up local police units during demonstrations and in cases involving high-risk arrests. Its primary function, however, would be to attack "hard targets," such as organized criminal groups, that were beyond the capacity of local police. U.S. officials made clear that they wanted the Europeans to provide experienced units and "not just a bunch of guys with guns." While unable to agree with the U.S. recommendation, EU officials did not close the door completely on the possibility of an armed constabulary unit in the EU police mission (EUPM). They held out the possibility that such a force might be added once the police mission was established, if it became clear that there was no real alternative to dealing with organized crime. They also wondered aloud about eventually shifting the MSU from SFOR to the EUPM, where it would report to the High Representative.[40]

THE TRANSITION TO A NEW INTERNATIONAL POLICE FORCE IN BOSNIA

In a situation reminiscent of Secretary of Defense Cohen's appeal to NATO defense ministers in December 1997, Secretary Rumsfeld's call for an armed European constabulary was made in the context of U.S. pressure for a reduction in the level of U.S. forces in Bosnia. In this case, however, there was the additional issue of the need to identify a follow-on force for the UN IPTF, which set a self-imposed deadline of December 31, 2002 for withdrawing from Bosnia. The United Nations decided to withdraw the IPTF despite the fact that six years after the signing of the Dayton Accords, deep divisions between the three ethnic groups in Bosnia continued to thwart the peace process. These divisions resulted from a "lethal combination of historical memories, recently perpetrated horrors, and the presence of conflict entrepreneurs—leaders determined to keep the conflict alive—on all sides." That these divisions persisted despite the presence of twenty-seven thousand peacekeepers and administrators, innumerable nongovernmental organizations, ample aid for reconstruction, and an open-ended international commitment was an indication of their tenacity. Peace had been maintained, but progress toward a unified, democratic state had been modest. No one believed Bosnia could continue functioning as a single country without continued international presence, including SFOR and an international civilian police force.[41]

As for the Bosnian police, a report by the influential International Crisis Group concluded that despite six years of effort by the IPTF, some fourteen separate, ethnically partial, underqualified, underpaid, and often corrupt local police forces still enforced the law selectively within a politicized and dysfunctional justice system controlled by nationalist interior ministers. In Bosnia, local police failed to deal with organized crime or prevent politicians from providing one law for the well connected and the ethnic majority and another for the poor and powerless minorities. According to the report, crime bosses operated with impunity, ethnic violence was tolerated, and official corruption was widespread. Politicians manipulated the justice system through their control of appointments and salaries. The communist-era doctrine that the police exist to serve the state persisted with the nationalist, obstructionist elite the primary beneficiaries.[42]

For the United Nations Mission in Bosnia and Herzegovina, advising the local police and monitoring relations between the police and the criminal justice system had become its sole responsibility. The strength of the International Police Task Force was allowed to shrink from 2,057 officers in 1997 to about 1,800 in November 2001 and was expected to decline further following the October 2002 elections. The number of Americans in the force had fallen from a high of 250 in 1997 to 87. The IPTF had abandoned its efforts to provide a security presence and had terminated its training programs for local police officers. Its central focus was a co-locator program, which placed IPTF advisers in Bosnian police stations, where they were able to mentor local counterparts. This program was conducted in conjunction with a new effort to certify local police by reviewing their records to determine their fitness to serve. UN efforts to monitor the judicial system were limited to the work of the Criminal Justice Advisory Unit, a remnant of a much larger UN Judicial System Assessment Program that operated between 1998 and 2000. The advisory unit focused most of its limited resources on court cases resulting from the IPTF Special Trafficking Operations Program that dealt with trafficking in women and high-profile trials such as those resulting from the assassinations of Bosnian political figures.[43]

The UN decision to culminate its mission and withdraw from Bosnia was based on a recommendation from Jacques Klein, the SRSG in Sarajevo, which was endorsed by IPTF commissioner Detlef Buwitt (of Germany) and his successor, Vincent Coeurderoy (of France). Klein's recommendation was based on his assessment that the IPTF was nearing a point where it had achieved what was possible within the confines of its mandate. Klein believed the time had come to begin planning for the handover to another international monitoring force with a more relevant structure and increased authority. He was encouraged by the fact that during the previous year, IPTF had begun to make the transition from monitoring local police operations to providing technical assistance and guidance to Bosnian police executives. Through its co-locator program, IPTF had placed advisers in the offices of local police officials, where they were able to observe and offer suggestions on a real-time basis. The IPTF had created the State Border Service and organized a truly multiethnic police force in Brcko. It had established the Law Enforcement Personnel Registry and completed a review and certification of about half the police officers in Bosnia. Local police had also performed professionally during recent municipal elections. A police academy was operating successfully in each entity, and initiatives were underway to accelerate recruitment of minorities into the police.[44]

At the same time, Klein's recommendation was informed by a clear-eyed assessment that there were limits to what the IPTF could accomplish. Klein felt it was time for the IPTF to disengage from activities and commitments, such as training local police, that were essentially open-ended. Given its limited mandate, it was not possible for the IPTF to affect such seemingly intractable problems as official corruption, organized crime, slowness of refugee returns, and the basic factors affecting the performance of local police (for example, inadequate housing, low pay, and political interference). It was also impossible for the IPTF to influence the development of the other two parts of the judicial system, courts and prisons. Preliminary findings of a two-year study of the Bosnian judiciary by the UNMIBH Judicial System Assessment Program had concluded that the "entire judiciary was—to a greater or lesser degree—politically, professionally, and structurally dysfunctional."[45]

Klein's road map for withdrawing the IPTF from Bosnia was set out in the UNMIBH "Mandate Implementation Plan for 2000–2002."[46] To leave behind "effective, democratic, and sustainable law enforcement agencies," the IPTF would implement six core programs to raise the performance of the Bosnian police to international standards by December 2002. The mandate implementation plan called for the IPTF to implement programs for—

+ *Police reform* to raise the professional competence and personal integrity of Bosnian law enforcement personnel.

+ *Police restructuring* to improve the organizational capacity and institutional integrity of Bosnian law enforcement agencies, while progressively approaching the benchmarks for multiethnic representation.

+ *Judicial cooperation* to improve police procedures and practices in order to enhance cooperation with the rest of the judicial system.

+ *Institution building* to improve internal coordination and increase capacity through the creation of a State Border Service and a specialized unit to combat international organized crime.

+ *Public awareness* to increase communication with the public and foster popular support for the police.

+ *International participation* to expand the involvement of Bosnian law enforcement agencies and personnel in the UN system and in European law enforcement institutions.

The plan would be implemented in four six-month phases starting in January 2001. Progress would be evaluated by a mandate implementation team in consultation with a consultative body of local and UN law enforcement officials. Assuming the UN Security Council would conclude that UNMIBH had achieved its core mandate, the plan anticipated the transfer of responsibility for monitoring the Bosnian police in 2002. Based on "past experience," the plan stated that Bosnia would continue to require an effective "follow-on presence of qualified international police personnel" provided by a European regional organization to prepare for "the eventual admission of Bosnia into the European family."[47]

The "past experience" referred to in the mandate implementation plan was the transfer from the United Nations to the OSCE of responsibility for the international police program in Eastern Slavonia. From January 1996 to January 1998, Klein served as the SRSG and transitional administrator for Eastern Slavonia. In October 1998, the OSCE mission in Croatia replaced the UN Transitional Administration in Eastern Slavonia (UNTAES) coincident with the return of Eastern Slavonia, Baranja, and Western Sirmium to Croatian sovereignty. During its two-year mission, UNTAES and its 453-member UN police support group had overseen the creation of a 1,400-member multi-ethnic transitional police force. Training for the initial three hundred members of the transitional force was conducted by the U.S. Department of Justice and UN CIVPOL at the International Law Enforcement Academy in Budapest. Subsequently, all members of the force received training in basic police skills, civil disorder management, human rights, and community policing from international instructors. At reintegration, some seven hundred ethnic Serb police officers accepted Croatian citizenship and the entire transitional force became part of the Croatian national police force.[48]

At the time of transition, responsibility for monitoring the local police passed from the United Nations to the one hundred and twenty officers of the OSCE Police Monitoring Mission in Croatia's Danube region. The OSCE mission was composed almost entirely of western European and American personnel who simply exchanged their UN blue berets for new OSCE headgear and remained in place to ensure a seamless transition. During the next two years, OSCE police monitors worked to improve the professionalism of the police, while ensuring that the Croatian government met its responsibilities to support the multiethnic force. On October 31, 2000, the OSCE police mission in Eastern Slavonia disbanded and transferred its residual responsibilities to the OSCE mission in Zagreb.[49]

On September 13, 2001, the political directors of the Peace Implementation Council steering board met in Brussels with the High Representative, the OSCE, the EU, and Bosnian government representatives to assess the current situation in Bosnia and discuss the forthcoming effort to direct the peace implementation process toward a "European end-state." The board stressed the necessity for "responsible governance" and for the Bosnians' "total, immediate, and professional commitment to fully implementing long-term, institutional, legal, and economic reforms as a prerequisite for full integration into EU structures." The OHR would draft a comprehensive international community action plan governing future cooperation between the international community and the Bosnian government. Among the many items included in the action plan would be "options for a follow-on police monitoring mission." OHR promised to have the action plan ready in time for consideration by the next meeting of the PIC steering board in December.[50]

To prepare for the December meeting, OSCE commissioned the "First Preliminary Report on a Follow-on Mission to UNMIBH and the UN International Police Task Force."[51] The purpose of the report was to "ensure OSCE would be in position to contribute positively to the forthcoming discussion on a successor mission to the IPTF." The report endorsed the UN's goal of creating a "Bosnian police force fit for Europe" by raising the level of professionalism to European standards. It also provided a frank review of the obstacles that lay on the path toward achieving that objective. The report noted that despite the best efforts of the IPTF, there remained "insufficient local willingness to embrace major concepts, which underpin progressive law enforcement reform and thereby build public trust and confidence in the police." Among the major areas requiring improvement, the report listed—

Depoliticization. The report noted that the twenty-three police administrations in Bosnia were run directly by their respective Interior Ministries and were responsible to nationalist officials who held party membership. The report stated that it was difficult to see how Bosnia, with its "separate and autonomous police forces, judiciaries, and intelligence services, could coordinate its efforts or its participation with European counterparts."

Openness and Transparency. The report noted that substantial changes were necessary to correct the legacy from the communist past and to create the "attitudes and practices" required to ensure that the "public may be informed about and have a voice in the mode and operation of policing."

Internal Control. The report noted that efforts to create "internal control units" within the various Bosnian police forces were inadequate. At the same time, there was "minimal interest" in creating organizations to provide external oversight of police conduct. On this issue, the report stated ominously that "dark political and nationalist motives condition the mindset of many senior police officials, and low pay and corruption produce negative forces that cancel much of the positive international contribution."

Crime. The report noted that while the level of street crime remained extremely low, organized crime and international trafficking posed a grave threat to Bosnian society. The report stated that the absence of organized crime statutes, blatant intimidation of police, political interference, and corruption of judges presented nearly "insurmountable obstacles."

Courts. The report noted that one of the major failures of the international effort in Bosnia had been the lack of attention paid to criminal and civil justice reform. The report stated that efforts to stiffen police resolve to fight crime were thwarted by "poor-quality prosecutors and judges who remain weak, fearful, or corrupt."

To correct this situation, the OSCE report recommended replacing the IPTF with a "rule-of-law mission" that would focus on both police and judicial reform. The police component would be made up entirely of highly experienced senior law enforcement professionals who would work shoulder-to-shoulder with their Bosnian counterparts. This group of senior police advisers would have superior skills in police management and would concentrate on providing advice and direction to midlevel and senior police executives. To deal with "foot draggers and spoilers," the new police mission would have a strong mandate with a "prepared list of ascending sanctions and a clear and unquestionable determination to enforce them." The mission would remain for three years and, hopefully, be replaced by a number of bilateral police assistance programs.[52]

Following circulation of the OSCE study, the OHR commissioned its own "Report On a Police Follow-on Mission to UNMIBH and the UN International Police Task Force,"[53] which built on the findings of the OSCE report. To ensure compatibility, the OHR also selected Richard Monk, who had drafted the OSCE report, to be the primary drafter of its contribution. A former British police officer, Monk previously served as IPTF commissioner and was the "police expert" on the Panel on United Nations Peace Operations. To emphasize the identity of views between the two documents, the OHR report began with the instruction that it should be read in conjunction with the OSCE report.

The OHR report endorsed the OSCE proposal for an executive-level police mission that would monitor and advise interior ministers and police commanders, with the goal of raising the level of police operations in Bosnia to European standards. This would be accomplished through "ministerial and senior command level technical assistance and by forcewide inspections and performance reviews." The proposal called for co-locating 498 experienced international police officers with senior Bosnian police officials to provide professional advice on a day-to-day basis. These advisers would be authorized to exercise oversight and to intervene, if necessary, to correct the actions of their local counterparts. A second group of international police executives and civilian experts in human rights and judicial affairs would work with local ministers to develop a police inspection and performance evaluation regimen that would measure improvements by "outcomes" rather than "outputs." The goal would be to improve management and planning capability and to empower the local police. Such assistance would expand on the IPTF co-locator program that had enjoyed considerable success.

According to the OHR proposals, the new executive police mission would be preceded by an extensive effort to create a strategic plan and set objectives for the follow-on mission and the development of the Bosnian police. This would include new units like the State Border Service and the court police. The plan would contain provisions for forcewide inspections and performance reviews that would document progress and identify shortfalls in performance. Emphasis would be placed on ensuring effective systems of internal control; financial accountability; provision of public services; decentralization of authority; and procedures for insuring transparency, public access, and dialogue. The mission would last three years with the objective end-state of a police force that is "mature, accountable, and self-critical."

The OHR report noted that international efforts for local police reform had been hindered not only by the limitations of the IPTF mandate and lack of resources but also by shortfalls in UN implementation and opposition from entrenched local interests. While the IPTF was mandated to conduct police training and reform, it was staffed like a traditional monitoring mission, with much of its strength drawn from countries where the police were poorly trained, ill equipped, and unfamiliar with community policing in a democratic society. Under the OHR plan, the provision of individually selected, highly qualified European law enforcement professionals would solve one of the basic problems that had plagued the IPTF—the inadequate quality of its personnel.

According to the OHR report, police in Bosnia must not only protect citizens but also deal effectively with organized crime, terrorism, and international trafficking. In this regard, the OHR would have to take the lead on depoliticizing the police and reducing the influence of corrupt and nationalist political elites on police leadership. Political interference in appointments, promotions, dismissals, and distribution of manpower would be reduced by the appointment of professional police commissioners on merit, as recommended by the IPTF police commissioner project. The report noted, however, that such efforts would not entirely remove the pernicious influence of political interference without additional support from the international community. The same was true for the issue of low police salaries, which were directly linked to low self-esteem, petty corruption, and poor performance. Finally, the report linked the prospects for the follow-on mission to the successful achievement of the objectives outlined in the UNMIBH mandate implementation plan. These objectives included police reform and restructuring, improved judicial cooperation, institution building, the creation of a border service, improved public awareness, and increased cooperation with regional and international law enforcement.

Judicial reform has been an afterthought in the Bosnian peace implementation process. Coherent assistance to the judicial sector did not begin until several years after the beginning of the UN mission. Failure of prosecutors and judges to resist corruption and withstand intimidation had earned the judiciary the deep distrust of the police. This was particularly true in the area of organized crime. While Bosnia had one of the world's lowest incidents of street crime, police did not arrest known organized crime figures because of fear of retribution. The OHR proposal stated that the new mission should be conceived as a rule-of-law mission, which would combine international efforts for both police and judicial reform. Recommendations for reinvigorating the work of the UN Independent Judicial Commission and reconstituting the Bosnian judiciary were contained in a companion OHR report, "Assessment of the Current Mandate of the Independent Judicial Commission and a Review of the Judicial Reform Follow-on Mission for Bosnia and Herzegovina."[54] The assessment confirmed the dismal findings of earlier studies and called for a restructuring and upgrading of the Bosnian judiciary to meet European standards.

At the meeting of the Peace Implementation Council in Brussels on December 5–6, 2001, the steering board, after hearing from SFOR, UNMIBH, OSCE, UNDP, the UN Human Rights Commission, and the World Bank, endorsed the recommendations in the OHR report and agreed on the transition to a new international police mission in Bosnia. The board recognized the need for a "robust police mission combining crisis management and capacity building." It noted the importance of taking a comprehensive approach and endorsed the recommendations in the OHR report for coordinating efforts for police and judicial reform. The board asked the OHR to develop options for such a program and noted that the mandate for a follow-on mission to the IPTF would require UN Security Council endorsement.[55] During this meeting it was determined that the goal of bringing the Bosnians to European standards could best be reached by handing off the responsibility for the follow-on mission to the EU and not the OSCE. A final decision on the EU candidacy for the follow-on mission was scheduled for the PIC steering board meeting on February 28, 2002.

As a first step in preparing to accept responsibility for providing the follow-on police mission for Bosnia, the Joint Council Secretariat of the EU and the European Commission dispatched a high-level joint delegation led by EU deputy director-general Pieter Feith to Sarajevo on December 16–19, 2001. The EU delegation met with UN and SFOR officials, who strongly endorsed the idea of an EU police mission as being consistent with Bosnia's "European aspirations." In its report, the EU delegation endorsed the recommendations made in the two OHR reports and concluded that an EU follow-on mission should be composed of about five hundred highly qualified European police executives working in a "monitoring, mentoring, and inspection function with the middle and higher levels" of the local police. The delegation also endorsed the idea of a joint rule-of-law mission and the need to support the Independent Judicial Commission through assistance from the European Commission. The delegation determined that the EU police mission should be supported by economic and material assistance from the European Commission and aim at raising police services in Bosnia to European standards. The mission would enforce such standards through its ability to remove noncompliant local police officers by a recommendation from the EU police commissioner to the High Representative. To accomplish its goals, the EUPM would concentrate on—

+ Providing continuity in order to preserve the achievements of the IPTF mission, specifically the institutional and personal proficiency of the local police.

+ Enhancing through monitoring, mentoring, and inspecting the operational planning, managerial, and crime analysis capabilities of the local police.

+ Strengthening professionalism at the higher levels of ministerial and police officials through advisory and inspection functions.

+ Monitoring the exercise of appropriate political control over the police.[56]

The European Union delegation specifically counseled against including armed police in the follow-on force. This appeared to be a response to Secretary Rumsfeld's call at the December 18 NATO defense ministers' meeting for replacing the IPTF with an armed European constabulary. In its report, the delegation stated that the EU's police mission should not have "executive powers or the deployment of an armed component." In this regard, the report assumed that the drawdown of SFOR would proceed at a measured pace, with the MSU remaining as part of the reduced troop presence. The report further assumed that if the local police met the standards established by the departing IPTF in its final mandate implementation plan, the existing public security gap "would not widen" by the end of 2002. The EU delegation arrived at this conclusion despite admitting in its report that the forthcoming October 2002 elections, refugee returns, economic deterioration, migrant smuggling, and the fight against organized crime were likely to result in a resurgence of nationalist extremism, violent confrontations, and social unrest.[57]

On January 28 2002, the EU foreign ministers met in

Brussels and decided, in principle, to take over the international policing role in Bosnia from the UN IPTF. The ministers endorsed the EU delegation's recommendations for an advisory force of five hundred that would not carry weapons or have executive authority. The EUPM would co-locate with the Bosnian police at command centers and at entity and canton interior ministries, where it would monitor and advise senior-level officers on their managerial and operational responsibilities. It would also conduct evaluations of lower-ranking officers and ensure they received proper training to improve their performance. On February 18, this decision in principle was formalized at a meeting of the EU Council, which confirmed that the EU, supported by the European Commission's institution-building programs, would provide a follow-on international police advisory program for Bosnia. Sven Frederiksen, a Danish police officer and former UNMIK police commissioner, was tapped to lead the EU police mission. Media reports noted that the ministers' decision would result in the first civilian police operation tied to the European Security and Defense Policy that aimed at creating a European rapid reaction military force of sixty thousand military and a European security and intelligence force of five thousand police by 2003.[58]

In the competition between the EU and the OSCE, there was a combination of factors favoring the EU that the OSCE could not overcome. In many ways, the Bosnian police mission represented something of a turnkey project for the EU. Of the 1,673 IPTF monitors, 636 were from EU member countries.[59] Most of these officers would simply remain in place, ensuring a seamless transition. In fact, because the EUPM would number about five hundred, there would actually be a 22-percent reduction in the number of EU police personnel. In addition, the cost to the EU of maintaining this number of police officers in Bosnia would be about the same. The EUPM's estimated annual cost of 38 million euros was roughly equivalent to what EU member states were contributing to provide European police officers to the IPTF. This estimate included: €17 million for per diem, €1 million for travel, €11 million for operations, €4 million for local staff, and €5 million for international staff.

There would be an additional one-time cost of €14 million for start up expenses. Salaries for police officers serving in the EUPM would be paid directly by their home countries. As the police mission would, in essence, be taking over the IPTF's successful co-locator program, Javier Solana, now the EU Council's secretary-general, saw the replacement of the United Nations as a way of beginning the European security and intelligence (police) force with a virtually assured success. Through the European Commission, the EU also had a ready source of development assistance, as the commission was already engaged in providing material aid to the Bosnian police through the IPTF. This assistance program would continue with the aid provided through the EUPM. The OSCE had no comparable assistance program.[60]

In political terms, the EU had important advantages as well. Bosnia was a member of the OSCE and was represented in the OSCE Assembly in Vienna. The assembly operated on the basis of consensus, making it extremely awkward, if not impossible, for the organization to conduct an intrusive police mission with the authority to sanction local officials in a member country. In contrast, the EU Council made decisions on the basis of majority vote, much like the UN Security Council, and Bosnia was not a member. It also appeared likely that the next High Representative in Bosnia would be selected from an EU member state. Giving the EU responsibility for the police program would help ensure a unified effort, replacing the current situation in which the UNMIBH was headed by an American who reported to New York. The international community's overall goal was the integration of Bosnia into Europe, and the EUPM was an obvious first step toward preparing Bosnian law enforcement agencies for integration into European institutions such as Europol. The OSCE, which included the United States, Canada, and the former Soviet republics, would not have been the appropriate agency to prepare Bosnia for EU membership.[61]

With the EU foreign ministers already in agreement, the formality of PIC approval of the EUPM was accomplished at the meeting of the PIC steering board political directors in

Brussels on February 28, 2002. The board accepted the offer of the EU General Affairs Council to ensure the continued professional development of the Bosnian police beginning on January 1, 2003 for a period of three years. This would be accomplished through mentoring, monitoring, and inspecting the Bosnian police with the assistance of the European Commission's institutional development programs. The board noted that the EUPM would work closely with the Independent Judicial Commission, the OSCE, and relevant bilateral programs under the coordination of the Rule of Law Task Force to ensure that EU assistance would address the entire spectrum of issues involved in establishing the rule of law. The board welcomed the agreement of the EU to invite non-EU member states to participate in the EUPM. It also offered its full support to the EU to achieve a "seamless transition" of responsibilities from the IPTF to the police mission. In this regard, it directed the OHR to inform the UN secretary-general of its decision.[62]

The EU agreement to involve nonmember states in the police mission followed consultations with the UN's SRSG in Bosnia, Jacques Klein, who strongly recommended including outside countries. Under the rubric of "continuing to include countries that had played a major role in the IPTF and the Bosnia police assistance program," Klein urged that five countries—the United States, Russia, Norway, Switzerland, and Turkey—be invited to participate. Klein's selections were made to ensure political and geographic balance and to facilitate continuation of the U.S. Department of Justice's ICITAP program. According to the understanding with the EU, some 70 percent of the new EUPM would come from EU member states, and 30 percent would come from the five nonmember countries. It was anticipated that the U.S. contingent would number thirty officers. Inclusion of nonmember states had the additional advantage of further reducing the number of police from EU member states serving in Bosnia from 636 with the IPTF to about 350. This would both hold down costs and free personnel resources for donor nations.[63]

At the same meeting, the PIC steering board took note of

another decision by the EU to better define the structure of the international community in Bosnia and to ensure effective coordination between the EU police mission and the OHR. The board acknowledged that the EU had "double hatted" the new High Representative, Lord Paddy Ashdown, as the EU special representative in Bosnia, to whom the incoming EU police mission commissioner would report directly. This would replace the existing situation, in which the IPTF commissioner reported to the SRSG, whose only obligation under the Dayton Accords was to "coordinate" with the High Representative. Behind the EU's action was the hope that Lord Ashdown, the former leader of the United Kingdom's Liberal Democratic party, would be able to place Bosnia firmly on the path toward EU membership and bring the period of international tutelage to an end.[64] The idea of "double hatting" the new High Representative was strongly encouraged by the United States as part of the Bush administration's effort to strengthen his position and to give the EU a greater role in peace implementation.

On March 5, 2002, the UN Security Council formally accepted the EU offer to replace UNMIBH beginning in 2003. In adopting Resolution 1396, the UN Security Council welcomed the appointment of Lord Ashdown as the new High Representative and unanimously approved the transfer of responsibility for police in Bosnia to the EUPM. In his address to the council, Secretary-General Annan reported that the IPTF was on track to complete its core mandate by the end of 2002. He told the council the UN could be very satisfied with the work the IPTF had performed. He listed transformation of the Bosnian police from a wartime militia of forty thousand to a professional force of sixteen thousand; establishment of two multiethnic police academies; completion of in-service training programs in human rights, organized crime, and crowd control; and creation of the State Border Service as highlights of the IPTF achievements. Although the IPTF would soon complete the "peace-keeping phase of police restructuring," Annan said problems of the Bosnian police, such as low salaries, poor housing, lack of funding, and political interference, remained to be resolved. As the Bosnian police would continue to require international monitoring and assistance, the secretary-general welcomed the EU's decision to provide the follow-on police mission to ensure consolidation of the progress made so far. Annan said the "next phase of capacity building in law enforcement, including judicial and penal systems, would be carried out in a European context." He said creation of the EUPM and the presence of EU Council secretary-general Solana at the UN session signaled the importance the European Union attached to the future of Bosnia.[65]

8

NATION BUILDING
✦ ✦ ✦ ✦ ✦ ✦ ✦ ✦ ✦ ✦ ✦ ✦ ✦ ✦
Biting the Bullet in
✦ ✦ ✦ ✦ ✦ ✦ ✦ ✦ ✦ ✦ ✦ ✦ ✦
Afghanistan and Iraq
✦ ✦ ✦ ✦ ✦ ✦ ✦ ✦ ✦ ✦ ✦ ✦ ✦

URING MOST OF ITS FIRST TWO YEARS IN OFFICE, the Bush administration did little to follow up on its initial interest in finding alternatives for military forces in peace operations. Despite the early indications from Condoleezza Rice, Secretary Powell, and others that the United States might look for civilian alternatives to reliance on the military, the administration did little to improve U.S. capacity to provide nonmilitary solutions to the problem of achieving postconflict security. Instead, the administration took a step backward and dismantled the limited framework for bureaucratic decision making created by its predecessor. As in previous administrations, the first National Security Presidential Directive (NSPD-1) signed by the president established a new bureaucratic framework and interagency process for dealing with issues related to national security and foreign affairs. The directive assigned to Rice, as the administration's national security adviser, the traditional powers of that post as chairperson of the Principals Committee and head of the National Security Council staff. Also, in accordance with established practice, NSPD-1 abolished the organizational innovations and cancelled the presidential directives of the previous administration.[1]

The need for this kind of periodic bureaucratic housecleaning is obvious—even more so with the Bush national security team's arrival at the Old Executive Office Building, right next to the White House. During its eight years in office, the Clinton administration had issued 75 Presidential Decision Directives and constructed a labyrinth of 102 Interagency Working Groups (IWGs). NSPD-1 nullified the directives, abolished 46 of the IWGs outright, and reorganized the remaining 56 as sub-groups of 21 new Policy Coordinating Committees (PCCs). The role of the PCCs was to serve as the focal point for interagency coordination of national security policy, provide analysis and recommendations for more senior committees in the policy process, and ensure timely implementation of decisions made by the president. Six of these committees would deal with geographic regions (for example, Africa, Asia, and Europe), the other fifteen with functional issues (such as human rights, arms control, and so forth). Issues related to the implementation of ongoing peace operations were consigned to the PCCs dealing with the relevant geographic regions.[2]

WHAT EVER HAPPENED TO PDD-71?

Among the casualties of this interagency reorganization was the Peacekeeping Core Group established by the Clinton administration to coordinate issues related to the conduct of peace operations and the three Presidential Decision Directives concerned with peacekeeping policy.[3] While imperfect in design and often ignored in practice, the three peacekeeping directives provided a bureaucratic framework and policy process for "complex contingencies" that sought to ensure the active involvement of all relevant government agencies. The three directives were not abolished outright but were consigned to a category of directives that required revision after further study. The residual functions of the IWG that had been established to oversee PDD-71 implementation were relegated to the new PCC on democracy, human rights, and international operations.[4]

Failure to explicitly renew or replace the Clinton administration's directives left the Bush administration without clear policy guidance on how the U.S. government should address peacekeeping. This was particularly true concerning issues related to justice and reconciliation that fell within the purview of PDD-71. In the absence of the directive, the new administration did not have a clear policy concerning what assistance the United States should provide toward restoring public order, law enforcement, justice, and the rule of law in postconflict environments. There was no indication of what agency, office, or individual was responsible for providing leadership or how interagency programs should be coordinated. There was also no policy guidance on funding responsibilities. This proved problematic for an administration that had announced its intention to re-examine U.S. programs and priorities.[5]

In the policy vacuum created by the administration's failure to renew or repeal PDD-71, implementation of the instructions contained in the directive was left to the State Department's Bureau of International Narcotics and Law Enforcement Affairs (INL). This responsibility included expending the $10 million that had been appropriated by Congress in FY 2001 and provided to State for that purpose. The problems that had been encountered in implementing PDD-71 at the end of the Clinton administration continued. In the new administration, inattention from the NSC staff was accompanied by a similar lack of interest from senior officers in the State Department, which was unable to resolve the gridlock of interagency differences. Implementation of the directive was left in the hands of a small group of midlevel INL officials who were responsible for managing the U.S. civilian police program.[6]

Acting largely on their own authority, these officials in INL took a number of useful steps toward CIVPOL reform. To improve accountability, U.S. CIVPOL contingent commanders were given greater authority to supervise and impose discipline on American police officers in the field. A system of personnel evaluations was also developed so that the State Department could create a record of the performance of individual officers. INL also took a number of actions to emphasize the fact that U.S. CIVPOL were participating in a government program, despite being hired by a commercial contractor. U.S. CIVPOL officers were honored in ceremonies, given medals, and sent letters of appreciation and commendation from the State Department to bolster a sense of pride and professionalism. To improve the quality of personnel, efforts were made to increase the percentage of active duty police officers and otherwise improve the caliber of officers participating in the CIVPOL program. A former deputy IPTF commissioner in Bosnia was hired to develop a program for expanding outreach to U.S. police departments and to involve the State Department more directly in recruiting policemen for CIVPOL service.[7]

To increase awareness of the U.S. CIVPOL program, representatives of U.S. police departments were invited to Washington for a briefing on the positive experience their officers would gain from serving in UN police missions. As a recruiting aid, INL produced an attractive color brochure describing the CIVPOL program that was mailed to police departments and distributed by INL staff at the national conferences of law enforcement associations. INL established an Internet web site (www.policemission. com) that was maintained by DynCorp, where police officers interested in CIVPOL service could learn about the program and complete an online application. To improve responsiveness, the State Department planned to create a "ready roster" of police officers who would be prepared to depart on short notice. INL prepared specific job descriptions as the first step in recruiting police officers for the roster. Yet it decided not to create the roster until the competition of the commercial contract for supporting the CIVPOL program was completed in 2003. Creation of the roster would be the responsibility of the service provider under the new contract.[8]

INL also hired an experienced police training coordinator to better prepare American police officers selected for CIVPOL duty. Among his first tasks was to improve the current orientation program. As an incentive for active duty police officers, INL sought to have the course accredited by the Police Officers Standards and Training organization so that it would satisfy the training requirements police officers must meet to qualify for promotions. In addition to INL's efforts, the U.S. CIVPOL program benefited from a growing number of officers who volunteered for second and third deployments following an initial one-year assignment. It also was helped by the growing presence of active duty police officers who were able to take leave from their departments. The seeding of U.S. CIVPOL contingents with experienced veterans and active duty officers increased the professionalism and improved the performance of U.S. contingents.[9] State Department efforts and the involvement of more experienced and better-qualified officers did little, however, to reverse the tendency of American CIVPOL to identify with the commercial firm that hired them rather than with the U.S. government. Even with increased State Department involvement, the average CIVPOL officer had little contact with U.S. government officials outside of their predeparture orientation program and their initial in-country briefings. Strengthening the authority of the U.S. contingent commanders (who also were contractors) did little to improve the State Department's ability to exercise effective supervision over U.S. CIVPOL officers in the field.

THE PROBLEM OF CIVPOL ACCOUNTABILITY

This lack of direct State Department supervision and the resulting inability to ensure accountability was evidenced by a slowly growing scandal resulting from allegations of misconduct, corruption, and involvement in human trafficking in the Balkans. On May 29, 2001, the *Washington Post* reported that accusations of criminal behavior and sexual impropriety against UN police officers, including Americans, had been hushed up by UN officials and that offenders had been sent home without further investigation or punishment. According to the newspaper, David McBride, the deputy commissioner of the IPTF and the most senior U.S. CIVPOL officer in Bosnia, had resigned in August 1999 after an IPTF internal disciplinary panel concluded that he had violated the UN code of conduct for police in peacekeeping missions. The panel charged that McBride had accepted favors from Bosnian Croat authorities, including gifts, hotel accommodations, a car, and a free cell phone, which created the appearance of a conflict of interest. McBride returned to the United States, claiming he had been the victim of character assassination by UN officials who disagreed with him on policy issues. The *Post* also reported that another American IPTF officer, Peter Alzugaray, had been fired by DynCorp following allegations of sexual misconduct resulting from his relationship with a thirteen-year-old Bosnian girl. In these cases and several others involving misbehavior, there was no follow-up by the State Department or U.S. law enforcement agencies after the CIVPOL officers returned to the United States.[10]

While these cases of misconduct were troubling, the most serious allegations concerned the involvement of IPTF officers, including Americans, in the growing problem of human trafficking and forced prostitution in Bosnia. According to UN reports, Bosnia was the destination for six thousand to ten thousand women from central Europe and the former Soviet republics who were brought there for illicit purposes.[11] While some women willingly emigrated in order to participate in the sex trade, most were lured from economically depressed areas, primarily in Moldova, Romania, and Ukraine, by false promises of jobs as secretaries, domestic workers, nannies, and barmaids. These women had their passports taken away and were physically abused. They were brought to the Balkans and sold as chattel to work in brothels in Bosnia and Kosovo. Prices ranged from $230 to $2000 with "ownership" often changing hands several times before the women reached their final destination. A major center for this trade were the nightclubs in the Arizona Market near Brcko. Girls appeared naked on stage at "sex slave auctions," where they were sold to the highest bidder after a teeth check and physical inspection. The buyers (usually women) were representatives of the owners of bars and brothels frequented primarily by internationals. Money paid for the women was considered a debt that had to be repaid before they could regain their freedom.[12]

The systemic basis for the trafficking problem was the criminal relationships between organized crime, local politicians, and Bosnian police. Much of the trafficking was overt and was carried out with at least the passive complicity of local law enforcement officials. Local police stations routinely issued work permits to nightclub owners for "foreign dancers" and "waitresses," an obvious ruse that the police simply ignored. There was also compelling evidence of corrupt local officials and police tipping off bar owners of impending raids. According to the United Nations, nearly three hundred nightclubs in Bosnia were involved in trafficking and forced prostitution. When queried about the lack of enforcement, local officials tended to dismiss the problem as one caused by the international presence— foreign women servicing a predominantly foreign clientele.[13]

In late November 2000, six IPTF officers, including two Americans, resigned rather than face disciplinary action for exceeding their authority in a November 13, 2000 raid on three nightclubs suspected of employing trafficked women as prostitutes. While the police action liberated thirty-three women who had been forced to engage in prostitution, the IPTF officers were reprimanded for exceeding their authority, which was limited to monitoring and advising the local police. The officers' resignations, according to the head of the Bosnian UN mission, Jacques Klein, resulted from the fact that they did not have executive authority and had failed to involve local police officers in the raid. In a statement to reporters, Klein denied the allegation of the local nightclub owner that the IPTF officers knew about the women because they had frequented his establishment and had previously engaged in improprieties.[14]

On June 22, 2001, a former American IPTF officer, Kathryn Bolkovac, filed a civil lawsuit in the United Kingdom against DynCorp, claiming she had been dismissed from the U.S. contingent of the IPTF for investigating allegations of sexual misconduct in Bosnia by her fellow officers. In the lawsuit, Bolkovac accused DynCorp of wrongful dismissal, sexual discrimination, and violation of the UK's whistle-blower laws. In July 2002, a British court ruled in favor of Bolkovac, finding that DynCorp had acted improperly when it dismissed her.[15] In Bosnia, Bolkovac served first as a human rights investigator and then as head of the IPTF Gender Office, a unit responsible for advising the local police on gender-related offenses, including human trafficking. Bolkovac said she discovered it was common practice for IPTF officers to frequent brothels and that some officers were actively assisting in the trafficking by forging documents, transporting women, and tipping off bar owners about raids. Other officers, Bolkovac said, had "purchased" women, some as young as fourteen years old, for their personal use and kept them in their apartments. When her efforts to raise the issue with her superiors were rejected or ignored, Bolkovac put her allegations in an e-mail message to her UN supervisors, IPTF colleagues, and DynCorp entitled, "Do Not Read This If You Have a Weak Stomach or a Guilty Conscience."[16]

Almost immediately, Bolkovac was removed from her position in the Gender Office and reassigned to a clerical job in another division. Twelve days later, she was dismissed by DynCorp on grounds that one year earlier she had falsified a time sheet, claimed unwarranted per diem expenses, and taken unauthorized leave to attend her daughter's state basketball championship game in Nebraska. Michael Stiers, the deputy IPTF commissioner and senior U.S. police officer in Bosnia, said Bolkovac was dismissed because "she had behaved unprofessionally in her quest to help trafficked women and had lost sight of the IPTF's main priority: ending the ethnic violence that threatened to unravel the country's fragile peace."[17]

The following December, the *Washington Post* carried another article alleging that UN officials in Bosnia had quashed an investigation into whether IPTF officers were directly involved in the trafficking and enslavement of women. According to the newspaper, David Lamb, an American IPTF human rights investigator, was subjected to official interference and threats of violence when he investigated allegations that six IPTF officers had recruited Romanian women, purchased false passports for them, and sold the women to brothel owners in Bosnia. Threats were also directed against Lamb's colleagues from Canada and Argentina when they attempted to follow up on his findings. In June 2001, the newspaper stated, Mary Robinson, the UN's High Commissioner for Human Rights, had requested an inquiry by the UN Office of Internal Oversight into allegations of UN police involvement in sexual trafficking. The office sent two investigators from New York to Bosnia, but the oversight team found no grounds for further investigation. Yet they did not talk to Lamb, his colleagues, or Kathryn Bolkovac. Following the team's departure, Jacques Klein stated in a letter to the OSCE that it would be a mistake to focus on the IPTF's involvement in human trafficking, as it would divert attention from organized crime and corrupt local officials who "perpetrated the trade and allowed it to flourish."[18]

According to Klein, there was no concrete evidence that members of the IPTF had engaged in trafficking, the "importation of women for immoral purposes." The United Nations had no authority to prosecute members of the IPTF; it could only repatriate them with a request that their own governments take appropriate action. Klein said the overwhelming majority of IPTF officers were morally responsible. Of the nineteen officers then under investigation by the UN for misconduct, most were accused of nothing more serious than drinking on duty or filing inaccurate reports. As for cracking down on prostitution, IPTF was at a disadvantage because Bosnian laws concerning prostitution were different in the RS and in all ten cantons in the Bosnian Federation. Under the various statutes concerning "public order and peace," prostitution was generally defined as a "minor," but not a "criminal," offense. It was, therefore, something less than a misdemeanor and offenders were usually subject only to a small fine. Local laws did, however, provide stiffer penalties of between five and ten years in prison if prostitution was combined with other offenses such as assault, rape, or kidnapping or if it involved minors.[19]

While the IPTF did not have executive authority and had to rely on the local police for law enforcement, the United Nations did initiate the only effective program to control trafficking of women in Bosnia. Under the leadership of an indomitable French woman, Celhia de Lavarene, the IPTF Special Trafficking Operations Program (STOP) sought to guide and monitor the local police, rescue women from sexual bondage, and keep UN personnel and other internationals out of trouble. In its first year of operation, STOP conducted 557 raids on 215 establishments that employed trafficked women and closed 120 of them. It interviewed 1,770 women and assisted 164 with repatriation. It also prosecuted sixty bar owners and traffickers and obtained fifty-nine convictions.[20] According to an IPTF spokesman, only fifteen of the ten thousand CIVPOL officers that had served in Bosnia had been repatriated for misconduct. Nine of these, however, were Americans, six of whom were involved in sexually related incidents.[21]

In the spring of 2002, concern about the alleged involvement of UN police in trafficking in women and sexual misconduct reached the halls of Congress. On April 24, the House Subcommittee on International Operations and Human Rights held a hearing on "UN Peacekeepers' Participation in the Sex Slave Trade in Bosnia: Isolated Case or Larger Problem in the UN System?" According to the chairperson, Representative Ileana Ros-Lehtinen (R–Florida), it was the responsibility of Congress to investigate reports that UN officials in Bosnia had sought to prevent investigations and cover up allegations of IPTF involvement in human trafficking. Ros-Lehtinen noted that the UN officials had denied such allegations and then admitted in the same statements that IPTF officers had used young girls' services, sometimes against their will. Congress had an obligation, she said, to address the participation of Americans in such activities and the response from U.S. government agencies. One would hope, she said, that it would not be necessary to tell American DynCorp contractors they could not "buy and sell women," but that it appeared "we need to send the message that such behavior will not be tolerated."[22]

Speaking on behalf of the administration, Ambassador Nancy Ely-Raphel, director of the State Department's Office to Monitor and Combat Trafficking, reviewed the steps the department had taken to address the problem. According to Ely-Raphel, State had adopted a "zero tolerance policy" with respect to involvement of U.S. CIVPOL officers in immoral, unethical, and illegal behavior. All American CIVPOL officers were now briefed prior to their departure from the United States that involvement in such activities, including sexual misconduct, would result in immediate dismissal and repatriation. Failure to report such behavior on the part of fellow officers would also result in termination. In such cases, officers would have to pay their return plane fare, forfeit their completion of service bonus, and become ineligible for future missions. After receiving the briefing, CIVPOL officers signed a "DynCorp letter of agreement" pledging not to engage in human trafficking and acknowledging that they would be dismissed if they violated the agreement. Ely-Raphel said there had been no complaints against U.S. CIVPOL since these procedures were implemented, but that previously there had been six cases of sexual misconduct involving American police officers. These officers were not tried in Bosnia because members of the IPTF are immune from prosecution under an agreement between the United Nations and the Bosnian government. If misconduct is discovered, IPTF officers are sent home for prosecution.[23]

Concerning the cases of misconduct by American CIVPOL officers, Ambassador Ely-Raphel said the two most serious ones had been referred by State to the Department of Justice for possible prosecution. No action was taken, however, because the Justice Department determined that U.S. courts did not have jurisdiction and there was no law that would allow them to be tried in the United States. To remedy this problem, the Criminal Division of the Department of Justice was considering drafting an amendment to the Military Extraterritorial Jurisdiction Act of 2000, which covered American citizens working for U.S. military forces abroad. The proposed amendment would extend federal jurisdiction to all U.S. government employees and civilian contractors working abroad in a law enforcement capacity. If adopted, this provision would enable the U.S. government to prosecute American CIVPOL officers for sexual misconduct and involvement in human trafficking. As for the United Nations, Ely-Raphel expressed confidence in the work of the Office of Internal Oversight Services, which she said had "become a highly effective oversight body, helping to instill a culture of accountability and management effectiveness" in UN programs.[24]

During the hearing, Ambassador Ely-Raphel's positive assessment was challenged by a panel of nongovernment witnesses who said they saw little effort by the United Nations or the U.S. government to deal with the problem. Martina Vandenberg of Human Rights Watch pointed out that a "de facto blanket of complete impunity" covered American and foreign IPTF officers. Under the Dayton Accords, IPTF officers could not be prosecuted in Bosnia, nor were they likely to face prosecution under the criminal laws of their own countries. This was the case in the United States, where, Vandenberg said, multiple Human Rights Watch requests filed under the Freedom of Information Act had failed to unearth any evidence of prosecutions of American CIVPOL officers for crimes committed abroad. Vandenberg said the fact that IPTF officers enjoyed immunity from prosecution was deeply troubling to all of those who were attempting to establish the rule of law in Bosnia.[25] David Lamb, the former IPTF human rights investigator, repeated the charges he made earlier that senior UN officials responded to his efforts to investigate IPTF involvement in human trafficking with indifference at best and with intimidation at worst. Lamb said donor governments were responsible for their personnel, and the U.S. State Department shared responsibility for failing to control this illicit activity. Lamb accused the department of "purposefully distancing itself from U.S. CIVPOL by hiring DynCorp as the middleman and making no attempt to know anything about the activities of American IPTF officers."[26]

The Bush administration's disinterest in the U.S. civilian police program was part of its aversion to peacekeeping in general. When it assumed office, the administration expressed profound skepticism about the value of U.S. military deployments in support of peacekeeping operations. Moreover, its commitment to the nonmilitary dimensions of peacebuilding was uncertain. After September 11, the administration acknowledged that U.S. support for postconflict stabilization and development could have important implications for regional stability. At the same time, the administration continued to resist a significant role for U.S. troops in peacekeeping operations. The first real test of the Bush administration in dealing with the problem of establishing postconflict security was Afghanistan.

POSTCONFLICT SECURITY IN AFGHANISTAN

Following the defeat of the Taliban and its al Qaeda allies, the starting point for rebuilding Afghanistan was the Agreement on Provisional Arrangements in Afghanistan Pending Re-establishment of Permanent Institutions—the Bonn agreement—signed by representatives of the Afghan people on December 5, 2001.[27] The agreement established an Interim Authority to run the country and provided the basis for an interim system of law and governance. In Annex I, the parties called for the deployment of an international military force to maintain security in Kabul. In response, UN Security Council Resolution 1386 of December 20, 2001 authorized the creation of an International Security Assistance Force (ISAF) for six months to assist the new Afghan government.[28] ISAF deployed in January 2002 and by summer had five thousand troops from nineteen countries. ISAF's responsibility was limited to providing security in the capital, where it conducted routine patrols with local police. The international force operated separately from Operation Enduring Freedom, the U.S.-led military mission, which was focused on destroying the remnants of the Taliban and al Qaeda. To ensure coordination, U.S. Central Command was given formal operational authority over ISAF, and U.S. military activities took precedence over ISAF operations. ISAF's purpose was to provide a "breathing space" during which the Afghans could create their own security forces and judicial system. On January 13, 2002, a Joint Coordination Committee was established, composed of ISAF, the United Nations, and the Interim Authority's defense and interior ministers; its role was to ensure close cooperation among those responsible for the security sector.[29]

The UN model for intervention in Afghanistan was vastly different from the prototype used in Kosovo and East Timor. In those missions, the United Nations established an interim authority that was responsible for civil administration and for guiding the local population toward democratic self-government. In Afghanistan, the UN sought to limit international involvement and to encourage the Afghans to assume responsibility for their own political reconciliation and economic reconstruction. Under the leadership of the SRSG, Ambassador Lakhdar Brahimi, the UN advocated a "light international footprint"—a euphemism for minimal international oversight and material assistance—despite initial promises of billions of dollars in foreign largess. This was particularly true concerning the international community's approach to ensuring internal security and assisting the Afghan police.[30]

The Bonn agreement did not provide a role for the United Nations in monitoring or training the Afghan police, nor did the Security Council authorize a CIVPOL mission. The UN CIVPOL Division did send a CIVPOL officer to Kabul to provide liaison between the SRSG and the Interim Authority on police matters. In May, UN secretary-general Kofi Annan dispatched four additional CIVPOL advisers. Their duties were to—

+ Advise the SRSG and coordinate with other international agencies and member states on police and security issues, including support for the Afghan police.

+ Advise the Interior Ministry and Afghan police officials.

+ Assist a German police team and its Afghan counterparts in recruiting and training the local police.

+ Assist the commander of the Kabul police with strategic and operational planning and provide advice and assistance on handling day-to-day police matters.[31]

According to the Bonn agreement, responsibility for maintaining security throughout the country rested with the Afghans. The Interim Authority, particularly Interior Minister Mohammad Yunis Qanooni, recognized that international assistance would be required to create a new Afghan national police. Given Afghanistan's size and population, creating a national police force represented a far greater challenge than anything the international community had ever attempted. While the United Kingdom (later Turkey) assumed the lead for ISAF, Germany was asked by the Afghans to take responsibility for training and equipping the local police. This request was based on the Afghans' positive experiences with German police assistance programs prior to the Soviet intervention.[32] On February 13 and March 14–15, 2002, representatives from eighteen potential donor countries met in Berlin to discuss international contributions to the Afghan police assistance program. The Germans developed an initial plan for police training and announced the commitment of $70 million toward renovating the police academy in Kabul, providing eleven police instructors, refurbishing Kabul police stations, and donating fifty police vehicles. The first team of German police advisors arrived in Kabul on March 16 and the German Coordination Office was opened on March 18, 2002. U.S. State Department representatives attended the Berlin meetings and subsequently assisted the Germans with planning the police mission. The United States also considered providing bilateral assistance to the Afghan police.[33]

Even before the U.S. intervention in Afghanistan, the Afghan Northern Alliance began training a police force as part of its long-term plan for occupying Kabul. Training took place at a police academy near the village of Dashtak in the Panjshir Valley. The majority of the Northern Alliance's two thousand–member police force were ethnic Tajiks, but the police academy's director and some of its cadets were from other ethnic groups. At the academy, recruits were taught eighteen subjects over a three-year period, including law, basic investigation techniques, criminology and human rights, plus martial arts and military drill. According to the academy's deputy director, a veteran Afghan police officer, it was important to send police rather than soldiers to maintain order in Kabul.[34]

When the Northern Alliance occupied Kabul, some four thousand police from the alliance were deployed. They were only partly trained and had only a few vehicles, little communications equipment, and a few dilapidated or damaged stations. They did, however, cooperate with ISAF and helped reduce the number of armed militia fighters in the city. The police were still organized on the Soviet-era model—with a two-track system of career officers and temporary conscripts that served for two years as patrolmen as an alternative to joining the military. While officers were trained at the academy, conscripts were untrained and often mistreated by their superiors. Without waiting for international assistance, the Afghans reopened the old police academy on the outskirts of Kabul. The academy had spacious wooded grounds, the remains of a large swimming pool, and the ruins of several buildings. A class of ninety-two cadets that transferred from the Northern Alliance police academy lived and took classes in the one habitable structure in the complex. The Afghans wanted to create a new professional police service, replacing conscripts with career noncommissioned officers who would receive a year of training. According to Interior Minister Qanooni, the Interim Authority intended to train an initial force of thirty-two hundred police (one hundred from each province) with the long-term goal of creating a force of seventy thousand officers.[35]

During his first visit to Washington in January 2002, Hamid Karzai, the leader of the Afghan Interim Authority, was profuse in his public praise for U.S. assistance in defeating the Taliban and for the promise of U.S. material assistance in rebuilding the country. Privately, Karzai expressed concern about growing insecurity outside of Kabul, which was delaying development and frightening away relief agencies, prospective investors, and returning refugees. In response, President Bush announced that the United States would help train a new Afghan army and police force and offered $297 million in American food, development and refugee aid, and investment credits. The president acknowledged the need to prevent Afghanistan from sliding back into the type of lawlessness that occurred after the Soviet withdrawal and said U.S. troops would "bail out" the ISAF if it got into trouble.[36]

In subsequent speeches at West Point and the Virginia Military Institute, the president appeared to embrace a major U.S. role in rebuilding Afghanistan, similar to the one General George C. Marshall devised for rebuilding Europe after World

War II. In a midmorning speech to the institute's cadets, Bush warned that military force alone could not bring peace and that stability in Afghanistan required the reconstruction of roads, schools, hospitals, and businesses. Bush said, "General Marshall knew our military victory had to be followed by a moral victory that resulted in better lives for individual human beings." The president's remarks raised hopes that the United States had finally recognized that weak and unstable states could threaten U.S. security and that political and economic reconstruction (that is, "nation building") was required to prevent them from becoming a spawning ground for terrorism.[37]

Hope that the president's speech marked a major change in administration policy did not survive lunch. At 11:30 A.M. on the same day, Secretary of Defense Rumsfeld told a Pentagon press conference that the president did not envision using American forces as part of ISAF, nor did the United States support the expansion of ISAF outside of Kabul. Rumsfeld said he was opposed to using Americans for peacekeeping because of the limited size of the U.S. military and the fact that soldiers should not perform nonmilitary jobs. As for U.S. policy toward Afghanistan, Deputy Secretary of Defense Paul Wolfowitz said the United States should help build a national army and police force, use international peacekeepers to preserve security in Kabul, and send small teams of U.S. Special Forces to work with the regional warlords. To do more, he said, would risk ignoring Afghanistan's history of regional power holders and intervening too actively on behalf of the central government. The U.S. goal, Wolfowitz said, was to create conditions so that Afghanistan would not revert to the kind of terrorist haven it became after the Soviets' departure.

The concerns created by the Defense Department's limited vision were reinforced by the growing gap between the administration's rhetoric about assisting Afghan recovery and the reality on the ground. Pledges of billions of dollars of international economic assistance failed to materialize. Tensions between rival warlords boiled over into armed clashes between their supporters. Even after his selection as president by the national grand council (*loya jirga*), Karzai remained "little more than the mayor of Kabul" who was protected by ISAF, which did not venture outside the capital. Most Afghans believed that without major international help, Karzai's government could not establish internal security, which was the key to rebuilding the country.[38]

The growing instability in Afghanistan led to mounting concern in Congress that the administration was "seizing defeat from the jaws of victory" by its refusal to support peacekeeping and nation building in Afghanistan. Senator Joseph Biden, chairman of the Senate Foreign Relations Committee, sent a letter to President Bush urging expansion of ISAF and its deployment throughout the country. Biden also proposed shifting $130 million in counterterrorism funding to support peacekeeping in Afghanistan.[39] Senator Chuck Hagel (R–Nebraska), another member of the Senate Foreign Relations Committee, said the administration was "adrift" and was "only doing enough in Afghanistan to stay in the game." According to the *Washington Post,* congressional staffers and some administration officials believed "U.S. policy was hamstrung by President Bush's aversion to broad-based nation building and his refusal to expand the role of ISAF. The resulting policy —high on rhetoric and low on engagement—amounted to a gamble that things would work out." In Afghanistan, growing anxiety about deteriorating security was emphasized by President Karzai's decision to replace his Afghan security force with U.S. Special Forces personnel.[40]

America's European allies shared congressional discomfort over the administration's aversion to peacekeeping and the growing insecurity in Afghanistan. The Europeans balked at U.S. suggestions that they should take responsibility for peacekeeping in Afghanistan. They also took exception when the United States indicated that the next step in its war against terrorism would be a military assault to drive Saddam Hussein from power in Iraq. Within six months after the September 11 attacks, the sense of solidarity between the United States and Europe had dissipated and the transatlantic allies were at odds over a broad range of issues. When President Bush visited Europe in March 2002, he was greeted by a barrage of criticism of U.S. policies on Afghan peacekeeping; global warming; nuclear proliferation; weapons of mass destruction; the Middle East; and the president's branding of Iran, North Korea, and Iraq as an "axis of evil." In contrast to September 12, when the French newspaper *Le Monde* declared, "We are all Americans now," the European media depicted the United States as a unilateralist, selfish, insular, bellicose, and gun-happy "hyperpower" that was determined to have its own way, regardless of the consequences. Europeans viewed the U.S. absorption with homeland security and global terrorism as obsessive—at a time when NATO expansion, European integration, and globalization required U.S. attention. Even long-time American friends like EU commissioner for external affairs Chris Patten were moved to advise that Washington could deal effectively with terrorism, organized crime, drugs, human trafficking, environmental degradation, poverty, and regional insecurity only through engaging in multilateralism.[41]

European exasperation with the United States reached a crescendo on June 30, 2002, when the United States vetoed a UN Security Council resolution extending the mandate of the UN mission in Bosnia. The U.S. cast its veto because the Security Council refused to grant the forty-six American police officers serving in the IPTF immunity from prosecution by the International Criminal Court (ICC), which was scheduled to come into existence on July 1. The ICC was established with initial American support as a court of last resort for prosecuting war crimes, human rights violations, and genocide. In explaining the U.S. position, UN ambassador John Negroponte said the U.S. did not oppose the UN mission in Bosnia but wanted to demonstrate its concern that American peacekeepers might be brought before the tribunal. Defense Secretary Rumsfeld warned that the United States might not join future peace operations without a grant of blanket immunity from the ICC. President Bush said the prospect of American soldiers being dragged into court was "very troubling."[42]

In response, European members of the Security Council criticized the U.S. veto as "extraordinary, unnecessary, and an attempt to misuse the council to rewrite a treaty." Secretary-General Annan warned that the United States was putting the entire UN peacekeeping system at risk when the type of politically motivated prosecution the U.S. feared was "highly improbable." In fact, there were only 677 American police, 34 military observers, and one soldier currently serving in UN peacekeeping missions, so the potential for the ICC to prosecute Americans was extremely limited. In Europe, NATO ambassadors were called into emergency session to consider the ramifications of the U.S. action. The president of the EU issued a statement regretting the American decision and reaffirming the EU commitment to the ICC.[43] At home, the *New York Times* warned editorially that U.S. actions "could unravel UN peacekeeping, destroying a mechanism that had quieted conflicts and spread a burden that might have fallen on American troops alone. It is bad enough that the Bush administration is trying to undermine the ICC. It should avoid damaging international peacekeeping as well."[44]

Stung by the outpouring of criticism, the United States relented and on July 12 voted in favor of UN Security Council Resolution 1423, which extended the mandate of the UN's Bosnian mission until December 31, 2002.[45] During the twelve days of hectic deliberations required to resolve the dispute, the EU bravely offered to step in immediately and take over the Bosnian police mission. In fact, the EU was completely unprepared to assume responsibility for monitoring the police and judicial system in Bosnia. Members of the EU advance team had just begun working with their IPTF counterparts and reportedly were overwhelmed by the complexity of the UN mission. After learning that UN vehicles and equipment had been procured from non-EU countries, the EU decided to purchase new vehicles and equipment, which would not arrive until September. Further, the EU program was predicated upon the IPTF completing the final phase of its mission implementation plan, which would not happen until December. If the UN mission had ended abruptly, the IPTF would have been required to immediately repatriate its complement of 1,552 officers and close down operations in 254 locations. It also would have had to remove or dispose of $60 million in material assets. The incident left the United Nations and the Europeans badly shaken. It also left them wondering whether the Bush administration's paranoia regarding the ICC and aversion to peacekeeping had blinded American officials to the negative impact of their single-minded pursuit of U.S. foreign policy objectives on the international community.[46]

By the first anniversary of the attacks of September 11, observers on both sides of the Atlantic were wondering whether the Bush administration's true intentions had been articulated in a blunt statement by Richard Haass, the State Department's director for policy planning. Haass said, "The principal aim of U.S. foreign policy is to integrate other countries and organizations into arrangements that will sustain a world consistent with U.S. interests and values."[47] In fact, the administration's policy of "unilaterialism" seemed increasingly at variance with the post–World War II "grand strategy of American foreign policy to create an international order based upon a tightly woven fabric of common values, shared understandings, and mutual obligations." President Bush had campaigned for the presidency by calling for a shift away from the Clinton administration's emphasis on multilateralism toward the pursuit of U.S. national interests and the rebuilding of the nation's military. The problem was that "the belief system the president brought into office—which condemned Clinton as a serial intervener and sought to withdraw from U.S. overcommitments to peacekeeping and nation building—was in direct conflict with the reality Bush was handed on September 11." The United States was attempting to lead a global coalition in a war against terrorism at the same time it appeared to ignore the interests of the global community it was ostensibly fighting to defend.[48]

The inevitable legacy of U.S. military action against regimes that harbored terrorism would be postconflict environments where the U.S. would have to engage in peacekeeping and nation building in order to create sustainable security and ensure the survivability of new democratic governments. In late 2002, the Pentagon responded to the continuing deterioration in the security situation in Afghanistan by shifting the focus of U.S. military operations toward greater involvement in civil affairs and reconstruction. American troops began providing humanitarian assistance and took on road and school construction. U.S. forces also assumed a policing role by ensuring that disputes between regional leaders did not end in violent confrontations.[49] In December, the Defense Department initiated a program to establish eight to ten Provincial Reconstruction Teams (PRTs) at bases near major cities throughout Afghanistan. The first three pilot teams were assigned to Bamyan, Kunduz, and Gardez. Each of these sixty-member contingents would be commanded by a senior U.S. military officer and consist of personnel from Special Forces, Civil Affairs, Army Engineers, the State Department, the Agency for International Development, and other coalition forces. The PRTs would provide assistance in rebuilding local infrastructure and ensuring local security, but would not perform police functions. Officially they would remain part of Operation Enduring Freedom and would not be part of ISAF or designated as peace-keepers.[50] The experience gained from this tentative engagement in nation building would be directly applicable if the Bush administration carried through on its announced intention to disarm Saddam Hussein and achieve a regime change in Iraq.

THE POSTCONFLICT CHALLENGE IN IRAQ

At the beginning of 2003, the United States faced an unprecedented security challenge. It arose from a global terrorism based on intolerant ideologies, the willingness of adherents to sacrifice their lives, and their determination to use weapons of mass destruction (WMD).[51] The United States was in the second phase of the war in Afghanistan. Coalition military forces and their Afghan allies had driven al Qaeda and the Taliban from Afghanistan, but the leadership had survived. Small groups of al Qaeda and Taliban fighters continued to harass U.S. forces from safe havens in the lawless tribal border area of Pakistan. An ongoing global search for al Qaeda operatives was punctuated by terrorist attacks in Asia, Africa, and the Middle East and periodic alerts of new attacks in the United States. Concurrently, the Bush administration sounded an alarm concerning the threat posed by an old enemy, President Saddam Hussein of Iraq. In a television address to the nation on October 7, 2002, President Bush warned that Iraq "possesses and produces chemical and biological weapons. It is seeking nuclear weapons. It has given shelter and support to terrorism and practices terror against its own people. While there are other dangers in the world, the threat from Iraq stands alone because it gathers the most serious dangers of our age in one place."[52]

In truth, Saddam Hussein had provided the United States with a long list of reasons for seeking a regime change in Iraq. In addition to invading Kuwait and precipitating the Gulf War, he had invaded other neighboring states, killed masses of Kurds and Iranians with poison gas, administered a brutal police state, accumulated chemical and biological weapons of mass destruction, and attempted to build nuclear weapons. He had murdered or taken revenge against anyone who might stand against him, including his two sons-in-law. He had also sought to assassinate a former American president, President Bush's father. While Saddam's links to al Qaeda and international terrorism remained open to question, he had conducted terrorist operations abroad and could provide extremist organizations with weapons of mass destruction.[53] Saddam was not insane, but he had repeatedly demonstrated that he was capable of bizarre actions, miscalculations, and egregious judgment. There were no constraints on his behavior within the Iraqi political structure. He was also willing to take enormous risks and to allow his country to absorb extensive damage and loss of life in his attempts to become the leader of the Arab world.[54]

In Iraq, Saddam Hussein exercised power through a sophisticated security structure and a vast network of informers, violence, and extreme brutality in dealing with dissent. He also skillfully balanced competing forces within the country, playing on ethnic and religious rivalries and using co-optation and financial inducements. He had concentrated decision making within a tight circle of family, close relatives, his Bani al-Nasiri tribe, and those from his hometown, Tikrit. Beyond this ruling group, he relied upon patronage, tribal allegiance, ethnic affiliation, and economic leverage. The core of this system was a pervasive security apparatus with the primary units supervised by his youngest son. At the same time, all state structures had been corrupted and transformed into instruments of support for one-man rule. The UN's sanctions regime and its Oil-for-Food Program allowed Saddam to decide which domestic and international firms were awarded contracts. This unintended consequence of UN efforts to ease the suffering of Iraq's people gave Saddam unprecedented control over the country's economy and enabled him to reward the loyal regime supporters. It also enabled him to direct lucrative contracts to firms in France, Russia, and China in a successful effort to build support on the Security Council. At the same time, regime-sanctioned smuggling provided lucrative incomes for Saddam's relatives, the Baath party elite, and corrupt businessmen. Iraq's impoverished middle class could only watch as a class of unsavory nouveau riches emerged to flout their fortunes made on the black market. "This combination of ruthlessness, an all-intrusive security and intelligence apparatus, close kinship and tribal connections, and an elaborate system of co-optation based on reward and punishment enabled the regime to withstand internal and external challenges."[55]

To ensure his rule, Saddam established an interlocking network of military and civilian security organizations with different official missions but with overlapping and redundant functions concerned with intelligence gathering and internal security. These security services were accountable to Saddam through the regime's National Security Council, which he chaired. Their redundant responsibilities and vaguely defined relationships ensured that plots against the regime were likely to be detected and that the various agencies would compete with each other. The result was a pervasive and encompassing system that converted Iraq into a police state. According to former CIA analyst Kenneth Pollack, "Everyone in Iraq must assume that he or she is surrounded by security agents, informants, surveillance devices, and would-be snitches. The result is that few Iraqis can summon the courage to take even the first step toward opposition, and most live their lives in constant fear."[56]

In Saddam's Iraq, the following civilian security organizations were created to preserve his rule.

Special Security Directorate (SSD: al-Amn al-Khas). Under the leadership of Saddam's youngest son, Qusay Saddam Hussein, the SSD's five thousand members were from the president's Tikriti clan and were hand picked by Qusay from other parts of the security apparatus for their loyalty. The SSD's responsibilities included protecting the president and his immediate family and securing the presidential palaces. It also supplied security details for other senior officials, both providing protection and reporting on their activities. The SSD was charged with the regime's most sensitive security tasks, such as concealing the WMD program, evading the embargo on sensitive technologies, and supervising the military forces that were responsible for protecting the president. The SSD included the Presidential Guard, the Palace Guard, the Special Republican Guard, and the Republican Guard, all of which reported to the head of the SSD.

General Intelligence Directorate (Jihaz al Mukhabbarat). Between 1973 and the Gulf War, the Mukhabbarat was headed by Saddam's brother, and its powers increased significantly. After the war, it lost influence and personnel with the rise of the SSD headed by Saddam's son. The Mukhabbarat's purview was all-inclusive, but its primary missions were foreign espionage and intelligence collection, supervision of Iraqi embassy personnel, covert action, assassinations, and terrorist operations. Domestically, its responsibilities included suppression of Kurdish and Shiite opposition, monitoring foreign embassies, and surveillance of all other intelligence and security agencies, government ministries, the Baath Party, and the Iraqi military.

General Security Directorate (GSD: al-Amn al-'Amm). The GSD was the oldest and largest of the security services. Its primary concern was internal security, and its operatives were located in every jurisdiction and kept abreast of everything that transpired within their area. GSD personnel were responsible for detecting dissent among the general public and monitoring the daily lives of Iraqi citizens, especially prominent personalities. A good part of the GSD's mission was intimidating the population. Its heavy-handed operatives were responsible for most of the official harassment suffered by Iraqi citizens.

Baath Party Security Agency (BPS: al-Amn al-Hizb). The ruling Baath party had an internal security apparatus that over-saw the activities of Iraqis through party security branches in organizations such as universities, factories, and trade unions. The BPS was responsible for security in all party offices, moni-toring the activities of party members, and security activities not directly related to the state.[57]

Iraqi National Police (INP: Shurta). Below these security agencies were the national police and border guards who were responsible for law enforcement. Under the monarchy, the INP force had grown to 23,400 personnel by the 1958 revolution. Established with the assistance of British advisers, the INP was under the jurisdiction of the Interior Ministry and performed routine police functions. The INP included representatives from all ethnic groups and religious denominations. In the 1960s, police academies were established to improve training. The INP had positive relations with the public and enjoyed a reputation for professionalism, political neutrality, and honesty. After 1968, the Baath party enacted legislation that led to the militarization of the INP and its close association with the army. By the beginning of 2003, the force strength of the INP was approximately sixty thousand.[58]

Over time, as Saddam consolidated power, the INP was increasingly marginalized and its responsibilities for internal security and protection of the regime were subsumed by the various security organizations. The INP remained responsible for law enforcement, but the persuasiveness of the regime's security appa-ratus and its brutal methods meant that crimes were more likely to be committed by regime operatives than criminals. In many cases, the INP was prevented from investigating criminal activity under orders from the security services. After the Gulf War, the INP suffered from years of neglect and deprivation. The INP suffered from repressive political leadership, which discouraged initiative and efforts to modernize the force. Under the impact of sanctions and the resulting decline in living standards, members of the INP were forced to turn to petty corruption.

Planning for the postwar period

On February 11, 2003, less than two months before U.S.-led coalition forces would enter Iraq, the Bush administration made its first formal statement concerning its plans for postwar Iraq. In testimony before the Senate Foreign Relations Committee, Marc Grossman, undersecretary of state for political affairs, and his Defense Department counterpart, Douglas Feith, provided a general outline of the administration's thinking. Grossman said the president had not made a final decision about how the United States would proceed, but he had provided clear guidance that the U.S. should be prepared to meet the humanitarian, reconstruction, and administrative challenges that would follow the "liberation" of Iraq. According to the undersecretary, the administration was planning a three-stage transition to a future democratic Iraq—

1. Stabilization, where an interim coalition military administration would ensure security, stability, and public order for a period of up to two years.

2. Transition, where authority would be passed to Iraqi institutions.

3. Transformation, where a democratically elected Iraqi government would govern Iraq on the basis of a new constitution drafted by representatives of the Iraqi people.[59]

To ensure the United States could meet its responsibilities, Undersecretary of Defense Feith said, the president signed National Security Presidential Directive 24 on January 20, creating the Office of Reconstruction and Humanitarian Assistance (ORHA) at the Pentagon. ORHA was responsible for detailed preplanning and for nation building in Iraq. In the event of war, Feith said, most of the people in this "expeditionary" unit would deploy to the region where they would supervise humanitarian assistance and relief operations. ORHA was headed by Lieutenant General Jay Garner, (U.S. Army, ret.), who in 1991 had played a leading role in Operation Provide Comfort, the post–Gulf War response to the humanitarian crisis created by Saddam's attacks on the Kurds. Garner reported through Feith to Secretary of Defense Donald Rumsfeld. ORHA was staffed by personnel on detail from State, Treasury, Energy, AID, Agriculture, and Justice, including experts on police training and judicial reform. It was responsible for three operations, each under a civilian coordinator: humanitarian relief, reconstruction, and humanitarian assistance. A fourth coordinator was responsible for communications, logistics, and the budget. Feith said the United States would try to share the postwar burden and would encourage participation by coalition partners, the UN, NGOs, and others. The U.S. goal was to transfer authority to the Iraqis as soon as possible. Feith said the United States would not, however, "foist burdens on those who were not prepared to carry them."[60]

Undersecretary Grossman noted that the State Department had been working with Iraqi exile organizations on the Future of Iraq Project—an ambitious endeavor involving seventeen working groups on topics ranging from transitional justice and democratic principles to education and energy. Among the results of this effort, Grossman said, was the drafting, in Arabic, of six hundred pages of proposals for the reform of Iraqi criminal and civil codes; the trial of Saddam Hussein; and reform of the police, courts, and prisons. While the Iraqi diaspora was a "great resource," Grossman made clear the United States would not create a provisional Iraqi government or simply hand power to the Iraqi exile organizations. He said the U.S. goal was the creation of an Iraq that was a democratic, unified, multiethnic state that would be at peace with its neighbors and devoid of weapons of mass destruction and ties to terrorism.[61]

Although Grossman's statement provided some initial insight into the Bush administration's intentions, the general nature of his comments sent a message that planning for post-

Saddam Iraq was still very much a work in progress. This unleashed criticism from Congress and the media that the administration was unprepared to managing a postconflict situation in Iraq that was likely to be chaotic and dangerous for coalition forces. On February 20, administration officials briefed reporters on a "finalized blueprint" for managing postwar Iraq. Under this plan, the commander of U.S. Central Command, General Tommy Franks, would head a U.S. military administration that would remove the Saddam regime, dismantle its terrorist infrastructure, and run the country until Iraq's WMD were located and neutralized. In the immediate aftermath of the fighting, U.S. military teams would deliver emergency humanitarian aid under a program directed by General Garner. This effort would demonstrate to Iraqis that they were better off under U.S. military rule than under Saddam. In addition, the military regime would patrol Iraq's borders and ensure the country remained a unitary state that was free of interference from its neighbors, particularly Iran.[62]

When conditions stabilized, Franks would hand over control to an American civilian administrator (a former state governor or ambassador) who would direct reconstruction. Administration officials indicated that they had developed several contingency plans for the second and third phases of the transition process, but they wanted to wait until they could assess conditions on the ground before making decisions. Among the possibilities was a plan for turning authority over to an interim UN administration that would oversee the transition to an Iraqi government. In any case, responsibility for food and humanitarian aid would be handed off to the UN World Food Program, which would utilize the distribution network that had been created by the Oil-for-Food Program.[63] For its part, the UN Department of Peacekeeping Operations was already engaged in contingency planning for creating an Afghanistan-style UN political office that would be able to help administer Iraq and deliver humanitarian assistance. In January, the United Nations issued an appeal for international donors to provide $37 million to finance initial preparedness for Iraq.[64]

On February 21, less than a month before the invasion, Garner convened the first joint meeting of military and civilian planners for a two-day "rock drill" at the National Defense University in Washington D.C.[65] Military planning had been underway since the previous summer, but Garner's staff had been preparing for postconflict reconstruction for just one month. Despite the administration's rhetoric, Garner was dismayed to discover that an overwhelming amount of work remained to be done. Although the president had directed DOD to lead the planning for the postconflict period, preparations continued in bureaucratic "stovepipes," with little coordination among agencies. In particular, ORHA ignored the findings of the State Department's $5 million Future of Iraq Project. Thomas Warrick, the project's director, and a number of other State Department nominees were pointedly not invited to join the ORHA staff. Instead, planning at DOD proceeded under a group of former generals brought back from retirement.[66]

Perhaps the biggest difference between Defense and State over postwar Iraq concerned the role of the Iraqi exile community. At Defense, supporters of Iraqi National Congress (INC) chairman Ahmed Chalabi argued that the United States should hurry up and create an Iraqi government under his leadership. In contrast, the State Department and CIA believed that ordinary Iraqis would rebel against any U.S. attempt to install a government composed of Chalabi and other expatriates. With war approaching, the Bush administration announced that the role of expatriate Iraqis would be limited to providing advice through a twenty-five-member "consultative council" that would be appointed by the United States. Iraqi expatriates would also be asked to form a commission to advise on judicial reform and the drafting of a new constitution. State Department officials made clear that any attempt by Iraqi exile groups to form a provisional government would not be tolerated.[67] Meanwhile, DOD began predeployment training of several hundred Iraqi exiles, mostly from the INC, at a military base in Taszar, Hungary. According to a Pentagon spokesman, the intention was to create a force of Iraqis that could assist coalition forces with nonmilitary duties in Iraq. Their one-month ori-entation program would not include military training, but it would prepare them to serve as liaison officers, guides, and translators for coalition forces. The Iraqis received training in first aid, self-defense, landmine identification, and how to use protective equipment in the event of an encounter with chemical or biological weapons. Major General David Barno, the commander of the training program, said they might also serve as police in liberated areas.[68]

At the end of February 2003, the United States was clearly headed toward military intervention in Iraq. On February 23, the United States, the United Kingdom, and Spain introduced a draft UN Security Council resolution stating that Iraq had ignored its "final opportunity" to disarm. The resolution reminded the Security Council that Resolution 1441 had warned Iraq of "serious consequences" if it failed to end its WMD programs and destroy existing stocks of nuclear, chemical, and biological weapons and long-range missiles. The proposed resolution did not provide explicit authorization for U.S. military action, yet American diplomats claimed that a statement in the resolution that Iraq was in "material breach" of previous UN resolutions would provide the United States with enough "legal cover" to justify intervention.[69] On February 25, President Bush served notice that he was prepared to go to war in Iraq even without passage of a new UN resolution. The president expressed irritation at opposition in the Security Council from Germany and France and at Saddam's efforts to buy time with new promises of cooperation with UN weapons inspectors. American envoys delivered a similar message of U.S. determination in meetings with leaders in European capitals and in Moscow.[70]

In a televised speech at the American Enterprise Institute in Washington on February 26, President Bush provided the first comprehensive view of U.S. aspirations for a post-Saddam Iraq. According to the president, a "liberated" Iraq would show the power of freedom to transform the Middle East by bringing hope and progress to the lives of millions of people. Bush noted that rebuilding Iraq would not be easy and would require sustained commitment from the United States and other nations. The U.S., the president said, would "remain in Iraq as long as necessary, but not a day more."[71] Meanwhile, the American and British troop buildup in the Persian Gulf topped two hundred twenty-five thousand. These forces included five carrier battle groups and Stealth and B-52 bombers deployed to bases close to Iraq. Press reports indicated that U.S. Special Forces were already engaged in operations inside the country. British and American aircraft had begun strikes beyond the "no-fly zone" aimed at crippling Iraq's air defenses.[72]

Establishing the Rule of Law in Iraq

On the eve of U.S. military action to remove Saddam Hussein, there were myriad warnings from inside and outside the government that postwar Iraq would be difficult, confusing, and dangerous for everyone involved. Since the 1950s, regime changes in Iraq had been significantly bloodier than those in other Arab states.[73] From inside the Bush administration, the CIA and other intelligence agencies were persistent in warning that postconflict reconstruction would be more difficult than achieving a military victory. The CIA predicted that Iraqis were likely to resort to "obstruction, resistance, and armed opposition," and that pro-Saddam groups were likely to attempt to sabotage reconstruction efforts.[74] In addition, Army Chief of Staff General Eric Shenseki warned that an occupation force of at least three hundred thousand soldiers would be needed to pacify Iraq.[75]

From outside the government, the Council on Foreign Relations, the Center for Strategic and International Studies, and the U.S. Institute of Peace warned that Iraq's recent history gave every indication that extreme violence would erupt immediately following the end of hostilities.[76] Following the Gulf War, returning Iraqi soldiers had ignited massive uprisings among the majority Shiites in the south and among the Kurds in the north. Rampaging crowds executed Baath party and government officials and took revenge for past injustices on members of the Sunni minority that has ruled the country since independence. A similarly violent uprising occurred in December

1998 following Operation Desert Fox, a four-day American and British air campaign that targeted biological weapons facilities and mostly empty Republican Guard barracks.[77]

Based on this experience, coalition military units would have to adjust quickly from combat to peacekeeping operations to avoid a new outbreak of ethnic, religious, and tribal strife. Without a total commitment by coalition forces to maintaining public order, it was likely that Iraq's ethnic and religious factions would again descend into a much deeper and more powerful vortex of revenge taking that would leave large areas of the country in chaos. If such a breakdown in public order occurred, neighboring states could be expected to intervene to support their proxies, protect their predominant ethnic kin, and promote their interests. Failure of coalition forces to control widespread civil disturbances would also prevent international humanitarian assistance agencies and nongovernmental relief organizations from reaching those in need. Intervention forces might also have to deal with areas affected by the release of chemical or biological weapons and to aid those affected.[78]

In the initial phase of the postwar transition, the U.S.-led coalition would be responsible for restoring public order, providing security, and ensuring effective law enforcement as part of its obligations as an occupying power under the 1949 Fourth Geneva Convention.[79] The intervention force would require substantial military personnel who were trained to interact with civilians and provide basic public services, including Civil Affairs officers, military police, medical units, and combat engineers. Troops trained in border control would also be needed to ensure that criminals and terrorists did not enter the country, and that war criminals and WMD did not leave Iraq.[80] Establishing the rule of law would require a two-phase process. First, the coalition would need to dismantle and disband the interlocking network of internal security services that were used to control the country. Second, the coalition would need to rehabilitate, retrain, and reform the Iraqi National Police (INP) so it could assume responsibility for local law enforcement. Given Iraq's population and size, the coalition would need the assistance of the INP to maintain public order.

Iraqi police officers could perform this function if they received international supervision, technical assistance, new equipment, and extensive retraining to make the difficult transition to community-oriented policing in Iraq's new democratic society.

Unlike previous peace operations, it was clear the U.S. could not depend on its allies to provide the military police, civilian constabulary, civil police, judicial personnel, and corrections officers in Iraq. Neither Great Britain nor Australia, the principal coalition partners, had constabulary forces, and the UK lacked a national police force. It was also unlikely that constabulary and civil police forces would come from NATO, the EU, or the OSCE—organizations that had staffed police missions in the Balkans. After September 11, NATO was quick to help defend the United States; NATO troops participated in the war in Afghanistan and staffed the ISAF. France and Germany, however, opposed military action to remove Saddam Hussein, and there was no indication that the European members of the Atlantic Alliance would provide constabulary and police this time if the United States intervened in Iraq.[81] As war approached, it seemed as if the United States would have to rely on its own resources to ensure postconflict stability in Iraq.

Postconflict Chaos in Iraq

Inexplicably, almost nothing was done to prepare for the inevitable outburst of civil disorder that began as U.S. military forces entered Baghdad on April 9. Remarkably, senior DOD officials assumed that, despite the trauma of war and the removal of the Saddam regime, coalition forces would inherit a fully functioning modern state with all of its institutions intact. They also believed the Iraqis would welcome American troops as liberators and that Iraqis would join coalition forces in quickly neutralizing the Baath party, Saddam Hussein's security services, and other opponents of the new order. Pentagon planners assumed that Iraqi police and the regular Iraqi army would remain on duty and would quickly assume responsibility for local security. This would enable coalition forces to tackle regime holdouts and remaining pockets of military resistance.

At the same time, Iraqi technocrats would take responsibility for managing the country's government ministries, public utilities, and other vital institutions. Instead, Iraqi security forces and all government authority simply vanished when Task Force 4-64 of the Second Brigade of the U.S Army's Third Infantry Division reached the center of Baghdad.[82]

In scenes reminiscent of the sacking of Panama City and the burning of the Sarajevo suburbs, U.S. military forces stood by and watched as mobs looted Baghdad's commercial district, ransacked government buildings, and pillaged the residences of former regime officials. The only exceptions were the Petroleum Ministry and the Palestine Hotel, which housed foreign journalists, where U.S. troops protected buildings and preserved their contents. As described by the *Washington Post's* Anthony Shadid,

> Baghdad descended into lawlessness. Scenes of mayhem were repeated across the city. Hospitals and embassies were looted, as were ministries, government offices, Baath party headquarters, and private residences. Ambulances were hijacked, as were public buses that ran their routes until the very moment of the government's collapse. Cars barreled the wrong way down streets deserted by traffic policemen. . . . Mohammed Abboud, piling a pickup truck ten feet high with booty, declared: "It's anarchy!"[83]

Once it became clear that the small number American soldiers in Baghdad were either unable or unwilling to intervene, public exuberance, joy at liberation, and economic opportunism quickly darkened into a systematic effort to strip the capital's stores and public institutions of everything of value. Families from Saddam City, the Baghdad slum inhabited by two million impoverished Shiites, and gangs of men armed with assault rifles worked their way through government ministry buildings, removing their contents, tearing out the plumbing and wiring, and then setting the buildings on fire. Looters ransacked Iraq's main medical center, the Al-Kindi Hospital, and the wards of Baghdad's other hospitals, which were jammed with victims of the U.S. bombing campaign. The mobs removed patients from their beds and carried away medical equipment that had been in use. Even the city's psychiatric hospital, the colleges of medicine and nursing, and the Red Cross headquarters were not spared. So complete was the pillaging that the International Committee of the Red Cross said the city's hospitals were unable to treat war wounded and other victims of the conflict. By night, families armed themselves and barricaded their homes to protect them from the "Ali Babas," the gangs of thieves that freely roamed the city.[84]

In the vast industrial parks south of the capital, mobs ransacked factories and warehouses, returning home in a parade of cars, trucks, and wheelbarrows, piled high with stolen goods. In heavy-equipment parking lots, thieves jump-started tractors and bulldozers and drove them away. More ominously, looters also ransacked and destroyed much of Iraq's nuclear facilities and industrial plants, which were suspected of housing or producing WMD components. With only twelve thousand soldiers to police a city of four and a half million, the U.S. military was unable to prevent these critical sites from being pillaged systematically by gangs of thieves and vandals. In many cases, the destruction looked like the work of professionally trained saboteurs intent on ensuring that U.S. authorities would never be able to determine what the facilities had actually manufactured.[85]

Mobs of looters and more sinister forces also attacked Baghdad's major cultural centers. During the initial wave of chaos, crowds burst into the National Museum of Antiquities, looting and destroying its irreplaceable Babylonian, Sumerian, and Assyrian collections. Most of the looters were local people bent on letting off steam, but there were also elements with a more sinister purpose: according to officials at the UN Economic, Scientific, and Cultural Organization (UNESCO), the pillaging was the work of organized criminal gangs that bribed museum guards and minor officials for keys to the vaults holding the most valuable works of art. UNESCO director-general Koichiro Matsuura said the looting was well planned by professionals who stole priceless historical and cultural items that could be sold by highly organized trafficking rings to collectors in Europe, the United States, and Japan. U.S. attorney general John Ashcroft told an Interpol meeting in Lyon, France that a "strong case could be made that the theft of artifacts was perpetrated by organized criminal groups who knew exactly what they were looking for."[86] Initial reports that the museum's entire collection of one hundred seventy thousand items was lost proved exaggerated, but careful accounting by the United States and international experts determined that at least six thousand artifacts had been removed by thieves who knew the value of the items.[87] Looters and arsonists also attacked the Iraqi National Library and Iraq's principal Islamic library, destroying their priceless collections of manuscripts and archives. The National Library housed a copy of all the books published in Iraq, plus all doctoral theses. It also had books from the Ottoman and Abbasid periods dating back a millennium.[88]

As a result of years of neglect and the recent wave of widespread looting, Baghdad's fragile infrastructure ceased to function: electricity failed, potable water stopped flowing, and telephone service ceased. Shops closed and Iraqis began to run short of basic necessities. Women were afraid to leave their homes, as stories of daylight kidnappings and rapes swept the city. Murders, muggings, and robberies went unreported by residents who could find no one in authority. Hundreds of Baath party members and informants were gunned down by former victims who were working from lists taken from security service headquarters. Into this void stepped a variety of opportunists, self-appointed officials, Sunni sheiks, and Shiite clerics who attempted to seize control of towns, government ministries, hospitals, universities, and other institutions. The situation became so chaotic that General David McKiernan, commander of U.S. forces in Iraq, issued a statement reminding Iraqis that the coalition "retained absolute authority." The same day, American soldiers arrested Muhammad Mohsen Zobeidi, the self-appointed "mayor" of Baghdad.[89]

U.S. military efforts to restore order and control lawlessness were hindered by a growing number of armed attacks on American soldiers. Baath party loyalists, remnants of the security services, former soldiers, Islamic extremists, and Arab terrorists ambushed military convoys, sniped at soldiers standing guard duty, and attacked isolated outposts with increasing sophistication and deadly result. At the same time, U.S. military spokesmen and soldiers alike made clear their lack of enthusiasm for performing law enforcement functions. In response to demands from Iraqis that the United States restore order, Brigadier General Vincent Brooks, U.S. Central Command spokesman, said the U.S. military would help rebuild civil administration but expected the Iraqis to assume responsibility for public order. "At no time," Brooks said, "do we see [the U.S. military] becoming a police force."[90] In a similar vein, Major General David Petraeus, commander of the 101st Airborne, told reporters, "We should discourage looting, but we're not going to stand between a crowd and a bunch of mattresses." Other American commanders said they lacked the personnel and the mandate to interfere with Iraqi civilians. Individual soldiers bluntly told reporters that they were neither trained nor equipped to do police work. In Baqubah, soldiers of the 588th Engineering Battalion, 2nd Brigade, 4th Infantry Division were trained in weapons demolition and bridge building, but they were ordered to use their M113 armored personnel carriers like squad cars to patrol the city. As one soldier explained, "By the time we get there, the bad guys are gone."[91]

With fires still burning in government ministries and the National Library, U.S. military authorities appealed publicly for Iraqi police to return to duty. On April 14, 2003, joint patrols of American soldiers and Iraqi police tentatively made their initial appearance on the streets of the capital. Iraqi police were not permitted to carry weapons, and the appearance of some officers produced outrage from citizens who claimed they were guilty of corruption and other abuses under Saddam Hussein. U.S. military Civil Affairs officers attempted to weed out the thugs while trying to encourage additional officers to join their colleagues.[92] Military commanders explained that rebuilding the police was one of the tasks assigned to General Garner and his staff of civilian administrators. Security conditions prevented Garner and a small advance team from reaching Baghdad until April 21, twelve days after U.S. forces arrived in the city. The remainder of his three-hundred-member staff arrived some days later.[93]

ORHA's plan for Iraq's reconstruction was based on the assumption that Garner's team would find government ministries intact. Instead, ORHA's "ministry teams" found that seventeen of twenty-one of Iraq's ministries had "simply evaporated." American officials found the burned out shells of public buildings, their contents looted and their staffs scattered, frightened, and demoralized. ORHA was prepared to handle oil fires, masses of refugees, the release of chemical and biological weapons, and mass starvation. The U.S. military, however, had followed a battle plan that called for pinpoint bombing, the immediate seizure of the oil fields, the bypassing of urban centers, and a rapid advance to Baghdad to neutralize WMD. As a result, there was no large-scale destruction of infrastructure, no widespread urban fighting, and no refugee crisis or other disasters for which ORHA had planned. Instead, there was a complete breakdown in public order and collapse of public services, problems that Garner's team was ill equipped to handle.[94]

Only a small number of Garner's staff had experience in previous peace operations and still fewer had ever visited Iraq. Almost none spoke Arabic. At their heavily guarded headquarters in one of Saddam Hussein's palaces, ORHA personnel found little or no office equipment and no provision for interoffice communication by e-mail or telephones. Staff members could communicate only by visiting one another's office; they could not call out from the palace without going outdoors to use a satellite telephone. Living accommodations were primitive, with many people sharing a single room; many ORHA staff members were unaccustomed to the one-hundred-and-twenty-degree heat of a typical Iraqi late spring day, and there was often no electricity to run air conditioners or fans.[95]

A New Start on Reconstruction

On May 1, 2003, President Bush stood on the deck of the USS *Abraham Lincoln,* an aircraft carrier returning to California

from the Persian Gulf, and proclaimed that major combat operations were over in Iraq and that the U.S.-led coalition had
achieved victory. Bush told the five thousand Naval personnel
gathered on the flight deck that "no terrorists will gain weapons
of mass destruction from the Iraqi regime because that regime is
no more." The president said that difficult work remained in
Iraq but that the U.S. would stay until it was finished.[96] Six days
later, on May 7, the president attempted to reverse the deteriorating situation in Iraq by appointing former ambassador L. Paul
Bremer III to replace General Garner. Bremer had previously
served as head of the State Department's Office of Counterterrorism and ambassador to the Netherlands; he had also
worked for Kissinger Associates in New York. Unlike Garner,
Bremer reported directly to Secretary Rumsfeld and enjoyed the
support of Secretary of State Powell. Bremer came with a
deserved reputation for decisiveness. In commenting on this
aspect of Bremer's character, senior Pentagon adviser Richard
Perle said Bremer was aggressive by "foreign-service standards"
but that he himself had "seen hummingbirds that were aggressive by foreign-service standards."[97]

Bremer's arrival in Baghdad brought both a more telegenic
public image and a new dynamism to what was now called the
Coalition Provisional Authority (CPA). Among his first acts was
to ban those who had held one of the top four ranks in the
Baath party from holding government jobs, reversing ORHA's
policy that banned only the most senior Baathists from public
service. The CPA's decision answered criticism from some Iraqis
that former Baathists were being allowed to remain in power.
Yet it deprived the Iraqi government of up to thirty thousand
senior bureaucrats, many of whom had either been forced to
join the party or did so to avoid harassment. This broad-brush
vetting removed an entire level of senior leadership from government ministries—including the police—and created bitter-
ness, mistrust, and confusion; it also further slowed the restoration of government services.[98] The deteriorating security situation was exacerbated even more by the CPA's decision to disband the Iraqi army and to order those few soldiers who had

remained in their barracks to return home. This action was taken without promise of pay or of a future in the new Iraq. Within days, crowds of former soldiers staged angry protests in front of CPA headquarters. Disbanding the military added approximately four hundred thousand unemployed young men to an already volatile situation and increased the security challenges facing the U.S. military and the Iraqi police. Disenfranchised former government officials, police, and soldiers were potential and ready recruits for anti-American groups and organized crime.

In a June 11, 2003 report on conditions in Baghdad, the International Crisis Group stated that Iraq's capital was in "distress, chaos, and ferment." Two months after the termination of major combat operations, the CPA had failed to provide personal security, restore essential services, or establish a positive rapport with the Iraqi public. The report noted that Iraqis had seen their public institutions destroyed by uncontrolled looters and saboteurs; they were not safe on the streets or in their homes, as the number of murders, revenge killings, rapes, carjackings, and armed robberies continued to rise without an effective coalition response. It was "conventional wisdom," the ICG report said, that the Americans had blundered by failing to protect vital institutions and impose public order in the first days of the occupation: "The subsequent failure to impose order once the extent of the problem became clear can only be considered a reckless abdication of the occupying power's obligation to protect the population." The report concluded that general lawlessness not only posed a constant danger to Iraqi citizens but also inhibited the restoration of the cities' destroyed infrastructure.[99]

In Baghdad, Bernard Kerik, a former New York City police commissioner and the CPA's senior police adviser, was severely handicapped in providing an effective response to the problem of general lawlessness. Kerik's teams consisted of twenty-six American police advisers from the U.S. Justice Department's ICITAP program. These veterans of previous peace operations were responsible for conducting a nationwide needs assessment and developing a plan of action while reconstituting the Iraqi police, customs, immigration, border patrol, fire departments, and emergency medical services.[100] This assignment proved to be something of a "Mission: Impossible," given the lack of financial resourses and the magnitude of the challenge.

The Iraqi National Police force was the only institution in Saddam's interlocking network of intelligence and security services to remain intact at the end of the war. Yet the INP was at the bottom of the bureaucratic hierarchy and clearly suffered from years of mismanagement, lack of resources, and few professional standards. ICITAP's assessment team found that the INP's sixty thousand members had little understanding of basic police skills. While most of its officers were graduates of a police college, its noncommissioned officers had little formal education. Under Saddam Hussein, the INP had been militarized, and its doctrine, procedures, and weapons were completely unsuited to policing in a democratic society. Iraqis saw the INP as part of a cruel and repressive regime and described its officers as brutal, corrupt, and untrustworthy. Furthermore, the police infrastructure was heavily damaged or completely destroyed by looters and arsonists following the collapse of the regime. Iraqi police officers who had remained at their posts until U.S. forces entered Baghdad took their personal weapons and went home. Rampaging mobs destroyed police stations, stole police vehicles, and walked away with weapons and equipment. Police returned to find their stations gutted or reduced to a pile of smoldering ruins.[101]

The assessment team concluded that the INP would require substantial international assistance to make the transition to a modern, community-oriented, and democratic police force. Given the INP's record, a thorough vetting of its personnel was required to remove Baath party loyalists and those who were guilty of human rights abuses and corruption. Second, those who survived the vetting process would require retraining, new weapons, and new equipment, plus a probationary period under the supervision of international police advisers who could monitor their performance. The ICITAP team prescribed a robust training program in basic police skills for all ranks and courses in police management and administration for the officer corps. To direct this effort, the team called for the deployment of more than sixty-six hundred international police advisers, including three hundred and sixty professional police trainers who would be assigned to the police college and other training sites, and one hundred and seventy advisers on border control functions.[102] To help meet this need, the State Department contracted with DynCorp to recruit one thousand American police and a limited number of former prosecutors, judges, and corrections officers. DynCorp located the personnel, but, as of the end of July 2003, the CPA had not decided whether to accept the ICITAP advisers' recommendations; hence, the project was put on hold. As for the remaining fifty-five hundred police, including ten constabulary units with a total of twenty-five hundred officers, the ICITAP assessment assumed that they would be provided by other countries. Unfortunately, U.S. diplomatic initiatives to encourage other countries to contribute forces produced only meager results.[103]

Despite the difficulties encountered in reconstituting the Iraqi police, the CPA announced plans to expand the role of Iraqis in establishing postconflict security. On July 20, 2003, General John Abizaid, the newly appointed head of U.S. Central Command, announced that the United States would create an Iraqi "militia-like civil defense force," which would operate initially with coalition forces and, eventually, alone. The new force of thirty-five hundred personnel would be organized into ten battalions, each of which would be "sponsored" by a different U.S. military unit. The force would be more heavily armed than the Iraqi police but would not be armed or trained to operate like an army. This new force would join the nearly nine thousand members of the Iraqi Facility Protection Service, a new security-guard force that would replace U.S. soldiers in protecting Iraq's public buildings and other vital sites. Creation of these new Iraqi units would remove Americans from dangerous sentry posts and increase the likelihood that attacks on coalition forces would also result in Iraqi casualties. Meanwhile, the number and sophistication of assaults on U.S. forces continued to mount. On the day of General Abizaid's announcement, the number of

Americans killed since President Bush had declared an end to combat operations reached thirty-six. It also seemed clear that the one hundred and fifty thousand American troops remaining in Iraq would continue to be there for some time.

Against a background of Iraqi discontent and growing congressional concern in the United States, the Pentagon asked a team of outside experts from the Center for Strategic and International Studies (CSIS) to assess the security situation and the reconstruction effort in Iraq. In a report issued on July 17, 2003, the CSIS team concluded that the Coalition Provisional Authority was isolated from Iraqis, lacked adequate personnel and financial resources, and faced growing anti-Americanism in parts of the country. The team warned that the window of opportunity for achieving successful postwar reconstruction was rapidly closing and that the next three months would be crucial, particularly for addressing the problem of security. Although the Iraqis would ultimately have to assume responsibility for their own security, the CSIS team pointed out that it was unrealistic to expect the newly reorganized and retrained Iraqi police to successfully handle determined groups of hardened and well-organized insurgents. The new Iraqi security forces would remain dependent on coalition forces for the foreseeable future. In this regard, there was an urgent need for international police advisers, trainers, and monitors to work with the Iraqis.[104]

Despite the lessons from more than a decade of postconflict stability operations, the U.S. government was almost as poorly equipped to address the public order challenge in Iraq as it had been in Bosnia and Kosovo. During that period, the U.S. military made major investments in improving the combat efficiency of its forces based on the experiences of the Gulf War and the interventions in the Balkans—an effort that was obviously worthwhile, as the U.S. military quickly defeated the Iraqi forces and captured Baghdad with minimum losses. Yet no similar effort at efficiency on the postconflict side was made by relevant U.S. civilian agencies and executive-branch departments; they simply had not adopted postconflict stability as a core mission.

Instead, the State and Defense Departments treated each new mission as if it were the first and as if it were going to be the last. No single department had responsibility for stabilization and no one at the planning table could present a coherent view of what the United States could offer or of what it would cost. Such contingency planning—or even lack thereof—was particularly true in the areas of restoring public security and establishing the rule of law. The United States did not have civilian constabulary forces; it still relied on commercial contractors for civil police, judicial experts, and corrections officers, although it was doubtful that contractors could meet the huge challenges of postwar Iraq. Justice Department programs for training indigenous police and prosecutors (but not judges and corrections officers) still relied on ad hoc State Department project funding that would have to come from supplemental budget requests to Congress.

During its two terms in office, the Clinton administration conducted a new postconflict peace operation every two years. The Bush administration quickened the pace, intervening in a new country every 18 months, despite its aversion to nation building. As a major study by the RAND Corporation pointed out, postconflict stability operations and nation building were an "inescapable responsibility of the world's only superpower." Once the U.S. government admitted that fact, there was much it could do to improve its ability to conduct such operations.[105]

9

WHERE IS THE
LONE RANGER WHEN
WE NEED HIM?

As the War on Terrorism progresses, U.S. ability to establish sustainable security in postconflict societies will become more important, not less. Even prior to September 11, the Pentagon had begun planning to reshape the U.S. military to address a range of new contingencies. The defense review reflected an emphasis on homeland defense against asymmetrical threats from international terrorism; cyberwarfare; transnational organized crime; illicit trafficking in drugs, weapons, and people; and the proliferation of weapons of mass destruction. The study concluded that such threats were likely to originate in countries experiencing political, ethnic, and religious turmoil. After September 11, it became unmistakably clear that failed states pose a direct threat to U.S. national security. Al Qaeda found sanctuary in Afghanistan, Albania, Bosnia, Sudan, Somalia, and other countries with intractable conflicts. The United States cannot afford to be grudging in its attention to messy situations in places that traditionally were not considered to be vital to U.S. national strategic interests. The United States also will need the capacity to project its power in a manner that ensures the rapid restoration of stability and the creation of an environment conducive to postconflict reconciliation and reconstruction. In the words of a former U.S. Army officer,

"The U.S. cannot be unprepared for missions it does not want, as if the lack of preparedness might prevent our going. We can not be like children who refuse to get dressed for school."[1]

To deal with rogue states and international terrorism, the United States will need new forces and a new approach to post-conflict intervention. It must maintain its war-fighting ability while becoming more adept at integrating civilian actors and processes. The mission of the military remains one of providing overall security; yet in postconflict environments, civilian actors also have critical roles to play in achieving sustainable security. The way forward was presaged by lessons learned from the international community's experience in Kosovo. In his predeparture press conference on December 17, 2000, Bernard Kouchner, the senior UN official in Kosovo, said the lesson of Kosovo was that "peacekeeping missions need to arrive with a law-and-order kit made up of trained police, judges, and prosecutors and a set of draconian security laws. This is the only way to stop criminal behavior from flourishing in a postwar vacuum of authority."[2] Such a judicial package must be supported by effective military and constabulary forces that can quickly subdue armed opposition, disarm opposing forces, handle civil disorder, and ensure that civil law enforcement officers and judicial and corrections officials can perform their functions in an atmosphere of relative security.

The importance of Kouchner's statement is that the current doctrine for peace operations—which dictates a linear transition from intervention and peace enforcement through a period of stabilization to a final phase of national institution building—is incorrect. Building rule-of-law institutions must begin as soon as the fighting stops. From the first day that U.S. Task Force Falcon entered Kosovo as part of KFOR, American troops were confronted by the same type of law-and-order mission they faced during the post–World War II occupation of Germany and Japan. In Kosovo, U.S. forces were immediately required to arrest local citizens for committing major criminal offenses, to detain them, to provide judicial review, and to establish and run prisons. Those arrested were criminals who had dynamited buildings and committed murder, arson, and rape. The perpetrators of these crimes threatened the viability of NATO's mission, which was to establish a safe and secure environment that would permit the withdrawal of U.S. troops.[3]

The international intervention force's first step in establishing sustainable postconflict security is to break the cycle of impunity for those who commit acts of violence. The intervention force must rapidly provide citizens with assurance of their personal safety and evidence that acts of revenge and other forms of violence will not be tolerated. Democratic societies, including postconflict states, must be rooted in the rule of law. Postconflict states must provide their people with the assurance that transparent processes provide the same protection and penalties for all citizens. If this does not happen, political reconciliation and economic reconstruction do not occur, and the spoilers consolidate their position and obstruct the peace process.

Paddy Ashdown, the High Representative in Bosnia, confirmed this view when he said, "In Bosnia, we thought that democracy was the highest priority, and we measured it by the number of elections we could organize. In hindsight, we should have put the establishment of rule of law first, for everything else depends on it: a functioning economy, a free and fair political system, the development of civil society, and public confidence in police and courts. We should do well to reflect on this as we formulate our plans for Afghanistan and, perhaps, Iraq."[4] Beyond the immediate restoration of public order, establishing the rule of law in postconflict societies also involves dealing with human rights violations and crimes committed during and prior to the war. The relatively rapid arrest, trial, and punishment of regime officials and military officers who have committed major abuses are important to achieving a sense of justice within society. It is also important to removing fear and to promoting reconciliation among opposing factions.

LESSONS LEARNED FROM PREVIOUS OPERATIONS

The experience with the use of international constabulary and police forces in the Balkans has been painful but instructive. The

NATO Multinational Specialized Units in Bosnia and Kosovo have been used sparingly. This has resulted from misunderstandings on the part of SFOR and KFOR commanders of their proper role and mission. Military commanders generally were unfamiliar with constabulary forces and assumed the MSUs were part of SFOR's strategic reserve, a "riot squad" that should be called only when needed. They failed to appreciate that the MSUs could perform a broad range of functions, including proactive patrolling, providing area security, and collecting intelligence. Problems with language and the absence of common doctrine also impeded efforts to use the MSUs more effectively. Commanders were unaware that the MSUs were subject to the same rules of engagement as other NATO forces. These units did not have executive authority and could not engage in law enforcement. This created additional misunderstandings within the military and between the MSUs, UN CIVPOL, and local police. As experienced law enforcement professionals in their own countries, members of the various MSU contingents, particularly the Italians, were frustrated by their lack of police powers and routinely exceeded their authority. In Kosovo, the MSU practice of detaining suspects and seizing contraband and then attempting to turn them over to the UN police was a source of constant friction between the two organizations.

The civilian UN Special Police Units in Kosovo fared better than their military counterparts, but many of the problems encountered by these units were the same. Senior police commanders, mostly from the United States and northern Europe, were unfamiliar with constabulary forces and underestimated their usefulness to the mission. In Kosovo, the SPUs eventually demonstrated their ability to perform a long list of tasks, but in nearly every case these heavily armed and highly capable units were engaged at levels well below their capacity. Apprehension on the part of senior UN officials and a lack of common doctrine and training meant the SPUs only recently were used for the first time for civil disorder management, their primary function. As part of the UNMIK police, the SPUs had executive authority and were subject to the same rules of engagement as other UN

CIVPOL. This was an advantage that was seldom utilized. The fact that members of the SPUs were not required to speak the mission language and could operate only in ten-member teams or thirty-member platoons severely limited their ability to perform a number of police functions. The fact that they were quartered in separate compounds and not in UNMIK police stations also meant that it was often a case of "out of sight, out of mind."

Many of the problems encountered by constabulary forces in the Balkans remained unresolved. However, making certain such problems would not trouble future stability operations would not be difficult. Constabulary units demonstrated that they were highly capable, versatile, and effective, if properly utilized. Missing were clear mandates, common doctrine, and joint training programs. There was also a failure to properly brief senior commanders on how these units could be used most effectively. Providing clear mandates and rules of engagement for constabulary forces would ensure that everyone understood their role and mission. Drafting common doctrine and developing joint training programs would require both unit commanders and their superiors to work together and to develop the understanding and trust that was missing in Bosnia and Kosovo.

As for civil police, the results of the experiment with international executive policing in Kosovo have been promising. At the outset, many observers warned that international police could not perform the full range of police functions in a peace operation because they would be unfamiliar with the local language, culture, and legal system. In fact, over time, the UNMIK police have proven effective in controlling crime, ensuring public safety, and providing police services. They have also demonstrated, in cooperation with the Kosovo Police School and police trainers from the OSCE, the ability to develop an effective indigenous police force. In the past year, the UNMIK police have provided Kosovo with comprehensive police services, including effective intelligence collection and a crackdown on organized crime.

The problems encountered by the UNMIK police have been those that have been experienced by previous international police missions: inadequate numbers, agonizingly slow deployment, and extreme variation in the quality of personnel. The solutions to these problems are well known but have not been implemented because of a lack of financial resources and a failure of political will. Recommendations for upgrading the Civilian Police Division at UN headquarters, creating "ready rosters," developing effective pre-mission training programs, and standardizing personnel requirements were contained in the Brahimi Report. Also included were recommendations for providing the UN police with judicial and penal counterparts so that future peace missions would include all three parts of the "justice triad"—police, courts, and prisons. Absent such a unified approach, international police are left with a situation in which criminals and violent offenders are arrested but cannot be properly detained or brought to trial.

THE MODEL FOR A U.S. STABILITY FORCE

The answer to the problem of creating sustainable security in postconflict environments is straightforward: In addition to a robust military component, a U.S. Stability Force must also comprise effective civilian constabulary, policing, and law enforcement elements (lawyers, judges, corrections officers) to maintain public order and security. These units are essential to prevent the emergence of a security gap following the cessation of hostilities and the emergence of a democratic government that can ensure public order through the rule of law. All elements of a U.S. Stability Force must be assembled and ready at the outset of military operations. They should be under the control of U.S. military authorities because unity of command in the initial phase of a stability operation is paramount. Civilian control of the civilian elements of the stability force should, however, be restored as quickly as possible.

As postconflict stability operations have shown, civilian constabulary, police, and law enforcement units deployed in a timely, fully equipped, and well coordinated manner provide an invaluable asset to U.S. military operations. The civilian units help establish police and judicial authority from the outset, thereby freeing the military to concentrate on performing other duties. Most important, they help create the vital foundation for the rule of law from which the other aspects of political, economic, and social reconstruction can go forward in an environment conducive to achieving success.

The Military

The first component of a U.S. Stability Force is a familiar one: robust military forces specifically designed, trained, and equipped for such missions. These forces must be able to deploy rapidly but still have the combat power to compel warring parties to cease fighting and abide by the terms of the peace agreement. Creating such forces will be a challenge, but the effort is already underway. The U.S. Army is already engaged in a long-term program that will transform the army from a heavy, armored force designed for duty in the Cold War to a futuristic "objective force" built around highly mobile units and information superiority on the battlefield. At Fort Lewis, Washington, the army is converting the Third Brigade, Second Infantry Division into one of as many as six new, 3,500-personnel Stryker Brigade Combat Teams (SBCTs) to be operational by 2010. These new units are built around a new medium-weight, wheeled combat vehicle, the "Stryker," that is highly maneuverable, armored, and lethal. The Department of Defense has committed to funding four units but is withholding judgment on the final two, pending a decision to add attack helicopters, 155 mm howitzers, and reconnaissance drones to increase firepower and command capabilities. The fact that the Stryker is transportable by C-130 aircraft means SBCTs can arrive anywhere in the world within ninety-six hours from bases in the United States. The brigade's one thousand–member dismounted infantry component and its own intelligence battalion give it adaptability and "situation awareness" to match its speed and firepower.[5]

Despite their considerable military prowess, the Stryker brigades are not designed to handle the type of general lawlessness that U.S. forces encountered at the beginning of stability operations in the Balkans and Iraq. In the initial stage of future missions, the most serious security challenges likely will come from civilians and ex-combatants in civilian attire. To deal with riots, looting, arson, and other forms of civil disorder, the U.S. Stability Force should include U.S. Army Military Police, who have demonstrated the ability to operate effectively in Kosovo. Trained to deal with civilians, MPs readily accepted a mission in which the goal was stability and the eventual hand-off of responsibility to civilian authorities. Military police assets within the U.S. Army are scarce; the Defense Department will need to increase the number of MPs, to shift more units from the reserves to active duty forces, and to integrate MPs with the Stryker brigades.

Special Police Units

A U.S. Stability Force should include the type of civilian Special Police Units that the United Nations developed for Kosovo. U.S. civilian constabulary forces would serve as a bridge between military and civil police forces and take on tasks that are not clearly set in either camp. Unlike military police, these civilian constabulary units could take on law enforcement functions as well as threats to public disorder. They could deploy rapidly with their own weapons, transport, communications, and logistical support. They could respond to situations requiring greater firepower, such as large-scale civil disturbances, than that maintained by civil police. They could also assist the police by performing law enforcement functions such as high-risk arrests in cases involving terrorism and organized crime.

While Special Police Units might be difficult to establish, their value in creating postconflict stability more than justifies the effort. Organizing the civilian constabulary element of the stability force will require drawing together the necessary resources. It will also require new funding and, eventually, new legislative authority. Currently, there is no funding or agency in the federal government responsible for such a program. Fortunately, personnel, skill sets, and equipment already are present in U.S. civilian law enforcement agencies in SWAT teams and special operations units. This personnel pool also includes retirees within two years of active service. The component parts need to be organized into formed, trained, and equipped units; this should be done by a federal law enforcement agency. Locating the force in a federal agency could provide a center for the development of doctrine and training programs for the use of such forces in postconflict scenarios. This would correct the primary problem that has impeded the effective use of constabulary forces in Bosnia and Kosovo. Once established, civilian constabulary forces could also contribute to U.S. security. General Barry McCaffrey, the former "drug czar" in the Clinton administration, has called for a U.S. constabulary force of forty thousand to protect America's borders against narcotics traffickers, illegal immigrants, and terrorists.[6] Civilian constabulary forces could improve homeland defense and give the United States the capability to provide such forces for postconflict stability operations.

The addition of military police and civilian constabulary to the capabilities of the Stryker brigades would give the U.S. Stability Force maximum flexibility in the use of armed force during the initial phases of the peacekeeping mission. It would also permit the rapid and seamless transition to lighter and more cost-effective forces, freeing the heavier military elements for other tasks or redeployment. The use of special U.S. military and constabulary forces for stability operations is consistent with the findings of the U.S. Commission on National Security in the Twenty-First Century (the Hart-Rudman Commission), which was tasked with developing a U.S. national security strategy for the next quarter-century. In its report, the commission concluded that the "spreading phenomena of weak and failed states, ethnic separatism, and violence and the crises they breed" will occur in the future "with sufficient regularity and simultaneity as to oblige the United States to adapt its force structure" to such contingencies. The commission recommended that the United States develop military and constabulary forces that "possess greater flexibility to operate in a range of environments," particularly those that call for "expeditionary interventions or stability operations."[7]

Civil Police

Military police and civilian constabulary forces have the technical skills to restore public order and engage in law enforcement, but they cannot serve as role models for indigenous civil police. They also should not be required to engage in the patient work of traffic control, community policing, and criminal investigation, which are normally the responsibilities of civil police in democratic societies. U.S. law prohibits the U.S. military from training foreign civilian police, and both Congress and common sense require the use of U.S. civil law-enforcement professionals to serve as role models for indigenous police in an emerging democracy. Failure to deploy a civil police force with executive authority to enforce a basic criminal code will result in prolonged deployment of military and constabulary forces.

Creating a U.S. civil police component for a U.S. Stability Force will require new funding and, possibly, new legislative authority. It will also require moving the U.S. civilian police program from the State Department to a federal law-enforcement agency. It will require federalizing U.S. police personnel, rather than relying upon commercial contractors. This will ensure that American police officers in stability operations are responsive to direction from Washington and accountable for their actions under U.S. law. Placing both the U.S. civilian constabulary force and the civil police program in one federal law-enforcement agency would provide an effective civilian police partner for the Defense Department in Washington and for the U.S. military abroad. It would provide an effective voice for the police program in the interagency process, freeing the State Department to concentrate on related foreign policy issues and diplomacy. It would also establish a cadre of law enforcement professionals that could develop doctrine, job descriptions, and training programs and interact with their UN and foreign counterparts. Federalizing the U.S. CIVPOL program would place American police officers in peace operations on a par with those of other nations. The United States now has several thousand police officers that have served in UN police missions. These veterans could form the core of a new, federalized civil police force that would be recruited specifically for service as part of a U.S. Stability Force.

Federalizing the U.S. CIVPOL program would have advantages similar to those achieved when Congress created the Transportation Security Administration (TSA) after September

11. The TSA replaced commercial contractors with federal officers to screen passengers and luggage at the nation's airports. When the first 221 federal baggage inspectors reported for duty at Baltimore-Washington International Airport on May 1, 2002, they had received forty hours of classroom instruction, five times more than their private-sector predecessors. They then underwent an additional sixty hours of on-the-job training. These new federal employees spoke English, had at least a high school diploma, and had passed a federal background examination. They also were older and most were retired military. In contrast, the contract hires they replaced were discovered to have problems with language, education, and personal finances, and some had criminal records.[8] Federalizing the U.S. civil police program would ensure that government regulations and standards of conduct would apply to the recruiting, training, and management of police personnel in this important program. It would also give the federal government the control it now lacks over American civil police officers in peace operations who wear U.S. uniforms, carry weapons provided by the U.S. government, have authority to use deadly force, but work for a commercial contractor.

Judicial and Penal Experts

In Somalia, Bosnia, East Timor, Afghanistan, and Iraq, the judicial systems literally lay in ruins. Courthouses and detention centers were destroyed. Law books and legal codes had been burned. Judges, prosecutors, and court administrators had either disappeared or were too intimidated to serve. Constabulary and police are important, but they cannot function effectively without the other two parts of the "justice triad," courts and prisons. Democracies require that those arrested are processed by a functioning judicial and penal system, without which restoration of public order is effectively and immediately compromised. In the long run, there is also a failure to provide a sense of justice for the victims of war crimes, human rights violations, and other criminal activities, which is essential to achieving sustainable security.

To complete the U.S. Stability Force, the United States

needs to quickly organize "justice teams" of lawyers, judges, court administrators, and corrections officers. These teams would be augmented by a headquarters staff, a cadre of paralegals and translators, and a training unit. They would have authority to act independently and could decide to handle sensitive cases on their own without reference to local authorities. While the teams could dispense justice directly, their primary mission would be to provide liaison and monitor local courts, which would continue to handle all but the most sensitive cases. They would provide international legal assistance and training to local attorneys, jurists, and penal officers and ensure that the courts function fairly and effectively. Judicial teams would also help ensure accountability for human rights violations, provide guidance on dealing with accused war criminals, and advise on and assist with the rehabilitation and reform of the justice system. International correction officers would take over the handling of important prisoners, supervise the release of those imprisoned for political offenses, ensure the humane treatment of prisoners, and assist with improving prison facilities.

In Kosovo and Bosnia, the United Nations discovered that in politically sensitive cases or those involving nationalist leaders or powerful gangsters, local jurists where either too intimidated or biased to render proper verdicts. The same was true of corrections officers, who were either afraid or unwilling to jail high-profile offenders. International personnel eventually were substituted to handle such cases and ensure that offenders were given fair trials and received appropriate sentences. Fortunately, the United States now has a cadre of experienced judicial experts who worked in Bosnia, Kosovo, and East Timor and can build on the experience they gained in those operations. In addition, the U.S. Institute of Peace has developed a model criminal code and set of criminal procedures for future stability operations. The creation of such a legal code was one of the recommendations in the Brahimi Report. The code and procedures are now available to the U.S. government and the United Nations for future missions.

Creating U.S. government justice teams for stability operations would complement similar planning underway among non-governmental organizations. In 1997, the Stanley Foundation began developing the concept of a rapid-reaction international legal assistance consortium (ILAC) that would enter postconflict environments simultaneously with the peacekeeping force to coordinate international legal assistance provided by nongovernmental organizations to local judicial and legal authorities. ILAC would support rehabilitation of local judicial systems and promote accountability for violations of international humanitarian and human rights law. It would also be capable of providing a "judicial accountability response team" to support efforts to bring war criminals and human rights offenders to justice.[9] Such private efforts could begin in partnership with U.S. government efforts and continue on after the U.S. intervention force and justice teams have departed.

SUMMING UP

In his book on his experiences as NATO commander, General Wesley Clark described the tactics employed by SFOR in Bosnia as "a modern way of waging war" by "using forces, not force." In Bosnia, Clark said NATO forces were not at war, but they did everything military forces do short of firing their weapons. This included deploying troops and using intelligence, presence, movement, observation, and intimidation to influence events. Clark concluded that in modern war there are "requirements for police activities, ranging from investigating crime through reaction to civil disturbances and urban violence. Most militaries are simply not capable of performing such functions effectively and should not be the primary element responsible for them. Nations will have to create a full range of deployable, robust, police-type capabilities, as well as provide a legal and judicial structure to support their responsibilities."[10]

A U.S. Stability Force would have such a capacity. With the inclusion of military, constabulary, police, and judicial personnel, this force would in fact have full-spectrum capability to enforce peace and to maintain stability through the introduction of the rule of law. In summary, the creation of a U.S. Stability Force would—

1. Join together all of the elements required to effectively achieve sustainable security under a single, unified authority.

2. Close the security gap that has plagued previous peace operations by providing for a smooth transition from warfighting to institution building.

3. Establish police and judicial authority from the outset, thus freeing the military to perform its functions and speeding the withdrawal of military forces.

4. Establish the rule of law as a platform from which the other aspects of political, economic, and social reconstruction could go forward in an environment conducive to achieving success.

5. Provide the United States with a force that could join with similar forces organized by the European Union, the OSCE, and other regional organizations.

6. Allow the United States to support much-needed UN reform by contributing a force that could assist the United Nations in meeting its responsibilities for international peacekeeping as envisioned in the Brahimi Report.

Again, creating a U.S. Stability Force will require extensive congressional involvement, new authorizing legislation, and new funding. Congress must hold hearings to determine what needs to be done and who should do it. In February 2001, Representative James McGovern (with seventeen co-sponsors) introduced the United Nations Rapid Deployment Act (HR 938), calling for the president to establish a UN rapid reaction military and police force, utilizing the army's interim combat brigade teams as the core of a U.S. Rapid Deployment Brigade. In May 2001, Senator Joseph Biden, chairman of the Senate Foreign Relations Committee, called for creation of a nonmilitary gendarmerie for use in crowd pacification and refugee return in peace operations.[11] Other members of Congress joined Senator Biden in urging the administration to play a role in postconflict security and reconstruction in Afghanistan and in Iraq. These are clear indications of congressional awareness of the importance of the United States creating the capacity to engage effectively in postconflict environments.

To accomplish this task, the Defense Department and Joint Chiefs of Staff must overcome their understandable reluctance to engage in stability operations. They must also engage fully in the interagency policy process at home as well as in the conduct of peacekeeping abroad. Only DOD has the prestige, the influence, and the resources to help create an effective stability force and close the existing security gaps. Most important, however, the White House must provide leadership—what a Defense Department official described as a "highly agitated individual" or "peacekeeping czar" on the NSC staff with the authority and commitment to put together a U.S. Stability Force and make it work.[12] Before this individual deals with the terrorists and the spoilers abroad, he or she will have to overcome even more difficult opponents, the knee-jerk critics and turf warriors in the U.S. government. Finally, the effort must begin now. U.S. troops are engaged in fighting terrorism in Afghanistan and the Philippines. With the significant problems in the postconflict phase of war in Iraq, this simply cannot wait.

As the United States pursues the global War on Terrorism, the U.S. military will be called upon to do more than hunt down terrorists and their protectors. It will continue to participate in peace operations, including those in countries where regimes that fostered terrorism have been replaced. The exit from such operations will demand a structured entry with a clear focus on establishing the rule of law and achieving sustainable security. In dealing with the security component of stability operations, America currently faces gaps in both force structure and political will. After September 11, the United States became very serious about fighting terrorism. It now needs to get equally serious about dealing with the security-related aspects of postconflict reconstruction. We cannot afford policies based on wishful thinking or passing off responsibility. In short, we owe those who perished on September 11 nothing less than our best effort.

NOTES

INTRODUCTION

1. Section 660 of the Foreign Assistance Act of 1961, as amended, entitled "Prohibiting Police Training," states that no money made available for U.S. foreign assistance programs can be used by the U.S. government to provide advice, training, or financial support for the law enforcement forces of any foreign government. The provision was enacted in 1974 and was subsequently amended to allow police assistance under certain programs for counternarcotics and counterterrorism training and for "reconstituting police forces" in "countries emerging from instability."

1. BRCKO: SFOR vs. THE "RENT-A-MOB"

1. David Bosco, "After Genocide: Building Peace in Bosnia," *The American Prospect,* July 1998, 16.

2. Edward Cody, "Bosnian Serb's Backers Stone American Troops: U.S. Support for Rival Angers Karadzic Allies," *Washington Post,* August 28, 1997, A1.

3. Wesley Clark, *Waging Modern War* (New York: Public Affairs, 2001), 86–87.

4. Misha Savic, "NATO Troops, Serbs Clash," *Stars and Stripes,* August 29, 1997, 1.

5. Interview with Ambassador Robert Farrand, Washington, D.C., November 7, 2001.

6. Ibid.

7. Daniel Pearl, "A Tough U.S. Cop with a Daunting Beat: Peace in the Balkans," *Wall Street Journal,* December 9, 1999.

8. General Framework Agreement for Peace in Bosnia and Herzegovina, Annex 11 (International Police Task Force).

9. Telephone interview with Donald Grady, January 16, 2002.

10. Jerry Merideth, "International Police Had to Flee Bottle-throwing Mobs," *Stars and Stripes,* August 30, 1997, 1.

11. Chris Stephen, "Farrand Reportedly 'Marooned' in Brcko Town Center," Agence France-Presse, August 29, 1997.

12. Ibid.

13. Merideth, "International Police Had to Flee."

14. Grady interview.

15. The constitution contained in the Dayton Accords established a three-member presidency, with one ethnic Serb, Croat, and Bosniak (Bosnian Muslim) member.

16. Savic, "NATO Troops, Serbs Clash," 1.

17. Ibid.

18. Telephone interview with Colonel James Greer, July 10, 2002.

19. Jerry Merideth, "They Got Me Good, GI Relates," *Stars and Stripes,* August 29, 1997, 1.

20. "Medals Given to Soldiers Who Braved Attack," *Stars and Stripes,* August 31, 1997, 1.

21. Clark, *Waging Modern War,* 86

22. Grady interview.

23. Merideth, "International Police Had to Flee," 1.

24. Interview with Sergeant Mike Agate, former member of the U.S. Army Force Protection Team, Camp McGovern, December 18, 2001.

25. Ibid.

26. Ibid.

27. Grady interview.

28. Greer interview.

29. Colonel James Greer, "The Urban Area During Stability Missions Case Study: Bosnia-Herzegovina, Part 2," RAND Online Publications, available at: www.rand.org/publications/cf/cf162.

30. Clark, *Waging Modern War,* 87.

31. "Bosnian Serb Leaders Krajisnik, Kalinic Arrive in Brcko," Pale SRNA, August 28, 1997; translated in Foreign Broadcast Information Service, doc. FTS19970828001239.

32. Greer interview.

33. Interview with former U.S. ambassador to Bosnia Richard Kauzlarich, Washington, D.C., January 3, 2002.

34. Ibid.

35. Cody, "Bosnian Serb's Backers Stone Americans."

36. Belgrade Tanjug, "Tanjug criticizes SFOR in Brcko," August 28, 1997; translated in Foreign Broadcast Information Service, doc. FTS19970828001415.

37. Alison Smale, "Tough and Sharp Words Exchanged," *Stars and Stripes*, August 31, 1997, 1.

38. Lee Hockstader, "U.S. Troops Pull Back from Bosnian Bridge, Stir Debate over Reasons and Results," *Washington Post*, September 4, 1997, A27.

39. Clark, *Waging Modern War*, 87.

40. Hockstader, "U.S. Troops Pull Back from Bosnian Bridge."

41. Office of the High Representative, "Press Conference by the Principal Deputy High Representative, Ambassador Jacques Klein, and Deputy High Representative/Supervisor for Brcko, Ambassador Robert Farrand," September 2, 1997; available at www.ohr.int/print/?content_id=4853.

42. Jerry Merideth, "Official Says SFOR Won't Leave," *Stars and Stripes*, August 30, 1997, 5.

43. Hockstader, "U.S. Troops Pull Back from Bosnian Bridge."

44. Bosco, "After Genocide."

45. The General Framework Agreement for Peace in Bosnia and Herzegovina (GFAP) is commonly referred to as the Dayton Accords.

46. Richard Holbrooke, *To End a War* (New York: Random House, 1998), 308.

47. International Crisis Group, *Brcko Arbitration: Proposal for Peace.* ICG Bosnia Report, no. 18 (Washington, D.C.: International Crisis Group, January 20, 1997), 1.

48. Bosco, "After Genocide."

49. Ivo Daalder, *Getting to Dayton: The Making of America's Bosnia Policy*, (Washington, D.C.: Brookings Institution Press, 2000), 140–50.

50. Holbrooke, *To End a War*, 216–17.

51. Greer, " The Urban Area During Stability Missions."

52. Kauzlarich interview.

53. Bill Gertz, "U.S. Peace Troops Get Non-lethal Arms for Use in Bosnia: Commanders Order Sponge Grenades," *Washington Post*, September 3, 1997, A7.

54. Ron Laytner, "You Can Hide But You Can't Run: Radar Will Stop Your Car," *Straits Times* (Singapore), January 4, 1998.

55. Laura Silber and Allan Little, *The Death of Yugoslavia* (London: Penguin Books, 1995), 335–50.

2. CONSTABULARY

1. *Webster's Desk Dictionary*, s.v. "constabulary."

2. Erwin A. Schmidl, "Police Functions in Peace Operations: A Historical Overview," in *Policing the New World Disorder*, ed. Robert Oakley, Michael Dziedzic, and Eliot Goldberg (Washington, D.C.: National Defense University Press, 1998), 22.

3. Morris Janowitz, *The Professional Soldier: A Social and Political Portrait* (New York: The Free Press of Glenco, 1960), 418.

4. Charles, Moskos, Jr., *Peace Soldiers: The Sociology of a United Nations Military Force* (Chicago: University of Chicago Press, 1976), 93 and 130.

5. Don M. Snider, Ph.D., and Maj. Kimberly Field, memorandum to the Strategic Studies Institute's Research and Publication Board on "A Constabulary Force: Impacts on Force Structure and Culture" project, U.S. Military Academy, August 11, 2000.

6. Andrew Scobell and Brad Hammitt, "Goons, Gunmen, and Gendarmerie: Toward Reconceptualizing Paramilitary Formations," *Journal of Political and Military Sociology* 26, no. 2 (1998): 213–21.

7. Ibid.

8. Alice Hills, "International Peace Support Operations and CIVPOL: Should There Be a Permanent Global Gendarmerie?" *International Peacekeeping* 5, no. 3 (Autumn 1998): 35–37.

9. Michael J. Dziedzic, introduction to Oakley, Dziedzic, and Goldberg, eds., *Policing the New World Disorder*, especially pp. 8–13.

10. Gendarmerie Nationale web site, http://www.defense.gouv.fr/gendarmerie/, "La Gendarmerie."

11. John Andrade, *World Police and Paramilitary Forces* (New York: Stockton Press, 1985), 67–71.

12. Gendarmerie Nationale web site, "Les missions."

13. Gendarmerie Nationale web site, "Les différentes composantes de la gendarmeries."

14. Gendarmerie Nationale web site, "Les relations internationales de la gendarmerie."

15. Gendarmerie Nationale web site, "Operations extérieures."

16. Carabinieri web site, www.carabinieri.it/, "I Reparti."

17. Andrade, *World Police and Paramilitary Forces*, 101–03.

18. Carabinieri web site, "I Reparti."

19. Carabinieri web site, "Missioni all'estero."

20. See the English-language brochure on the Marechaussee published by the Netherlands Ministry of Defense, *The Royal Marechaussee* (Amsterdam: Ministry of Defense, January 1977), 3–4; available at http://www.defensie.nl/nieuws/media/content/200601_royal marechaussee.html.

21. Ibid., 9–13.

22. Andrade, *World Police and Paramilitary Forces*, 124–43.

23. Ministry of Defense, *The Royal Marechaussee*, 17–19.

24. Ibid., 4.

25. Ibid., 5.

26. Ibid., 16.

27. Information on Spain's Civil Guard can be found on the Federation of American Scientists' Intelligence Resource Program web site of "World Intelligence and Security Agencies" at http://www.fas.org/irp/world/spain/guard/htm.

28. Ibid.

29. Ibid.

30. Ibid.

31. Andrade, *World Police and Paramilitary Forces*, 142–43.

32. www.fas.org/irp/world/spain/guard/htm.

33. Ibid.

34. Ibid. See also NATO/SFOR Informer Online official homepage: http://www.nato.int/sfor/.

35. Ibid.

36 Juan A. Pina, "Guardia Civil in SFOR," SFOR Informer Online, April 26, 2000; available at www.nato.int/sfor/indexinf/86/guardia/t000427l.htm.

37. Andrade, *World Police and Paramilitary Forces*, 9.

38. Argentine National Gendarmerie (Gendarmeria Nacional Argentina) web site: http://www.gendarmeria.gov.ar/ingles/texto/indiceing.htm.

39. Andrade, *World Police and Paramilitary Forces*, 9.

40. Argentine National Gendarmerie web site, "Organization."

41. Argentine National Gendamerie web site, "Mission."

42. Ibid.

43. Argentine National Gendarmerie web site, "Scope of Performance."

44. William Rosenau, "Peace Operations, Emergency Law Enforcement, and Constabulary Forces," in *Peace Operations: Developing an American Strategy*, ed. Antonia Chayes and George T. Raach (Washington, D.C.: National Defense University Press, 1995).

45. Charles M. Robinson III, *The Men Who Wear the Star: The Story of the Texas Rangers* (New York: Random House, 2000), 7.

46. Ibid., 14.

47. "Texas Rangers Historical Development," Texas Department of Public Safety; available at http://www.txdps.state.tx.us/director_staff/texas_rangers/index.htm.

48. Robinson, *The Men Who Wear the Star*, 31–38.

49. Texas Department of Public Safety web site.

50. Robinson, 159.

51. Ibid., 155.

52. An Act to Provide for the Protection of the Frontier of the State of Texas, September 21, 1866, Texas Legislature, *General Laws of the State of Texas—1866*, pp. 10–12, cited in Robinson, *The Men Who Wear the Star*, 157.

53. Texas State Department of Public Safety web site.

54. Robinson, *The Men Who Wear the Star*, 168.

55. Texas State Department of Public Safety web site.

56. Robinson, *The Men Who Wear the Star*, 273.

57. Ibid., 285.

58. Ethan Nadelmann, *Cops across Borders: The Internationalization of U.S. Criminal Law Enforcement* (University Park: The Pennsylvania State University Press, 1993), 111–12.

59. Ivan Musicant, *The Banana Wars: A History of United States Military Intervention in Latin America from the Spanish-American War to the Invasion of Panama* (New York: Macmillan, 1990), 46.

60. Allan Millett, "The Rise and Fall of the Cuban Rural Guard," *The Americas*, October 1972, 191–94.

61. Ibid.

62. Musicant, *The Banana Wars*, 132–36.

63. Robert Harding, *Military Foundations of Panamanian Politics* (New Brunswick, N.J.: Transaction Publishers, 2001), 29–31.

64. Sandra Meditz and Dennis Hanratty, eds., *Panama: A Country Study* (Washington, D.C.: Federal Research Division, 1989), 22, 28, 34, 224.

65. Thomas Walker, *Nicaragua without Illusions: Regime Transition and Structural Adjustment in the 1990s* (Wilmington, Del.: Scholarly Resources, Inc., 1997), 3.

66. Musicant, *The Banana Wars*, 287.

67. Ibid., 298.

69. Marvin Goldwert, *The Constabulary in the Dominican Republic and Nicaragua: Progeny and Legacy of United States Intervention* (Gainesville: University of Florida Press, 1962), 32–36.

70. Ibid., 340–61.

70. Ibid., 42–47.

71. Walker, *Nicaragua without Illusions*, 4–5.

72. Goldwert, *The Constabulary in the Dominican Republic and Nicaragua*, 5–7.

73. Martha Huggins, *Political Policing: The United States and Latin America* (Durham, N.C.: Duke University Press, 1998), 27.

74. Musicant, *The Banana Wars*, 235–37, 274–75.

75. Ibid., 275–84.

76. Goldwert, *The Constabulary in the Dominican Republic and Nicaragua*, 15–21.

77. Hans Schmidt, *The United States Occupation of Haiti, 1915–1934* (New Brunswick, N.J.: Rutgers University Press, 1995), 230.

78. Ibid.

79. Emily Balch, *Occupied Haiti* (New York: Writers Publishing, 1927), vii.

80. Michel Laguerre, *The Military and Society in Haiti* (Knoxville: University of Tennessee Press, 1993), 63.

81. Balch, *Occupied Haiti*, 130.

82. Laguerre, *The Military and Society in Haiti*, 79–80.

83. John Brown, "Combat Cops?" *Armed Forces Journal*, September 2000; available at http://www.afji.com/AFJI.Mags/2000/September/combat_2.html.

84. Major James Snyder, "The Establishment and Operations of the United States Constabulary, October 3, 1945–June 30, 1947," Historical Sub-Section C-3; available at www.carlisle.army.mil/usamhi/DL/chron.htm#AworldWarII19391945.

85. United States Army Europe, U.S. Army Center of Military History, "History of the U.S. Constabulary January 10, 1946 to December 31, 1946," Historical Manuscripts Collection, File number 8-3.1 CA 37; available at http://www.army.mil/cmh-pg/reference/cstb46.htm.

86. Ibid.

87. Ibid.

88. Snyder, "The Establishment and Operations of the United States Constabulary."

89. Ibid.

90. Ibid.

91. Ibid.

92. United States Army Europe, U.S. Army Center of Military History, "The U.S. Constabulary in Post-War Germany (1946–52)," Historical Manuscripts Collection, October 24, 2001; available at http://www.army.mil/cmh-pg/lineage/Constab-IP.htm.

93. Roy Licklider, "The American Way of State Building: Germany, Japan, Somalia, and Panama," *Small Wars and Insurgencies* 10, no. 3 (Winter 1999): 85–86.

94. Richard Finn, *Winners in Peace: MacArthur, Yoshida, and Postwar Japan* (Berkeley: University of California Press, 1992), 35, 165.

95. Licklider, "The American Way of State Building," 87.

96. Brown, "Combat Cops?"

97. James Schnabel, *The United States Army in the Korean War, Policy and Direction: The First Year* (Washington, D.C.: Center of Military History, United States Army, 1972).

98. Jack Siemieniec, "Task Force Smith Recalls Historic Days," *Army News Service*, June 29, 2000; available at www.dtic.mil/armylink/news/jun2000/a20000629smithrecalls.htm.

99. Schnabel, *The United States Army in the Korean War.*

100. Brown, "Combat Cops?"

101. Interview with Scott Feil, executive director of the Role of American Military Power Program, Association of the U.S. Army, Washington D.C., August 12, 2002.

102. National Guard Bureau, *About Us–National Guard History;* available at http://www.ngb.dtc.mil/about_us/ng_hist.shtml.

103. Army National Guard History, available at http://www.arng.army.mil/history.

104. Rex Applegate, "Riot Control: Army and National Guard Unprepared to Rule the Mob," *Soldier of Fortune,* December 1992, 43–44.

105. Ibid., 45.

106. Clark Staten, "Three Days of Hell in Los Angeles," Emergencynet News Service, April 29–May 1, 1992, available at http://www.emergency.com/la-riots.htm; Christopher Schnaubelt, "Lessons in Command and Control for the Los Angeles Riots," *Parameters,* Summer 1997, 88–109.

107. Bob Haskell, "Seattle Civil Disturbance Puts Guard on Duty," *Air Force News,* December 3, 1999, available at http://www.af.mil/news/Dec1999/n19991203_992177.html; Ed Offley, "Guardsmen Protect WTO Delegates and Protesters Alike," *Seattle Post-Intelligencer,* December 2, 1999.

108. Cable News Network, "National Guard Protecting Nation's Airports," September 29, 2001; available at http://www.cnn.com/2001/Travel/NEWS/09/29/rec.attacks.airports/index.html.

109. 18 United States Code, Section 1385 (1994). Currently, the fine is up to $250,000 for individuals.

110. Matthew Carlton Hammond, "The Posse Comitatus Act: A Principle in Need of Renewal," *Washington University Law Quarterly* 75, no. 2 (Summer 1997).

111. The legal interpretation of 10 United States Code, Sections 331–335, is from Sean Byrne, "Defending Sovereignty: Domestic Operations and Legal Precedents"; available at http://www cgsc.army.mil/milrev/English/MarApr00/byrne.htm.

112. See United States Army, Field Manual 100-19, *Domestic Support Operations* (Washington, D.C.: Department of the Army, July 1993), particularly chapter 7, "Missions in Support of Law Enforcement."

113. Bryne, "Defending Sovereignty."

114. "Major Jay D. Wells and Major Thomas P. Baltazar, "Counter-Drug (CD) Operations," Center for Army Lessons Learned *Newsletter,* no. 91-4 (November 1991).

115. Eric Schmitt, "Military Role in U.S. Gains Favor," *New York Times,* July 22, 2002.

116. Bill Miller, "National Guard Awaits Niche in Homeland Security Plan," *Washington Post,* August 11, 2002, A1.

117. United States Army, Field Manual 3-19.1, *Military Police Operations* (Washington, D.C.: Department of the Army, March 22, 2001).

118. Ibid.

119. Interview with Col. Larry Forester, former director of the U.S. Army Peacekeeping Institute, U.S. Army War College, Carlisle Barracks, Pennsylvania, February 27, 2002.

120. Ibid.

121. Thomas Ricks, "U.S. Military Police Embrace Kosovo Role," *Washington Post,* March 25, 2001, A21.

3. CIVPOL: Police in Peacekeeping

1. Bernard Miyet, "Opening Statement to the Special Committee on Peacekeeping Operations" (speech by the UN undersecretary-general for peacekeeping, United Nations, February 11, 2000, photocopy), 4.

2. Henry L. Stimson Center, Future of Peace Operations Project, "U.S. Personnel Contributions to UN Peacekeeping Operations," April 30, 2002; available at www.stimson.org./fopo.

3. U.S. Department of State, "Strengthening Criminal Justice Systems in Support of Peace Operations and Other Complex Contingencies," Press Fact Sheet, Washington, D.C., February 24, 2000.

4. Schmidl, "Police Functions in Peace Operations," 25–29.

5. See the chapters on major armed conflicts in the Stockholm International Peace Research Institute's (SIPRI) *Yearbook* for the years 1991 to 1996, and the "Status of Armed Conflict" in *The Military Balance, 1997/98* (London: International Institute for Strategic Studies, 1997).

6. Michael Lund, *Preventing Violent Conflicts: A Strategy for Preventive Diplomacy* (Washington, D.C.: United States Institute of Peace Press, 1996), 18–22.

7. Rosenau, "Peace Operations," 127–28.

8. Janowitz, *The Professional Soldier,* 248.

9. Jeffery Smith, "Fired On, Marines Kill Gunman in Kosovo," *Washington Post,* June 26, 1999, A17.

10. Mark Bowden, *Black Hawk Down: A Story of Modern War* (New York: Atlantic Monthly Press, 1999).

11. Swedish Ministry for Foreign Affairs, *Police in the Service of Peace*. Excerpts from the Report by the Swedish Committee of Inquiry on Civilian Police in International Activities (Stockholm: Ministry for Foreign Affairs, 1997), 11.

12. Jules Lalancette, "A Police Officer's Perspective on Peace-keeping with Muscle," in *Peacekeeping with Muscle: The Use of Force in International Conflict Resolution,* ed. Alex Morrison, Douglas A. Fraser, and James D. Kiras (Clementsport, Nova Scotia: Canadian Peacekeeping Press, 1997), 108–109.

13. James Delk, *Fires and Furies: The L.A. Riots* (Palm Springs, Calif.: ETC Publications, 1995), chapter 1.

14. Bernard Miyet, "Remarks for the DPKO Seminar" (speech by the UN undersecretary general for peacekeeping, UN seminar on the "Role of Police in Peacekeeping Operations," March 20–21, 1998, photocopy), 3–4.

15. Halvor Hartz, "CIVPOL: The UN Instrument for Police Reform," *International Peacekeeping* 6, no. 4 (1999): 31.

16. Roxane Sismanidis, *Police Functions in Peace Operations.* Peaceworks, no. 14 (Washington, D.C.: United States Institute of Peace, 1997), 2–3.

17. Ibid.

18. United Nations, Department of Peacekeeping Operations, *United Nations Civilian Police Course Curriculum* (New York: United Nations, 1995), 19–20.

19. Ibid.

20. Om Prakash Rathor, "Briefing" (speech by the senior UN police adviser, DPKO seminar on "The Role of CIVPOL in Peacekeeping," UN headquarters, New York, March 20–21, 1998, photocopy), 1.

21. Charles Call and Michael Barnett, "Looking for a Few Good Cops: Peacekeeping, Peacebuilding, and UN Civilian Police" (paper prepared for the annual meeting of the International Studies Association, March 18–22, 1997, Toronto, Ontario), 16–18.

22. Duncan Chappell and John Evans, "The Role, Preparation and Performance of Civilian Police in United Nations Peacekeeping Operations" (paper prepared for the International Center for Criminal Law Reform and Criminal Justice Policy, University of British Columbia, Vancouver, British Columbia, 1997), 58.

23. Barbara Crossette, "The UN's Unhappy Lot: Perilous Police Duties Multiplying," *New York Times,* February 22, 2000, A30.

24. Tonya Cook, "Toward Better Practices to Train International Civilian Police for Peace Operations" (paper presented at the symposium on "Best Practices for Training for Humanitarian and Peace Operations," U.S. Institute of Peace, Washington, D.C., June 25–26, 2001), 11.

25. Richard Fought, "American Cops Keeping the Peace in War-Ravaged Bosnia," *Police,* September 1999, 14–21.

26. U.S. Institute of Peace, *American Civilian Police in UN Peace Operations: Lessons Learned and Ideas for the Future.* Special Report, no. 71 (Washington, D.C.: U.S. Institute of Peace, July 6, 2001), 7, 9.

27. Robert Perito, *The American Experience with Police in Peace Operations* (Clementsport, Nova Scotia: Canadian Peacekeeping Press, 2002), 5–6.

28. United Nations, Department of Peacekeeping Operations, *Selection Standards and Training Guidelines for United Nations Civilian Police* (New York: United Nations, 1997).

29. United Nations, Department of Peacekeeping Operations, *United Nations Police Officers Course* (New York: United Nations, 2000).

30. Cook, "Toward Better Practices," 3–4.

31. Harry Broer and Michael Emery, "Civilian Police in UN Peacekeeping Operations," in Oakley, Dziedzic, and Goldberg, eds., *Policing the New World Disorder,* 374–76.

32. Ibid.

33. Om Prakash Rathor, "United Nations Requirements for Civilian Police: Mechanisms to Address Them" (speech by the UN senior police adviser, UN seminar on the "Role of Police in Peace Operations," UN headquarters, New York, July 29–30, 1999, photocopy), 5–6.

34. Nassrine Azimi, ed., *The Role and Functions of Civilian Police in United Nations Peacekeeping Operations: Debriefing and Lessons.* Report of the 1995 Singapore Conference (London: Kluwer Law International Press, 1996), 6–7.

35. Broer and Emery, "Civilian Police in UN Peacekeeping Operations," 385–86.

36. Michael Emery, "Civilian Police in a Climate of Peace Enforcement: Redefining the Role of UNCIVPOL," in Morrison, Fraser, and Kiras, eds., *Peacekeeping with Muscle*, 114.

37. John McFarlane and William Maley, "Civilian Police in UN Peace Operations: Some Lessons from Recent Australian Experience," in *United Nations Peacekeeping Operations: Ad Hoc Missions, Permanent Engagement*, ed. Ramesh Thakur and Albrecht Schnabel (New York: United Nations University Press, 2001), 198.

38. Espen Barth Eide, "Norwegian Experiences with UN Civilian Police Operations" (paper for the joint Carnegie Commission on Preventing Deadly Conflict/National Defense University/Canadian International Peacekeeping Training Center conference on "Policing the New World Disorder," Washington, D.C., September 15–16, 1997, photocopy), 13–15.

39. Peter Fitzgerald, "The Role of Police in Peacekeeping Operations" (speech by the former IPTF commissioner in Bosnia at the UN seminar on the "Role of Police in Peacekeeping Operations," March 20–21, 1998, photocopy), 5–8.

40. United Nations, Department of Public Information, *The Blue Helmets: A Review of United Nations Peacekeeping*, 3d ed. (New York: United Nations, 1996), 453–58.

41. John Sanderson, "The Cambodian Experience: A Success Story Still?" in Thakur and Schnabel, eds., *United Nations Peacekeeping Operations*, 163–65.

42. James Schear and Karl Farris, "Policing Cambodia: The Public Security Dimensions of UN Peace Operations," in Oakley, Dziedzic, and Goldberg, eds., *Policing the New World Disorder*, 82–83.

43. Klaas Roos, "Debriefing of Civilian Police Components: UN Transitional Authority in Cambodia," in Azimi, ed., *The Role and Functions of Civilian Police in United Nations Peacekeeping Operations*, 123–25.

44. Ibid.

45. Schear and Farris, "Policing Cambodia," 88–90.

46. Terrence Lyons and Ahmed Samatar, *Somalia: State Collapse, Multilateral Intervention, and Strategies for Political Reconstruction* (Washington, D.C.: Brookings Institution Press, 1995), 25–30.

47. Ibid., 32–33.

48. Samuel Makinda, *Seeking Peace from Chaos: Humanitarian Intervention in Somalia* (Boulder, Colo.: Lynne Rienner, 1994), 69–70.

49. John Hirsch and Robert Oakley, *Somalia and Operation Restore Hope* (Washington, D.C.: U.S. Institute of Peace Press, 1995), 87–88.

50. Lynn Thomas and Steve Spataro, "Peacekeeping and Policing in Somalia," in Oakley, Dziedzic, and Goldberg, eds., *Policing the New World Disorder,* 188.

51. Ibid.

52. Ibid.

53. Ibid., 192–93.

54. Hirsch and Oakley, *Somalia and Operation Restore Hope,* 89.

55. Ibid., 196.

56. Vernon Loeb, "After-Action Report: Warlords, Peacekeepers, and Spies," *Washington Post Magazine,* February 27, 2000, 8.

57. Makinda, *Seeking Peace from Chaos,* 76–81.

58. David Bentley and Robert Oakley, "Peace Operations: A Comparison of Somalia and Haiti," *Strategic Forum,* no. 30 (May 1995): 3.

59. Ibid.

60. Ambassador Walter E. Stadtler, "The Lessons of Somalia" (speech at the Lester B. Pearson Canadian International Peacekeeping Training Center, Clementsport, Nova Scotia, October 20, 1995, photocopy), 4.

61. U.S. House of Representatives, *Message from the President of the United States Transmitting a Report on the Military Operations in Somalia,* 103d Cong., 1st Sess., H. Doc. 103-149, October 1993.

62. Interview with Ambassador Walter Stadler, director of the Somalia Task Force during UNOSOM II, Washington, D.C., October 5, 1999.

63. United Nations, *The Blue Helmets,* 298.

64. Thomas and Spataro, "Peacekeeping and Policing in Somalia," 200–01.

65. Ibid.

66. Ibid., 202.

67. United Nations, *The Blue Helmets,* 318.

68. Ibid., 202–10.

69. Charles Call, "Institutional Learning Within ICITAP," in Oakley, Dziedzic, and Goldberg, eds., *Policing the New World Disorder*, 338–42.

70. United Nations, *The Blue Helmets*, 315.

71. Interview with Michael Kozak, State Department Haiti Working Group, Washington, D.C., February 3, 2000.

72. Michael Bailey, Robert Maguire, and Neil Pouliot, "Haiti: Military-Police Partnership for Public Security," in Oakley, Dziedzic, and Goldberg, eds., *Policing the New World Disorder*, 205–21.

73. Rachel Neild, *Policing Haiti: Preliminary Assessment of the New Civilian Security Force* (Washington, D.C.: Washington Office on Latin America, 1995), 12–18.

74. Raymond Kelly, "American Law Enforcement Perspectives on Policing in Emerging Democracies," in *Policing in Emerging Democracies: Workshop Papers and Highlights*. Report of the National Institute of Justice Workshop on Policing in Emerging Democracies, ed. Jeremy Travis (Collingdale, Pa.: Diane Publishing, 1997), 25–28.

75. Robert Perito, "The Experience of ICITAP in Assisting the Institutional Development of Foreign Police Forces" (paper presented at the 35th Annual Program of the Academy of Criminal Justice Systems, Albuquerque, March 10–14, 1998), 4.

76. David Bentley and Robert Oakley, "Peace Operations: A Comparison of Somalia and Haiti," *Strategic Forum*, no. 78 (June 1998): 1–2.

77. Julian Harston, "MIPONUH: A Case Study of the Civilian Police Element in United Nations Peacekeeping" (paper presented at the 3rd Nordic/UN Peacekeeping Senior Management Seminar, Helsinki, September 2, 1998, photocopy), 1–9.

4. TEST CASE: Creating Postconflict Security in Bosnia

1. General Framework Agreement for Peace in Bosnia and Herzegovina (GFAP), Annex 11 (International Police Task Force), Article I.1-2.

2. Interviews with a State Department legal adviser and with Robert Gallucci, State Department official in charge of Dayton Accords civilian implementation, Washington, D.C., January 21, 2000.

3. Ibid.

4. Ibid.

5. Ibid.

6. Carl Bildt, *Peace Journey: The Struggle for Peace in Bosnia* (New York: Orion Press, 1999), 132–33.

7. International Crisis Group, *Policing the Police in Bosnia: A Further Reform Agenda.* Balkans Report, no. 130 (Brussels: International Crisis Group, May 10, 2002), 5.

8. Holbrooke, *To End a War,* 216–17.

9. Gallucci interview.

10. International Crisis Group, *Policing the Police in Bosnia,* 5.

11. GFAP, Article II.1

12. James Gow, *Triumph of the Lack of Will: International Diplomacy and the Yugoslav War* (New York: Columbia University Press, 1997), 294–95.

13. Michael J. Dziedzic and Andrew Bair, "Bosnia and the International Police Task Force," in Oakley, Dziedzic, and Goldberg, eds., *Policing the New World Disorder,* 270.

14. United Nations Report of the Secretary-General Pursuant to Security Council Resolution 1026 (1995), December 13, 1995, 6–7.

15. Bruce Pirnie, *Civilians and Soldiers: Achieving Better Coordination* (Santa Monica, Calif.: Rand Corporation, 1998), 72.

16. United Nations, *The Blue Helmets,* 562–63.

17. Larry Wentz, *Lessons from Bosnia: The IFOR Experience* (Washington, D.C.: National Defense University Press, 1998), 149–50.

18. United Nations, *The Blue Helmets,* 563.

19. Bildt, *Peace Journey,* 196–97.

20. Holbrooke, *To End a War,* 327–37.

21. United Nations Secretariat, Report of the Secretary-General Pursuant to Resolution 1035 (1995), March 29, 1996. UN Doc. S/1996/210, p. 3.

22. Hills, "International Peace Support Operations and CIVPOL," 35.

23. Bair and Dziedzic, "Bosnia and the International Police Task Force," 264.

24. Robert Wasserman, "Remarks" (speech by the IPTF deputy commissioner, Contributors Meeting, United Nations Headquarters, June 26, 1996, photocopy), 3–4.

25. Wentz, *Lessons from Bosnia,* 153–56.

26. Agreement on Restructuring the Police, Federation of Bosnia and Herzegovina, Bonn, Germany, April 25, 1996, 1–4.

27. International Crisis Group, *Policing the Police in Bosnia,* 7.

28. United Nations Secretariat, Report of the Secretary-General Pursuant to Security Council Resolution 1088 (1996), March 14, 1997, 1–4.

29. UN Security Council Resolution 1103 (1997), March 31, 1997.

30. International Crisis Group, *Brcko: What Bosnia Could Be.* ICG Bosnia Project Report, no. 31 (Sarajevo: International Crisis Group, February 10, 1998), 6–8.

31. Alexander Nicoll, "NATO Studies Staying On in Bosnia," *Financial Times* (London), October 6, 1997, 2.

32. Lizette Alvarez, "Senate Is Cool to GI Mission in Bosnia but Doesn't Cut Off Funds," *New York Times,* July 11, 1997, 3.

33. Steven Bowman, Julie Kim, and Steven Woehrel, *Bosnia Stabilization Force and U.S. Policy* (Washington, D.C.: Congressional Research Service, September 19, 1998), 12–14.

34. Ivo Daalder, "Bosnia after SFOR: Options for Continued U.S. Engagement," *Survival* 39, no. 4 (Winter 1997–98): 8–9.

35. John Maher, "Part of the Resources Needed for Bosnian Police Raised at Dublin Meeting," *The Irish Times* (Dublin), September 30, 1996, 4.

36. The author was a member of the U.S. delegation to the Dublin meeting.

37. Interview with Robert Gelbard, August 20, 2002, Washington D.C.

38. Telephone interview with Andrew Bair, former special assistant to Ambassador Robert Gelbard, January 24, 2002.

39. Clark, *Waging Modern War,* 77–87.

40. Ibid.

41. Bowman, Kim, and Woehrel, *Bosnia Stabilization Force and U.S. Policy,* 10–11; Gelbard interview.

42. "Bosnia: NATO Prepares New Force Options," *World News Digest,* December 4, 1997; available at: http://mutex.gmu.edu.2283/stories/index/1997083180.asp.

43. Bradley Graham, "Cohen Plays Skeptic Role on Bosnia: Defense Chief to Insist on Europe Doing More," *Washington Post,* November 30, 1997, A1.

44. Hills, "International Peace Support Operations and CIVPOL," 26–28.

45. Ennio Caretto, "America Wants Out, Looks to Allies for Relief," *Corriere della Sera* (Milan), December 1, 1997.

46. William Drozdiak, "NATO Commander Urges Follow-On Force in Bosnia," *Washington Post,* December 3, 1997, A41.

47. Jim Mannion, "Police Role in Bosnia a Point of Contention Among Allies," Agence France-Presse, December 2, 1997.

48. Drozdiak, "NATO Commander Urges Follow-on Force in Bosnia."

49. Steven Meyers, "Britain Presses U.S. for Pledge on Bosnia GI's," *New York Times,* December 5, 1997, A8.

50. Agence France-Presse, "Obstacles Strew the Way of Bosnia's Future Force," January 22, 1998.

51. "Mr. Cohen's Caution on Bosnia," *New York Times,* December 8, 1997, A24.

52. "Call the Police: Cohen's Plan to Replace Bosnia Peacekeepers with a NATO Police Force Makes Sense," *Newsday,* December 8, 1997, A30.

53. "Bonn Peace Implementation Conference 1997," December 10, 1997, p. 11; available from the OSCE's web site at http://www.oscebih.org/documents/bonnpic.htm.

54. Interview with Gregory Schulte, senior director, National Security Council, Washington, D.C., August 20, 2002.

55. Norman Kempster, "NATO Seeks Plan to Extend Its Peace Mission in Bosnia," *Los Angeles Times,* December 17, 1997, A1; "NATO Stays in Bosnia Another Year," *Toronto Star,* December 17, 1997, A17.

56. Martin Walker, "No Exit for NATO's Bosnia Force" *The Guardian* (London), December 17, 1997, 12; U.S. Mission to NATO, "Statement by Secretary of State Madeleine Albright During the North Atlantic Council Ministerial Meeting," Brussels, December 1997, available at NATO's web site at http://www.nato.int/usa/state/s19971216a.html.

57. Schulte interview.

58. Federal News Service, "Decision in Bosnia," *New York Times,* December 19, 1997, A20.

59. Ibid.

60. James Bennet, "Clinton on Tour, Presses Bosnians and Salutes GI's," *New York Times,* December 23, 1997, A1.

61. Kauzlarich interview.

62. Holbrooke, *To End a War,* 357.

63. Kempster, "NATO Seeks Plan to Extend its Mission in Bosnia."

64. "Military Police Units Considered for SFOR Follow-On," Agence France-Presse, January 16, 1998.

65. North Atlantic Treaty Organization, "Statement by the North Atlantic Council on the Continuation of a NATO-led Multinational Military Presence in Bosnia and Herzegovina," press release, February 20, 1998; available at http://www.nato.int/docu/pr/1998/p98018e.htm.

66. Norman Kempster, "NATO to Create New Police Force in Bosnia," *Los Angeles Times,* February 20, 1998, A10.

67. Elizabeth Neuffer, "NATO Plans Paramilitary Force in Bosnia," *Boston Globe,* February 23, 1998, A2.

68. Carlo Scognamiglio-Pasini, "Increasing Italy's Input," *NATO Review,* Summer 2001, 26–27.

69. Carabinieri web site, "Missioni all'estero."

70. Luc Rosenzweig, "NATO Debates Mission of New Multi-national Force," *Le Monde* (Paris), February 4, 1998.

71. Miguel Gonzalez, "Civil Guard to Send Its Men to Bosnia Under Order of NATO," *El Pais* (Madrid), December 28, 1997.

72. Agence France-Presse, "Spain Rejects Military Police Plan for Bosnia," May 4, 1998.

73. The White House, Office of the Press Secretary, "President Seeks $2.5 Billion for 1998 to Support Military Operations in Bosnia and Southwest Asia," March 4, 1998; available at http://Clinton6.nara.gov/ 1998-03-04-supplemental-appropriations-for-bosnia-and-southwest-asia.htm.

74. Agence France-Presse, "Slight Reduction in American Contingent of International Force in June," March 4, 1998.

75. Interview with Ambassador Robert Oakley, Washington D.C., August 23, 2002.

76. Dziedzic, introduction, p. 12, and Robert B. Oakley and Michael J. Dziedzic, conclusions, p. 519, in Oakley, Dziedzic, and Goldberg, eds., *Policing the New World Disorder.*

77. Interview with Colonel Michael Dziedzic, Washington D.C., August 28, 2002.

78. Ibid.

79. United Nations Secretariat, Report of the Secretary-General on the United Nations Mission in Bosnia and Herzegovina, UN Doc. S/1998/491 (June 10 1998), 5.

80. International Crisis Group, *Impunity in Drvar.* ICG Balkans Report, no. 40 (Sarajevo: International Crisis Group, August 20, 1998), 3–8; Kauzlarich interview.

81. International Crisis Group, *Impunity in Drvar.*

82. E-mail interview with Vincenzo Coppola, former MSU executive officer, August 29, 2002.

83. Ibid.

84. North Atlantic Treaty Organization, "Statement on Bosnia and Herzegovina Issued at the Ministerial Meeting of the North Atlantic Council held in Luxembourg on May 28, 1998," press release M-NAC-1(98)60, May 28, 1998; available at http://www.nato.int/docu/pr/1998/p98-060e.htm.

85. Philippe Rater, "Third NATO Peace Mission to be Named 'Joint Forge,'" Agence France-Presse, April 22, 1998.

86. Gelbard interview.

87. North Atlantic Treaty Organization, "Final Communique, Ministerial Meeting of the North Atlantic Council" NATO Headquarters, Brussels, Belgium, June 11, 1998," press release M-NAC-D-1(98)71, June 11, 1998; available at http://www.nato.int/docu/pr/1998/p98-071e.htm.

88. UN Security Council Resolution 1174 (1998), June 15, 1998.

89. "SFOR Continued" (speech by Gregory Schulte, director, Bosnia Task Force, NATO International Staff, NATO Information Seminar, Sarajevo, July 2, 1998); available at http://www.nato.int/docu.speech/1998/s980702b.htm.

5. BLUE BOX: The Multinational Specialized Unit in Bosnia

1. "MSU Arrives in BiH," SFOR Informer Online, August 12, 1998; available at http://www.nato.int/sfor/indexinf/92/msufor.htm.

2. Interviews with American SFOR officers, Sarajevo, August 3–8, 1998.

3. "MSU Arrives in BiH."

4. Bonn Peace Implementation Conference, Section IV, Public Order and Police Issues, paras. 1 and 3, Bonn, December 10, 1997, OSCE Essential Documents; available at www.oscebih.org/documents/ bonnpic.htm.

5. UN Security Council Resolution 1144 (1997), December 19, 1997.

6. Interview with ICITAP project manager James Tillman, Sarajevo, July 1, 2002.

7. Telephone interview with former UN IPTF deputy commissioner Mark Kroeker, February 5, 2002.

8. Ibid.

9. Interviews with UN and Bosnian officials, Sarajevo, August 3–8, 1998.

10. Vincenzo Coppola, "Briefing on the Multinational Specialized Unit" (paper presented at the U.S. Army Peacekeeping Institute, Carlisle Barracks, Pa., June 16, 1999, photocopy), 1.

11. Ibid., 2–3.

12. Paolo Valpolini, "The Role of Police-Military Units in Peacekeeping," Jane's Europe News, July/August 1999; available at http://www.janes.com/regional_news/europe/news/ipr/ipr990801_1. shtml.

13. Alexander Montagna, "MSU Dog Team," SFOR Informer Online, January 6, 2000; available at http://www.nato.int/sfor/indexinf/ 92/msufor/t000719l.htm.

14. Valpolini, "The Role of Police-Military Units in Peacekeeping."

15. Luis Barber, "SFOR Argentinean Contingent," SFOR Informer Online, November 8, 2000; available at http://www.nato.int/ sfor/index-inf/100/s100p03a/t0011083a.htm.

16. Kroeker interview.

17. Angel Brufau, "MSU Certification Ceremony," SFOR Informer Online, September 23, 1998; available at http://www.nato.int/ sfor/indexinf.

18. Information provided by the Office of the Commander of Multinational Specialized Unit, Camp Butmir, Bosnia, June 28, 2002.

19. "History of the NATO-led Stabilization Force in Bosnia and Herzegovina," available from the SFOR web site at http://www.nato.int/ sfor/duc/d981116a.htm.

20. Coppola, "Briefing on the Multinational Specialized Unit," 4–5.

21. Ibid.

22. Ibid.

23. HINA News Agency, "Official Condemns SFOR Action to Unblock Road at Capljina," October 2, 1998; translated in Foreign Broadcast Information Service, doc. FBIS-EEU-98-275.

24. "NATO/SFOR Joint Press Conference," Coalition Press Information Center, Tito Barracks, October 7, 1998; available at http://web.lexis-nexis.com/universe/printdoc.

25. Coppola, "Briefing on the Multinational Specialized Unit."

26. Ibid.

27. Belgrade Tanjug Domestic Service, "B-H: Workers Protest Against SFOR Using Factory Premises," November 2, 1998; translated in Foreign Broadcast Information Service, doc. FTS19981102002064.

28. Coppola, "Briefing on the Multinational Specialized Unit."

29. Srpski Radio, "RS Minister to Help Get SFOR to Vacate Firm's Premises," November 10, 1998; translated in Foreign Broadcast Information Service, doc. FTS19981110001587.

30. "Final Award of the Arbitral Tribunal for Dispute Over the Inter-Entity Boundary in the Brcko Area," March 5, 1999, pp. 3–6; available at www.state.gov/www/regions/eur/bosnia/990305_arbiter_brcko.html.

31. "Bosnian Serbs United in Anger," BBC News Online, March 8, 1999, available at http://news.bbc.co.uk/hi/english.world/europe/newsid_292000/292441.stm; Ivo Daalder and Michael O'Hanlon, *Winning Ugly: NATO's War to Save Kosovo* (Washington, D.C.: Brookings Institution Press, 2000), 230–31; interview with former Brcko Supervisor Robert Farrand, Washington, D.C., July 31, 2002.

32. Jane's Europe News, "The Role of Police-Military Units."

33. Nick Thorpe, "Returning to Brcko," BBC News Online, March 15, 1999; available at http://news.bbc.co.uk/hi/english.world/from_our_own_correspondent/newsid_294000/294839.stm.

34. Interview with Lieutenant Colonel Michael Meese, executive officer, assistant chief of staff (Operations), SFOR, Camp Butmir, Sarajevo, June 28, 2002.

35. Ibid.

36. Dziedzic and Bair, "Bosnia and the International Police Task Force," 260.

37. Mac Warner, "SFOR Lessons Learned in Creating a Secure Environment with Respect for the Rule of Law," (paper prepared for the Joint Chiefs of Staff Peace Operations Seminar on "The Role of the Military in Establishing the Rule of Law in Peace Operations," U.S. Army Peacekeeping Institute, Carlisle Barracks, Pa., June 13–15, 2000, photocopy), 5.

38. R. Jeffrey Smith, "Bosnian Mart Becomes Den of Criminal Enterprise: Thieves, Tax Cheats Thrive in U.S.-Sponsored Venture," *Washington Post*, December 26, 1999, A33.

39. Warner, "SFOR Lessons Learned," 22.

40. Meese interview.

41. "Police Arrest Croat Accused of Organized Crime in Stolac," HINA News Agency, January 18, 1999; translated in Foreign Broadcast Information Service, doc. FTS1999121700319.

42. HINA News Agency, "B-H: More on Illegal Intelligence Activities Discovery," December 17, 1999; translated in Foreign Broadcast Information Service, doc. FTS19991217001319.

43. "B-H Croat SNS Secret 'Operations' Details," *Slobodna Bosna* (Sarajevo), December 23, 1999, 18–19; translated in Foreign Broadcast Information Service, doc. FTS19991225000291.

44. Amra Kebo, "Croat Troops Mutiny: Tension Mounts in Bosnia as Croat Officers Leave the Federation Army," *Balkans Crisis Report*, no. 229 (March 23, 2001).

45. R. Jeffery Smith, "Criminal Gangs Challenging West in Bosnia: Separatist Croat Threat Alters Troops' Mission," *Washington Post*, June 24, 2001, A1.

46. Ibid.

47. Aida Cerkez-Robinson, "Bosnian Croats Stoned NATO," Associated Press, April 7, 2001.

48. Smith, "Criminal Gangs Challenging West in Bosnia."

49. Lisa Simpson, "MSU Trains Solvenians and Romanians," SFOR Informer Online, April 25, 2002; available at http://www.nato.int/sfor/indexinf/137/p07a/t02p07a.htm.

50. Meese interview.

51. Interview with Colonel Antonio Colacicco, MSU commander, Camp Butmir, Sarajevo, June 30, 2002.

52. Reuters, "NATO Prepares to End Its Patrols of U.S. Skies," May 2, 2002.

53. Associated Press, "NATO: Terrorists Are Still in Bosnia," April 2, 2002.

54. BBC World News, "Bosnia Terror Suspects Quizzed," October 2, 2001; available at http://news.bbc.co.uk/hi/english/world/europe/newsid_1547000/1574678.stm.

55. Andrew Purvis, "Targeting 'Eagle Base,'" *Time Europe,* October 16, 2001.

56. Peter Finn, "U.S. Troops Seize 6 Terror Suspects Freed by Bosnia," *Washington Post,* January 18, 2002, A16.

57. BBC World Service, "UN Condemns Serb 'Sickness,'" May 8, 2001; available at http://news.bbc.co.uk/hi/english/world/europe/newsid_1318000/1318283.stm.

58. Cable News Network, "Diplomats Freed After Bosnia Riot," May 7, 2002; available at http://www.cnn.com/2001/world/europe/05/07/bosnia.violence.02.

59. Tillman interview.

60. Meese interview.

61. Colacicco interview.

62. Meese interview.

6. ODD JOBS: Constabulary Forces in Kosovo

1. Steven Meyers, "2,000 Monitors Go to Kosovo, but Their Power Is Unclear," *New York Times,* October 15, 1998, A6.

2. UN Security Council Resolution 1244 (1999), June 10, 1999.

3. United Nations Secretariat, Report of the Secretary-General on the United Nations Interim Administration in Kosovo, UN Doc. S/1999/779 (July 12, 1999), 9.

4. For more on the Kosovo Force's Multinational Brigades, see the page on "KFOR Structure" on the KFOR web site at http://www.nato.int/kfor/structure.htm.

5. Peter Jakobsen, "The Role of Military Forces in Managing Public Security Challenges: As Little as Possible or Filling the Gap?," (paper presented at the International Studies Association's, 43rd Annual Convention, New Orleans, March 27, 2002), 10–12.

6. "Multinational Specialized Unit" available from the KFOR web site at http://www.nato.int/kfor/kfor/msu.htm.

7. Annika Hansen, *From Congo to Kosovo: Civilian Police in*

Peace Operations (London: International Institute for Strategic Studies, 2002), 73.

8. Carabinieri web site, "Missioni all'estero."

9. International Crisis Group, *Kosovo Report Card.* ICG Balkans Report, no. 100 (Pristina/Brussels: International Crisis Group, August 28, 2000), 42–43.

10. OSCE Mission in Kosovo, "Kosovo Police Service School Fact Sheet," Pristina, August 2, 2001.

11. OSCE Mission in Kosovo, "Kosovo Police Service School," Pristina, May 1, 2002.

12. Eileen Kovchok, "Kosovo Police Service Trainers," *Law and Order,* March 2001, 57–61.

13. Ibid.

14. United Nations, Civilian Police Division, *Concept of Operations for the UNMIK Police* (New York: United Nations, May 2001), 1–8.

15. UN Secretariat, Report of the Secretary-General on the United Nations Interim Administration in Kosovo, 12.

16. Interview with Joelle Vatcher, UN CIVPOL Division desk officer, New York, December 1, 2001.

17. Interview with William De Meyer, UNMIK police special adviser, New York, December 1, 2001.

18. Interview with Adalbert Gross, UNMIK police deputy commissioner of operations, Washington, D.C., February 21, 2002.

19. UN CIVPOL Division, *Concept of Operations,* 11.

20. Interview with Colonel Gery Plane, SPU special adviser to the UNMIK police commissioner, Pristina, June 24, 2002.

21. UN CIVPOL Division, *Concept of Operations,* 11.

22. United Nations Secretariat, "Memorandum of Understanding with Jordan for UNMIK," October 9, 2000, A-1.

23. Ibid.

24. Interview with Colonel Hameed Iqbal Khaled, Pakistani SPU commander, Mitrovica, Kosovo, June 26, 2002.

25. Ibid.

26. Ibid.

27. Ibid.

28. Interview with Lieutenant Colonel Ovidiu Bratulescu, Roma-

nian SPU commander, Ferizaj, Kosovo, June 25, 2002.

29. Ibid.

30. Ibid.

31. Ibid.

32. United Nations Secretariat, Report of the Secretary-General on the United Nations Interim Administration Mission in Kosovo, UN Doc. S/1999/987 (September 16, 1999), 4.

33. International Crisis Group, *Kosovo Report Card*, 44.

34. Vatcher interview.

35. De Meyer interview.

36. Interview with UN CIVPOL Division official, New York, February 22, 2002.

37. Ibid.

38. Bradley Graham, "Pentagon Faults UN in Kosovo," *Washington Post*, July 21, 1999, A17.

39. United Nations Secretariat, Report of the Secretary-General on the United Nations Interim Administration Mission in Kosovo, UN Doc. S/1999/779 (July 12, 1999), 5.

40. United Nations Secretariat, Report of the Secretary-General on the United Nations Interim Administration Mission in Kosovo, UN Doc. S/1999.1250 (December 23, 1999), 5.

41. UN Secretariat, Report of the Secretary-General, S/1999/987, 1.

42. R. Jeffery Smith, "With Few Police to Stop It, Crime Flourishes in Kosovo," *Washington Post*, October 23, 1999, A19.

43. UN Secretariat, Report of the Secretary-General, S/1999/1250, 5–6.

44. Peter Finn, "Gunman Kills Serb in Café in Kosovo," *Washington Post*, December 19, 1999, A51.

45. Carlotta Gall, "German General's Kosovo Peacekeepers Are Fighting Crime," *New York Times*, December 21, 1999, A10.

46. UN Secretariat, Report of the Secretary-General, S/1999/1250, 5.

47. Guy Lawson, "The View From the Bridge," *New York Times*, August 20, 2000, 48.

48. International Crisis Group, *Kosovo Report Card*, 9 and 19.

49. International Crisis Group, *UNMIK's Kosovo Albatross: Tackling Division in Mitrovica*. Balkans Report, no. 131 (Pristina/Belgrade/Brussels: International Crisis Group, June 3, 2002), 1–10.

50. R. Jeffrey Smith, "French Troops in Kosovo Accused of

Retreat," *Washington Post,* February 2, 2000, A14.

51. United Nations Secretariat, Report of the Secretary-General on the United Nations Interim Mission in Kosovo, UN Doc. S/2000/177 (March 3, 2000).

52. United Nations Secretariat, Report of the Secretary-General on the United Nations Interim Administration Mission in Kosovo, UN Doc. S/2000/538 (June 6, 2000), 10.

53. UN Secretariat, Report of the Secretary General, S/2000/538, 6.

54. Musa Mustafa, "Serbs Burned Police Vehicles and Attacked Albanians in Their Apartments," *Koha Ditore* (Pristina), June 21, 2000, 4.

55. Interview with General William Nash (U.S. Army, ret.), former UNMIK commissioner for Mitrovica, Washington, D.C., February 5, 2002.

56. Ibid.

57. Interview with official in the Office of the SPU Special Adviser to the UNMIK Police Commissioner, Pristina, June 24, 2002.

58. Reuters, "Kosovo Serbs React Angrily to NATO Shutting Smelter," August 15, 2000.

59. BBC World Service, "Serbs and NATO Clash in Mitrovica," August 14, 2000; available at http://news.bbc.co.uk/english/world/europe/newsid_880000/880130.stm.

60. Interview with Joelle Vatcher, UN CIVPOL Division desk officer, New York, March 4, 2002.

61. United Nations Secretariat, Report of the Secretary-General on the United Nations Interim Administration Mission in Kosovo, UN Doc. S/2001/218 (March 13, 2001), 2–3.

62. BBC World Service, "Kosovo Serbs Attack UN Police," March 14, 2001; available at http://newssearch.bbc.co.uk/cgi-bin/results.pl/tab=news &scope=news&q=kosovo+riots.

63. UN Secretariat, Report of the Secretary-General, S/2001/565, 3.

64. BBC World Service, "Serbs Stone KFOR Troops," April 19, 2001; available at http://news.bbc.co.uk/hi/english/world/europe/newsid_1286000/1286203.stm.

65. Interview with Gary Matthews, former deputy SRSG in Kovoso, Washington, D.C., April 16, 2002.

66. UN Secretariat, Report of the Secretary-General, S/2001/565, 12.

67. De Meyer interview.

68. UN Secretariat, Report of the Secretary-General, S/2000/538, 6.

69. De Meyer interview.

70. Halvor Hartz, "The Role of Civilian Police" (paper presented at the conference on "Building a Durable Peace in Kosovo," sponsored by the Role of American Military Power Program of the Association of the United States Army, Arlington, Virginia, October 16, 2001, photocopy).

71. Interview with police adviser, U.S. Office Pristina, June 26, 2002.

72. De Meyer interview.

73. International Crisis Group, A Kosovo Roadmap (II): Internal Benchmarks. Balkans Report, no. 125 (Pristina/Brussels: International Crisis Group, March 1, 2002), 13–18.

74. United Nations Secretariat, Report of the Secretary-General on the United Nations Interim Administration Mission in Kosovo, UN Doc. S/2000/878 (September 18, 2000), 6. Specific incident reports were provided by the Office of the SPU Special Adviser, Pristina, July 10, 2002.

75. Interviews with UNMIK police officials, Pristina, June 26, 2002.

76. David Mullins, "UN Crime Crackdown Provoked a Backlash by Kosovo Albanian Radicals," Balkan Crisis Report, no. 317 (February 13, 2002).

77. Plane interview.

78. Gross interview.

79. UNMIK Police Situation Center, "Security Situation Summary for April 10, 2002" (Pristina, April 10, 2002, photocopy), item 6.5; interviews with staff members of UN Department of Peacekeeping Operations/Civilian Police Division, New York, April 8, 2002.

80. Ibid.

81. BBC World Service, "UN Kosovo Police Attacked," April 8, 2002; available at http://news.bbc.co.uk/hi/english/world/europe/newssid_1917000/1917278.stm.

82. Interview with senior UNMIK police officer, Washington, D.C., February 21, 2002.

83. Nick Woods, "Polish PM Visits Kosovo Wounded," BBC World Service, April 9, 2002, available at http://news.bbc.co.uk/ hi/english/world/europe/newsid_1917000/1917278.stm; idem., "Analysis: Gangs Target Kosovo Police," BBC World Service, April 9, 2002, available at http://www.bbc.co.uk/hi/english/world/europe/newsid_

1919000/1919546.stm; UNMIK Press Office, "Kosovo: UN Mission Chief Condemns Recent Attacks on UN Police," *UNMIK News*, April 9, 2002, available at http://www.unmikonline.org/news.htm#0904.

84. International Crisis Group, *UNMIK's Kosovo Albatross*, 5.

85. United Nations Secretariat, Report of the Secretary-General on the United Nations Interim Administration Mission in Kosovo, UN Doc. S/2002779 (July 17, 2002), 5.

86. Arben Qirezi, "Kosovo: New Crime Crackdown," *Balkan Crisis Report*, no. 349 (July 10, 2002).

87. United Nations Secretariat, "Briefing by the Special Representative of the Secretary-General for Kosovo," press release, July 30, 2002; available at http://www.un.org/News/Press/docs/2002/sc7472.doc.htm.

88. Interview with Thomas Hacker, acting UNMIK police commissioner, Pristina, June 25, 2002.

89. Ibid.

90. Interviews with UNMIK police and OSCE police training officers, Pristina, June 24–26, 2002.

91. Ibid.

92. Ibid.

93. Ibid.

94. UN Secretariat, Report of the Secretary-General, S/2002/779, p. 4.

95. Police adviser interview.

96. Erjon Kruja, "Kosovo: Serbs Return Blow," *Balkan Crisis Report*, no. 356 (August 8, 2002).

7. POLICEKEEPING: U.S. Policy on Peace Operations

1. Interview with an official in the Office of the Secretary of Defense, Washington D.C., August 12, 2002.

2. Ibid.

3. The White House, "The Clinton Administration's Policy on Strengthening Criminal Justice Systems in Support of Peace Operations," Washington, D.C., February 2000.

4. U.S. Department of State, Office of the Spokesman, "Secretary of State Madeleine Albright: Press Briefing on the Presidential Decision Directive for Peace Operations," Washington, D.C., February 24, 2000.

5. Ibid.

6. The White House, "The Clinton Administration's Policy on Strengthening Criminal Justice Systems in Support of Peace Operations," 11.

7. Ibid., 10.

8. Ibid., 3–5.

9. Ibid.

10. William Lewis and Edward Marks, *Strengthening International Civilian Police Operations* (Washington, D.C.: Center for Strategic and International Studies, December 2000), 2–3.

11. Cook, "Toward Better Practices."

12. William Lewis, Edward Marks, and Robert Perito, *Enhancing International Civilian Police in Peace Operations.* Special Report, no. 85 (Washington, D.C.: U.S. Institute of Peace, April 2002), 4–5.

13. Perito, *The American Experience with Police in Peace Operations,* 97–98.

14. United Nations Secretariat, *Report of the Panel on United Nations Peace Operations,* UN Doc. A/ff/305, S/2000/809 (August, 21, 2000), 7; available at http://www.un.org/peace/report/peace_operations/.

15. Ibid., 20.

16. Gary Dempsey and Roger Fontaine, *Fool's Errands: America's Recent Encounters with Nation Building* (Washington, D.C.: Cato Institute, 2001), 1–25.

17. ABC News–sponsored "Roundtable on the Confederate Flag and Iowa Caucuses," January 23, 2000; available at http://www.foreign policy2000.org/library.

18. "Statement on Defense at a Campaign Rally in Kansas City," February 22, 2000; available at http://www.foreignpolicy2000.org/library.

19. Second Presidential Debate, October 11, 2000; available at http://www.foreign policy2000.org/library.

20. Chester Crocker and Richard Solomon, "The Lone Ranger No More," *Washington Post,* January 17, 2001, A24.

21. Elaine Sciolino, "Bush Aide Hints Police Are Better Peacekeepers than Military," *New York Times,* November 17, 2000, A7.

22. President-elect Bush, Colin Powell Press Conference Transcript, "Powell Chosen to be Secretary of State in the Bush Administration,"

U.S. State Department, Office of International Information Programs, Crawford, Texas, December 16, 2000, 6.

23. Edith Wilkie and Beth DeGrasse, *A Force for Peace and Security: U.S. and Allied Commanders' Views of the Military's Role in Peace Operations and the Impact on Terrorism of States in Conflict* (Washington, D.C.: Peace Through Law Education Fund, February 2002).

24. Alan Sipress, "Balkans Uprisings Condemned," *Washington Post*, April 12, 2001, A27.

25. Agence France-Presse, "NATO Rejects Big Bosnia Drawdown, Leaves Room for Tinkering," May 29, 2001.

26. Secretary of State Colin Powell, "Remarks to the Press," International Media Center, Budapest, May 29, 2001; available at http://www.state.gov/secretary/rm/2001/ index.cfm?docid=3126.

27. Philip Gordon, "Bush's Unilateralism Risks Alienating America's Allies," *Handelsblatt* (Dusseldorf), April 2, 2001.

28. Frederick Bonnart, "In NATO, the Bush Reformers Are Getting Things Backward," *International Herald Tribune*, June 11, 2001, 8.

29. Ivo Daalder, "Are the United States and Europe Heading for Divorce?" *International Affairs* 77, no. 3 (Summer 2001): 553–55.

30. George W. Bush, "The Hour is Coming When America Will Act." Address to a Joint Session of Congress. *Washington Post*, September 21, 2001, A24.

31. Nationally televised speech given by President Bush on the one-month anniversary of the September 11 attacks. A transcript of President Bush's speech is available from Cable News Network at: www.cnn.com/2001/U.S./10/11/gen.bush.transcript.

32. Sebastian Mallaby, "Lots of Talk, Precious Little Walk," *Washington Post*, March 11, 2002, A21; Richard Holbrooke, "Rebuilding Nations," *Washington Post*, April 1, 2002, A15; and Barnett Rubin, "Is America Abandoning Afghanistan?" *New York Times*, April 10, 2002, A25.

33. Charles Krauthammer, "We Don't Peacekeep," *Washington Post*, December 18, 2001, A27.

34. Interview with John Hulsman, research fellow in European affairs, Heritage Foundation, Washington, D.C., March 4, 2002.

35. Peter Finn, "Military Gap Grows between U.S. and NATO Allies," *Washington Post*, May 19, 2002, A22; Jeffrey Gedmin, "The Alliance is Doomed," *Washington Post*, May 20, 2002, A21.

36. Vernon Loeb, "Rumsfeld Asks NATO for Bosnia Troop Cuts," *International Herald Tribune*, December 19, 2001; Alexander Nicoll, "Europe: U.S. Moots NATO Exit from Bosnia," *Financial Times* (London), December 19, 2001.

37. North Atlantic Treaty Organization, "Statement on the Situation in the Balkans Issued at the Meeting of the North Atlantic Council in Defense Ministers Session," Press Release (2001) 172, December 18, 2001; available at http://www.nato.int/docu/pr/2001/p01-172e.htm.

38. Telephone interview with an official in the Office of Secretary of Defense, July 16, 2002.

39. Ibid.

40. Statement made by a National Security Council staff member at a U.S. Institute of Peace conference on "The Balkans: Taking Stock and Looking Forward," Washington D.C., January 22, 2002.

41. Marina Ottaway, "International Actors in Postconflict Democracy Promotion" (paper presented at the conference on "Democratization after War," Brown University, Providence, R.I., April 4–5, 2002), 4.

42. International Crisis Group, *Policing the Police in Bosnia: A Further Reform Agenda*. Balkans Report, no. 130 (Brussels: International Crisis Group, May 10, 2002), i.

43. International Crisis Group, *Courting Disaster: The Misrule of Law in Bosnia and Herzegovina*. Balkans Report, no. 127 (Sarajevo/Brussels: International Crisis Group, March 25, 2002), 10.

44. United Nations Secretariat, Report of the Secretary-General on the United Nations Mission in Bosnia and Herzegovina, UN Doc. S/2000/529 (June 2, 2000), 4–8.

45. Ibid.

46. United Nations Mission in Bosnia and Herzegovina, "Mandate Implementation Plan 2000–2002," Sarajevo, March 13, 2001.

47. Ibid.

48. Jacques Paul Klein, "The Prospects for Eastern Croatia: The Significance of the UN's Undiscovered Mission," *RUSI Journal* 142, no. 2 (April 1997): 23.

49. Alexander Nitzsche, "Support for Democratic Policing Gradually Moves Up Agenda for OSCE in Southeastern Europe," *OSCE Newsletter* 8, no. 8 (September 2001), 9–10.

50. Office of the High Representative, Peace Implementation Council, "Communiqué of the Steering Board of the Peace Imple-

mentation Council," Brussels, September 13, 2001; available at http://www.ohr.int/pic/default.asp?content_id=5810.

51. Richard Monk, "First Preliminary Report on a Follow-on Mission to UNMIBH and the UN International Police Task Force" (OSCE, Vienna, October 2001, photocopy).

52. Ibid.

53. Richard Monk, Tor Tanke Holm, and Serge Rumin, "Report on a Follow-on Mission to UNMIBH and the UN International Police Task Force" (Office of the High Representative, Sarajevo, November 2001, photocopy).

54. Charles Erdmann, "Assessment of the Current Mandate of the Independent Judicial Commission and a Review of the Judicial Reform Follow-on Mission for Bosnia and Herzegovina" (Office of the High Representative, Sarajevo, November 2001, photocopy).

55. Office of the High Representative, Peace Implementation Council, "Communiqué of the Meeting of the Steering Board of the Peace Implementation Council," Brussels, December 5–6, 2001.

56. European Union Joint Council Secretariat, "Report on a Possible Follow-on Mission to the UN IPTF," Brussels, December 21, 2001.

57. Ibid.

58. Judy Dempsey, "EU to Take Over Police Operations in Bosnia," *Financial Times* (London), January 29, 2002; BBC News, "EU Paves Way for Bosnia Police Force," February 18, 2002, available at http://news.bbc.co.uk/hi/english/world/europe.newsid_1826000/1826821.stm; Daniel Korski, "EU Bid to Police Bosnia Under Scrutiny," *Balkan Crisis Report,* no. 310 (January 18, 2002).

59. United Nations Secretariat, Report of the Secretary-General on the United Nations Mission in Bosnia and Herzegovina, UN Doc. S/2001/1132 (November 29, 2001), 7–8.

60. Interviews with Souren Seraydarian, deputy SRSG, and Paraskevi Nazou, task manager, delegation of the European Commission to Bosnia, Sarajevo, July 1, 2002.

61. Ibid.

62. Office of the High Representative, Peace Implementation Council, "Communiqué of the Peace Implementation Council Steering Board," Brussels, March 1, 2002.

63. Interview with SRSG Jacques Klein, Sarajevo, July 2, 2002.

64. International Crisis Group, *Policing the Police in Bosnia,* 9.

65. United Nations, "Bosnia and Herzegovina Mission on Track to Completing its Core Mandate in 2002 Secretary-General Tells Security Council," Press Release SG/SM/8149 SC/7320, March 5, 2002; available at http://www.un.org/News/Press/docs/2002/ sgsm8149.doc.htm.

8. NATION BUILDING: Biting the Bullet in Afghanistan and Iraq

1. Jane Perlez, "Directive Says Rice, Bush Aide, Won't Be Upstaged by Cheney," *New York Times*, February 16, 2001.

2. The White House, National Security Presidential Directive (NSPD)-1, "Organization of the National Security Council System," February 13, 2001.

3. The three Presidential Decision Directives (PDDs) on peacekeeping signed by President Clinton were PDD-25, "Reforming Multilateral Peace Operations," issued on May 6, 1994; PDD-56, "Managing Complex Contingency Operations," issued in May 1997; and PDD-71, "Strengthening Criminal Justice Systems in Support of Peace Operations," issued on February 24, 2000.

4. Telephone interview with NSC staff member, May 22, 2002.

5. Michele Flournoy and Michael Pan, "Supporting Postconflict Justice and Reconciliation" (paper prepared for the Joint Project on Post-Conflict Reconstruction of the Center for Strategic and International Studies and the Association of the U.S. Army, Washington, D.C., July 9, 2002), 3.

6. Lewis, Marks, and Perito, *Enhancing International Civilian Police in Peace Operations,* 4–6.

7. Ibid.

8. Ibid.

9. Robert Schoenhaus, *Training for Peace and Humanitarian Relief Operations: Advancing Best Practices.* Peaceworks, no. 43 (Washington, D.C.: U.S. Institute of Peace, April 2002), 31–32.

10. Colum Lynch, "Misconduct, Corruption by U.S. Police Mar Bosnia Mission," *Washington Post,* May 29, 2001, A1.

11. International Crisis Group, *Policing the Police in Bosnia,* 29; UN Mission in Bosnia and Herzegovina, "Background Paper on Efforts against Human Trafficking," (paper submitted to the House Committee on International Relations, Washington, D.C., April 23, 2002).

12. Nidzara Ahmetasevic with Julie Poucher Harbin, "Thousands of Women Lured in Bosnian Brothels," *Balkan Investigative Report* (April 18, 2002).

13. "Testimony of Martina E. Vandenberg, J.D., Europe Researcher, Women's Rights Division, Human Rights Watch," House Committee on International Relations, Subcommittee on International Operations and Human Rights hearing on "The UN and the Sex Slave Trade in Bosnia: Isolated Case or Larger Problem in the UN System?" 107th Cong., 2d Sess., April 24, 2002.

14. Rick Emert, "UN Officers Resign after Unauthorized Raid," *Stars and Stripes,* December 1, 2000, 3.

15. Robert Capps, "Sex-Slave Whistle-Blowers Vindicated," Salon.com News, August 6, 2002; available at www.salon.com/news/feature/2002/08/06/dyncopr/print.html.

16. Michael Kaplan, "One Woman's War on Sexual Slavery," *Glamour,* May 2002, 296–306.

17. Colum Lynch, "Ex-UN Officer Sues U.S. Firm on Dismissal," *Washington Post,* June 23, 2001, A20.

18. Colum Lynch, "UN Halted Probe of Officers' Alleged Role in Sex Trafficking," *Washington Post,* December 27, 2001, A17.

19. Klein interview.

20. International Crisis Group, *Policing the Police in Bosnia,* 30.

21. Robert Capps, "Crime Without Punishment," Salon.com News, June 27, 2002; available at www.salon.com/news/feature/ 2002/06/27/military/print.html.

22. Statement by the Honorable Ilena Ros-Lehtinen, chair, House Committee on International Relations, Subcommittee on International Operations and Human Rights hearing on "The UN and the Sex Slave Trade in Bosnia: Isolated Case or Larger Problem in the UN System?" 107th Cong., 2d Sess., April 24, 2002.

23. Statement by Ambassador Nancy Ely-Raphel before the House Subcommittee on International Operations and Human Rights hearing on "The UN and the Sex Slave Trade in Bosnia: Isolated Case or Larger Problem in the UN System?" 107th Cong., 2d Sess., April 24, 2002.

24. Ibid.

25. Vandenberg testimony.

26. Statement by former IPTF officer David Lamb before the House Subcommittee on International Operations and Human Rights

hearing on "UN Peacekeepers' Participation in the Sex Slave Trade in Bosnia: Isolated Case or Larger Problem in the UN System?" 107th Cong., 2d Sess., April 24, 2002.

27. United Nations Secretariat, "Agreement on Provisional Arrangements in Afghanistan Pending the Re-establishment of Permanent Government Institutions"; available at http://www.un/News/dh/latest/afghan/afghan-agree.htm.

28. United Nations Secretariat, Security Council Resolution 1386 (December 20, 2001).

29. Henry L. Stimson Center, *Security in Afghanistan: The International Security Assistance Force*. Peace Operations Backgrounder (Washington, D.C.: Henry L. Stimson Center, June 2002), 2.

30. International Resources Group, American Bar Association/Asia Law Initiative, International Foundation for Election Systems, and International Human Rights Law Group, *Filling the Vacuum: Prerequisites to Security in Afghanistan*. Report of the Consortium for Response to the Afghanistan Transition (Washington, D.C.: International Resources Group, March 2002), 10–14.

31. Ibid., 12.

32. United Nations Secretariat, Report of the Secretary-General on the Situation in Afghanistan and Its Implications for International Peace and Security, UN Doc. S/2002/278-A/56/875 (March 18, 2002), 9–12.

33. Interview with U.S. Department of State official, Washington, D.C., April 14, 2002.

34. William Branigin, "Afghan Rebels Ready Police Force for Kabul: Officers Part of Plan to Control Capital," *Washington Post*, November 7, 2001, A20.

35. Doug Struck, "National Police Force Sought in Afghanistan," *Washington Post*, February 5, 2002, A8; International Resources Group, et al., *Filling the Vacuum*, 28.

36. Karen DeYoung, "Bush Says U.S. Will Help Train Afghan Army, Police," *Washington Post*, January 29, 2002, A8.

37. James Dao, "Bush Sets Role for U.S. in Afghan Rebuilding," *New York Times*, April 18, 2002; "The Evolving President," *Washington Post*, April 21, 2002, B6.

38. Fred Hiatt, "Underachieving on Afghanistan," *Washington Post*, May 20, 2002, A21; Peter Baker and Susan Glasser, "Miles Before Kabul Can Be Left Behind," *Washington Post*, June 9, 2002,

B1; Bill Gertz, "Rumsfeld Takes Dim View of Peacekeeping Role," *Washington Times*, February 27, 2002, A1.

39. Glenn Kessler, "Bush's Afghan Plan Questioned: Legislators Fear Poor Security Will Impede Democracy," *Washington Post*, May 21, 2002, A1.

40. Glenn Kessler, "U.S. Fears Grow over Turmoil in Afghanistan," *Washington Post*, August 8, 2002, A1.

41. Judy Dempsey, "Afghan Dilemmas," *Financial Times* (London), March 8, 2002; Keith Richburg, "Europe, U.S. Diverging on Key Policy Approaches," *Washington Post*, March 4, 2002, A13; Todd Purdum, "A Wider Atlantic: Europe Sees a Grotesque U.S.," *New York Times*, May 16, 2002; and T. R. Reid, "Resurfacing Animosity Awaits Bush in Europe," *Washington Post*, May 22, 2002, A29.

42. Colum Lynch, "Dispute Threatens UN Role in Bosnia," *Washington Post*, July 1, 2002, A1; Serge Schmemann, "U.S. Votes to Extend UN Bosnia Mission," *New York Times*, July 4, 2002; Barnaby Mason, "Peacekeeping Row Deepens Transatlantic Rift," BBC News, July 1, 2002, available at http://news.bbc.co.uk/hi/english/world/americas/newsaid_2079000/2079161.stm; and Colum Lynch, "Bush Promises to Try to Save Bosnia Mission," *Washington Post*, July 3, 2002, A16.

43. Ibid.

44. "Doubling the Damage at the UN," *New York Times*, July 2, 2002.

45. United Nations, "Security Council Extends Bosnia Mission's Mandate Until December 31," Press Release SC/7451, July 12, 2002; available at http://www.un.org/News/Press/docs/2002/sc7451.doc.htm.

46. Klein interview; Reuters, "EU Ready to Take Over UN Bosnia Mission, Raps U.S.," July 3, 2002.

47. G. John Ikenberry, "America's Imperial Ambitions," *Foreign Affairs*, September/October 2002, 48.

48. Michael Hirsch, "Bush and the World," *Foreign Affairs*, September/October 2002, 23.

49. Bradley Graham, "Pentagon Plans a Redirection in Afghanistan," *Washington Post*, November 20, 2002, A1.

50. Thomas Ricks, "U.S. to Set Up New Bases to Help Afghanistan Rebuild," *Washington Post*, December 20, 2002.

51. Alexandra Vondra and Sally Painter, "No Time to Go It Alone: Europe and the United States and Their Mutual Need for NATO," *Washington Post*, November 18, 2002, A21.

52. Associated Press, "Text of President Bush's Address to the Nation," October 8, 2002.

53. Philip Gordon, Martin Indyk, and Michael O'Hanlon, "Getting Serious About Iraq," *Survival* 44, no.3 (Autumn 2002), 9.

54. Kenneth Pollack, *The Threatening Storm: The Case for Invading Iraq* (New York: Random House, 2002), 253–57.

55. International Crisis Group, *Iraq Backgrounder: What Lies Beneath.* ICG Middle East Report, no. 6 (Amman/Brussels: International Crisis Group, October 1, 2002), 9–10.

56. Pollack, *The Threatening Storm,* 117.

57. Conference of the Iraqi Opposition, "Final Report on the Transition to Democracy in Iraq (final version of the working document as amended by the members of the Iraqi Democratic Principles Working Group, Iraq Foundation, Washington, D.C., November 2002).

58. Ibid.

59. Marc Grossman, "Post-Saddam Iraq" (testimony presented before the Senate Foreign Relations Committee hearing on "The Future of Iraq," 108th Cong., 1st Sess., February 11, 2003); Associated Press, "Bush Creates Office in Post-Saddam Plan," January 22, 2003.

60. Douglas Feith, "Post-War Planning" (testimony presented before the Senate Foreign Relations Committee hearing on "The Future of Iraq," 108th Cong., 1st Sess., February 11, 2003).

61. Grossman, "Post-Saddam Iraq."

62. Karen DeYoung and Peter Slevin, "Full U.S. Control Planned for Iraq," *Washington Post,* February 21, 2003, A1.

63. Ibid.

64. Colum Lynch, "Iraq War Could Put 10 Million in Need of Aid, UN Reports," *Washington Post,* January 7, 2003, A12.

65. "Rock drill" is a military expression referring to a meeting in which issues are closely considered by "turning over all the rocks."

66. Mark Fineman, Robin Wright, and Doyle McManus, "Washington's Battle Plan: Preparing for War, Stumbling to Peace," *Los Angles Times,* July 18, 2003, 1.

67. Ibid.

68. Daniel Williams, "U.S. Army to Train 1,000 Iraqi Exiles," *Washington Post,* December 18, 2002, A23; Daniel Williams, "Iraqi Exiles Mass for Training," *Washington Post,* February 1, 2003, A17;

and Peter Green, "Anti-Hussein Iraqis in Hungary for Training by U.S. Military," *New York Times,* February 19, 2003, A17.

69. Colum Lynch," U.S., Britain, Spain Unveil New Iraq Resolution," *Washington Post,* February 25. 2003, A1.

70. Glenn Kessler and Colum Lynch, "Bush Firm on Warning Iraq," *Washington Post,* February 26, 1003, A1.

71. Dana Milbank and Peter Slevin, "President Details Vision for Iraq," *Washington Post,* February 27, 2003. A1.

72. Thomas E. Ricks, "War Plan for Iraq Largely in Place," *Washington Post,* March 2, 2003, A1.

73. Charles Tripp, *A History of Iraq* (New York: Cambridge University Press, 2001), 7.

74. Fineman, Wright, and McManus, "Washington's Battle Plan."

75. Peter Slevin and Dana Priest, "Wolfowitz Concedes Iraq Errors," *Washington Post,* July 24, 2003, A1.

76. Council on Foreign Relations, *Iraq: The Day After.* Report of an Independent Task Force sponsored by the Council on Foreign Relations (New York: Council on Foreign Relations, 2003), 25–26; United States Institute of Peace, *Establishing the Rule of Law in Iraq.* Special Report, no. 104 (Washington, D.C.: United States Institute of Peace, April 2003), 11–12; Bathsheba N. Crocker, *Postwar Iraq: Are We Ready?* (Washington, D.C.: Center for Strategic and International Studies, March 25, 2003), 7–8.

77. Andrew Cockburn and Patrick Cockburn, *Out of the Ashes: The Resurrection of Saddam Hussein* (New York: HarperCollins, 1999), 4–34.

78. Rachel Bronson and Andrew Weiss, "Guiding Principles for U.S. Postconflict Policy in Iraq" (report of an independent working group cosponsored by the Council on Foreign Relations and the James A. Baker III Institute for Public Policy of Rice University, Washington D.C., December 18, 2002), 1–6.

79. Michael Kelly, "Legitimacy and the Public Security Function," in Oakley, Dziedzic, and Goldberg, eds., *Policing the New World Disorder,* 399–431.

80. "Iraq: Looking Beyond Saddam's Rule" (report on a workshop sponsored by the National Defense University's Institute for National Strategic Studies and the Naval Postgraduate School, Washington, D.C., November 20–21, 2002, photocopy), 2.

81. Michael Dobbs, "Allies Slow U.S. War Plans," *Washington Post*, January 11, 2002, A1.

82. Slevin and Priest, "Wolfowitz Concedes Iraq Errors."

83. Anthony Shadid, "A City Freed from Tyranny Descends into Lawlessness," *Washington Post*, April 11, 2003, A1.

84. John Burns, "Loot and a Suicide Attack in Baghdad," *New York Times*, April 11, 2003, A1; Jonathan Weisman, "Iraq Chaos, No Surprise, but Too Few Troops to Quell It," *Washington Post*, April 14, 2003, A28; and Dexter Filkins, "U.S. Troops Move to Restore Order in Edgy Bagdad," *New York Times*, April 13, 2003, A1.

85. Barton Gellman, "Seven Nuclear Sites Looted; Iraqi Scientific Files, Some Containers Missing," *Washington Post*, May 10, 2003, A1.

86. Robert McCartney, "Expert Thieves Took Artifacts, UNESCO Says," *Washington Post*, April 18, 2003, A1; Joseph Coleman, "Ashcroft: Looting in Iraq Done by Criminal Groups, Not Just Civilians," Associated Press, May 5, 2003.

87. Guy Gugliotta, "Looters Stole 6,000 Artifacts: Number Expected to Rise as Officials Take Inventory," *Washington Post*, June 21, 2003, A16.

88. Charles Hanley, "Looters Ransack Iraq's National Library," Associated Press, April 15, 2003.

89. Michael Gordon and John Kifner, "U.S. Warns Iraqis against Claiming Authority in Void," *New York Times*, April 24, 2003, A1; Scott Wilson, "Iraqis Killing Former Baath Party Members," *Washington Post*, May 20, 2003, A8.

90. Associated Press, "Lawlessness and Looting Spread in Baghdad," April 11, 2003.

91. William Branigin and Rick Atkinson, "Anything and Everything Goes," *Washington Post*, April 11, 2003, A1; Daniel Williams, "U.S. Troops Frustrated with Role in Iraq," *Washington Post*, June 20, 2003, A1.

92. Douglas Jehl, "As Order Breaks Down, Allies Try to Rebuild Iraqi Police," *New York Times*, April 12, 2003, A1; John Burns, "Joint Patrols Begin in Baghdad," *New York Times*, April 14, 2003, A1.

93. Monte Reel, "Garner Arrives in Iraq to Begin Reconstruction," *Washington Post*, April 22, 2003, A1.

94. Joshua Hammer and Colin Soloway, "Who's in Charge Here?" *Newsweek*, May 26, 2003; Rajiv Chandrasekaran, "Iraq's Ragged Reconstruction," *Washington Post*, May 9, 2003, A1.

95. Ibid.

96. Karen De Young, "Bush Proclaims Victory in Iraq," *Washington Post,* May 2, 2003, A1.

97. Mike Allen, "Expert on Terrorism to Direct Rebuilding," *Washington Post,* May 2, 2003, A1.

98. Peter Slevin, "Many More Iraqis Banned from Government Positions: U.S. Is Purging High-Ranking Members of Hussein's Party," *Washington Post,* May 18, 2003, A18.

99. International Crisis Group, *Baghdad: A Race against the Clock.* ICG Middle East Briefing (Baghdad/Amman/Brussels: International Crisis Group, June 11, 2003), 1–8.

100. Amy Waldman, "After the War: Law Enforcement," *Washington Post,* June 30, 2003, A1.

101. Coalition Provisional Authority/Interior Ministry, "Iraq Police: An Assessment of Their Present and Recommendations for the Future" (Coalition Provisional Authority, Baghdad, May 30, 2003, photocopy), 4–5.

102. Ibid.

103. Peter Slevin, "Policing Iraq to Stay U.S. Job," *Washington Post,* June 22, 2003, A20.

104. "Field Report on Iraq's Postconflict Reconstruction" (joint statement by John Hamre, Frederick Barton, and Bathsheba Crocker, Center for Strategic and International Studies; Johanna Mendelson Forman, United Nations Foundation; and Robert Orr, Council on Foreign Relations before the Senate Foreign Relations Committee hearing on "Iraq: Status and Prospects for Reconstruction—Next Steps," 108th Cong., 1st Sess., July 23, 2003), 2–3.

105. Rachel Bronson, "When Soldiers Become Cops," *Foreign Affairs,* November/December 2002, 122–30; James Dobbins, et al., *America's Role in Nation-Building: From Germany to Iraq* (Santa Monica, Calif.: RAND Corporation, 2003), xxix.

9. WHERE IS THE LONE RANGER WHEN WE NEED HIM?

1. Ralph Peters, "Heavy Peace," *Parameters* 29, no. 1 (Spring 1999): 73.

2. R. Jeffrey Smith, "Kosovo Still Seethes as UN Official Nears Exit," *Washington Post,* December 18, 2000, A20.

3. Alton Gwaltney, "Law and Order in Kosovo: A Look at Criminal Justice During the First Year of Operation Joint Guardian" (paper prepared for the Center for Law and Military Operations, Judge Advocate General's School of the Army, Charlottesville, Virginia, July 2001), 1–5.

4. Paddy Ashdown, "What I Learned in Bosnia," *New York Times*, October 28, 2002.

5. Vernon Loeb, "Army Shows Off Its New Strykers," *Washington Post*, October 17, 2002, A19; Jim Lynch, "Army Is Testing a Leaner Fighting Machine," *San Diego Union-Tribune*, January 5, 2003, A19.

6. "National Security for a New Era: Focusing National Power" (final report of the Thirty-First Annual Institute for Foreign Policy Analysis–Fletcher Security Conference, Washington D.C., November 14–15, 2001), 35.

7. U.S. Commission on National Security/21st Century, "Seeking a National Strategy: A Concert for Preserving Security and Promoting Freedom" (report of the U.S. Commission on National Security Phase Two, July 24, 2002); available at www.nssg.gov?PhaseII.pfd.

8. Sara Goo, "Federal Screeners Take Up Posts at BWI Checkpoints," *Washington Post*, May 1, 2002, A10.

9. Stanley Foundation, "Accountability and Judicial Response: Building Mechanisms for Postconflict Justice" (report of the Thirty-Eighth "Strategy for Peace, U.S. Foreign Policy Conference," Airlie Center, Warrenton, Virginia, October 23–25, 1997), 7–10.

10. Clark, *Waging Modern War*, 86, 98.

11. Senator Joseph Biden, "Against Withdrawal from Bosnia," press statement, May 23, 2001; available at http://biden.senate.gov/press/statmts/2001/may/052301.htm.

12. Lewis, Marks, and Perito, *Enhancing International Civilian Police in Peace Operations*, 4.

INDEX

381

Robert M. Perito is a visiting lecturer at Princeton University's Woodrow Wilson School of Public and International Affairs and an adjunct professor at George Mason and American Universities. He was deputy director of the International Criminal Investigative Training Assistance Program at the U.S. Department of Justice, where he supervised police training programs in peace operations in Haiti, Bosnia, Kosovo, and East Timor. Prior to serving at the Department of Justice, Perito was a career Foreign Service officer at the U.S. State Department. His diplomatic assignments included Beijing, Hong Kong, and Geneva; he was also the director of the State Department's Office of International Criminal Justice. In 1992, he received a Presidential Meritorious Honor Award for leading the U.S. delegation to the Angola peace talks. Perito has also served in the White House as deputy executive secretary of the National Security Council (1988–89). Before joining the Foreign Service, he was a Peace Corps volunteer in Nigeria. Perito holds an M.A. in peace operations policy from George Mason University. He was a senior fellow at the U.S. Institute of Peace in 2000–2001.

United States Institute of Peace

The United States Institute of Peace is an independent, nonpartisan federal institution created by Congress to promote the prevention, management, and peaceful resolution of international conflicts. Established in 1984, the Institute meets its congressional mandate through an array of programs, including research grants, fellowships, professional training, education programs from high school through graduate school, conferences and workshops, library services, and publications. The Institute's Board of Directors is appointed by the President of the United States and confirmed by the Senate.

Chairman of the Board: Chester A. Crocker
Vice Chairman: Seymour Martin Lipset
President: Richard H. Solomon
Executive Vice President: Harriet Hentges
Vice President: Charles E. Nelson

Jennings Randolph Program for International Peace

This book is a fine example of the work produced by senior fellows in the Jennings Randolph fellowship program of the United States Institute of Peace. As part of the statute establishing the Institute, Congress envisioned a program that would appoint "scholars and leaders of peace from the United States and abroad to pursue scholarly inquiry and other appropriate forms of communication on international peace and conflict resolution." The program was named after Senator Jennings Randolph of West Virginia, whose efforts over four decades helped to establish the Institute.

Since 1987, the Jennings Randolph Program has played a key role in the Institute's effort to build a national center of research, dialogue, and education on critical problems of conflict and peace. Nearly two hundred senior fellows from some thirty nations have carried out projects on the sources and nature of violent international conflict and the ways such conflict can be peacefully managed or resolved. Fellows come from a wide variety of academic and other professional backgrounds. They conduct research at the Institute and participate in the Institute's outreach activities to policymakers, the academic community, and the American public.

Each year approximately fifteen senior fellows are in residence at the Institute. Fellowship recipients are selected by the Institute's board of directors in a competitive process. For further information on the program, or to receive an application form, please contact the program staff at (202) 457-1700, or visit our web site at www.usip.org.

Joseph Klaits
Director

Where Is the Lone Ranger When We Need Him?
America's Search for a Postconflict Stability Force

This book was set in the typeface Sabon; the display type is Sabon Bold. Cover design by The Creative Shop, Rockville, Md. Interior design and page makeup by Mike Chase. Copyediting and proofreading by EEI Communications, Inc., Alexandria, Va. Production supervised by Marie Marr. Peter Pavilionis was the book's editor.